CONTENTS

INTRODUCTION

Conversations about money and investing tend toward the terrifying for most folks. Seldom do people take the time to slog through the long, deep, gray tables tucked into the back of their newspapers. The television programming aimed at investment is filled with arcane phrases such as "Dutch auction" and foreign-sounding words: "arbitrage," "backwardation," "contango." Sometimes it seems as if those in the know would prefer us not to understand. They'd prefer we move along so they can revel in their own coded language about Wall Street, money and investing.

But their gambits aren't that tough to unlock. You don't need a four-year degree or years spent toiling on the stock exchange to understand Wall Street. This book will help unravel the mysteries. By the end of this book, you will not only understand stocks and bonds, but also more complex investment instruments such as futures and options, as well as how to be smart about money and investing matters. Increasingly, individuals are responsible for organizing their own retirement planning. Investments make up the core of college-funding strategies. Even thinking about health care can benefit from a more thorough understanding of money and investing.

In this book, we will provide the keys to unlocking the mysteries of money and investing, so that when you are at a cocktail or dinner party you can deftly slip into a conversation about the markets, should one arise. In easy-to-understand fashion, this book will tell you about how the market works—the world of stocks, bonds, mutual funds and other investments—so that you can use this knowledge to make investing decisions that are right for you. We will provide history and show you how to read those long gray tables in the back of your newspaper. We will even decode many of the phrases that so-called experts toss around so easily and carelessly on television. And we will place the world of investing in the context of the broader economy and the monetary system of dollars, cents, credit cards and other means of money.

Think of yourself as traveling to a new place and this as your guidebook. Culture and history are explained. Maps to points of interest are enclosed. Recommended reading lists to delve deeper into specific topics have been selected by *The Wall Street Journal*'s experts.

So, without delay, let's journey into the land of money and investing.

CHAPTER 1

STOCKS

M any people have heard of the New York Stock Exchange; maybe some have even seen footage of people scurrying around in strangely colored jackets. But just what are all those people doing at the NYSE, and what does it mean to you as an investor?

First, we should take a step back. Buying and selling stocks involve financial markets. And markets sound more complex than they are. In fact, many of us start learning about markets from a very early age.

As kids, many of us set up lemonade stands. We had a product we wanted to sell, and we went looking for buyers. We needed information to set prices. What were the kids on the next block charging? What kind of demand did we see? The corner of a block seemed to offer more opportunity than the middle of the block. None of us considered working from the alley. We also needed to know how much our sugar, plastic cups and water cost, in order to see if we were making any money at five cents a cup.

A stock market isn't that different. It's about buyers and sellers. It's about finding a place where the most buyers and sellers are located. It's about supply and demand. Basically, all the transactions in our life, from selling a used car to running a garage sale, contain elements of what happens among those brightly dressed folks running around the stock exchange floor (by the way, those jackets help traders quickly identify who a fellow trader works for). But in the world of stock markets, things happen faster and on a much larger scale than at a lemonade stand.

TWO TYPES OF MARKETS

In the United States, stocks trade in two main markets: the New York Stock Exchange and the Nasdaq Stock Market. A number of other markets exist, but they make markets mainly in stocks that are primarily traded at one of these two marketplaces. When companies go public, they can seek to list on any of these exchanges.

THE NEW YORK STOCK EXCHANGE

The New York Stock Exchange is the oldest stock market in the United States. It began in 1792 under a buttonwood tree in lower Manhattan, with folks trading shares back and forth among one another. Since then it has grown to become the largest stock market in the world.

It's now located on the corner of Wall Street and Broad Street in lower Manhattan, but its physical place is less and less important. In a world of high-speed information, stock market participants can work from Whitefish, Montana, as easily as from the floor of the exchange itself.

Trading at the New York Stock Exchange, often called the NYSE or the Big Board, uses a so-called specialist trading system. In this system, a single person is in charge of the trading in a particular stock. For instance, if you want to buy a share of IBM, your bid will ultimately go to the specialist assigned to trade IBM. That specialist acts as a kind of traffic cop, directing movement among buyers and sellers. He or she looks around to find someone who wants to sell a share of IBM at the price you want to buy. The matching up of buyers and sellers occurs throughout the trading day, and sometimes the specialist buys or sells for his own account if an order can't be matched.

When the NYSE is on television, sometimes you see a gaggle of folks standing in front of the specialist, hollering out buy and sell orders. That's when the specialist looks most like a traffic cop—pointing, gesturing, yelling. It looks confusing, but it's just a simple matching up of buyers and sellers so they can trade stocks.

Along with shouting and pointing, specialists also match buyers and sellers electronically. This kind of high-tech activity makes up a growing amount of the trading that happens at the New York Stock Exchange. While the trading volume and the number of stocks trading at the NYSE have grown dramatically in the past twenty years, the number of people working on the floor of the stock exchange has remained about the same, thanks largely to the growth of high-tech, all-electronic trading. All aspects of NYSE trading, including electronic trading, are refereed by the specialists.

THE HISTORY OF THE NYSE

The New York Stock Exchange, the world's largest and best-known stock market, traces its history to 1792, when a group of brokers in our young nation agreed to trade stocks and other securities for a commission (securities being another name for financial assets such as stock and bonds). The Buttonwood Agreement—so named since it was reached under a button-wood tree in lower Manhattan—initiated trading in five securities, a small start for a market that now lists stocks with a value of about $20 trillion.

In 1817, the group of brokers and traders adopted a set of rules and the name "The New York Stock & Exchange Board." Over the following decades, the exchange would trim its name but add greatly to the number of stocks traded: banks, insurance companies, canal companies and, as the century rolled forward and America moved westward, rail, mining and steel companies.

The stock market swelled in importance and popularity as the years passed by, helping to finance the growing nation's infrastructure through projects such as the Transcontinental Railroad and the Erie Canal. But the NYSE became the heart of various financial panics, too. Jay Cooke, who played a role in financing the Union efforts in the Civil War, was a large dealer in the bond market through his eponymous company. In 1873, Jay Cooke & Co. collapsed due to large, bad bets on railroad stocks, forcing the market to close for ten days and triggering a national uproar.

In 1896, *The Wall Street Journal* published its first Dow Jones Industrial Average (DJIA). It was the first popular measuring stick for the NYSE and remains a cultural touchstone more than a hundred years later. Its initial value was 40.74. The DJIA, a price-weighted average, reached its initial value by totaling the share prices of its twelve component stocks (today it has thirty component stocks) and dividing that figure by a "divisor" to reach the average price. (For more on the DJIA, see page 22.)

In 1903, the NYSE moved into its current location. Three years later, the Dow Jones Industrial Average closed above 100 for the first time.

The stock exchange closed for four and a half months in 1914—its longest closure ever—just before the start of World War I. Concerns about the market's health amid so much uncertainty, compounded by trading

losses ahead of open conflict, led market officials to shut down operations. The NYSE reopened later in the year. After the war ended in 1918, the NYSE became the center of the stock market world, supplanting the London Stock Exchange.

The exchange's most infamous events occurred in 1929. The Roaring Twenties led to widespread speculation, roaring stock prices and newfound wealth. But the dreams of getting rich on stocks ended badly. On Black Tuesday, October 29, the DJIA fell 11%, to 230 points. The DJIA, which had peaked in September 1929 at 381.17, wouldn't reach that level again until 1954.

In the wake of the crash, the Great Depression unfolded, and the Securities and Exchange Commission (SEC) was created to police the stock markets. Prior to its establishment, few rules governed the buying and selling of stocks. Politicians believed that the watchdog function of the SEC was needed to restore confidence in the stock market.

But during the Depression, few people cared much for the market. Trading was thin, as the memory of the 1929 crash and the wealth lost remained far too vivid.

In the late 1960s, a steady increase in trading volume led to a paperwork crisis. Eventually, greater automation was adopted to stave off a problem that had back offices processing trades around the clock for months in order to keep up with trading volume.

In 1987, the stock market crashed once more, with the Dow Jones Industrial Average dropping 22% in a single day. NYSE volume topped a then-record 500 million shares, yet the NYSE was able to maintain a relatively orderly market, something that competing markets, such as the Nasdaq Stock Market, failed to do. The following day, as prices stabilized, volume set another record, topping 600 million shares.

By 1990, the stock market had evolved from its clubby beginnings to include wide swaths of America. More than 50 million individuals owned shares of stocks traded on the exchange. This rise of individual investment in stocks continues today.

Daily trading volume passed 1 billion shares in 1997 during a selling panic that prompted officials to halt trading briefly. The downdraft became a blip in an otherwise impressive move in share prices. From 1995 to 2000, the Dow Jones industrials rose from 5000 to 10,000, eventually clipping past 11,000.

But the good times—or the bubble, as many came to see it—didn't last. Starting in the spring of 2000, major market measures peaked (the DJIA at 11,722.98 and the Nasdaq at 5048.62) and then slid. Over the next few years, the Dow slipped toward 7000 and the Nasdaq Composite Index lost more than half its value, dropping below 2000.

In the wake of the September 11, 2001, attacks, which destroyed the nearby World Trade Center, the NYSE closed for four sessions, its longest closure since 1933. Trading reopened on September 17, with a record 2.37 billion shares traded.

Today, daily trading volume routinely tops 1 billion shares, and about 2,800 stocks trade on the New York Stock Exchange. While trading still takes place via a specialist system established in the late 1800s, most transactions move through the exchange electronically. Listed companies are based all over the world, including in Japan, China, Latin America, Europe and Africa.

STOCKS ON THE NYSE AND STOCKS ON THE NASDAQ

NYSE

Name	Symbol
Exxon Mobil	XOM
General Electric	GE
Citigroup	C
Wal-Mart	WMT
Pfizer	PFE
Johnson & Johnson	JNJ
Bank of America	BAC
AIG	AIG
IBM	IBM
Berkshire Hathaway	BRKA
Procter & Gamble	PG
Altria Group	MO
ChevronTexaco	CVX
J.P. Morgan Chase	JPM
Coca-Cola	KO
Wells Fargo	WFC
Verizon Communications	VZ
PepsiCo	PEP
Home Depot	HD
United Parcel Service	UPS

NASDAQ

Name	Symbol
Microsoft	MSFT
Intel	INTC
Cisco Systems	CSCO
Dell	DELL
Amgen	AMGN
Comcast	CMCSA
Oracle	ORCL
Qualcomm	QCOM
eBay	EBAY
Google	GOOG
Yahoo!	YHOO
Apple Computer	AAPL
Nextel Communications	NXTL
Applied Materials	AMAT
Fifth Third Bancorp	FITB
Biogen Idec	BIIB
Costco Wholesale	COST
Starbucks	SBUX
Electronic Arts	ERTS
Staples	SPLS

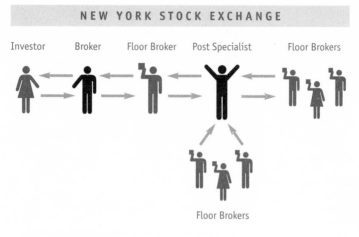

How an Individual Buys Stock on the NYSE

THE NASDAQ STOCK MARKET

The NYSE has tough listing requirements, so many less-proven companies, especially young technology companies, begin life on the Nasdaq Stock Market. The Nasdaq, known for its high-tech stocks such as Microsoft and Intel, trades in a different way. Rather than having specialists who manage the trading in specific stocks, the Nasdaq Stock Market relies on an army of so-called market makers to trade stocks. Market makers are like specialists, in the sense that they focus on the trading of one stock or a specific group of stocks. But rather than a single referee, the Nasdaq has groups of market makers all making deals in a single stock. These market makers post bid (sell) and ask (buy) prices and trade shares among themselves, usually on behalf of investors.

Interestingly, the Nasdaq Stock Market doesn't have a floor like the NYSE. Its trading world is all electronic, living in the phone lines and computers of various brokerage firms around the country. Market makers advertise their buy and sell orders through this network; they can see one another's orders and match buys against sells.

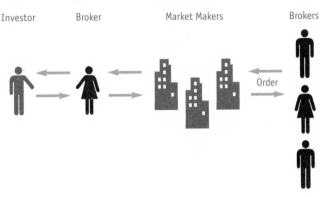

NASDAQ STOCK MARKET

Investor   Broker   Market Makers   Brokers

Order

How an Individual Buys Stock on the NASDAQ

ECNs

Electronic communications networks are the newest way to trade. These all-electronic networks enable buyers and sellers to find one another in a manner similar to the Nasdaq Stock Market, but large investors favor the speed of ECNs. ECNs also often provide for lower transaction costs and a degree of anonymity that is favored by very large investors. Large investors like a bit of shielding so that competitors don't know their trading moves. If others know a large investor is buying a big chunk of a certain stock, they may want to join the buying fray. More buyers mean more demand, making the stock more expensive for our large investor. By staying anonymous, the large investor can accumulate a large chunk of stock without the trouble of attracting hangers-on.

ECNs trade all sorts of stocks, but various regulatory rules make it easier for ECNs to trade Nasdaq Stock Market stocks than New York Stock Exchange stocks.

THE HISTORY OF THE NASDAQ

The Nasdaq Stock Market today is a well-known market that trades some of the marquee names in corporate America. Microsoft, Cisco Systems, Oracle and Kmart all trade on the Nasdaq, and its major measure, the Nasdaq Composite Index, is quoted nearly as widely as the Dow Jones Industrial Average.

But today's modern trappings have wilder origins. Prior to the establishment of the Nasdaq Stock Market, stocks either traded at the exchanges, notably the New York Stock Exchange and the American Stock Exchange, or "over the counter" (OTC). The over-the-counter market was fragmented and often included companies with sketchy track records. Trading OTC meant taking bigger risks than investing in stocks at the NYSE or the smaller AMEX.

That began to change in the early 1960s, when the Securities and Exchange Commission asked the National Association of Securities Dealers (NASD) to automate and better organize the OTC market. The solution: the National Association of Securities Dealers Automated Quotation (Nasdaq) stock market.

On February 8, 1971, the Nasdaq began trading more than 2,500 securities in the new system. Even with the launch of Nasdaq, securities traders had a very defined view of stocks. Think of it like baseball: the NYSE was the major leagues, the American Stock Exchange (Amex) was Triple-A, and the Nasdaq was akin to Double-A ball. Companies sought to move up from Nasdaq to Amex to the Big Board, seeking more market respectability as they moved up the chain.

Nasdaq, however, didn't like playing in the lower league, so it sought to muscle into the exchanges' territory. In 1975, it sharpened its listing requirements, separating stronger Nasdaq stocks from drabber OTC stocks. In 1982, the best of the Nasdaq companies broke away once again, forming the Nasdaq National Market. Again, the move strengthened listing standards for the best Nasdaq companies and placed the market in a position to compete more effectively against the exchanges.

In 1991, regulators placed Nasdaq National Market stocks on an essentially even footing with NYSE and AMEX stocks. This move makes it less enticing to migrate from Nasdaq to the NYSE or AMEX. The impact: the

American Stock Exchange began to diminish as a stock market wait station for public companies. By the early 2000s, the American Stock Exchange was focused much more on options and other markets. Its stock-trading business has become tiny.

Nasdaq, meantime, continued to grow. The technology boom of the late 1990s functioned as the market's coming-out party. Boasting some of the biggest names in the boom, Nasdaq became known as a technology-rich market. Microsoft, Intel, Sun Microsystems and a bushel of Internet companies such as Yahoo! and eBay dominate its list of companies. During this heady period, the market that was once a humble OTC exchange sought to expand globally, pushing efforts in Japan and Europe.

But the bubble burst, Nasdaq's global ambitions came undone and the exchange retrenched. In the mid-2000s, Nasdaq remains a formidable domestic market, and it retains many of the big technology names that give it competitive heft. On many days, the Nasdaq trades more shares than the NYSE. It has more than 3,000 listed companies trading. And the Nasdaq continues to attract young, entrepreneurial companies that give the market a reputation for verve and innovation.

INDEXES AND HOW THEY ARE CALCULATED

When most people think about the stock market, one of the first things that comes to mind is the Dow Jones Industrial Average. Newscasts, cocktail party conversations and idle chatter about stocks often revolve around "how the market is doing." With thousands of stocks trading, "the market" is a slippery notion. But the Dow Jones Industrial Average enables people to take a measure of the market. Often called simply "the Dow," the industrial average is the most popular such measure.

The Dow has thirty large stocks in it, representing major industries such as finance, technology and retailing. The measure is more than a hundred years old, and of the original group of components only General Electric remains (and even it spent a little time outside the Dow during the past century). The components of the Dow Jones averages are determined by the editors of *The Wall Street Journal*. The editors make changes to maintain the relevance of the Dow Jones average in relation to the overall market. For instance, as the U.S. economy has evolved away from a manufacturing focus, steel companies have fallen off the Dow industrials. At the same time, technol-

THE DOW JONES INDUSTRIAL AVERAGE, THEN AND NOW *(Dow Jones)*

THE 12 ORIGINAL STOCKS

American Cotton Oil	Laclede Gas
American Sugar	National Lead
American Tobacco	North American
Chicago Gas	Tennessee Coal & Iron
Distilling & Cattle Feeding	U.S. Leather Preferred
General Electric	U.S. Rubber

THE 30 CURRENT STOCKS

Alcoa	IBM
Altria Group	Intel Corporation
American Express Company	J.P. Morgan Chase
American International Group	Johnson & Johnson
Boeing Company	McDonald's Corporation
Caterpillar	Merck & Company
Citigroup	Microsoft Corporation
Coca-Cola Company	Pfizer
DuPont	Procter & Gamble
Exxon Mobil Corporation	SBC Communications
General Electric Company	3M
General Motors Corporation	United Technologies Corporation
Hewlett-Packard Company	Verizon Communications
Home Depot	Wal-Mart
Honeywell International	Walt Disney Company

ogy companies, such as Microsoft and Intel, have been added in recent years.

Other popular measures of the market include the Standard & Poor's 500-stock index, which tracks the performance of 500 blue-chip stocks, or stocks of companies (including stocks in the Dow Jones Industrial Average) known for their long-established record of earning profits and paying dividends. The Nasdaq Composite Index, wildly popular during the Internet bubble of the late 1990s, measures the performance of all the stocks in the Nasdaq market. The Nasdaq Composite, which includes technology giants such as Microsoft and Cisco Systems, is often seen as a proxy for that important sector. The most popular measure of smaller stocks is the Russell 2000, which tracks the performance of 2,000 small-capitalization stocks. (Capitalization refers to the market value of the company, and that figure is reached by multiplying the share price by the number of shares outstanding.) The Russell 2000 stocks have an average market capitalization (often shortened to simply "market cap") of about $1 billion. By comparison, stocks in the DJIA often have market caps of many billions of dollars.

As computer technology has advanced, the number of market measures has proliferated. Broad measures, such as the New York Stock Exchange Composite Index and the Wilshire Total Market Index, calculate the performance of large groups of stocks. These indexes provide a more complete measure of how the market is doing. But despite these technological improvements, the thirty-stock Dow remains the most frequently cited gauge of how the stock market is doing.

As mentioned earlier, the Dow is a "price-weighted" average. Here's how it works. To get a closing figure of the Dow, add up all the price moves of the thirty stocks. If each stock rose by $1, that would come to $30. Then divide that number by the "divisor." The divisor is determined by the editors of *The Wall Street Journal* and is published on page C2 of the paper. The divisor has been less than 1 since 1986, and thus it now acts as a multiplier. In mid 2005, the divisor was 0.13033708. Thus, a $30 total would lead to a gain of more than 220 points in the Dow. If each stock lost $1, the calculation would be the same, except that the result would be a loss of more than 220 points.

Other market measures, such as the S&P 500, are market cap weighted. A market-cap-weighted index gives large companies proportionally a bigger impact on the index. A price-weighted index ignores market cap altogether and focuses on price moves.

The Dow Jones Industrial Average was created in 1896 by Charles Dow to help him figure out a way to gauge the market's overall performance. Mr. Dow also invented the Dow Jones Transportation Average, a popular measure of an important subsector of the market, in 1896. Dow Theory investing, which is one of the oldest investment ideas, holds that when the industrials and transports are moving in the same direction, they confirm a market trend. The undergirding theory: "What the industrials make, the transports take." Though far more complex investment concepts have developed in the last century, the Dow Theory remains popular, with a number of newsletters tracking its signals to determine if the stock market is in a bullish (positive) or bearish (negative) phase.

Charles Dow (WSJ)

THE DOW JONES INDUSTRIALS THROUGH THE YEARS

As we have moved from the rail era to the plane era into a world of microchips and wireless phones, the Dow Jones Industrial Average has marked the milestones. The Roaring Twenties roared partly because the stock market soared. The association of the Dow with the Roaring Twenties, the stock market crash and the Great Depression has led many casual economic historians to believe that the crashing Dow *led* to the Great Depression. But scholars don't see the linkage so clearly. Instead, steps by the government, especially in the form of higher tariffs, along with sluggish action by the Federal Reserve—it didn't manage the economy with the same skill as the current Fed does—may have played a bigger role in launching the Great Depression.

Regardless of its role in that economic calamity, the Dow did drop dramatically in 1929, falling 23% over two days and wiping out vast fortunes in the process. After the crash, individual investors moved away from the stock market, fearing that it was a rigged game. Indeed, not until 1954 did the Dow reach the high-water mark of 1929. Stocks do take time to go up, but that was a twenty-five-year wait between highs.

In early 1942, the Dow suffered another funk. The Japanese had attacked Pearl Harbor, Germany controlled much of Europe and it appeared that capitalism was on the run around the world. But an old stock market saw is "Buy to the sound of cannons." And those who bought stocks in early 1942 were richly rewarded. The U.S. postwar economy boomed. Even as the Dow achieved its pre-Depression high in 1954, however, politicians held hearings to examine the possibility of another market crash. It took a long time for investors to regain comfort with stocks.

The Dow had a tumultuous decade in the 1960s, rising above 1000 in 1968 before dipping again. It didn't manage to close above 1000 again until 1972. As the 1980s opened, dislike for stocks was widespread. But that dislike turned out to be misplaced. From 1982 to 2000, the Dow industrials put on a mighty show, racing past 4000 in 1995 and eventually crossing 11,000 in 2000. Of course, that terrific run had one memorable hiccup in 1987.

Following the 1987 crash and another sharp drop in 1989, the New York Stock Exchange altered its rules by implementing so-called circuit breakers, which would slow certain trading when the Dow Jones Industrial Average made big moves.

THE DOW JONES INDUSTRIAL AVERAGE, FROM 1990–2005 *(WSJ)*

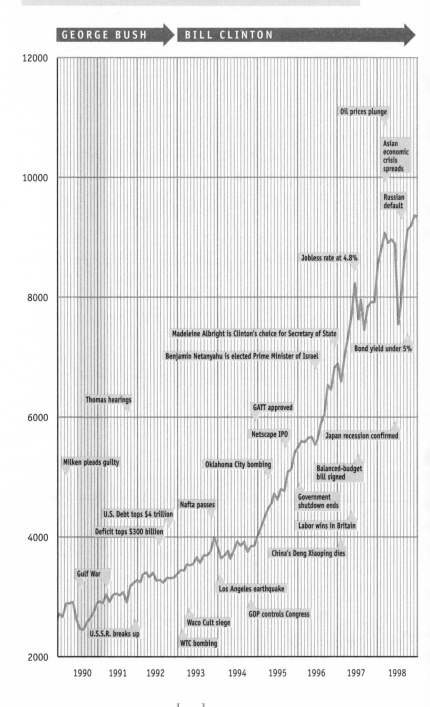

GEORGE BUSH → BILL CLINTON →

Oil prices plunge

Asian economic crisis spreads

Russian default

Jobless rate at 4.8%

Madeleine Albright is Clinton's choice for Secretary of State

Benjamin Netanyahu is elected Prime Minister of Israel

Bond yield under 5%

Thomas hearings

GATT approved

Netscape IPO

Japan recession confirmed

Milken pleads guilty

Oklahoma City bombing

Balanced-budget bill signed

Government shutdown ends

Nafta passes

U.S. Debt tops $4 trillion

Labor wins in Britain

Deficit tops $300 billion

China's Deng Xiaoping dies

Gulf War

Los Angeles earthquake

GOP controls Congress

U.S.S.R. breaks up

Waco Cult siege

WTC bombing

Indicates a recession

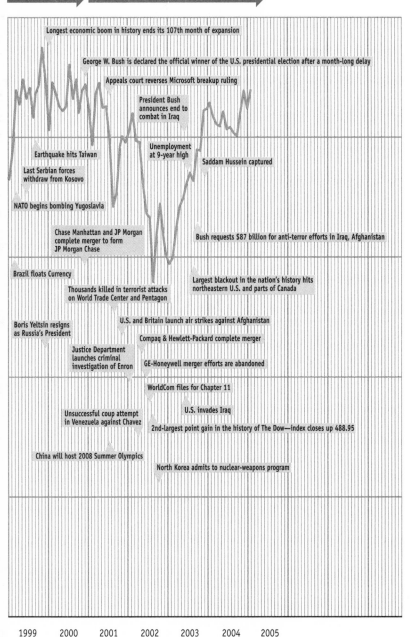

GEORGE W. BUSH

Longest economic boom in history ends its 107th month of expansion

George W. Bush is declared the official winner of the U.S. presidential election after a month-long delay

Appeals court reverses Microsoft breakup ruling

President Bush announces end to combat in Iraq

Unemployment at 9-year high

Earthquake hits Taiwan

Saddam Hussein captured

Last Serbian forces withdraw from Kosovo

NATO begins bombing Yugoslavia

Chase Manhattan and JP Morgan complete merger to form JP Morgan Chase

Bush requests $87 billion for anti-terror efforts in Iraq, Afghanistan

Brazil floats Currency

Largest blackout in the nation's history hits northeastern U.S. and parts of Canada

Thousands killed in terrorist attacks on World Trade Center and Pentagon

Boris Yeltsin resigns as Russia's President

U.S. and Britain launch air strikes against Afghanistan

Compaq & Hewlett-Packard complete merger

Justice Department launches criminal investigation of Enron

GE-Honeywell merger efforts are abandoned

WorldCom files for Chapter 11

Unsuccessful coup attempt in Venezuela against Chavez

U.S. invades Iraq

2nd-largest point gain in the history of The Dow—index closes up 488.95

China will host 2008 Summer Olympics

North Korea admits to nuclear-weapons program

1999   2000   2001   2002   2003   2004   2005

These rules throw sand into the electronic gears that drive a lot of automated trading, thereby limiting the chance of a runaway up-or-down market. The size of a DJIA move that will trigger these circuit breakers is adjusted quarterly. In the second quarter of 2005, that size was 210 points.

The NYSE rules also provided for *closing* the markets during sharp declines. Under those rules, a 350-point drop in the DJIA would lead to a 30-minute trading halt, and a 550-point drop would lead to a one-hour trading halt. Those points were reached during a single trading session in October 1997 during the Asian financial crisis.

The NYSE amended those rules in 1998, adjusting various trigger points for periods of extreme declines. According to the rules adopted at that time, a 10% decline in the DJIA before 2 P.M. would lead to a one-hour trading halt, the same movement between 2 and 2:30 would lead to a half-hour stop, and after 2:30 the market would simply close at 4 P.M. as usual. There are triggers for even more severe scenarios, topping out with the mandate that a 30% drop in the DJIA at any time would lead to the market closing for the day.

GROWTH, VALUE AND OTHER KINDS OF STOCKS

Along with broad measures of the market, investors often seek to define narrower slices. Among the broadest measures are "growth" and "cyclical" stocks. Growth stocks are shares of companies that have steady growth paths, even when the economy turns sour. Traditionally, this includes food companies such as Kellogg, drug companies such as Pfizer and Merck, and other health-related companies, such as UnitedHealthcare and Aetna. The notion is that even when the economy isn't going well, people still have to eat and they still want to remain healthy. Investors also refer to growth stocks as "defensive" stocks, since they are a place to invest even when the economic outlook isn't upbeat.

BULLS AND BEARS

Animals on Wall Street? As a matter of fact, a huge bronze bull flares its nostrils on Broadway in lower Manhattan, not far from the New York Stock Exchange. "Bull" may mean something else in slang, but on Wall Street "bull" means that the market's going higher. The origins of the term "bull market" are obscure. The most common explanation is that bulls drive their horns upward when going for the kill. Any toreador can tell you that their horns do indeed jerk upward as they move at the red cape. A bear market means that stocks are in a downward trend. The origins of that phrase? Also obscure, though two ideas persist. One is that London bearskin brokers would often sell the skins before they actually had them in hand, hoping their price would decline before they had to deliver them. That's a form of short selling that we'll dig into shortly.

The other idea is that bears kill by coming down on something, such as a fish. Wall Street loves its blood sport, apparently.

Technically, bull and bear markets stem from the movements of major averages, such as the Dow Jones Industrial Average. A decline of more than 10% from the high is called a correction. A decline of 20% or more is termed a bear market. The opposite holds for the bull. A rise of 20% or more from the low constitutes a bull market. Some market observers contend that these moves have to be "confirmed" over a period of time. And a market may be termed bearish or bullish ahead of the 20% triggers, due to changes in investor confidence or broad market characteristics.

BULL AND BEAR TRENDS

Bull	Bear
Rising stock prices	Falling stock prices
Rising earnings	Falling earnings
Low inflation	Rising inflation
Low interest rates	High or rising interest rates
Fund inflows	Fund outflows

Cyclical stocks are shares that move in anticipation of economic growth. When the economic cycle turns positive, cyclical stocks tend to benefit. Cyclical sectors include automakers such as General Motors, steel companies such as Nucor, heavy machinery makers such as Caterpillar and mining companies such as Newmont. When the economy emerges from a downturn, companies and individuals start making bigger purchases that they have put off, increasing the demand for cars as well as for the steel and commodities that go into these items.

The market is also broken down into several industry groups, separating everything from computer software to agricultural producers into their own categories. With thousands of stocks trading in the United States, the categorization helps investors understand how different parts of the stock market are behaving. And the Internet allows investors to check out how many different pockets of the market are churning to get a more precise picture of the overall movement. One of the sharpest illustrations of this is SmartMoney.com's "Map of the Market" (www.smartmoney.com).

The Internet has also made getting information on different stocks or sectors much easier. The Securities and Exchange Commission, which regulates stock trading in the United States, requires companies to file a huge volume of documents electronically. All of these documents are available at www.sec.gov. They include everything from quarterly earnings reports to filings concerning major corporate events.

GOING PUBLIC

About 10,000 stocks trade in the United States. Nearly all of them began life as private companies and subsequently decided they wanted to tap the public markets. In so doing, these companies went through an initial public offering, or IPO. An IPO is a way for a company to raise money to fund its operations or expand its business. An IPO also gives investors a chance to own a piece of a company in a manner similar to

WWW.SEC.GOV *(SEC)*

The Securities and Exchange Commission's Web site has a treasure trove of information available free to the public. The home page includes a quick guide for investors seeking various types of information, including regulatory rules information and recent actions taken by the SEC. For investors, the most important area pertains to **Forms & Filings.** This area of the site, referred to as EDGAR (Electronic Data Gathering, Analysis, and Retrieval) contains all the corporate filings and forms that public companies or companies seeking to go public must file. These include earnings statements, annual reports, initial public offering forms and reports about changes in business conditions. The SEC provides a helpful EDGAR tutorial that can help carve through the numerous filings. Another key area of interest on the SEC site is **Investor Information.** From this part of the site, an investor can provide a tip to the SEC's enforcement arm or find out information about a broker via the Central Registration Depository. Maintained by the NASD (www.nasd.com), this is a searchable database that provides information about brokers and the brokerage firms they work for. The SEC site also provides background on regulatory action and a detailed list of enforcement actions and investigations regarding brokers.

STANDARD IPO

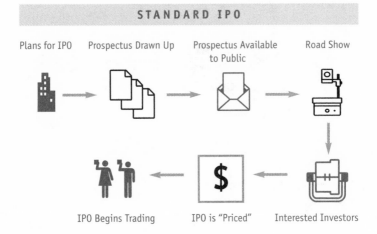

How a standard IPO works *(WSJ)*

buying the traded shares of an existing company, such as General Motors.

In the United States, the IPO process is highly regimented. Let's take an example. Bob owns Widgets Inc., and it is a successful private company. But Bob decides his company needs to expand, especially in Asia. The profits generated by the business won't provide enough money for the proposed expansion. So Bob decides he needs to sell a portion of the company. After careful consideration, Bob decides to sell that portion to the "public." This decision will lead to an IPO. But before Bob gets to his IPO, he has to go through a lengthy regulatory process. He has to hire an underwriter, or investment bank, that will help take the company public. He has to get his financial history in order. He has to tell everyone how much he and the other executives make. He has to describe the business, the risks and outline any outstanding litigation or other problems Widgets Inc. might have. This treasure trove of information is compiled into a prospectus, or S-1 filing, that is sent to the Securities and Exchange Commission and made available electronically to anyone who has any interest whatsoever in Bob's company. After filing the prospectus, Bob travels

DUTCH-AUCTION IPO

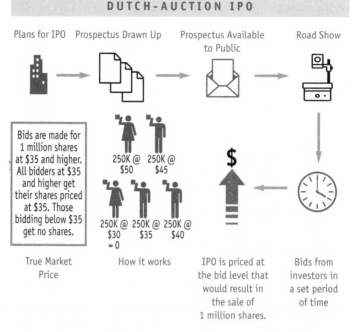

Plans for IPO Prospectus Drawn Up Prospectus Available to Public Road Show

Bids are made for 1 million shares at $35 and higher. All bidders at $35 and higher get their shares priced at $35. Those bidding below $35 get no shares.

250K @ $50   250K @ $45

250K @ $30   250K @ $35   250K @ $40
= 0

$

True Market Price

How it works

IPO is priced at the bid level that would result in the sale of 1 million shares.

Bids from investors in a set period of time

How a Dutch-auction IPO works *(WSJ)*

around with his investment bankers in what's called a "road show," visiting with interested investors in an effort to build support for the company's IPO. Eventually, the SEC approves the filing, and Widgets Inc. goes public. Bob gets his money, and Widgets Inc. can expand into Asia.

Investing in IPOs became very popular in the late 1990s, especially if you could get shares at the offering price. When filing for its IPO, a company tells the market how many shares it will be selling and also provides an estimated price. Along with its investment bank, the company decides how many shares it will sell by determining how much money it wants to raise in the offering and how much of the company it wants to permit the public to own. Some companies issue only a minority amount of the company, thereby retaining effective ownership but sharing a bit of it with the public.

In the late 1990s, IPOs became huge marketing events, with share prices soaring on the first day of trading as equity-mania swept the nation. But a lot of people who bought shares on an IPO's opening trading day got something they hadn't bargained for: a bad price. An IPO is priced the night before trading begins. The first trade of an IPO, however, may bear little relation to the official price.

Let's take a real-life example. In May 1999, TheStreet.com, an online financial news outfit, went public. Its shares were priced at $19. This means that the shares on offer were sold first to a group of investors, a mixture of institutions and individuals lined up by the investment bank, or underwriter. (The investment bank is called an underwriter because technically it acquires the shares from the company and then resells them to the investors it has lined up to buy the shares. This transaction occurs the night before public trading begins and is referred to as the "pricing" of the IPO.) The next day, the so-called opening trade, however, was at $72. This high price came about because of overwhelming demand for the shares by investors not involved in the initial pricing of the deal. At the time, individuals couldn't get enough dot-com shares, so a good number of these told their broker, "Buy me some shares in TheStreet.com at any price." These investors would've been buying at $72 or near there, rather than at $19. But because a lot of people who bought shares at the initial price sold quickly after the first trade, the selling pressure quickly outweighed the buying enthusiasm. Thus, shares in TSCM steadily dropped from the first day, and most first-day buyers were money losers.

IPOs are usually not as surreal as they were back in the days of stockmania, but there are still pockets of excitement. Google's summer 2004 IPO had a strong first-day pop in price, and its shares raced higher from there. The IPO was priced at $85 a share. It ended its first day of trading at $100.34 on about 22 million shares of trading volume.

This model has come under fire in recent years. Regulators found that investment banks and companies at times abused the allocation process. The most common abuse stemmed from allocating shares to favored business partners or in exchange for favors, such as buying other shares. The government cracked down on this practice, called "spinning," in the wake of the stock market bubble's bursting in 2000. Moreover, critics argued that the traditional model led to mispricing of shares. For instance, how could TSCM sell itself for $19 a share and find out the next day that investors were willing to pay $72 a share? The company is selling the shares to raise money for its business, and while those who got shares at $19 and could sell at $72 were happy, the company didn't raise as much money as it could have. It's a bit like selling a car to your neighbor for $1,000 and then finding out he drove it to a dealer the next day and sold it for $10,000. Your neighbor's happy, but you feel as though you left a lot of money on the table.

Most people on Wall Street think the IPO system works just fine. But others have proposed new IPO models, notably the so-called Dutch auction model. Modeled after the style of auction used to sell tulips (yes, they still sell 'em!), a Dutch auction seeks to sell an allotment of shares at the highest price that would result in selling the entire allotment.

Let's take an example. Grinnell Corp. decides it wants to go public in a Dutch auction. It has 100,000 shares to sell. So it seeks bids for its 100,000 shares. These bids are made blindly, meaning that none of the bidders knows what anyone else is bidding. The bid consists of the number of shares desired and the price the bidder is willing to pay for those shares. In the simplest example, BTB Mutual Fund makes the highest bid and wants 100,000 shares. Its bid becomes the highest price at which all the shares would sell, and it therefore gets all the shares at its price.

In practice, it's a bit more complicated. Usually, there are a number of bids of varying prices and sizes. The auctioneer collects the bids and finds the highest price that would sell all the shares; the shares are then all distributed at that price, no matter what anyone bid.

Here's a basic multiple-bid example of bidders vying for Grinnell Corp.'s 100,000 shares. (Usually a Dutch auction has dozens or hundreds of bids, but we're going to keep it simple in order to explain the concept.) Aragorn Mutual Fund bids to pay $50 a share and wants 20,000 shares. Frodo Mutual Fund bids to pay $55 a share for 20,000 shares. Gandalf Mutual Fund bids to pay $70 a share for 50,000 shares. Pippin Mutual Fund bids to pay $75 a share for 30,000 shares. There are no other bids. Under the Dutch model, there are bids for 100,000 shares at $55 a share and higher. Therefore, all bids above $55 a share are filled at that price. Thus, Frodo, Gandalf and Pippin all get their requested share allotments priced at $55—the highest price at which all 100,000 shares would be sold. Aragorn gets nothing, and Gandalf and Pippin get a better price than they expected. The Dutch model, in theory, finds the best market price and eliminates first-day price pops. But it has its drawbacks. Unlike in a typical auction, there's a great deal of mystery. Nobody really knows what other bidders are doing. Thus, investors have to analyze the company going public and make their best guess in terms of valuation. Partly because of their blind nature, Dutch auctions have had only intermittent usage for stock offerings. Google went public with what it called a modified Dutch auction. But its IPO, with a dramatic first-day gain, seemed to act just like a traditional IPO.

STOCK SPLITS, BUYBACKS AND DIVIDENDS

Investors often get excited about stock splits. A stock split occurs when a company decides to "split" its shares. In other words, if a company has 1 million shares outstanding, a two-for-one split gives it 2 million shares outstanding. Correspondingly, the price of the stock also splits. Thus 1 million shares at $100 a share become 2 million shares at $50 a share. Generally, investors see this activity as a bullish sign and bid up shares that have split. But there's no logic to this idea. If I give you an apple and you cut it in half and give it back to me, it's still an apple. Proponents of stock splits say that splitting shares can make a share price more affordable to a broader array of investors or that a split signals a company's confidence in the future. Most investment professionals, however, think this argument is hooey. Ultimately, the company is worth what it is worth, regardless of the number of shares outstanding. Warren Buffett, one of the sagest investors of the past 100 years, hasn't split his stock, Berkshire Hathaway. In the spring of 2005, it traded at $88,300 a share.

Companies also employ "reverse splits." In this case, rather than creating more shares, the company is consolidating its shares. For instance, if a company has 1 million shares, it may do a one-for-two reverse split to get to 500,000 shares. This tactic is often used by companies that have a woefully low share price. By reducing the number of shares, a reverse split makes each remaining share more valuable. Doing a reverse split is not often a sign of optimism. Among the many big companies that have resorted to reverse stock splits are AT&T and Nortel.

Another stock strategy companies use is share buybacks. This has more fundamental advantages to the shareholder. In chapter 2 we'll dig deeper into price/earnings ratios and other valuation measures, but for now it's enough to know that this is a key way to valuate a stock. The earnings are calculated on a per-share basis. If a company buys back shares, there are fewer shares, thus increasing the per-share earnings for each shareholder. Companies often announce share repurchase programs, but it is sometimes difficult to tell if the companies are, in fact, buying back their stock. One way to determine if they are following through on the program is to examine the quarterly financial statements of a company. Each quarter, the company discloses its average shares outstanding. If that figure is shrinking, the company is buying.

Along with splits and buybacks, some companies seek to entice investors' interest by paying a dividend. A dividend payment is usually quarterly, and the company announces a record date and a payment date. The record date is the date that an investor must own the share, and the payment date comes a few days after the record date. A stock trading after

TICKER SYMBOLS

Watching CNBC, the business cable television channel, first-time viewers may be flummoxed by the information that races across the bottom of the screen. Several series of letters—from one to five letters long—flies by, accompanied by numbers and subscripts. It looks like gobbledygook.

But of course, it's not. These letters and numbers, often called the ticker tape, or sometimes just "the ticker" or just "the tape," are telling the informed viewer what's happening in the stock market. Let's break it down so that the next time you see the ticker swinging through, you can decipher its meaning. The ticker consists of stock symbols, share prices, share price changes and, in some cases, the size of the trade being reported.

Symbols are one to five letters long, as noted above. Like football jersey numbers, the length of the ticker symbol tells you something about the stock. In football, players with numbers from 50 to 79 are ineligible to catch a pass, unless they check in with the referee or the ball is tipped. On the ticker, symbols with three letters or fewer are listed on the New York Stock Exchange. Symbols with four letters are members of the Nasdaq Stock Market. Symbols with five letters are unsponsored American depositary receipts or shares, basically companies that are primarily listed on an overseas market. There are also ADRs and ADSs in the one-to-four-symbol range.

The Nasdaq and the NYSE monitor the issuance of stock symbols. When a company is going public, or having its IPO, it can select an available stock symbol, which the Nasdaq or NYSE must approve. Usually, the symbol is closely associated with the company name. Dow Jones & Company, for instance, trades on the NYSE under the symbol DJ. Cisco Systems trades on the Nasdaq under the symbol CSCO.

The NYSE closely watches the issuance of single-letter symbols, since these are considered to have more cachet. For years, the Big Board has kept I and M available in case it ever manages to woo Intel (INTC) or Microsoft (MSFT) over to the NYSE. In recent years, other single-letter symbols have become available. C, which belonged to Chrysler, went to Citigroup after Germany's Daimler-Benz acquired Chrysler. S (Sears) became available after Kmart (KMRT) acquired the venerable retailer. G belonged to Gillette, but that company was bought by Procter & Gamble (PG).

Some companies choose unconventional symbols, sometimes giving a nod to corporate history. Southwest Airlines trades under LUV, because its operations began out of Dallas's Love Field. Sprint chose FON, reflecting its phone business. Nextel Communications, another phone business that merged with Sprint, used the symbol CALL for a long time but eventually opted for the more conventional NXTL. (A company called CallWave now has the CALL symbol.) Among the better-known five-symbol foreign companies are the British-based news agency Reuters (RTRSY) and the Swedish-based telecom equipment company LM Ericsson (ERICY). But, as noted, ADRs and ADSs are traded in the smaller varieties, too.

Once you understand the symbols, the rest of the ticker falls into place. The main number next to the symbol is the share price. If the price is green, the shares are heading higher. Red means the opposite. And when a longish number appears next to the share price, that indicates the volume of a large trade that has just been reported.

Trades appearing on the ticker tape are called "printed" trades. While the ticker is today all electronic, its origins were paper-based, and thus a literal ticker tape would print all trades. On particularly busy days, the tape might print for a long period of time after the market closed.

the record date and prior to the payment date is said to trade "ex-dividend." What that means is that purchasers of the stock after the record date don't get the dividend at the payment date. Instead, they will get the subsequent dividend payment.

Companies flush with cash also sometimes pay a special, onetime dividend. For example, Microsoft, in 2004, paid shareholders a special, onetime dividend of $3 a share. Its standard dividend in 2004 was 32 cents a share.

Some financial analysts talk about a stock's "total return." This is the stock's gain plus the dividend yield. If IBM, with a dividend yield of 0.90% on July 18, 2005, returned 5% during the next twelve months, its "total return" would be 5.90%. (The dividend yield is determined by dividing the annual dividend—in IBM's case, 74 cents in July 2005—by the share price, $82.24 on July 18 2005.) Companies most likely to pay dividends are large, steady performers such as the companies found in the Dow Jones Industrial Average.

The Wall Street Journal publishes dividend information in the Money & Investing section. The Online Journal also has information on dividends.

STOCK OPTIONS

During the late 1990s, it seemed that the road to riches was paved with stock options. For some people, stock options did provide great enrichment. And for corporate executives, stock options continue to provide a fat portion of their generous compensation packages.

What are stock options? Essentially, a stock option is a chance to buy a share of stock at a future date at a certain price. Here's how it works. You work for Humbert Humbert Enterprises, and it likes the things you do. So it decides to give you 100 stock options priced at $25 a share. The options "vest" after three years, which means you can exercise the options three years after receiving them. In most cases, you need to stick with your company until the options vest in order to take advantage of the award. Vesting periods vary. Some vesting periods can be longer, and many companies vest a portion of your shares each year (or month) over a set period, rather than all at once.

The idea behind stock options is simple. The vesting period encourages you to continue working at HHE. Since the options gain value as the share price rises, you are encouraged not to just hang around but to help the company make more money, thereby getting a bigger stock option payout.

Let's go back to HHE. Since it's publicly traded, your options are priced at the share price level the day the options are

GUIDE TO *WSJ* DIVIDEND INFORMATION *(WSJ)*

The Wall Street Journal provides daily information about recently announced dividends and about dividends that are about to trade ex-dividend.

(A) (B) (C) (D)

Corporate Dividend News
Dividends Reported Feb. 25

COMPANY	PERIOD	AMT	PAYABLE DATE	RECORD DATE
REGULAR				
Abrams Indus	Q	.04	3-31-05	3-14
Allegheny Tech	Q	.06	3-29-05	3-21
CBRL Group Inc	Q	.12	5-09-05	4-15
Cato Corp A	Q	.175	3-28-05	3-14
Cavalry Bancorp	Q	.07	4-15-05	3-31
Center Bancorp Inc	Q	.09	5-02-05	4-18
Champion Indus	Q	.05	3-28-05	3-11
Chester Valley Bcp	Q	.105	3-31-05	3-14
Commercial Fed'l	Q	.135	4-07-05	3-24
Community Bkshr-IN	Q	.145	3-28-05	3-09
Domtar Inc	Q	b.06	4-01-05	3-04
Eastern Amer Spers	Q	.6169	3-15-05	2-28
Erie Indemnity A	Q	.325	4-20-05	4-06
Federated Dept Str	Q	.135	4-01-05	3-15
Fst Capital	Q	.15	3-30-05	3-16
Jefferson Bncshrs	Q	.05	4-08-05	3-31
Macatawa Bank	Q	.15	3-30-05	3-09
Midwest Banc-IL	Q	.12	4-04-05	3-25
MississippiPwr pfD	Q	.328125	4-01-05	3-15
New England Realty	Q	.70	r3-31-05	3-17
r-Revised to include payable date.				
Placer Dome Inc	S	b.05	4-11-05	3-11
Potlatch Corp	Q	.15	6-06-05	5-13
Star Buffet Inc	A	.50	6-08-05	5-12
Team Fin'l	Q	.08	4-20-05	3-31
Torchmark Corp	Q	.11	4-29-05	4-01
United Bncp-Ohio	Q	.13	3-18-05	3-08
Valley Nat'l Bancp	Q	.225	4-01-05	3-07
Westmorld Coal pf	Q	.25	4-01-05	3-10
IRREGULAR				
Reinhold Indus A	Q	.50	3-24-05	3-10
Synthetc Strat GJI	M	.062392	2-28-05	2-25
FUNDS, REITS, INVESTMENT COS, LPS				
Corporate Off Prp	Q	.255	4-15-05	3-31
Corporate Off PrpE	Q	.6406	4-15-05	3-31
Corporate Off PrpF	Q	.6172	4-15-05	3-31
Corporate Off PrpG	Q	.50	4-15-05	3-31
Corporate Off PrpH	Q	.4688	4-15-05	3-31
CP Holds HCH	-	b.0684	4-05-05	3-15
Dreyfus HiYld Strt	M	.04	4-01-05	3-10
Getty Rlty	Q	.435	4-14-05	3-31
Retail Hldrs RTH	-	.0138	4-05-05	3-04
Mkt2000+ Hldrs MKH	-	.0015	3-22-05	3-04
Regionl Hldrs RKH	-	.0146	4-05-05	3-24
Regionl Hldrs RKH	-	.035	5-04-05	4-15
LL&E Royalty Tr	M	.027967	3-15-05	3-07
Mid-Amer Apt pfF	M	.1927	3-15-05	3-01
New Plan Excel pfE	Q	.47656	4-15-05	4-01
New Plan Excel RI	Q	.4125	4-15-05	4-01
Pope Resources	Q	.15	3-23-05	3-09
Sunstone Hotel Inv	Q	.285	4-15-05	3-31
Vornado Rlty pfA	-	.4219	4-01-05	3-15
Vornado Rlty pfA	Q	.8125	4-01-05	3-15
Vornado Rlty pfG	Q	.4375	4-01-05	3-15
Vornado Rlty pfG	-	.4141	4-01-05	3-15
Vornado Rlty Tr	Q	.76	5-13-05	5-05

COMPANY	PERIOD	AMT	PAYABLE DATE	RECORD DATE
STOCKS				
BFC Fin'l Corp A		s	3-14-05	3-07
s-5-for-4 stock split.				
Quality Systems		s	3-25-05	3-04
s-2-for-1 stock split revised to include payable date.				
R&B Inc		s	3-28-05	3-15
s-2-for-1 stock split.				
FOREIGN				
Cadbury Schw ADS	-	t.6612	6-06-05	4-29
ING Groep ADS	-	t.7656	5-11-05	4-27
Imperial Chem Ind	-	t.297898	4-22-05	3-04
Knightsbridge Tnkr	Q	t1.75	3-11-05	2-25
Norsk Hydro ADS	-	t3.20194	-	5-09
Tomkins PLC ADS	S	t.5937	6-06-05	4-22

INCREASED

	AMOUNTS			
	NEW	OLD		
Kenneth Cole Prods....Q	.16	.14	3-25-05	3-09
PAB Bankshares....Q	.11	.10	4-15-05	3-31
PPL Corp....Q	.46	.41	4-01-05	3-10
Penns Woods Bncp....Q	.45	.41	3-28-05	3-14
PepsiAmericas Inc....Q	.085	.075	4-01-05	3-15
Southwest Bncp-OK....Q	.075	.07	4-01-05	3-17
Staples Inc....A	.25	.20	c4-14-05	3-28
WesBanco....Q	.26	.25	4-01-05	3-11
White Mountain Ins....Q	v2.00	.25	3-23-05	3-14
v-Company previously paid on an annual basis.				

INITIAL				
Wilshire Bancorp	-	.04	4-14-05	3-31
SPECIAL				
Star Buffet Inc	-	.25	6-08-05	5-12
EXTRA				
NuCor Corp	-	mc.25	5-11-05	3-31

m-Represents supplemental dividend.
A-Annual. M-Monthly. Q-Quarterly. S-Semi-annual. b-Payable in Canadian funds. c-Corrected. h-From Income. k-From capital gains. r-Revised. t-Approximate U.S. dollar amount per American Depositary Receipt/Share before adjustment for foreign taxes.

Stocks Ex-Dividend March 1

COMPANY	AMOUNT	COMPANY	AMOUNT
Aaron Rents	.013	MN Muni Inco	.078
Aaron Rents A	.013	Newmont Mining	.10
American Inco Fund	.0475	Novartis AG ADS	1.86348
Amer Muni Inco	.078	Petro-Canada	b.15
Amer Select Port	.07	Sadia S/A ADS	1.0508
Amer Strtgc Incl	.0725	Scientific-Atlanta	.01
Amer Strtgc Incll	.08	Sodexho Allian ADS	t.9076
Amer Strtgc Incll	.08	Southwest Airlines	.0045
Banco Itau Fin ADS	t.0327	Synthetc Strat GJI	.062392
Fst Amern MN Muni	.06625	Suncor Energy	b.06
Halliburton Co	.125	Triarc Cos A	.065
Europe Hldrs EKH	t.043317	Triarc Cos B	.075
Mkt2000+ Hldrs MKH	.043174	Westlake Chemical	.02125
Oil Svc Hldrs OIH	.0275	t-Approximate U.S. dollar amount per	
Imperial Oil	b.22	American Depositary Receipt/Share be-	
Legg Mason Inc	.15	fore adjustment for foreign taxes.	
Minerals Technol	.05		

A. Period: Can be quarterly, annually, monthly or semiannually.

B. Amount: Is reflected in a per-share figure.

C. Payable date: This is when the shareholder gets the dividend payout.

D. Record date: This is the date a shareholder must own the stock in order to receive the payout. The record date precedes the payable date.

E. Ex-dividend stocks: Stocks trade ex-dividend between the payable and record date. During the period, buyers of the shares are eligible for the following dividend, if any, not the current dividend.

F. Special dividends: These are onetime dividends, as opposed to the standard recurring dividends.

G. Initial dividends: These are the first dividends paid by a company.

H. Stock splits: Stock splits are reported as dividends, with a similar pay and record date formula.

I. The table also shows which companies have increased (or decreased) dividends.

J. Securities such as funds and REITS pay "distributions" that can change based on a company's performance, and therefore are less steady than a regular corporate dividend.

INSIDER TRADING

Insider trading often evokes images of whispered secrets and illicit activity. And indeed, many forms of insider trading are illegal. But insider trading also refers to perfectly legal trading activity.

As for the sexier, illegal version: it isn't legal for employees to use material (potentially market-moving), nonpublic information to make investment bets. Thus, if Bob in marketing hears that his company is about to be taken over but that information isn't public, he's not supposed to buy shares in his stock to take advantage of that information. That would violate the rules governing insider trading. Those rules, however, aren't easy to enforce. And despite lots of market activity ahead of market-moving news, few individuals find themselves in the dock for violating insider trading rules.

The law has become so difficult to enforce that the most famous recent case involving trading on allegedly secret tips didn't even try to prove an insider trading violation. Martha Stewart decided to sell her ImClone Systems stock after getting a call from her broker. The question: did she get a secret tip from her broker that ImClone insiders were dumping their stock since they knew bad news was about to come out? The government didn't pursue that case. Instead, it said that Ms. Stewart had obstructed justice and given false statements as the government sought to investigate the curious trading in ImClone stock. She was convicted and served time for her offense. Despite having served her time, Ms. Stewart has appealed the conviction.

As for the plain-vanilla legal insider trading, it involves how corporate executives and board members handle trading in their own shares. Executives and directors must file information about their sales and purchases with the Securities and Exchange Commission in a timely manner, and this information can be gleaned from many Web sites, including the Online Wall Street Journal and Yahoo! Finance. In addition, *The Wall Street Journal* provides details on insider transactions in each Wednesday's paper.

Investors often track the activity of insiders for clues about how they are feeling about a company's prospects. If insiders are big buyers, that can often be a sign of confidence. If insiders are big sellers, that can be a hint that trouble may be ahead. Of course, insiders can't buy and sell based on material, nonpublic information. So they may be buying and selling based on their longer-term guesses as to the company's prospects. Some insiders also sell to diversify their portfolios, which can be heavily weighted toward their own company's stock.

There are important exceptions to this broad rule about insider buying and selling. Sometimes executives are plain wrong. For instance, Bernie Ebbers, the disgraced former chief of the defunct WorldCom, was a big buyer of his company's shares. That didn't work out for him—or for the investors who followed his lead. And on the buying side, many executives have a good deal of net worth tied up in their company stock. They might be selling simply to diversify. Bill Gates, for instance, has sold billions of dollars' worth of Microsoft stock, but that has more to do with funding his philanthropic efforts and diversifying his Microsoft-centric holdings than with any terrible feelings he has about his company's future.

issued. So HHE is trading at $25 and you get your 100 stock options. Three years later, HHE, thanks to your excellent work, trades at $50. You can now exercise your option on the 100 shares. That means you can buy 100 shares at $25 and then sell them at $50—in a sense, a free $25 gain, minus various taxes and trading fees. This is a small, simple example. Some executives get hundreds of thousands of options, meaning that just a few dollars' gain in the share price results in a big payday.

Going back to the 1990s, the options-to-riches scenario didn't depend on an individual becoming a top executive. Instead, workers were given options to join nonpublic companies. Since these companies were generally in start-up phases, the value of the nonpublic stock was quite low—pennies, in some cases. Options priced in pennies had plenty of potential upside. As these companies went public, the public share prices soared, and workers with options at a few cents could exercise their options and sell the shares with tremendous gains.

Enough people managed to find the stock options gold mine that stock options became a highly popular phrase during the go-go 1990s.

But since then, stock options have taken on a different sheen. With stock prices not soaring in the same way, some companies see little motivational value in issuing options. Microsoft, for instance, abandoned its stock option program in favor of issuing restricted stock. Restricted stock works like options, in the vesting sense (you have to stick around for a period of time before you can sell the shares). But unlike options, restricted stock is just stock. When it vests, you can sell it for its value, no matter if the stock is higher or lower. Take HHE again. Instead of options, you get 100 restricted shares. HHE hits a hard patch, and the share drops to $20 when your restricted shares vest three years later. Your $25 options would've been worthless. But you can still make $20 a share on your vested restricted shares.

Companies, under fire to improve executive compensation programs, have also started moving high-level pay packages from options to restricted stock. The thinking: stock options may have motivated some executives to do dark things in order to goose profits up and get the share price higher, at least for a little while. In some scenarios, executives employed accounting chicanery to improve a company's earnings and share price just long enough to cash out their stash of stock options. Subsequently, the shenanigans came to light and the companies imploded, but not before a lot of executives holding options made out like, well, bandits.

Stock options have also come under fire from accounting aficionados. Under current accounting rules, stock options, unlike other compensation, don't need to be expensed. Thus, issuing stock options seems, at least when reading a company's financial statement, a cost-free exercise. But since options have value, the idea of not expensing them has struck good corporate governance types as fishy. Accounting regulators are trying to enforce the expensing of stock options in a company's financial tables and may yet succeed. But many companies, especially technology companies, are fighting such a move.

INTERNATIONAL MARKETS

Stocks and bonds trade all around the globe. Indeed, the week's trading action gets under way early Sunday evening New York time with the opening of the Tokyo Stock Exchange, the largest exchange in the Asian hemisphere. The London Stock Exchange begins action in the wee hours New York time, and the NYSE itself opens for trading at 9:30 A.M. EST. (U.S. trading closes at 4 P.M. EST.) Several stocks trade in markets outside their home market. A number of Chinese stocks, for instance, trade in both Hong Kong and New York. A number of European stocks also trade in the United States. These foreign companies' shares trade in the United States as American depositary receipts (ADRs) or American depositary shares (ADSs).

In the twenty-first century, global financial markets interact in a number of ways. Often, when the U.S. market is doing well, so are other global markets. One of the reasons is the increasing connectivity and globalization of business. IBM, for instance, has large business interests in Asia, as well as in America. The same goes for Procter & Gamble and other multinational firms.

Measuring the global markets is the same as measuring the U.S. markets. The Dow Jones index group publishes a broad range of world stock indexes in *The Wall Street Journal* and online.

LARGE STOCK MARKETS OUTSIDE THE UNITED STATES

London Stock Exchange

Deutsche Börse (Frankfurt)

Tokyo Stock Exchange

Hong Kong Stock Exchange

Online Resources

www.sec.gov A repository of corporate filings, disciplinary actions and the latest information from the nation's top market watchdog. Among its best features is the EDGAR filing system, which contains electronic documents filed by companies pertaining to earnings, public offerings and executive compensation.

www.nasd.com Information from the organization charged with overseeing brokers and Wall Street firms. The site includes information about brokers and brokerage firms at NASD BrokerCheck. The information in BrokerCheck comes from the Central Registration Depository. The site also includes information about common stock scams and an investor complaint center.

www.nyse.com The latest news and information from the world's largest stock market. The Big Board site includes basic market information, regulatory information and records of disciplinary activity.

www.wsj.com The Web site of *The Wall Street Journal,* including its robust Market Data Center and all the stories from *The Wall Street Journal,* updated regularly day and night. The subscription site also includes many exclusive, nonnewspaper elements, such as columnists and interactive features.

www.marketwatch.com Up-to-the-second headlines and news. The site includes commentary, personal finance stories, global markets information and investor tools. MarketWatch is owned by Dow Jones.

www.ft.com The London-based *Financial Times* provides news, commentary and headlines from around the world. It charges subscription fees to access certain areas of its Web site.

Suggested Reading

Want to learn more about stocks and investing? Here are some good books to check out.

Origins of the Crash by Roger Lowenstein. A readable examination of how the stock market got so crazy in the late 1990s—and how it ended so badly.

Reminiscences of a Stock Operator by Edwin Lefèvre. This book is about a trader in the 1920s, but it still gives a good idea of how a trader thinks and operates.

The Number by Alex Berenson. A good history of markets in the twentieth century, as well as a good explanation of how the corporate accounting scandals of recent years came to pass.

Wall Street Meat by Andy Kessler. A tale from the inside by a former research analyst turned writer/investor.

CHAPTER 2

MAIN STREET

Market watchers like to talk about Wall Street and Main Street. Wall Street is the land of the market pros; Main Street is the realm of the individual investors. And in the course of doing business, Wall Street is always seeking to get Main Street interested in plowing its money into stocks, bonds and mutual funds.

Buying stock is like buying anything else. As a consumer, you research a purchase, usually spending more time on more expensive items. Looking into a purchase includes evaluating quality, value and affordability. It's a rare person who is brave enough to walk onto a car lot and purchase a car on a whim. It's just not wise to purchase a car—or a stock—when you haven't done your homework. Doing your homework isn't a guarantee, of course: a car can break down, and a stock pick can turn sour. But understanding how to research a purchase—whether a car or a stock—can help you reduce the chance of buying a clunker.

EVALUATING STOCKS

In assessing investments such as stock, investors consider valuation, strategy, diversification and appetite for risk. Stocks are evaluated in many ways, and most of the common measuring sticks are easily available online or in the printed version of *The Wall Street Journal*. The most basic measure involves a company's earnings. When you buy a stock, you're acquiring a piece of the company, and profitability is an important consideration. Imagine buying a store. Before deciding how much to spend, you want to know how much money that store makes. If it makes a lot, you'll have to pay more to acquire it. Now imagine dividing the store into a thousand ownership pieces. These pieces are similar to stock shares, in the sense that you are acquiring a piece of the business, rather than the whole thing. The business can pay you for your ownership stake in several ways. It can give you a portion of the profits, which for shareholders comes in the form of a dividend. It can continue to expand the business, increasing profitability and thereby increasing the overall value of the business. In such cases, a more valuable business makes each piece, or share, of the business more valuable. In such a scenario, the more valuable share merits a higher price, giving the shareowner capital appreciation, or a rising stock price.

To further illustrate, let's take a well-known stock, IBM. In 2004, the computer and services giant had revenue of $96 billion and net income of $8.4 billion. The company had 1.7 billion shares outstanding. So each share of ownership amounted to $4.94 in net income. IBM pays its shareholders 74 cents a year in dividends. That means investors are counting on IBM to use the rest of that net income to make its business more profitable and valuable.

Not every company pays a dividend. In fact, many fast-growing companies prefer to reinvest their cash rather than pay a dividend. Large, steadier companies are more likely to pay a dividend than are their smaller, more volatile counterparts.

As we mentioned in chapter 1, the most common measure for stocks is the price/earnings ratio. This measure, available in stock tables, takes the share price and divides it by a company's annual net income. So a stock trading for $20 and boasting annual net income of $2 a share would have a price/earnings

THE WALL STREET JOURNAL
STOCK MARKET TABLES *(WSJ)*

The Wall Street Journal provides daily information about stock movements.

Ⓐ	Ⓑ Ⓒ		Ⓓ	Ⓔ Ⓕ	Ⓖ	Ⓗ	

| 52-WEEK | | | YLD | | VOL | | NET |
HI	LO	STOCK (DIV)	%	PE	100s	CLOSE	CHG
60.19	28.29	Hallibrtn .50	.9	62	40098	57.67	−0.89
13.21	5.28	HnckFabrcs .24	4.1	dd	787	5.91	0.01
23.84	12	Handleman .32	2.2	11	2759	14.27	0.39
8.39	4.45	HangerOrtho	...	...	1402	7.99	0.15
14.93	10.13	HanovrCmprsr	...	dd	4209	14.58	0.03
53.39	33.99	Hanson ADS 1.74e	3.4	...	133	51.70	0.49
42.50	29.25	Harland .60f	1.5	17	790	41.24	−0.13
63.23	45.14	HarleyDav .64f	1.3	16	7337	50.30	0.25
131.74	68.54	HarmanInt .05	...	33	8591	107.97	−0.31
14.29	5.96	HrmnyGld ADS .05e	.7	...	13350	7.59	−0.19
79.69	47.08	HarrahEntn 1.45f	2.0	21	20952	73.37	2.96
38.10	23.46	Harris s .24	.6	26	8487	37.90	0.63
63.74	42.75	Harsco 1.20	2.1	18	1164	57.97	1.08
31.47	24.10	HarteHanks .20	.7	22	1202	27.10	0.30
82.50	52.73	HrtfrdFnl 1.16	1.5	10	5554	75.72	0.11

A. 52-WEEK HI LO: These two figures show the highest and lowest price of the stock during the preceding fifty-two weeks, plus the current week, but not the latest trading day. These ranges are adjusted to reflect stock payouts of 1% or more, and cash dividends or other distributions of 10% or more.

B. STOCK: An abbreviation of the company name (stock listings are ordered alphabetically based on the company's name). The abbreviations are made for space considerations. Harley-Davidson Inc., the motorcycle maker, thus becomes HarleyDav in the stock tables.

C. DIV: This figure represents annual dividends based on the latest public declaration by the company.

D. YLD %: This is defined as the dividends or other distributions paid by a company on its securities, or stock, expressed as a percentage of share price. A company that pays a $1 dividend and trades for $20 a share has a dividend yield of 5%.

E. PE: The PE reflects the stock's price/earnings ratio. This is determined by dividing the closing market stock price by the company's diluted per-share earnings, as available, for the most recent four quarters. ("Diluted" refers to all potential shares outstanding of a company's stock.)

F. Vol 100s: The unofficial daily total of shares traded, quoted in 100s. Thus, in the Harley-Davidson example, it traded 733,700 shares. (7337 plus 00 at the end.) In *WSJ* tables, a footnote on the trading volume of "f" means that the figure is quoted in 10,000s, so a reader must add four zeros to the end of the number to reach the volume.

G. Close: This is the closing price of the stock from the previous session.

H. Net Chg: This reflects the change in price in dollars and cents. Harley-Davidson stock rose 25 cents to $50.30.

The Wall Street Journal tables also have additional features that help a reader suss out what's happening with their stocks. Two of them:

Boldfaced quotes highlight those issues whose price changed by 5% or more in the previous day, if the shares started the session priced at greater than $2. (The price limit helps weed out the big moves made by tiny stocks.)

Underlined quotes are stocks with large changes in trading volume, compared with the issue's average trading volume. The calculation applies to stocks of $5 a share or more with an average volume over 65 trading days of at least 5,000 shares. The underlined quotes are for the forty largest-volume percentage leaders on the NYSE and the Nasdaq Stock Market.

The tables also have a lot of helpful footnotes. Not all elements appear in the chart on page 48.

↑ Arrow Up (Symbol): New fifty-two-week high.

↓ Arrow Down (Symbol): New fifty-two-week low.

a. Extra dividend or extras in addition to the regular dividend.

b. Indicates annual rate of the cash dividend and that a stock dividend was paid.

c. Liquidating dividend, paid when shutting down a company or division.

cc. P/E ratio is 100 or more. The tables have room for only two figures.

dd. Loss in the most recent four quarters, therefore no P/E.

e. Indicates a dividend was declared in the preceding 12 months, but that there isn't a regular dividend rate. Amount shown may have been adjusted to reflect stock split, spinoff or other distribution.

FD. First day of trading.

f. Annual rate, increased on latest declaration. This figure applies to dividends.

g. Indicates that the dividend and earnings are expressed in Canadian money. The stock trades in U.S. dollars. No yield or P/E ratio is shown on these stocks.

gg. Special sales condition; no regular way of trading.

h. Does not meet continued listing standards.

i. Indicates that amount declared or paid after a stock dividend or split.

j. Indicates that dividend was paid this year and that at the last dividend meeting a dividend was omitted or deferred.

k. Indicates a dividend declared this year on cumulative issues with dividends in arrears.

lf. Late filing.

m. Annual dividend rate, reduced on latest declaration.

n. Newly issued in the past fifty-two weeks. The high-low range begins with the start of trading and doesn't cover the entire period.

p. Initial dividend. No yield calculated.

pf. Preferred issue. Shares that generally pay a certain dividend.

pp. Holder owes installments of purchase price.

pr. Preference shares. Similar to preferreds. Preferreds and preference shares usually have first call on dividend payments.

q. Temporary exemption from Nasdaq requirements.

r. Indicates a cash dividend declared in the preceding 12 months, plus a stock dividend.

rt. Rights, a share that gives holders rights to purchase other securities.

s. Stock split or stock dividend, or cash or cash equivalent distribution, amounting to 10% or more in the past fifty-two weeks. The high-low price is adjusted from the old stock. Dividend calculations begin with the date the split was paid or the stock dividend occurred.

stk. Paid in stock in the past twelve months. Company doesn't pay a cash dividend.

t. NYSE bankruptcy.

un. Units. Some securities trade as units rather than shares.

v. Trading halted in primary market.

vj. In bankruptcy or receivership or being reorganized under the bankruptcy code, or securities assumed by such companies.

wd. When distributed.

wi. When issued.

wt. Warrants, which are similar to rights.

ww. With warrants.

x. Ex-dividend, ex-distribution, ex-rights or without warrants.

z. Sales in full, not in 100s.

ratio, or P/E, of 10. Market experts disagree about what constitutes a cheap or expensive stock. Historically, stocks have averaged a P/E in the midteens, though in recent years, the market P/E has been higher, often nearer to 20.

Let's go back to IBM. In mid 2005, its shares traded for $82. Taking that price and dividing it by the net income of $5.03 a share gives IBM a P/E of about 16. At that time, the Standard & Poor's 500-stock index, a broad measure of the market, had a P/E of 20. In basic analysis, a P/E lower than the broader market, such as IBM's in this example, would be described as trading at a "discount" to the market. As a general rule of thumb, stocks with P/Es higher than the broader market P/E are considered expensive, while lower-P/E stocks are considered not so expensive.

But P/Es aren't a perfect measure. A company that is small and growing fast may have a very high P/E. It earns little but has a high stock price. If the company can maintain a strong growth rate and rapidly increase its earnings, a stock that looks expensive on a P/E basis can quickly become a bargain. Conversely, a company may have a low P/E because its stock has been slammed in anticipation of poor future earnings. Thus, what looks like a "cheap" stock may be cheap because most people have decided that it's a bad investment. Such a temptingly low P/E related to a bad company is called a "value trap."

Other popular measures include the dividend yield, price-to-book and, sometimes, price-to-sales. These are simple ratios that examine the stock price against the second figure, and these measures can also be easily found by studying stock tables. Let's go back to IBM. Its yield, based on an $82 stock price, is determined by dividing the dividend payout by the stock price. IBM pays a 74-cent dividend per year. Thus, the yield .74/82 = 0.90%. Investors will compare IBM's yield to the market's overall yield. In July 2005, the S&P 500-stock index had a dividend yield of 1.98%. That means that IBM had a lower yield than the broader market. Investors seeking better value seek out stocks paying higher yields than the overall mar-

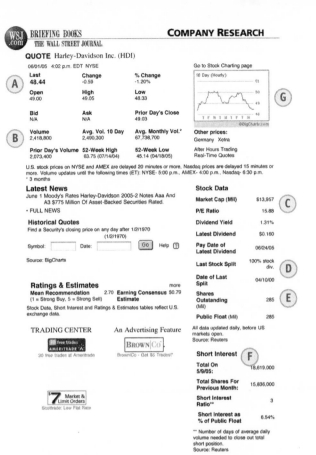

The Wall Street Journal Online has a robust market data center at **http://online.wsj.com/documents/mktindex.htm** that includes wide-ranging stock information as well as market data on even the most obscure markets. Unlike the static paper version, online stock quotes can reflect current market conditions and provide postclose data and information.

In terms of stock listings, here's a look at the Harley-Davidson quote online. Along with many of the newspaper elements, like the trading price, fifty-two-week high and low and volume, the online version has some additional bells and whistles:

A. Previous-day close and **B.** volume figures place the current day in context. In addition, on the right-hand side the site offers **C.** market cap information, **D.** stock split data, **E.** shares outstanding and **F.** a snapshot of short interest information. The page also includes a **G.** nifty stock chart that can be manipulated to expand the dates included or to compare the Harley chart to other stocks.

Down the left-hand side of the page, one click can take a viewer to all kinds of financial information that would be impossible to put in a newspaper: income statements, balance sheets and analysts reports, among other things. *(WSJ)* ket, but that's just one consideration for an investor when deciding whether or not to purchase a stock.

EARNINGS

Public companies report their earnings quarterly, and those reports provide a lot of information for investors. In *The Wall Street Journal,* readers can find a collection of corporate earnings news that provides a portion of the information released by a company. Most companies report on a "calendar" basis, meaning that their quarters end on the last day of March, June, September and December. Not long after the quarter ends, companies issue their earnings releases. At the same time, the companies file a more exhaustive financial statement, called a 10Q (for quarterly reports), with the Securities and Exchange Commission. An annual financial report, the 10K, has even more detail and is filed after the completion of a company's fiscal year, which is usually December 31. These reports include income statements, balance sheets and other items that express the financial health of a public company. Also, companies have to file footnotes to their financial statements, and that's where a number of interesting items, such as related-party transactions, can be found. If a company's CEO is doing a lot of business with a company owned by his brother, which may or may not be a good thing, that information should be in the footnotes to the financial statements.

These quarterly and annual filings can cause eyes to glaze over, but if you are determined to pick stocks on your own, understanding how to read these statements is crucial. We will walk through some of the basics, but keep in mind that an in-depth investment book will provide a more extensive look.

BUYING AND SELLING STOCKS

Now that you know how to evaluate stocks, you need to know how to buy them. Investors set up an account with a broker by

ANNUAL INCOME STATEMENT/ EARNINGS INFORMATION *(SEC FILINGS)*

This sheet is a barrel of information, but for most of us, just a few of the figures are key to understanding a company.

CONSOLIDATED STATEMENT OF INCOME

IN MILLIONS, EXCEPT PER SHARE DATA	Years ended December 31, **2003**	2002	2001
REVENUES			
(A) Sales by Company-operated restaurants	$12,795.4	$11,499.6	$11,040.7
Revenues from franchised and affiliated restaurants	4,345.1	3,906.1	3,829.3
Total revenues	**17,140.5**	**15,405.7**	**14,870.0**
Company-operated restaurant expenses			
Food & paper	4,314.8	3,917.4	3,802.1
Payroll & employee benefits	3,411.4	3,078.2	2,901.2
Occupancy & other operating expenses	3,279.8	2,911.0	2,750.4
Franchised restaurants—occupancy expenses	937.7	840.1	800.2
Selling, general & administrative expenses	1,833.0	1,712.8	1,661.7
(B) Other operating expense, net	531.6	833.3	257.4
Total operating costs and expenses	**14,308.3**	**13,292.8**	**12,173.0**
Operating income	**2,832.2**	**2,112.9**	**2,697.0**
Interest expense—net of capitalized interest of $7.8, $14.3 and $15.2	388.0	374.1	452.4
McDonald's Japan IPO gain			(137.1)
Nonoperating expense, net	97.8	76.7	52.0
Income before provision for income taxes and cumulative effect of accounting changes	2,346.4	1,662.1	2,329.7
Provision for income taxes	838.2	670.0	693.1
(C) Income before cumulative effect of accounting changes	1,508.2	992.1	1,636.6
Cumulative effect of accounting changes, net of tax benefits of $9.4 and $17.6	(36.8)	(98.6)	
Net income	**$ 1,471.4**	**$ 893.5**	**$ 1,636.6**
(D) Dividends per common share	$ .40	$ .24	$ .23
Weighted-average shares outstanding–basic	1,269.8	1,273.1	1,289.7
Weighted-average shares outstanding–diluted	1,276.5	1,281.5	1,309.3
Per common share–basic:			
Income before cumulative effect of accounting changes	$ 1.19	$ .78	$ 1.27
Cumulative effect of accounting changes	(.03)	(.08)	
Net income	$ 1.16	$ .70	$ 1.27
Per common share–diluted:			
Income before cumulative effect of accounting changes	$ 1.18	$ .77	$ 1.25
Cumulative effect of accounting changes	(.03)	(.07)	
Net income	$ 1.15	$ .70	$ 1.25

See notes to consolidated financial statements.

A. TOTAL REVENUE: This is often called the "top line" because it's the top line in the earnings statement. Companies often talk of driving "top-line" growth, which means they want to sell more goods or services. An investor likes to see this figure growing.

B. OPERATING INCOME: This figure represents how efficient the company is at turning revenue into profits, after various costs of doing business.

C. NET INCOME: After operating income, companies have to do a number of things, including pay taxes. There are other accounting issues sometimes happening between operating income and net income, and the more of these an investor sees, the more wary she should be about the stock. Net income, at the bottom of the earnings statement, represents the "bottom line."

D. BASIC EPS and DILUTED EPS: The basic figure, sometimes called the primary figure, refers to the shares outstanding. EPS is the earnings per share, essentially dividing the net income by the number of shares outstanding. The diluted figure, which includes all potential outstanding stock, is the same or, usually lower than the basic EPS. An investor likes to see this figure growing, too.

depositing cash or stocks into a brokerage account. Some investors do this with human brokers; others do it via online brokers. A number of firms offer brokerage accounts. Among the best known are Merrill Lynch, Charles Schwab and Citigroup's Smith Barney unit. Online, investors flock to E*Trade and Ameritrade, though the big brokers, such as Merrill Lynch, also have online operations.

After opening an account, an investor delivers an order to the broker, who executes trades on behalf of his customers. The broker is paid by commission, usually several cents a share, with the commission varying based on the size of the order and the investor's position as a client. More favored clients, those who have lots of money or trade actively, can get lower commissions. Some brokers offer a simple bulk charge per trade, regardless of the shares bought or sold. Other brokers provide accounts that charge a fee based on the assets in the account and allow unlimited, commission-free trading from the account. What the best fee structure is depends on how often an investor wants to trade during the year: not so many trades, stick with commissions; trading a lot, a flat fee generally makes more sense. Online trading sites offer lower commissions, partly because the transaction is handled electronically rather than by brokers.

Once you've decided to purchase a stock or build a position, it's a fairly straightforward exercise. If you want to buy 100 shares of Exxon Mobil, the oil giant, you can call your broker and put in an order to purchase those shares. As an investor, you have a handful of options on how to purchase the shares. You can place a "market order," in which you ask your broker to buy 100 shares of Exxon Mobil at the prevailing market price. You can also place a "limit order." This kind of purchasing strategy sets a specific price for acquiring the shares. Say Exxon Mobil trades at $50 a share, and you want to buy it at $45 a share. You give your broker a limit order to acquire those shares when they drop to $45 a share.

TRADING ONLINE

Trading online became very popular during the Internet bubble of the late 1990s, primarily because all transactions seemed to have one thing in common: they made money. Some online brokers created television ads that included tales of quickly found riches, personally owned islands and early retirement. Many of the online traders moved quickly into and out of their positions, earning the moniker "day traders." While day traders didn't necessarily trade every day, as the market mania rose in the late 1990s, many of them did trade every day—and often. Some companies set up special day-trading facilities where individuals could use high-tech equipment to chase their day-trading dreams. By the start of 2000, hearing of someone quitting his or her job to get rich day trading wasn't uncommon.

After the stock market bubble burst in the spring of 2000, online trading diminished in popularity. The reason: making money trading stocks became extremely difficult. Today, online trading has become popular again, but its adherents are more sober-minded than their gold-rush forebears.

POPULAR ONLINE TRADING SITES AND THEIR FEES

Site	Fee	URL
Fidelity Investments	$8 to $19.95	www.fidelity.com
Ameritrade	10.99	www.ameritrade.com
ShareBuilder	$4 or less	www.sharebuilder.com
Charles Schwab	$9.95 to $19.95	www.schwab.com
E*Trade Financial Corporation	$6.99 to $9.99	www.etrade.com
Scottrade	$7 and up	www.scottrade.com
Harris*direct*	9.95	www.harrisdirect.com

(Source: comScore Media Metrix)

ANNUAL BALANCE SHEET STATEMENT *(SEC FILINGS)*

Again, this is a table replete with figures. Investors often like to look at a few of them.

CONSOLIDATED BALANCE SHEET

IN MILLIONS, EXCEPT PER SHARE DATA	December 31, 2003	2002
(A) ASSETS		
Current assets		
Cash and equivalents	$ 492.8	$ 330.4
Accounts and notes receivable	734.5	855.3
Inventories, at cost, not in excess of market	129.4	111.7
Prepaid expenses and other current assets	528.7	418.0
Total current assets	1,885.4	1,715.4
Other assets		
Investments in and advances to affiliates	1,089.6	1,037.7
Goodwill, net	1,665.1	1,558.5
Miscellaneous	960.3	1,075.5
Total other assets	3,715.0	3,671.7
Property and equipment		
Property and equipment, at cost	28,740.2	26,218.6
Accumulated depreciation and amortization	(8,815.5)	(7,635.2)
Net property and equipment	19,924.7	18,583.4
Total assets	$25,525.1	$23,970.5
LIABILITIES AND SHAREHOLDERS' EQUITY		
Current liabilities		
Accounts payable	$ 577.4	$ 635.8
Income taxes	71.5	16.3
Other taxes	222.0	191.8
Accrued interest	193.1	199.4
Accrued restructuring and restaurant closing costs	115.7	328.5
Accrued payroll and other liabilities	918.1	774.7
Current maturities of long-term debt	388.0	275.8
(B) Total current liabilities	2,485.8	2,422.3
Long-term debt	9,342.5	9,703.6
Other long-term liabilities and minority interests	699.6	560.0
Deferred income taxes	1,015.1	1,003.7
Shareholders' equity		
Preferred stock, no par value; authorized–165.0 million shares; issued–none		
Common stock, $.01 par value; authorized–3.5 billion shares;		
issued–1,660.6 million shares	16.6	16.6
Additional paid-in capital	1,837.5	1,747.3
Unearned ESOP compensation	(90.5)	(98.4)
Retained earnings	20,172.3	19,204.4
Accumulated other comprehensive income (loss)	(635.5)	(1,601.3)
Common stock in treasury, at cost; 398.7 and 392.4 million shares	(9,318.5)	(8,987.7)
Total shareholders' equity	11,981.9	10,280.9
Total liabilities and shareholders' equity	$25,525.1	$23,970.5

See notes to consolidated financial statements.

A. CASH & CASH EQUIVALENTS: A healthy company usually has a store of cash, but not too much! A company accumulating cash quickly has investors hankering for a bigger dividend or better investments. Too little cash means a company is running the risk of being unable to deal with unforeseen trouble.

B. TOTAL LONG-TERM DEBT: This is a good measure to see if a company is loading up on debt. Big jumps in this figure, which can be seen by looking at the year-to-year movements, can mean trouble.

Selling stock is similar to buying stock. You can do a market order sale or a limit order sale. In addition, sellers can set "stop-loss" targets for their shares. If you own Exxon Mobil and want to avoid losing too much money, you can give your broker a stop-loss order, which is similar to a limit order. Say Exxon Mobil trades at $50, and you want to get out if it falls to $40. You set a stop-loss order with your broker, and if the shares reach $40, he automatically sells the shares at that price.

Most investment advisers recommend that investors use limit orders when buying and selling shares. This provides a discipline to your investment strategy, ensuring that you get both in and out at specific prices. In a volatile market, a market order can work against you. If the share price shoots higher, a market order could mean acquiring shares at a higher price than you intended. You always want to buy low and sell high, as the Wall Street saying goes. Setting a limit order provides more assurance that you can get the best possible price when acquiring shares.

Most investors buy shares in "lots," or groups of 100 shares. A purchase of fewer than 100 shares is called an "odd lot." Some investors track odd-lot activity as a way of measuring small-investor interest in a stock. Institutional investors, such as mutual funds, almost always make transactions in lots, rather than odd lots.

SHORT SELLING

You might have read or heard about an executive complaining about the shorts. "The shorts" are Wall Street shorthand for short sellers, or investors betting on a stock's decline. So much time and energy is spent figuring out which stocks will go up that the concept of short selling may seem odd. But short sellers play a valuable role in the market. They are constantly on the lookout for flawed accounting or questionable corporate assertions. They are hunting for problems that the broader market may have overlooked. Going short on a stock is difficult

NOTES TO FINANCIAL STATEMENTS *(SEC FILINGS)*

Each public company files quarterly (10-Q) and annual (10-K) financial statements with the SEC. These filings include all kinds of data, including earnings statements, balance sheets and statements about business activities. In addition, the filings include "notes to financial statements" at the very end of the report. These "notes" can include all kinds of interesting tidbits of information. Among them: important statements about various accounting choices, related-party transactions and information about key business issues. In this filing, a 2003 10-K from Martha Stewart Living

---

NOTES TO CONSOLIDATED FINANCIAL STATEMENTS
(in thousands except share data)

Inventories

Inventories consisting of paper and product merchandise are stated at the lower of cost or market. Cost is determined using the first-in, first-out (FIFO) method.

Advertising Costs

Advertising costs, consisting primarily of direct-response advertising, are expensed in the year incurred.

Reclassification Adjustments

Certain prior year financial information has been reclassified to conform with fiscal 2003 financial statement presentation.

Earnings Per Share

Basic earnings per share is computed using the weighted average number of actual common shares outstanding during the period. Diluted earnings per share reflect the potential dilution that would occur from the exercise of common stock options outstanding and the vesting of restricted shares. For the years ended December 31, 2003, 2002, and 2001 the dilutive effect of stock options included in the determination of diluted weighted average common shares outstanding were approximately 128,000, 375,000, and 401,000 respectively. The antidilutive options excluded from this amount totaled 1,069,000, 4,409,000 and 5,014,000 with a weighted average exercise price of $9.15, $13.58, and $19.05 in 2003, 2002, and 2001, respectively.

Options granted under the Martha Stewart Living Omnimedia LLC Nonqualified Class A LLC Unit/Stock Option Plan are not included as they are not dilutive (see Note 8).

Property, Plant and Equipment

Property, plant and equipment is stated at cost and depreciated using the straight-line method over the estimated useful lives of the assets. Leasehold improvements are amortized using the straight-line method over the lease term or, if shorter, the estimated useful lives of the related assets. The useful lives are as follows:

Studios and studio equipment	3-10 years
Furniture, fixtures and equipment	3-5 years
Computer hardware and software	3-5 years
Leasehold improvements	life of lease

Use of Estimates

The preparation of financial statements in conformity with accounting principles generally accepted in the United States requires management to make estimates and assumptions that affect the amounts reported in the financial statements and accompanying notes. Actual results could differ from those estimates. Management does not expect such differences to have a material effect on the Company's consolidated financial position or results of operations.

On March 5, 2004, Martha Stewart was found guilty of conspiracy, obstruction of an agency proceeding, and making false statements to federal investigators concerning a personal sale of non-Company stock. Management is currently unable to predict the effect of the outcome of Ms. Stewart's trial on the Company's business, although management anticipates that the Company may experience declines in circulation results and advertising revenues, softness in its Internet/Direct Commerce business and softness in sales of licensed products by its merchandising partners. Since March 5, 2004, the Company has experienced substantial declines in coverage of its syndicated television program. While the Company does not believe the conviction of Ms. Stewart affects the carrying amounts of its assets and liabilities on its December 31, 2003 balance sheet, uncertainties exist with respect to projections of future operating results which could impact the realization of certain of the Company's assets in the future.

Omnimedia, the financial statements notes include a reference, under "earnings estimates" to Martha Stewart's conviction on several charges related to sale of a noncompany stock (ImClone).

On page F-28, Martha Stewart Living Omnimedia tells investors that the company did work with a law firm where her son-in-law is a partner. Not all "notes to financial statements" are as interesting as the Martha Stewart Living Omnimedia filing. But for investors interested in digging in behind the numbers, the notes are a good place to look.

NOTES TO CONSOLIDATED FINANCIAL STATEMENTS
(in thousands except share data)

The Company has a NOL of approximately $14,964 as of December 31, 2003. The majority of the NOL will expire as of December 31, 2023. The Company expects to utilize the entire NOL and therefore has not established any related valuation allowance. The Company is undergoing various federal and state tax audits that have not yet concluded; therefore, no final adjustments have been assessed. Management believes the ultimate outcome of these audits will not have a material effect on the financial position of the Company.

10 RELATED PARTY TRANSACTIONS

Oxmoor House Inc., an affiliate of Time, currently publishes the *Martha Stewart Living* series of books. The Company has a contract with Oxmoor House whereby the Company and Oxmoor House split net profits from the sale of books. Income recognized under these agreements was approximately $125, $3,440 and $2,296 in 2003, 2002 and 2001, respectively.

The Company has entered into a location rental agreement with Martha Stewart, whereby the Company uses various properties owned by Martha Stewart. The fees for use of these properties amounted to $2,500 in 2003 and $2,000 in each of 2002 and 2001.

During 2003, 2002 and 2001 the Company paid $12, $452 and $255, respectively, to a company owned by Martha Stewart for various expenses incurred on the Company's behalf in connection with her properties.

In 2001, the Company entered into a split-dollar life insurance arrangement with Martha Stewart and a partnership controlled by her (the "Partnership") pursuant to which the Company agreed to pay a significant portion of the premiums on a whole life insurance policy insuring Ms. Stewart and owned by and benefiting the Partnership. The Company will be repaid the cumulative premium payments it has made upon the earlier of Ms. Stewart's death or the voluntary termination of the arrangement by Ms. Stewart out of the policies' existing surrender value at the time of repayment. If the arrangement lasts more than 16 years, the Company will no longer be obligated to make premium payments and will receive interest on the outstanding amount paid by the Company as of such time. As of December 31, 2003, the aggregate amount paid by the Company under this arrangement is $2,238. In 2002, the arrangement was amended such that the Company would not be obligated to make further premium payments unless legislation permits such payments.

From time to time, the Company uses the service of a law firm of which Martha Stewart's son-in-law is a partner. The Company paid an aggregate of approximately $91, $75 and $16 in fees and expenses in respect of such services in 2003, 2002, and 2001, respectively.

charged to operations for all such leases was approximately $8,582, $8,192, and $8,390 for the years ended December 31, 2003, 2002, and 2001, respectively.

F-28

INVESTMENT CLUBS

In the late 1990s, when the stock market seemed to provide the answer to every investor's hopes and dreams, investor clubs become as popular as ice-cold lemonade in deep July. Small groups of neighbors and friends, rather than gathering to discuss a book, started pooling cash to invest in the ever-rising stock market. Since the Internet and tech stock bubble burst in 2000 and the stock market has become less central to the national discussion, investment clubs have moved a bit to the background.

But investment clubs existed well before the late 1990s and continue today. They are often touted as educational tools—a chance for a group of people to learn about the stock markets and investing—and many universities and high schools use investment clubs for precisely that reason.

Forming an investment club is pretty simple. You gather together a group of people—friends or family—pool some assets, and then set about deciding how to invest the group's assets. The National Association of Investors Corporation provides a great deal of basic information about investment clubs at its Web site, www.better-investing.org.

Investment clubs provide a chance to test ideas with fellow members. And, the thinking goes, having a roomful of thoughtful investors makes it more likely that a clever idea will emerge than if you just sat in front of a computer all on your own.

Of course, money, friends and family can be a volatile mix. When things are going well in the market, clubs can be very happy places. But markets are fickle beasts, and stocks don't go up all the time. So it is prudent to keep a few things in mind:

- Managing risk is key. Since these clubs are social as well as educational, risking your nest egg will create massive tension, especially when things aren't going well.

- Set ground rules. Make sure the club members agree on an investment philosophy before stock picking gets under way. Also, establish the basic parameters of the group's operations: How often will you meet? What kind of attendance is expected? Who will prepare the agenda? How many stock ideas are members expected to provide? Agreeing on these rules ahead of time will diminish the risk inherent in all volunteer groups, such as someone not doing his or her share of the work.

- Be prepared to lose money. If you enter an investment club with the idea of getting filthy rich, you probably shouldn't be in it. Such clubs are educational, social—and then potentially profitable. Remember, not every dinner party has good food, but it's still nice to have the conversations.

Investment clubs provide a chance to learn firsthand about the market and investing. Sharing ideas, examining various investment theses, enjoying success and weathering failure can make an investment club a lively way to get to know the markets. If you decide to join or form a club, check out the NAIC Web site or pick up an investment club book, such as *Investment Clubs for Dummies*.

and expensive, so shorts do a great deal of homework before making an investment. Short sellers, at their best, style themselves as lonely sheriffs in the market, seeking to point out where the emperor has no clothes. Short sellers, at their worst, can get into all kinds of games—some of them in the gray shadow zone—in order to get their target stocks to go down. For example, some short sellers spread false rumors to try to get a stock price moving down. Others will try to use trading strategies to manipulate the market.

Here's how shorting works. Sally has done a lot of research on General Mills and has decided that its shares, at $50, are overvalued. It has a price/earnings ratio of 22, which is higher than the historical norm. The recent price increases for Cheerios aren't sticking. And the company's new business initiatives look moribund. She wants to bet that General Mills stock will go down. To do so, she goes to her broker and asks to borrow 100 shares of General Mills. She has to pay a "rent" (typically a single-digit percentage of the shares' overall value) to her broker on the borrowed shares and at a certain point will have to return them. She takes the borrowed shares and sells them on the open market for $50, reaping $5,000. Now the shorting waiting game begins. Her bet is that General Mills stock will decline, which it does. She watches General Mills shares fall to $40. She now purchases 100 shares for $4,000 and returns the shares to the lender, pocketing the $1,000 gain, less various trading fees and the "rent" for borrowing the shares.

It sounds easy, but it really isn't. Once borrowed, the shares must at some future date be returned. The future date isn't firmly set, but a broker might "call in" the shares, especially if the short bet is going wrong. The bottom line is that at some point the shares have to be returned. In the worst-case scenario, Sally goes short, but General Mills shares go from her borrowing price of $50 a share to $60. And then $70. Owners of General Mills shares (called "long" investors, the opposite of shorts) become increasingly enthusiastic. The broker who loaned Sally the shares starts to get a bit nervous about Sally's ability to repay the loan of shares. Sally watches the General Mills share price rise and rise. She is getting "squeezed," and a short squeeze isn't any fun. Eventually she surrenders, buying General Mills shares at $75 a share, meaning that she has had to fork out $7,500 to buy the shares and return them to her broker. Her overall loss: $2,500 plus fees and rent (remember, she received $5,000 for selling the borrowed shares at $50). Because there are no sure things on Wall Street, a short seller can triumph or get crushed. Short selling is not a game part-time investors should be playing. Even professional short sellers struggle. A handful of hedge funds, lightly regulated investment pools that cater to institutions and the wealthy, focus only on shorting stocks, but the number of pure short-selling hedge funds has shrunk in recent years, even as the number of hedge funds has exploded.

Each month, the New York Stock Exchange and the Nasdaq Stock Market release data on short interest. (The short interest reflects the number of shares borrowed by short sellers.) This data, published in *The Wall Street Journal* and available at the Online Journal, provides investors with information on the short interest outstanding in specific stocks. Information comes out in the middle of each month, providing a snapshot of the previous month's short interest. The tables indicate if the short interest in a company is rising or falling. The tables also show where the biggest increases and decreases in short interest have occurred. If you own General Mills, for example, keeping an eye on the monthly short interest can provide you with a clue to broader market sentiment about the stock. If General Mills' short interest is soaring, it might pay to look at recent earnings and news events related to General Mills to try to figure out why.

MARGIN

Another aspect of stock purchasing is margin. "Margin" refers to using borrowed money to make an investment. Regulators set rules about how much margin an investor can use to purchase stocks. Margin requirements are maintained by the Federal Reserve, the New York Stock Exchange and the National Association of Securities Dealers (NASD). Under current rules, most stock purchases require at least 50% cash up front, which means half of the purchase can be done on margin. Investors must maintain at least 25% of the investment position in cash after the initial purchase. So if you wanted to buy $100,000 of Microsoft stock, you'd need to put up only $50,000 in cash to acquire that stock. This means your broker is lending you the other 50% and charging you interest on that loan while you hold the Microsoft shares.

A more common—and riskier—form of margin is using stocks you already own, rather than cash, to buy stock. Here's how this works. You have $200,000 in Merrill Lynch shares. You want to buy $100,000 of Microsoft. You can use the "equivalent"

WARREN BUFFETT AND BERKSHIRE HATHAWAY

Warren Buffett is one of the best-known—and richest—investors in the United States. Over the past forty years, he has amassed an impressive track record, consistently beating the stock market. In so doing, Mr. Buffett has become one of the richest men in the world. According to *Forbes'* 2004 list of richest people, Mr. Buffett came in at number two (behind his friend Microsoft founder Bill Gates), with an estimated net worth of $42.9 billion. Mr. Buffett built that awesome fortune through a combination of acquiring undervalued assets and making clever deals.

Mr. Buffett does his investing through Berkshire Hathaway, a holding company. Among his longtime holdings are household stocks such as Coca-Cola and the Washington Post Company.

Investors who bought a share of Berkshire back in the early 1960s for less than $20 would have quite a story to tell today. Mr. Buffett doesn't split his stock, so its price has continued to rise steadily over time. A single share of Berkshire stock now goes for about $84,000. (A newer share class, so-called Baby Berkshires, trade for about $1/30$ the price of the standard Berkshire shares.) Over that same period, the Dow Jones Industrial Average rose from less than 1,000 to more than 11,000.

Mr. Buffett is generally associated with value investing. Sometimes value investors are called "buy-and-hold" investors. This is partly true, in the sense that they hold stocks for a long time. But they also sell. Mr. Buffett, for instance, moves deliberately, but he does enter and exit positions over time.

As Mr. Buffett has continued to record strong investment performance, he has become an investment-world icon. Each year, his letter to shareholders is a soapbox for his ideas. He often uses the letter to chastise bad business practices or to make broader societal points. In recent years, he has argued for better corporate governance and more reasonable executive compensation programs, among many other things.

Each spring, Mr. Buffett hosts his shareholders at the Berkshire annual meeting in Omaha, Nebraska. This has become a veritable investment-world Woodstock, with throngs of participants going to see Mr. Buffett and hear his opinions.

Mr. Buffett's success as an investor has provided him with other opportunities. He advised Arnold Schwarzenegger on his successful run for the California governor's mansion. When big companies get into trouble, he is often one of the first folks called. In 1991, Salomon Brothers, a venerable Wall Street firm, ran into a nasty Treasury bond–trading scandal. Mr. Buffett took a large stake in the firm and came on board to help clean things up.

Dubbed the "Oracle of Omaha," Mr. Buffett has maintained a reputation as a folksy, avuncular investing hero. He still lives in Omaha and, unlike many other very rich people, eschews large armies of handlers or ostentatious displays of his wealth.

of $50,000 in Merrill Lynch shares to satisfy the 50% cash margin requirement. (You could sell the Merrill Lynch shares and use just cash to invest in Microsoft. But you believe that both Merrill Lynch and Microsoft shares are headed higher, so you'd prefer not to sell.)

Remember, the rules say you have to maintain 50% of your Microsoft investment in cash. So if the Merrill Lynch shares start to skid, the broker makes a "margin call." In this case, the broker offers you a choice: add more stock and/or cash to bring your position back up to 50%. If you have no more stock and no more cash, the broker will force you to sell either the Merrill Lynch shares or the Microsoft shares in order to bring your account back up to the 50% cash level. In bad markets, where many investors are "margined up," or investing with lots of borrowed money, margin calls can lead to a cascade of forced selling.

It is wise to remember that margin means risk. Playing with other people's money is great when the market is going your way. When the market goes against you, other people often want their money back.

STOCK STRATEGIES

How to make sure your money does the most for you? Investment strategies abound. If you've had a thought today, there's probably an investment strategy to suit that thought. The number of investment strategy books written could fill libraries. This isn't an investment strategy book but a book aimed at providing you the basic structure of the investment and money world. Still, it helps to know about some of the basic investment strategies that exist. And in the world of investing, there are essentially two basic approaches.

FUNDAMENTAL INVESTING

This is probably the most widely practiced investment strategy. It relies on studying the fundamentals of a company before making an investment decision. This includes analyzing valuation measures, such as a company's price/earnings ratio, competitive landscape, corporate initiatives, earnings history and dividend payout. A fundamentalist tries to ascertain if the business justifies the current share price or, better yet, if the share price is lower than the business would justify.

Fundamentalists fall into several categories, including so-called value investors. These investors analyze a company's financial situation and competitive position to see if the share price reflects the value of the company. If the share price is lower than the analysis suggests, the stock is a "value." In this theory, eventually the market will come to realize the true value of the stock, making the share price rise to that value. Warren Buffett is a famed practitioner of value investing. Through Berkshire Hathaway, the company he controls, he acquires companies that look like values to him, based on his analysis. He often cites the book *Security Analysis* by Benjamin Graham and David Dodd as being key to his thinking. The book outlines how to analyze a company and come up with its intrinsic value. If the shares are priced lower than that value, it's a stock worth acquiring. Often value stocks are unpopular or out of favor with investors, something that the value investor anticipates will change as the value of the company is discovered. Among the value plays Berkshire has made is a large investment in the Washington Post Company. In Mr. Buffett's 2004 letter to shareholders, he reported that an $11 million investment in the Washington Post Company had grown to $1.7 billion.

Growth investors also rely on fundamentals, but in a different way. They are looking at the company's rate of earnings and revenue growth. If it is steady and strong, a growth investor will be interested. The growth investor is less interested in "value" and will often acquire shares that would make a value investor wince. Some of the more aggressive growth investors are called "momentum" investors. They see a stock moving higher, and they invest in the stock primarily because they think the stock will keep moving higher. This confidence in the stock continuing to rise is based on some fundamentals, such as strong earnings growth. As soon as the fundamental piece erodes, momentum investors bail out. Krispy Kreme was a classic high-flying momentum stock. But in the spring of 2004, the doughnut maker announced earnings problems and the stock fell sharply. When the momentum crowd loved Krispy Kreme in early 2004, it traded at $40. After the bad news, the momentum investors scurried for the exits, and the shares collapsed. One year later, Krispy Kreme shares traded in the single digits.

TECHNICAL OR CHART-BASED INVESTING

Some investors eschew the fundamentals, studying charts instead. Many growth and momentum investors rely heavily on charts, and some use charts exclusively when looking for growth or momentum plays. But growth investors, as noted above, also like to look at some fundamentals.

The charts favored by technicians depict stock price movement, volume and other technical indicators. A chart can be simple, but it can also quickly get complicated, depending on how arcane the chartists' strategy is. In theory, a pure chartist doesn't even need to know a company's name or what business it does. The chart tells him all he needs to know about making an investment decision.

Fundamentalists tend to dismiss chartists, but charts abound. *The Wall Street Journal* publishes a number of charts illustrating technical trends in the market on page C2 each publishing day. Charting can be very simple or very complex. A simple charting strategy is to plot a stock's price against a moving average. For instance, Cisco Systems trades at $20 a share. The average share price of the last 200 trading days, the so-called 200-day moving average, is $18. (The average is called "moving" because it moves with each day. Tomorrow, the moving average will include today's price and those of the previous 199 days. Technicians use several moving averages of varying lengths.) A stock trading above its moving average can be described as having positive momentum. A stock that trades below the moving average can be described as having negative momentum.

Two common words among chartists are "support" and "resistance." Using no more than a ruler, a chartist can trace a line across the chart that shows where the price rises and declines. A stock has support if it is bouncing off a certain price level. A stock faces resistance when it can't break through a certain price level. Let's take Cisco again. If it moves lower, hitting $16 a share, and then moves higher, doing so a few times over several sessions, the chartist will say that Cisco has support of $16 a share. Conversely, if Cisco moves higher and can't seem to get past $22 a share, it is said to face resistance at that level. A stock that falls through its support level must find a new level of support at a lower level; thus this is bad news for the stock. Alternatively, once Cisco smashes through $22, that level often becomes a new support level as a new high point of resistance is sought out.

Technicians also see patterns in the charts. The most common is the "head-and-shoulders" pattern. This is simply a stock that rises to a level, finds support, rises to a new high and faces resistance, then makes a return trip to the first level of support. A chart that depicts this would look like a head-and-shoulders. This is usually considered a negative technical indicator.

Chartists also place great faith in volume. A stock's trading higher on strong volume is a good sign. A stock's trading lower on light volume is a bad sign. Most basic charts include not just historical price patterns but also daily volume activity.

Fundamentalists scoff at chartists, but the prevalence of charts and their followers indicates that something must be working. Most of the charting work, however, is done by short-term traders.

For most of us, the proper approach to investing requires homework, diversification and patience. In the stock market, get-rich-quick schemes come and go all the time. The prudent approach is to set up a strategy with a financial adviser and stick to that strategy. Don't forget: If it's too good to be true, it probably is.

Online Resources

www.aaii.com The American Association of Individual Investors' site includes educational information for investors, tips on financial planning and a free newsletter.

www.finance.yahoo.com An easy-to-use resource center for investors including filings, stock charts, chat boards, recent headlines and basic share price information. The site has about everything a beginning investor would require, and it's free!

www.fool.com A populist site aimed at individual investors. Investment ideas, information and commentary.

www.thestreet.com The free portion of the site includes news, information and commentary. The site also has subscription portions that have more robust commentary and real-time information.

Suggested Reading

Want to learn more about stocks and investing? Here are some good books to check out.

Barron's Guide to Making Investment Decisions by John Prestbo and Doug Sease. A good basic primer on how investment decisions are made.

Bull! by Maggie Mahar. A rich tale of how the great bull market of 1982 to 1999 unfolded—and eventually ended badly.

Extraordinary Popular Delusions and the Madness of Crowds by Charles Mackay. A good book that explains how markets can go nuts, as they sometimes do.

A Random Walk down Wall Street by Burton Malkiel. A classic on "fundamentalist" investors and how they see the market.

Wall Street: How It Works and for Whom by Doug Henwood. Written from a critical perspective, it provides a view of Wall Street that the industry would certainly disagree with.

CHAPTER 3

BONDS

What exactly are bonds, and how are they different from stocks?

Stocks are more familiar than bonds to most investors, but the bond market is actually far larger. Bonds are essentially a form of debt. Companies and governments sell bonds to raise money, promising to pay those who buy bonds a return on the investment, which usually comes in the form of interest payments. The biggest seller of bonds is the U.S. government. It sells Treasury bonds of different varieties to finance the government's operation and its obligations. Because the U.S. government has a large debt, it sells a lot of Treasurys to finance it. Companies, similarly, issue bonds to finance acquisitions, operations or to pay down other debt obligations. Also, states, cities, counties and other government authorities sell bonds, usually called municipal bonds, to finance their various operations. The bond market is enmeshed in our everyday lives. A new sports stadium inevitably is built by selling bonds. The local utility sells bonds to build a new power plant. Car companies sell bonds to support the financing of the cars they sell. We are awash in bonds! So understanding what they are and why people invest in them is an important part of understanding money and investing.

THE HISTORY OF BONDS

Bonds play a major role in financial markets around the world. They also have a rich history for investors. Indeed, it is only in the last hundred years that stocks have slowly moved ahead of bonds in investors' imagination. Still, despite the popularity of stocks, the world's bond markets are much larger than the world's stock markets. Debt, it seems, never goes out of style.

Bonds have been used to finance many things and events in world history. Perhaps most familiar are bonds used to finance wars. Famously, after the Revolutionary War, Alexander Hamilton insisted that the new young American nation repay its war debts in full. This was initially an unpopular decision, but it helped set the tone for both the United States and the debt markets. The United States has never defaulted on its bonds. Liberty bonds were sold to fund U.S. efforts in World War I, and about 85 million Americans bought war bonds during World War II.

Infrastructure has also benefited from bonds. New York used bonds to finance the Erie Canal. The massive expansion of railroads across the United States during the nineteenth century was financed by a proliferation of bonds. Bonds have funded subways, sports stadiums and government buildings.

Government bonds have developed quirky names. While "Treasurys" sound dull, the United States also sells "TIPS," or Treasury Inflation-Protected Securities. The United Kingdom's debt is called "gilts" for gilt-edged securities. German debt is called "bunds" for the nation's central bank, the Bundesbank.

Bonds are considered less risky than stocks. But curiously, they usually pay investors a higher yield—an annual rate of return as paid in interest—than stocks. This wasn't always so. Indeed, before 1959, stocks paid a better yield than bonds, because investors saw stocks as being notoriously riskier than bonds. But in that year, the financial markets shifted their view of risk. Stocks, it seemed, now looked like less of a gamble. Moreover, stocks could benefit from a company's growth, which would lead to a rising share price. The stock's yield—or dividend payment—became secondary to its price. That shift in view has helped propel stocks to the forefront of investors' minds.

Today, bonds are sold by companies, governments and municipalities, but they also come in quirkier forms. In 1997, so-called Bowie bonds were sold against the future income from singer David Bowie's songs.

TREASURY BONDS

The U.S. government usually doesn't take in enough in taxes to fund itself. So in order for the government to keep functioning, it needs to raise money, and it does so by selling Treasury bonds. And since the U.S. government has a large accumulated debt, the government often goes to the debt markets to either raise funds for operations or to refinance the outstanding debt. (The debt is the amount of borrowing by the government accumulated over time. The deficit is the annual difference between income—taxes—and obligations—everything from Social Security to defense spending.)

Treasury bonds come in many forms. "Treasury bonds" is a catchall term that includes the issuance of debt with other names, such as notes and bills. Treasury *bonds* refer specifically to the ten-year bond. Treasury *notes* are generally from two to ten years in duration. Treasury *bills,* or T-bills, are much shorter term bonds, usually measured in weeks. Typical T-bills are thirteen weeks or twenty-six weeks in duration. Treasury debt is considered the safest debt investment, because the debt is backed by the full faith and credit of the United States, and the United States has never defaulted on its debt. Because Treasurys are considered the safest investment, they act as a pricing "benchmark" for other nongovernment bonds. The interest rates paid by Treasurys (and other nongovernment bonds) tend to be higher for longer-duration bonds and lower for shorter-duration bonds. This is because the longer you hold an investment, the greater the implied risk, and thus the investor demand for higher returns.

The most familiar and most important Treasury for individual investors is the ten-year bond. This is the longest-term Treasury sold by the U.S. government. (The thirty-year bond is the longest-term Treasury sold. After a brief hiatus, the 30-year bond will return in 2006.) Other nations also sell longer-term government bonds. France, for example, sold a fifty-year bond in 2005.) The term, or duration, of a bond is important in understanding its risk. A ten-year government bond promises the buyer that it will return the original investment of the bond, plus pay a fixed interest rate, or coupon. (The term "coupon" comes from the old practice of attaching coupons to a bond certificate that could be redeemed for the interest payment. Someone who buys bonds and collects interest, rather than trading the bonds, is called a "coupon clipper.") So, say you wanted to buy $1,000 in ten-year bonds ($1,000 is the minimum purchase amount). You would expect to get an annual return which in recent years has been about 4 to 5%, plus the original $1,000 at the end of the ten years. This interest rate payment, or yield, is set in the marketplace when the bonds are originally sold. Since the interest rate on the bond is fixed for the life of the bond at that first sale, investors in ten-year bonds are betting that inflation won't be so great during that decade as to erode the value of the bond. If inflation were to rise to 6 or 7%, that 4 to 5% fixed return would mean the holder of the ten-year bond would be losing money. Thus, while stock investors focus on profits, bond investors are obsessed with inflation.

The government initially sells bonds by auction. The dominant buyers at these auctions are large institutions and foreign governments, but individuals can also make bids either directly through the U.S. Treasury (www.treasurydirect.gov) or through their bank or broker. Notes, bills and bonds are sold throughout the year, and a calendar of these auctions can be found on financial Web sites, such as the Wall Street Journal Online. In addition, the government also sells loads of debt at

Bonds & Interest
10-Year Treasury Note Yield (4 p.m. ET)

	Price Chg.	Yield
	▼ - 6/32	4.268%

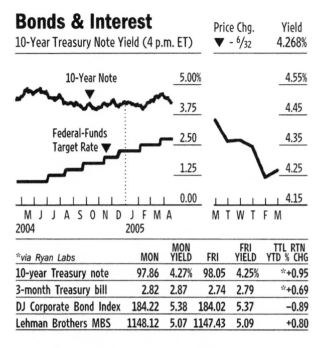

*via Ryan Labs	MON	MON YIELD	FRI	FRI YIELD	TTL RTN YTD % CHG
10-year Treasury note	97.86	4.27%	98.05	4.25%	*+0.95
3-month Treasury bill	2.82	2.87	2.74	2.79	*+0.69
DJ Corporate Bond Index	184.22	5.38	184.02	5.37	−0.89
Lehman Brothers MBS	1148.12	5.07	1147.43	5.09	+0.80

The 10-year Treasury note yield versus the federal funds target rate, which shows that right now 10-year Treasurys are beating inflation. *(WSJ)*

its quarterly refunding auction. This refunding, which usually consists of longer-dated bonds, is conducted in February, May, August and November.

Once these bonds, bills and notes are sold by the government, they then can be traded like any other security in the secondary market. The interest payment is fixed. So if the price of a bond falls, the yield, or the percentage return of the interest payment versus the price of the bond, will rise, and vice versa if the price of the bond rises.

The ten-year bond also plays a role in setting a number of other important interest rates. The most familiar is mortgage rates. Banks establish mortgage interest rates by checking in on the yield being paid by the ten-year bond. Thus, when the ten-year bond price falls and its yield begins to rise, home buyers see their mortgage rates start to go higher. In the early part of the new century, ten-year Treasury yields sank to their lowest levels in forty years. Mortgage rates followed, sparking a housing and mortgage-refinancing boom.

As mentioned, bond investors are inflation obsessed. In 1997, the government introduced a new Treasury that adjusted its yield to inflation. These bonds, called TIPS (Treasury Inflation-Protected Securities), provide investors with protection against surprising moves in inflation by resetting the yield on the bond annually. The TIPS market isn't nearly as large as the traditional Treasury market, but it has grown in popularity, especially among smaller investors.

Finding information about Treasurys isn't as simple as finding information about stocks. But, thanks to the Internet, more information than ever is available. Some of the most complete information about Treasurys is in *The Wall Street Journal* and on its Web site. Bond tables provide the current yield on traded Treasurys. Most individuals buy bonds and hold them for the duration. But some like to sell them before the end date. In that case, checking the tables in *The Wall Street Journal* will give you an understanding of what those bonds are worth in the trading market. Since Treasury prices aren't broadly disseminated in a manner similar to stock prices, understanding how to read the Treasury tables is important for those seeking to buy or sell Treasury bonds.

MUNICIPAL BONDS

Many states, cities and counties also sell debt. These municipalities peddle their bonds in the municipal bond market, and a lot of individual investors buy municipal bonds because of their tax advantages and slightly higher yields, because as good a debtor as a city or state may be, they are not considered as bullet-proof as the U.S. government. Therefore, municipalities have to pay a slightly higher yield in order to attract investors.

Municipal bonds, often called "muni bonds" or "munis," function basically the same way Treasury bonds do. They have a duration, pay a yield and are backed by the full faith and

Bond Yields
Treasury Issues*

(A) MATURITY	(B) COUPON	(C) PRICE	YIELD (D)
02/28/07	3.375	99.14	3.680
03/15/10	4.000	99.13	4.131
02/15/15	4.000	96.09	4.468
02/15/31	5.375	109.04	4.759

*Source: Reuters Group PLC.

A. Maturity: This refers to when the bond expires. In 2005, a bond that expires in 2007 is a two-year bond. Since the government no longer issues thirty-year bonds, the oldest maturity bond in the table expires in February 2031, which makes that "thirty-year bond" really a twenty-six-year bond.

B. Coupon: This refers to the fixed annual interest rate payment for the bond. This payment is set at issue, and when the price of the bond is at par, or 100, then the coupon and the yield are the same.

C. Price: Prices move as bonds are traded. In this case, the two-year bond has fallen below 100, which would mean its yield, or interest rate divided by the price, rises.

D. Yield: The table does the math for you.

credit of the issuing entity. Many muni bond issues are aimed at specific projects, such as building a bridge or expanding a local school. Often, localized bond issues are subject to a vote. In 2004, California asked residents to approve a massive $15 billion muni bond issue aimed at fixing the state's financial situation. And voters gave the thumbs-up.

Not every city or county has the same kind of credit. It's kind of like your friends: Sally may always pay you back, but Bob rarely has. Because of this, bond-rating agencies have become an important part of the municipal bond market. These agencies, which also rate federal government and corporate debt issues, focus on how strong a government entity's finances are. If its income is shrinking and its obligations are rising, the rating agencies might give a debt issue a bad grade. As in school, these grades are letter-based. Triple A is the best; anything below Triple B is increasingly risky. Issues below Triple B often carry the moniker "junk bonds." But we will delve into the world of junk when we discuss corporate bonds. The riskier the bond, the higher the yield the bond issuer has to pay to attract investors. The issue of risk and bonds is fairly straight forward: if you want someone to cross the street, he might do it with just a bit of encouragement; if you want him to bungee jump from a balloon, he might want some more incentive than a kind word. (Of course, there are plenty of thrill seekers who would gladly jump out of a balloon. Thrill seeking in the financial markets, however, is often a short-lived exercise.)

Investment returns on municipal bonds are tax-exempt at the federal level and, in many cases, at the state and local level for investors who reside where the bonds are issued. New York City muni bonds, for example—and the city sells a lot of them—are "triple tax free"; the feds, state and city all exempt the returns on New York City bonds from taxes. Not all localities have income tax, and some states don't have state income tax. So not everyone can enjoy triple-tax-free bonds.

One interesting aspect of muni bond issuance is that many bonds, especially bonds coming from dodgier governments, are insured. This kind of insurance means that should an issuer default on the debt, the insurer will come in and pick up some or all of the slack. The use of insurance can help a municipality sell debt with slightly lower interest rates—insurance means a bit less risk—when selling bonds. By selling at slightly lower interest rates, a municipality saves money by paying less in interest payments to its bond investors over time. Among the firms that provide such insurance are MBIA and Ambac.

Municipal bond information is far scarcer than Treasury information. While billions of dollars in Treasurys trade every day, the bonds for the Jasper County courthouse, for example, are generally bought and held. There are some exceptions, of course. Some states (California) and cities (New York) are quite active issuers of debt, and therefore mini secondary markets grow up around those muni bonds. In some cases, those bonds are listed in *The Wall Street Journal*'s Money & Investing section or carried in the Online Journal.

THE RATINGS AGENCIES

Who decides if El Paso, Texas, or Fargo, North Dakota, has good credit? The powerful ratings agencies. Establishing the creditworthiness of the bond issuer—the risk of default—defines what kind of yield the municipality will have to pay. The higher the risk, the higher the yield must be to attract enough buyers. The same applies to all bond issuers, including corporations. The credit ratings agencies study budgets, income trends and recent repayments of other debts. It's a practice similar to how individual credit ratings are developed. Having a good credit rating means it costs less to sell debt and raise money, because good credit means a lower yield.

The two biggest credit-rating agencies are Moody's Investors Service and Standard & Poor's. There is a smattering of smaller raters, but these two set the standard, and their view can save or sink debt offerings. These two not only rate the creditworthiness of small companies issuing debt, they also weigh in on the creditworthiness of nations issuing debt. The U.S. government, for instance, has a top, Triple-A rating from both agencies. Argentina, which has defaulted on its federal debt in recent years, has struggled to improve its rating. It has a B-minus rating, which is considered "junk," or high risk.

The two big dogs use slightly different rating systems. The different systems aren't quite as crazy as comparing Fahrenheit and Celsius, but a translation table below tells you precisely what is what in the bond-rating world.

THE RATINGS AGENCIES

Moody's Investors Service (From Best to Worst)	Standard & Poor's (From Best to Worst)
Aaa	AAA
Aa1	AA+
Aa2	AA
Aa3	AA−
A1	A+
A2	A
A3	A−
Baa1	BBB+
Baa2	BBB
Baa3	BBB−

The above are investment grade. Anything worse is considered "junk."

BOND LADDERING

Bond investors are often considered a boring lot, unless they're junk bond investors, which is a very risky (read: non-boring) game. But like their stock-investing cousins, bond investors have a few tricks they like to employ. Among the most popular tricks, or strategies, if you prefer, is bond laddering.

Bonds come in many forms, as this chapter points out. One of the most significant concerns the term, or duration, of a bond. A bond can have a very short duration—a matter of months in the Treasury markets—or a very long one. Some companies have issued bonds with 100-year durations.

Laddering is a way to balance the risk of a bond portfolio. A simple way to think about laddering is to consider horse-race betting. Some track rats will bet on their horse to win, place and show. This way, if their horse just doesn't quite win, they can still get a payout for a second- or third-place finish. This kind of track betting means less risk and therefore less payout. But as many shoddily dressed track rats will confess, some payout is better than no payout.

In laddering, a bond investor will build a portfolio with varying durations. Say the investment horizon is ten years; a ten-year laddered portfolio could include bonds of one year, two years, three years, on up to ten years in duration. When the ten-year bond matures, the laddered investor buys another ten-year bond, thereby keeping the ladder spread consistent.

The theory behind laddering is simple: risk management. Shorter-term bonds are less risky than longer-term bonds and thus have lower yields. In our example, putting all your eggs in the ten-year bond, which would generally have the highest yield in the laddered portfolio, would be the maximum risk strategy for a ten-year time frame. Putting everything in a one-year bond and rolling it over to a new one-year bond each year for ten years is much less risky, but the corresponding return is also not so great. Like the win-place-show bettor, laddering provides a chance at good returns (win) and balances them out with lesser short-term returns (show).

A laddered portfolio also cushions against changes in the yield environment. If yields fall, you'd be buying bonds with lower returns when you reinvest each year. But at the same time, the rest of the portfolio is making above-market returns. If rates rise, you might get below-market returns on your portfolio, but you start catching up to the market when you reinvest each year in new ten-year bonds.

The laddering strategy can be applied to different classes of bonds, depending on your appetite for risk. Treasurys are safest. Corporate bonds are rated from very safe to very risky. And municipal bonds are also rated from very safe to not so very safe. An investor seeking to balance risk could combine the laddering method with a mixture of bonds ranging from very safe to more risky.

AGENCY DEBT

Somewhere between government debt and corporate debt lives agency debt. Agency debt is so called because it is issued by government-sponsored enterprises, such as the Federal Home Loan Mortgage Corporation (Freddie Mac) and the Federal Home Mortgage Corporation (Fannie Mae). Other smaller GSEs, such as the Federal Agricultural Mortgage Corporation (Farmer Mac), also issue debt, but Fannie and Freddie issue the most.

These agencies issue enormous amounts of debt in order to fulfill their mission: to help generate broader home ownership, especially among the less fortunate. Some individuals buy Fannie and Freddie debt, but in recent years the big buyers of so-called agency debt have been other nations, notably China and Japan. These countries buy dollar-denominated debt, such as Treasurys, in order to manage their currency exchange rates between their currencies and the U.S. dollar. Since agency debt isn't as pristine and riskless as U.S. Treasury debt, it pays a bit more yield than a Treasury would. At the same time, because the issuers of agency debt have government backing of some sort, most investors see the risk of default as very remote. Like Treasury debt, returns on agency debt are taxable.

CORPORATE BONDS

Not only governments issue debt; companies do, too. The basics of corporate bond issuance—risk, yield, duration—are the same as for government debt. The big difference is the range of risks involved. Corporate bonds can be nearly as safe as a Treasury, or they can be as terrifyingly risky as driving blindfolded down an interstate highway. Bonds may sound boring, but there are areas where the more daring would feel right at home.

Unlike government debt, corporate bond returns are taxed. Thus, yields have to take into account that the government will take its share of the bond return. In other words, corporate bonds have to pay more than a Treasury bond would. Also, corporate bonds rely on the creditworthiness of the company issuing them. That's similar to how a city or state's creditworthiness comes into play, but states and cities have been around a lot longer than a lot of companies. So the ratings agencies have more work to do when analyzing corporate bonds.

Corporate bonds are split into two main worlds: investment-grade bonds and junk bonds. Within each world, many gradations occur. Again, the less risky the bond, the lower the yield. Many bond mutual funds can invest only in investment-grade bonds. And most individual investors will buy only investment-grade corporate bonds.

Corporate debt comes in varying durations. Most corporate debt is long term, and measured in years. The most common long-term corporate debt is five or ten years in duration, though IBM and Walt Disney have issued 100-year bonds. Companies also issue debt of much shorter durations, similar to the T-bills issued by the government. Such short-term debt, measured in

CORPORATE BOND TABLES (WSJ)

Each day *The Wall Street Journal* publishes a sample of actively traded corporate bonds. Here's how to decipher those tables:

Corporate Bonds

Wednesday, March 16, 2005

Forty most active fixed-coupon corporate bonds

COMPANY (TICKER)	COUPON	MATURITY	LAST PRICE	LAST YIELD	*EST SPREAD	UST†	EST $ VOL (000's)
General Motors (GM)	8.375	Jul 15, 2033	90.955	9.282	449	30	864,124
General Motors Acceptance (GM)	8.000	Nov 01, 2031	92.137	8.766	397	30	458,530
General Motors Acceptance (GM)	6.750	Dec 01, 2014	90.276	8.222	371	10	326,447
General Motors Acceptance (GM)	6.875	Sep 15, 2011	94.440	7.990	381	5	254,911
Ford Motor Co (F)	7.450	Jul 16, 2031	90.573	8.338	354	30	188,986
Time Warner (TWX)	7.700	May 01, 2032	120.573	6.133	134	30	165,466
Ford Motor Credit (F)	7.000	Oct 01, 2013	98.576	7.226	271	10	157,973
Comcast Cable Communications Holdings Inc (CMCSA)	8.375	Mar 15, 2013	119.805	5.300	79	10	129,051
Time Warner (TWX)	6.875	May 01, 2012	110.168	5.148	64	10	108,157
JP Morgan Chase and Co (JPM)	4.750	Mar 01, 2015	95.995	5.272	76	10	105,175
Wachovia Bank (WB)	4.875	Feb 01, 2015	97.398	5.215	71	10	101,720
Sprint Capital (FON)	8.750	Mar 15, 2032	131.866	6.283	149	30	99,532
General Motors (GM)	7.200	Jan 15, 2011	93.690	8.597	442	5	97,473
Kinder Morgan Energy Partners, L.P. (KMP)	5.800	Mar 15, 2035	96.518	6.053	126	30	96,000
General Motors Acceptance (GM)	7.750	Jan 19, 2010	98.997	8.000	382	5	95,822
Clear Channel Communications Inc (CCU)	5.500	Sep 15, 2014	96.717	5.958	145	10	95,775
Pacific Gas and Electric (PCG)	6.050	Mar 01, 2034	103.880	5.772	98	30	94,268
General Motors (GM)	8.250	Jul 15, 2023	89.625	9.449	466	30	88,013
Kroger Co. (KR)	7.500	Apr 01, 2031	117.207	6.164	139	30	84,700
Morgan Stanley (MWD)	4.750	Apr 01, 2014	95.915	5.326	82	10	77,281
Lehman Brothers Holdings (LEH)	4.800	Mar 13, 2014	97.158	5.200	74	10	76,535
Ford Motor Credit (F)	6.875	Feb 01, 2006	102.018	4.451	74	2	76,124
Pulte Homes (PHM)	5.200	Feb 15, 2015	96.142	5.715	121	10	76,010
General Motors Acceptance (GM)	6.875	Aug 28, 2012	92.681	8.208	370	10	74,695
Merrill Lynch (MER)	5.000	Jan 15, 2015	97.369	5.347	84	10	71,171
General Motors (GM)	7.125	Jul 15, 2013	90.795	8.700	418	10	68,680
General Motors Acceptance (GM)	5.625	May 15, 2009	92.920	7.645	347	5	68,287
Pioneer Natural Resources Co (PXD)	5.875	Jul 15, 2016	103.562	5.448	95	10	66,024
General Motors (GM)	8.800	Mar 01, 2021	95.083	9.400	461	30	64,583
Goldman Sachs Group (GS)	5.125	Jan 15, 2015	98.321	5.346	84	10	61,566
Washington Mutual (WM)	5.625	Jan 15, 2007	102.570	4.138	41	2	61,495
General Electric Capital (GE)	4.250	Dec 01, 2010	97.700	4.714	53	5	60,860
General Dynamics Corp (GD)	3.000	May 15, 2008	96.193	4.304	40	3	60,078
UnitedHealth Group Incorporated (UNH)	4.875	Mar 15, 2015	97.916	5.144	66	10	57,000
Wal-Mart Stores (WMT)	6.875	Aug 10, 2009	109.258	4.523	35	5	56,444
Comcast Holdings (CMCSA)	5.300	Jan 15, 2014	100.243	5.264	79	10	54,203

Volume represents total volume for each issue; price/yield data are for trades of $1 million and greater. * Estimated spreads, in basis points (100 basis points is one percentage point), over the 2, 3, 5, 10 or 30-year hot run Treasury note/bond. 2-year: 3.375 02/07; 3-year: 3.375 02/08; 5-year: 4.000 03/10; 10-year: 4.000 02/15; 30-year: 5.375 02/31. †Comparable U.S. Treasury issue.

Source: MarketAxess Corporate BondTicker

A. Company (Ticker): The company name of the bond, along with the company's stock ticker symbol. Bonds issued by Time Warner, for instance, include the NYSE ticker symbol of TWX.

B. Coupon: Like Treasurys and munis, corporates have a fixed coupon set at issuance. Time Warner's bonds in this table pay 7.7%.

C. Maturity: This is when the bonds expire. Time Warner's expire in 2032!

D. Last price: This is the price where the bonds last traded in the previous session. At 120.573, Time Warner bonds are trading above par, or 100.

E. Last yield: A price below par, or 100, will mean a higher yield than the coupon rate. With a high price, Time Warner's current yield is below the coupon.

F. Est. Spread: This is the spread between the corporate bond yield and the comparable Treasury bond yield,

expressed in "basis points." 100 basis points equals one percentage point. The wider the "spread" from Treasurys, the riskier the bond is. That's because Treasurys are considered very safe. If a corporate bond is considered safe, its spread is narrow. The riskier, the higher the corporate bond yield and the wider the spread. Time Warner has a relatively small spread, but it's still wider than many others.

G. UST: This tells you what comparable Treasury the data maestros are using to calculate the spread—a 30-year Treasury in Time Warner's case.

H. EST $ Vol (000s): This is the estimated dollar volume in thousands. In this table, Time Warner bonds traded $165,466,000 in bonds.

JUNK BONDS

Michael Milken
(WSJ)

Junk bonds are commonplace in today's financial markets. Mutual fund companies offer funds focused on junk bonds, and junk bond tables are sprinkled through the financial sections of newspapers.

But junk bonds aren't very old. Before junk bonds, companies raising money via bond, or debt, offerings needed to get a sufficient rating to go forward. Without a good credit rating, most companies didn't proceed with a bond offering. Indeed, most junk bonds were so-called fallen angels, bonds of companies that had fallen on hard times.

Michael Milken changed all that. He believed that a market existed for junk debt. And, while working at Drexel Burnham Lambert, a securities firm, Mr. Milken succeeded in selling junk bond offerings. His first such offering, in 1977, was for Texas International. Subsequent to that deal, Mr. Milken used the junk bond market to finance companies that are well known today, but had risky prospects at the start. Among them were CNN and MCI.

While others joined in the fray, Mr. Milken essentially became the father of an entire investment industry. He helped leveraged buyout companies raise massive amounts of money via the junk bond market, helping to fuel the 1980s takeover boom. On Wall Street, inventors of profit centers receive handsome rewards. According to the government, Mr. Milken earned $296 million in 1986 and $550 million in 1987.

But Mr. Milken's massive successes came to an ugly end. He pleaded guilty to federal racketeering and breaking securities laws in 1989 and was sentenced to ten years in prison and a $600 million fine. His sentence was later reduced, but he was barred from the securities industry for life. His firm, Drexel Burnham Lambert, collapsed in the wake of Mr. Milken's legal troubles. Before it crumbled, however, a Milken-less Drexel did manage to issue the junk debt to finance one of the most famous leveraged buyouts ever: Kohlberg Kravis Roberts' acquisition of RJR Nabisco. The deal became the subject of the best-selling book *Barbarians at the Gate*.

Even though Mr. Milken exited the game and Drexel Burnham failed, junk bonds continued to grow in popularity. No longer considered some strange creation, the junk bond market today moves in cycles like just about any other part of the financial markets. Untested companies continue to tap the junk bond market, and mutual funds and other investors hungry for higher-yielding assets make bets in the risky arena. And of course, leveraged buyout firms still make use of the junk bond market to finance their various deals.

Today, Mr. Milken is involved in philanthropic work and oversees the Milken Institute, a research organization.

weeks, is commonly called "commercial paper." Companies issue commercial paper to finance short-term obligations such as accounts receivable or to manage inventory.

Investors hungry for yield have increasingly looked at the so-called junk bond market. Wall Street likes to call this arena the "high-yield" market. Sounds safe. Those outside Wall Street, however, prefer to use the term "junk." That's because these bonds are the riskiest. Some have terrible credit ratings or no credit ratings at all. The reason the yields on these bonds are so high (when compared with safe Treasurys) is that smart people worry that the issuer won't be able to pay back the bondholders when the cash comes due. Therefore, to attract enough interested investors, a company with bad credit must pay a much higher yield. Perversely, paying this higher yield strains the creditworthiness of the institution, but often issuers of junk bonds have few choices.

The Wall Street Journal provides extensive corporate bond tables, as does the Online Journal. But the amount of information on corporate bonds is enormous. While Ford Motor Company has only one stock, it might have dozens of outstanding bond issues. Thus, most of the corporate bond information has moved online, where space and newsprint aren't an issue.

CONVERTIBLES AND OTHER TYPES OF BONDS

Since 2000, companies have issued an increasing amount of so-called convertible bonds. These aren't bonds with the top down. Rather, these are bonds that can convert into stock at a specified time and/or price. Originally issued as debt, convertibles pay a yield, based on the creditworthiness of the issuer.

But rather than being paid out at the end of a bond's duration, a convertible can "convert" into a stock at the option of the convertible-bond holder. This sounds more confusing than it actually is. Take General Motors: It issues $1 billion in ten-year convertible bonds with a yield of 5%. The bond pays the yield every year until such time as the holder opts to convert the bond into stock. The conversion term varies for each bond, but it typically is a preset ratio of the value of the bond held, such as 25 shares for each $1,000 in bonds held. If a convertible holder doesn't convert, because of poor stock performance or other matters, the company pays the yield for the duration of the bond. Thus, a convertible doesn't always convert and can sometimes remain just a bond. More than $98 billion in convertible bonds was issued in 2004.

For investors, the attraction of the convertible bond is that it pays an interest rate regardless of a stock's price movement. If a stock rises, the convertible holder has the advantage of converting the bond into shares, taking advantage of the share price gain. The downside of convertibles is that they pay lower interest rates than standard corporate bonds; if the stock price falls, the benefit of conversion diminishes. If the stock price rises, convertibles are more likely to be bought back, or called, by the issuer, because the company doesn't want conversion to take place at too high a price.

As noted above, holders of debt don't always get to hold their debt as long as they'd like. Issuers of bonds, including the government, sometimes take advantage of shifting interest rate environments to refinance their debt positions. In so doing, they will sometimes "call" in a previous offering. Typically this occurs in a falling-interest-rate environment. If an issuer can get more favorable terms (lower rates), it will issue a new set of bonds or notes and use the proceeds to call, or buy back, an earlier, more expensive issue. Issuers of debt also sell "noncallable" bonds, which can't be bought back in the future. But most debt, even U.S. Treasury debt, can be bought back before the term of the debt expires.

Bonds, as we've discovered, come in several flavors. Traders take Treasurys and break them into all kinds of bondlike vehicles to trade. Some bear just the yield of the Treasury, others just the price. Some companies issue "zero-coupon" bonds, which means they pay out the interest only at the very end of the issue, rather than on a quarterly or annual basis. Governments also come up with special bond issues, such as the Liberty bonds that supported World War I. Also, while most bonds are linked to a registered owner, some bonds are called "bearer bonds." This means that whoever has the bond—the bearer—has the right to sell them. Bearer bonds show up more in thriller movies and plot-heavy books than in the marketplace. Most people like to have their bonds registered in their name.

So many bonds of different shapes, sizes and tastes! But it's important to remember the basic truth of bonds: they're a way to borrow money. And the person lending the money (the investor) wants a return that reflects the creditworthiness of the issuer. The U.S. government pays rock-bottom rates. Hank's Two-Bit Automotive would pay higher rates than the government. Don't be flummoxed by the big world of bonds. Basically, bonds start with how Treasurys are faring, and risk (the yield, or interest rate payment) is measured from that benchmark.

Online Resources

www.treasurydirect.gov Information provided by the government about how to invest in Treasury bonds and other federal government bonds.

www.investinginbonds.com A wide array of bond-investing information, including information about corporate, municipal and Treasury bonds. Run by the Bond Market Association.

www.msrb.org The home page of the Municipal Securities Rulemaking Board, the group that oversees the muni bond industry.

www.convertbond.com Information about investing in convertible bonds, produced by Morgan Stanley.

Suggested Reading

The Bond Bible by Marilyn Cohen. A comprehensive overview of bonds and bond investing.

The Strategic Bond Investor by Anthony Crescenzi. An investment guide from a frequently quoted bond expert from Miller Tabak, a bond specialty financial services company. Lots of tips and tools.

Bill Gross on Investing by William H. Gross. Straight from the mouth of the bond market's Warren Buffett. Mr. Gross is a quirky character who writes about bonds but also nonbond issues. His comments can move markets.

CHAPTER 4

WALL STREET

At the center of all this talk about money and investing is Wall Street. Most of the folks on Main Street have heard of Wall Street, and many of them know it's in New York. But as technology has advanced, the idea of Wall Street has come to cover more than a geographical area. Indeed, thanks to computers and connectivity, Wall Street lives more in cyberspace than any single place. Mutual fund firms are based in Denver, Boston and Dallas. Trading desks are in Los Angeles, Chicago and Atlanta. In New York, financial firms are likely to be miles away from lower Manhattan, which is where Wall Street actually is.

Wall Street is as short as it is famous. It begins in a graveyard and ends in a river, spanning less than a mile. It derives its reputation from the early days of investment, when the New York Stock Exchange set up shop in lower Manhattan. Because communication meant sending runners from place to place, proximity to the trading center was key. Thus, financial firms started along and around Wall Street, and soon enough, people involved in investing started referring to the investment world simply as "Wall Street." (For more on the NYSE, see page 10.)

Today, the New York Stock Exchange is the most visible symbol of what we call Wall Street, seen by millions on television and in newspaper pictures. But the Wall Street picture is

far wider than this narrow frame reflects. Collectively, Wall Street is everything that makes the financial markets function.

SECURITIES FIRMS

Securities firms, sometimes called brokerage firms or investment banks, get their name because their business is centered around investments known as securities. (Stocks, bonds and other investment vehicles are lumped under this single term.) Big securities firms, such as Goldman Sachs, Merrill Lynch and Morgan Stanley, are at the center of Wall Street. When it comes to financial markets, the securities firms are at the heart of the action.

With Wall Street virtual and financial markets global, the securities firms on Wall Street now have signposts up everywhere, from London to Beijing to Los Angeles to Zurich. Indeed, American securities firms dominate the global financial markets, with only a handful of exceptions.

What do these dominant firms do? Make money—lots of it. And along with making a lot of money, they help make the financial markets function, for the most part. These firms have many divisions. Chief among them are: brokerage, trading, research, investment banking and asset management. The brokerage arm helps clients manage their investments. The trading group trades stocks, bonds, and other securities. The research group, which includes analysts, issues all kinds of data and information that examine bonds and stocks. Investment bankers take companies public, advise on mergers and acquisitions and help drum up financing for companies. Asset management invests money on behalf of clients, often in the form of mutual funds.

BROKERAGE

Most Wall Street firms have a brokerage arm aimed at servicing individual investors. These days some Wall Street types prefer grander terms, such as "financial adviser," but in the end these people are brokers. Brokers conduct transactions on behalf of their clients and advise on the management of individual investors' assets. On Wall Street, individual investors are called "retail" investors. The big dogs—mutual funds, hedge funds and the like—are called "institutional" investors. Among the biggest players on the retail side are Merrill Lynch, Morgan Stanley and Citigroup. While some firms, notably Goldman Sachs, don't cater to the masses, they do have businesses that cater to the very rich. While still retail, this crowd is usually defined as either private client or high net worth. Some of the high-net-worth folks have as much money as, or even more money than, some of the smaller institutional players.

Stockbrokers are paid in several ways. Some are paid based on the commissions of trades they execute. Others are paid based on a percentage of the assets they are overseeing. After the stock market bubble popped in 2000, individuals started trading a lot less. That has led Wall Street firms to push for more fee-based service.

Financial services advertisements often talk about brokers' great love for and devotion to their clients. One television spot in 2005 showed a broker making a speech at a client's daughter's wedding, a function that would normally be reserved for family. They care that much, you see! But brokers aren't paid by love and affection, but by commissions or asset fees. And while stocks go up and stocks go down, brokers, much like their investment banking cousins, seems to do just fine in any market. Stocks aren't working? Why don't we buy some bonds? Bonds aren't working? Maybe we should buy some commodities. Back in 1940, a book captured the sense many have about brokers. Its title: *Where Are the Customers' Yachts?*—the joke being, of course, that brokers could fund a flotilla on customer commissions. In the end, the broker isn't out to get you, but he or she isn't going to do all your thinking for you. There are lots of customers to handle and mouths to feed at home. Understanding money and investing is vital to handling your broker. *You* are the customer, and you should play an informed, active role in deploying your assets. By making intelligent choices, perhaps you, too, will generate returns sufficient to buy a yacht.

TRADING

When a broker makes a trade for an investor, he or she often sends the trade through a trading desk. Wall Street trading desks, however, do much more than handle trades for individual clients; they handle trades for mutual funds, hedge funds, pension funds and for companies. Firms also trade just for themselves, something called proprietary trading. Wall Street firms have traders handling just about anything traded: stocks, bonds, commodities, options and complex derivative instruments.

Traders live in a meritocratic world: if you are a good trader, it doesn't matter what school you went to. The best traders on Wall Street can sometimes earn even more than some top executives at the firm. Trading desks are a raucous place, and sometimes traders have a cowboylike image. But with rising technology and increasingly sophisticated trading strategies, most of the cowboys have given way to intense, agile thinkers who trade less and less on sheer gut instinct.

RESEARCH

Analysts today fit the part of the green eyeshade gang at Wall Street firms. Financially adept, research analysts evaluate stocks and tend to focus on specific sectors, such as retailing, banking or telecommunications. The stockbroker talking to a client wants to have good ideas to generate trades and investments. This is where the analyst comes in. By providing investment research, he or she gives the broker some investing suggestions to pitch to clients.

Research groups also include economists, who study generic economic trends, and strategists, who study the overall market environment. The strategist is usually the main mouthpiece for a research department, and his proclamations help frame the firm's overall public view of the stock market. For instance, in 2004, a Merrill Lynch strategist, Rich Bernstein, maintained a bearish view on stocks, even as the market rallied. That caused some grumbling among the stockbrokers who were trying to entice clients to do trades. But Mr. Bernstein's reputation as a sharp thinker has helped keep his ultimate bosses happy.

The research department publishes reports, which consist of lengthy analyses of a given stock (or bond or other security), as well as an investment recommendation—"buy," "hold," or "sell"—related to that stock. Until very recently, many analysts tended to push "strong buy," "buy" and "hold." Rare as a unicorn was the "sell" rating. Most on Wall Street grew used to this arrangement and therefore simply translated everything down a notch, meaning that "strong buy" meant "buy," "buy" meant "hold" and "hold" meant "run for the high hills."

But not everyone read through the language dodge, especially individual investors. After the stock market bubble popped, angry investors demanded to know why they'd been told to keep on buying or holding as stocks collapsed in value. Regulators examined the research processes and found that the analysts had been misleading when offering recommendations to the public.

In public, analysts would scream "Buy!," while in private they'd talk about the dreck they had to peddle to the masses. Henry Blodget, an analyst at Merrill Lynch, became notorious for his internal assessments of stocks he recommended publicly. In one e-mail he called Excite@Home "a piece of crap" even as he recommended that clients buy the shares. Internet Capital Group was "a disaster" in internal e-mail, even as he publicly proclaimed its praises. Mr. Blodget was fined $4 million and banned from the securities industry, and Merrill Lynch ended up paying a $100 million fine for its research woes.

Mr. Blodget's practices were widespread, but none of this mattered in the go-go late 1990s, when everyone thought he was getting rich and could retire at thirty-eight. But when the bottom fell out of the market, investors wondered why they had been told to buy stocks as they went to zero. In one instance, Smith Barney recommended WorldCom shares all the way from more than $100 down to $1. Once it was at $1 a share, and not far from bankruptcy, Smith Barney reduced its rating on the stock. Thanks!

Regulators found that much of the misleading research stemmed from how analysts were paid. Large securities firms have people doing research on a company as well as trying to win investment banking business from that same company. In theory, there is supposed to be a separation between the research analysts and the investment bankers. But during the stock market craze of the late 1990s, the separation broke down. Rather than being paid on the genius of their research, analysts were paid for bringing in investment banking clients and keeping them happy. Therefore, Smith Barney's World-Com analyst, Jack Grubman, was largely paid for his nonresearch work, especially on mergers, initial public offerings, and other investment banking work. The accuracy and quality of his work as a research analyst, where he examined various stocks and recommended them to investors, hardly mattered at all when it came to his compensation. (Mr. Grubman was fined $15 million and barred from the securities industry for his research work.)

These research practices came to an end with a large settlement in 2003 between Wall Street firms and regulators. As part of the settlement, firms had to pay a fine of $1.4 billion and change the way they do research. Indeed, in the wake of that settlement, research has become a bit more like, well, research. Securities firms do issue sell calls today, and analysts are now compensated by how accurate their investment ratings are.

Also, an increasing number of independent research outfits provide good investment information to clients of securities firms. "Independent" research means that the outside research operation is not also trying to win business with the companies being analyzed. Under the terms of the research settlement, brokerage firms are required to provide independent research to clients along with their own research.

What can you as an investor glean from all this research? Finding good ideas can be frustrating. A research analyst can help, but often an analyst's insights are so widely reported that it's hard to get much of an investing edge from them. Indeed, it's important to understand how information flows in the investing world. The sad truth is that by the time you read about an idea, it's usually too late to do much good.

Here's how it generally works. Frank, a big hedge fund manager, sees that Hank's Software Company, or HSC, has started to turn its business around. Quarterly numbers are looking better, sales are perking up, new markets are improving. He starts to build a position in HSC, stealthily buying up

RESEARCH ANALYSTS' RATINGS

At the end of 2002, regulators reached a global settlement with Wall Street firms concerning allegedly faulty stock research, and under the settlement analysts have a number of new restrictions. They must certify their reports, saying that they believe what they're writing about. They also must disclose if they're writing about an investment banking client or potential client of their firm. And research analysts are no longer allowed to participate in pitches to solicit new clients, to do IPOs or to sell stock in other public offerings, something that was commonplace prior to the settlement. Last, analysts can't be paid based on the clients they help lure to the firm.

The new rules have meant that "buy," "sell" and "hold" ratings have more weight than before the settlement. And many firms now have a reasonable distribution of buy, sell and hold ratings. A 2005 Morgan Stanley research report indicated that of the 1,870 stocks it tracked globally, 35% had buy ratings, 45% had hold ratings and 20% had sell ratings. Of that list, about one third were investment banking clients.

Here's how the new basic ratings stack up.

- *Buy:* When an analyst places a buy rating on a stock, that means he or she believes the stock will outperform its industry group over the next year or so. Usually the analyst includes a price target on that buy recommendation. Sometimes, when that target is met, the analyst will reduce the rating. Other times, he or she will reiterate the rating and raise the target price.

- *Hold:* When an analyst thinks the stock is okay but not likely to outperform the industry group, he or she places a rating of hold on the stock. This means that a new investor should probably look elsewhere. For an investor already holding the stock, consideration of selling should be made, especially if the investor finds an attractive buy candidate to replace it. Of course, selling means paying commissions and taxes, so selling is not a simple one-for-one swap.

- *Sell:* This means the analyst is pretty glum about a stock's prospects. While in the past few analysts said "Sell," many more do so today.

Caveat emptor: analysts aren't perfect; some are great, and some are terrible. It would be unwise to fly with just one analyst's thought. If you are going to buy a stock, it's important to check more than one analyst and to do some homework of your own.

Many organizations rate analysts, which makes it easier to find a good one. *The Wall Street Journal's Best on the Street* guide to analysts offers a wealth of information. It's published each spring, and it highlights the best stock pickers on Wall Street. *The Best on the Street* guide is also available online.

Some other Web sites also analyze research analysts. Two to check out are www.starmine.com and www.investars.com.

stock. He's being quiet, because he has a reputation as a shrewd investor. Once others know Frank is buying, they'll jump right in after him, pushing the stock price higher before Frank has bought all the shares he wants to buy. Once Frank has established his stake, he might mention to some guys at a brokerage firm that HSC is sure looking better. These folks will take a look, buy a few shares themselves, and kick the tip upstairs to the research department. The software analyst takes another look at HSC's filings. He's hated HSC for years, but as he studies the numbers, he discovers that HSC has, in fact, turned things around. He issues a research report raising his rating from hold to buy. A newspaper reporter sees the report, makes a few calls, and two days later publishes a story highlighting the turnaround at HSC.

It's important to note that at each step along the information trail, another investor is buying up a bit more HSC and, in so doing, amping up the stock price. Say Frank bought HSC from $15 to $18 a share. By the time the brokerage firm guy—and his other investing buddies—start buying, the stock has bumped up to $20. The analyst's report pushes the stock to $23. Thus the newspaper reader is seeing an idea that looked smart at $15 at a price nearly 50% higher. This lesson isn't meant to discourage, rather to explain how a hot tip may not be so hot by the time you hear about it. Is it fair that Frank figures out a good idea early or that the brokerage firm guys grab ahead of the general public? Maybe, maybe not, but nobody broke any rules. This trading didn't stem from secret, nonpublic information. But place this in the context of the non–Wall Street world. Do you think Wal-Mart pays the same as the local store for toilet paper or cereal? Big players, such as a big hedge fund similar to Frank's hedge fund, have some natural advantages, and all the rules in the world won't change that. Don't fight the fact; just know it and approach the hot tips in the magazines or on television with the appropriate skepticism.

Investment Banking

Investment bankers advise client companies on acquisitions, sales of divisions, initial public offerings, debt offerings and any other kind of securities transaction. For providing these services, bankers receive handsome fees, usually a percentage of an offering or deal's value.

Underwriting

When a stock goes public, a Wall Street firm underwrites the offering. Underwriting means that the securities firm guarantees a certain price for an offering, thereby taking on the risk of ensuring that the price is met. As part of the underwriting process, it helps a company, or issuer, prepare financial statements, takes the company on a "road show" to woo potential investors and prices the shares for trading. Wall Street firms also underwrite corporate bond offerings and other kinds of investments, such as convertible bonds. In a sense, the securities firms are market gatekeepers. If a company wants to issue stock or debt, it needs to go to the gatekeepers. The gatekeepers, naturally, charge a nice toll for bringing the company to the financial markets. In a typical stock IPO, underwriters command fees of 5 to 7% of the total value of the stock offered. The underwriters aren't in a risk-free position. Depending on market conditions, they may need to take on some of the offered stock in order to successfully complete a deal. Also, if an underwriter mishandles the presentation of a company to the investment community, interest could wane and an offering could be delayed or canceled altogether. The underwriting process takes several months, so in an erratic market, an underwriter faces real challenges in successfully completing an IPO.

Mergers and Acquisitions

Wall Street firms also act as highly paid matchmakers. Say General Electric wants to buy the Walt Disney Company. Setting aside the antitrust hurdles involved in such a combination, here's how Wall Street works such a deal. Both sides have their own investment bankers providing advice. The investment bankers negotiate a takeover price, often with management deeply involved. Other investment banks provide "fairness" opinions, i.e., whether the offered price is fair. Since investment bankers, including those offering opinions, usually are paid only when the deal gets done, it is a rare thing to see a bank provide an "unfair" opinion. (In the case of J.P. Morgan Chase buying Bank One in 2004, J.P. Morgan gave itself a "fairness" opinion to cement the deal. Though unusual, such an opinion is fair under the current rules, though regulators are examining those rules and may revise them.) For providing advice and a nifty corporate matchmaking service, bankers are paid fees; these can vary from deal to deal but are substantial.

Mergers and acquisitions ebb and flow like the sea. And Wall Street is ever adept at making sure its matchmaking efforts are needed. During a wave of mergers, investment bankers coo to corporations that bigger is better! Cobble together a mighty giant that can dominate your industry, and your profits will rise and the share price will soar! Corporate titans like this kind of whispering, so once a merger wave gets under way, it gathers up a good deal of momentum.

Eventually, dealmania dies down. And often, the big, merged companies find that meshing together their corporate cultures isn't so simple. Profits struggle, the share price wavers, and, presto: at the door is the investment banker with some more advice: Be nimble! That's the ticket! Time to hive off some of these units, perhaps spin off that other division. We will unlock the value in this company! The corporate titan, nervously eyeing the declining stock price, agrees to follow the banker's advice, and a wave of deconsolidation gets under way. In this scenario, bankers are paid to arrange the sales and spin-offs.

Not long after, of course, the same investment banker is cajoling some other corporate titan to begin the great merger cavalcade once again. It's a lovely business for Wall Street, since the bankers providing sage advice are paid to put together and take apart entire industries over and over again.

Asset Management

Some Wall Street firms also run money management operations. Merrill Lynch and Morgan Stanley (which owns the old Dean Witter), for instance, have a large array of mutual funds that they sell to clients. These money managers oversee assets and invest them as do mutual fund managers at fund companies such as Fidelity Investments or Vanguard.

Prime Brokerage

The fastest-growing area of Wall Street is in prime brokerage. This group caters not to individuals or companies but to hedge funds, to investment pools that cater to the rich and to institutions. They provide trading services and just about anything else that a hedge fund would require. Prime brokerage also pitches investment ideas to hedge fund clients, hoping to win more trading business from them. Hedge funds have grown rapidly in the past several years, and Wall Street knows how to follow the money. Morgan Stanley and Goldman Sachs have strong prime brokerage operations.

RISK MANAGERS AND COMPLIANCE

After the regulatory problems of the early 2000s, Wall Street firms are awash in lawyers, all of them helping the firms comply with a new array of rules and regulations governing everything from research to how IPOs are handled. Along with the lawyers, the firms also have stepped up their efforts to keep track of their risk exposure. With an increasingly complex mix of investments available to Wall Street firms and their clients, keeping track of risk exposure is essential.

WALL STREET'S POLICE

The regulators, as investors have learned in the past few years, play an important role in making sure that Wall Street is behaving properly. Regulators oversee everything from IPOs to insider trading to how firms communicate with customers. Regulators also police publicly traded companies and mutual funds. Their mandate is broad.

SECURITIES AND EXCHANGE COMMISSION

This is the lead federal regulatory agency, and it is tasked with overseeing everything that happens in the financial markets. Remarkably, federal regulatory oversight of the financial markets came into existence only in 1933. After the great stock market crash of 1929, federal lawmakers decided that more oversight of the markets was needed. So, through one securities act in 1933 and another in 1934, the SEC was formed to police the markets.

The SEC is part of the executive branch of the government and is governed by a five-member commission. The commission has two Democrats and two Republicans, and the president gets to name the chairman of the commission, thereby giving the party currently in power the decisive vote on any thorny issues. The SEC has several divisions, including market regulation and enforcement. It also has regional offices across the country that are tasked with overseeing local financial market issues.

William
Donaldson
(WSJ)

In recent years the SEC has been headed by a number of well-known figures. During the booming stock market, Arthur Levitt, once chairman of the American Stock Exchange, was the SEC chief. More recently, in the midst of various corporate scandals that bedeviled the investment world, William Donaldson was the chairman of the SEC. Mr. Donaldson, a longtime lion of Wall Street, had founded a brokerage firm, Donaldson, Lufkin & Jenrette, and the Yale School of Management. He vastly strengthened the SEC's regulatory function and enacted a number of rules to improve corporate governance and smooth the operations of the nation's stock markets. He stepped down in the summer of 2005, and former congressman Chris Cox took the helm.

The SEC is also the repository of a massive amount of financial information. All public companies must file financial statements with the SEC. All fund companies must file information about their investment holdings. Companies seeking to go public must also file their offering documents with the SEC. And there are many other such public filings that the SEC oversees. It used to be that filings arrived in paper form and were difficult to get at without paying a third party to gather the information. Today, filings are all electronic, and the SEC maintains these files on its Web site, www.sec.gov. So if an investor is curious about the latest financial statements for 3M, it can go to the SEC Web site and swiftly find them and read them. It is an invaluable resource for investors.

Self-Regulatory Organizations

The SEC can't do it all, so it also permits certain organizations to regulate themselves, while at the same time maintaining the right to do some regulatory snooping. The New York Stock Exchange and the National Association of Securities Dealers (NASD), for instance, are self-regulatory organizations (SROs). Both the NYSE and the NASD have active regulatory arms that oversee trading on their markets as well as their members' activity. Each organization regularly takes disciplinary actions, and records of these are maintained on their Web sites as well as published by *The Wall Street Journal*. The NASD disciplinary information is particularly important for investors, since it oversees the nation's stockbrokers. If you want to check out your broker, you can do so at www.nasd.com.

State Regulators

Each state also has a regulatory function, usually overseen by the state attorney general's office. The New York attorney general, because of Wall Street's hub in Manhattan, tends to be the most active state regulator when it comes to watching the financial markets. Eliot Spitzer, the New York AG, has made a national name for himself from his regulatory perch. He spearheaded the Wall Street research settlement, has uncovered fishy trading in mutual funds and investigated corruption in the insurance industry. Other states have been involved as well, with Massachusetts and Utah, among others, working with Mr. Spitzer on the research settlement.

Elliot Spitzer
(WSJ)

Other Regulators

Other federal bodies also have oversight in financial market activities. The Commodity Futures Trading Commission (www.cftc.gov) oversees trading in the futures markets. The Office of the Comptroller of the Currency (www.occ.gov) polices the na-

INVESTOR ADVOCACY GROUPS

Along with the feds, states and SROs, private organizations offer assistance to investors who either are seeking more information or who want to report problems with brokers or mutual funds. Many of these groups provide free information for investors curious to learn more about a particular discipline.

Among the most popular are:

CFA Institute (www.cfainstitute.org). This organization runs the Chartered Financial Analyst program, provides investor education, and advocates for rigorous financial research.

American Association of Individual Investors (www.aaii.com). This organization provides educational information on stocks, bonds and investing, along with a free newsletter.

Investment Company Institute (www.ici.org). The ICI is the trade organization for the mutual fund industry. It lobbies on the industry's behalf, but it also provides fund investors with lots of educational information about the fund industry.

National Association of Securities Dealers (www.nasd.com). Not only a regulatory body, the NASD provides lots of information about investing, brokers and mutual funds.

tional banks. The Federal Reserve (www.federalreserve.gov) monitors the banking system and also oversees bank activity.

For more information and lore about Wall Street, see below.

Online Resources

www.nyse.com Web site of the biggest stock exchange in the world, featuring market data and educational information.

www.sia.com Web site of the Securities Industry Association, a trade group representing Wall Street firms.

www.nyssa.org Web site of the New York Society of Security Analysts. Offering educational information and news related to research analysts.

www.financialhistory.org Web site of the Museum of American Financial History, located in lower Manhattan.

Suggested Reading

The House of Morgan: An American Banking Dynasty and the Rise of American Finance by Ron Chernow. Provides a history of J. P. Morgan and the early beginnings of what has become the most potent financial center in the world.

Where Are the Customers' Yachts? By Fred Schwed. A wry look at how Wall Street tends to treat its smaller clients.

Liar's Poker: Rising Through the Wreckage on Wall Street by Michael Lewis. An inside tale of working at a Wall Street firm.

Den of Thieves by James Stewart. An investigative book that shows what happens when Wall Street goes bad.

The Great Game: The Emergence of Wall Street as a World Power by John Steele Gordon. A historian's view of Wall Street beginning in 1653.

CHAPTER 5

ECONOMICS AND MONEY

The buying and selling of stocks and bonds is ultimately heavily influenced by the state of the economy. "The economy" is a vast term that encompasses the idea of how people interact to produce, buy and sell things. We create economic systems together, forging relationships and responsibilities that lead to buying a car or putting food on the table. Experts have written enormous amounts about the economy, and varying theories about economics abound. While it may be fun to dig into some of the hazier aspects of economics, we will keep things basic. Our goal isn't to become academic economic aces; rather, it is to understand how the economy intersects with investing. At the end of this chapter, the resources section will provide Web sites and additional reading material for those most curious about economics.

For investors, the focus is on whether or not the economy is growing. A growing economy is in expansion. When the economy is shrinking, it is dubbed a recession. The movement from growth to recession and back to growth is known as the "business cycle." Most economists believe that the economy moves through the business cycle over time. An expansion leads to excess capacity and excess goods. When there's too much stuff out there, profits dwindle, corporations retrench and the economy slows and then shrinks. As the excesses are

THE BUSINESS CYCLE *(South-Western)*

The economy moves through cycles over time. The cycles are an alternating world of growth and recession. Usually growth leads to overgrowth, which is followed by a slowdown and a recession. After excesses have been squeezed out of the system, the economy recovers and returns to growth. In the past twenty years, growth cycles have become longer and recessions shorter.

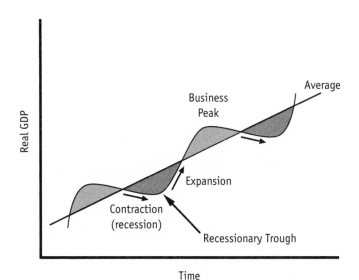

whittled away, the economy moves into recovery mode and then into expansion. The business cycle can be viewed as a circle or a clock face, with growth at twelve o'clock and recession at six o'clock. Slowdown is at three, and recovery is at nine. Round and round it goes.

Since World War II, the expansions have grown longer and the recessions briefer and narrower. Economists attribute this expansion of expansions to better technology, more intelligent planning and the broadening of globalization. In the late 1990s, when the Internet and technology boom gripped the stock markets (and more than a few wild-eyed individual investors), talk of a New Economy surfaced. This New Economy, proponents claimed, would eliminate the business cycle altogether, creating a nirvana of slow, steady growth as far as the eye could see. The New Economists argued that connectivity, technology, productivity growth and globalization would all combine to wipe out the growth–recession business cycle that had existed for centuries. (Way back in the nineteenth century, the business cycle wasn't called "growth–recession," it was called "boom and bust.") But in 2000 the New Economists found that the business cycle is a rather resilient force. The stock market stumbled (in the case of high-tech stocks, crashed), and the economy slowed, eventually falling into recession.

Many of the New Economists' claims, however, shouldn't be sneered at. The postbubble recession wasn't very deep, nor was it very long. The underlying ideas, such as productivity growth, more intelligent use of technology to manage excess, and the march of globalization have all combined to make economies stronger, expansions longer and recessions shallower and less nasty.

INVESTORS AND THE ECONOMY

Economic chatter may sound like a lot of claptrap to people who are interested in buying stocks and bonds. But the economy plays a starring role in determining what investments are worth. Knowing what's happening in the economy can help you understand if it makes more sense to buy shares of AT&T or Treasury bonds. Of course, divining the direction and strength of the economy isn't easy. Governments get it wrong, even with all their data and number crunchers. Recall how, in the early 2000s, the United States had budget surpluses to the moon, which swiftly evolved into deep, sinking deficits. That just underscores why wise investors diversify their holdings, combining various stocks, bonds, real estate and other items to ensure against bad guessing about the economy.

Even though forecasting the economy is fraught with peril, there are a number of ways for investors to figure out what's happening. Economic data provided by the government and other organizations offer important clues as to whether the economy is getting stronger or weaker—or, as some like to say, experiencing a "Goldilocks" phase, neither too hot nor too cold. The Goldilocks economy is the best environment for stocks and bonds since it means steady growth (profits for stocks) and little threat of inflation, which makes bonds valuable. Of course, staying on the Goldilocks glide path isn't simple in a multi-trillion-dollar economy that produces everything from soybeans to semiconductors.

GOVERNMENT DATA

The government issues oodles of economic data. It measures employment, productivity, consumer inflation, factory capacity, food prices, inventories, retail sales—the list goes on. It's a bit like baseball, where just about every aspect is measured by some statistic. For our purposes, we're going to look at some of the most important reports that Wall Street monitors particularly closely. Lots of this economic data can be found in *The Wall Street Journal.*

Jobs Data

On the first Friday of every month, the Labor Department releases its monthly payroll data. Among investors, this is one of the most highly anticipated reports. The two main parts of the monthly jobs report are the number of jobs created in the last month and the unemployment rate. During an expansion phase, payroll figures grow in the hundreds of thousands. During a recession, the opposite can occur. The unemployment rate measures the percentage of the work force unable to find work. When the unemployment rate gets very low, it raises fears of inflation, the idea being that too few workers means that companies have to pay more to get talent on board. But let's not get too deep into economic theory. The basic reading of the monthly jobs report is that if the economy is growing, companies are adding jobs. If it's not, payrolls are

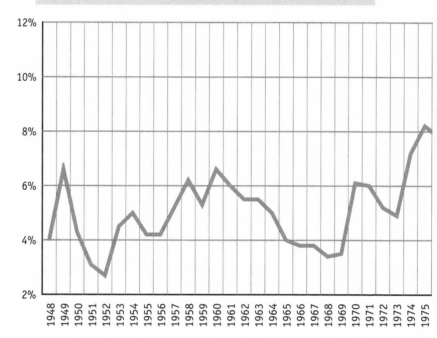

U.S. UNEMPLOYMENT RATE, 1948–2004
(Department of Labor)

shrinking. A rising unemployment rate can also indicate that job seekers are having a tough time, another clue that the economy isn't doing well. The jobs data also include several other figures, such as the average number of hours worked each week. But the payroll figures and unemployment rate provide the best look at the big picture.

Another jobs figure is the weekly unemployment claims number. When people lose their jobs, they often file for unemployment insurance. Those figures are reported on a weekly basis and can provide an additional clue about the economy's strength.

INFLATION MEASURES

You will recall that bond investors are obsessed with inflation (rising prices). That's because rising inflation erodes the value of their bonds, which pay a fixed interest rate. More inflation

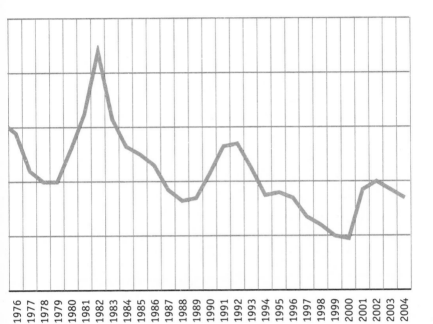

means the fixed payment is worth less over time. Stock investors also care about inflation because rising inflation means higher interest rates and more expensive financing. Rising inflation can also bring out the Federal Reserve to play (more on the Fed in a bit). The Federal Reserve dislikes inflation because it can crimp economic growth, and so it will use its powers to halt rising prices. That means the Fed takes steps to slow down the economy, sometimes even driving it into recession to curtail inflationary pressures. While reducing inflation is good, the recession cure is painful, leading to lost jobs and a shrinking economy.

The Department of Commerce releases inflation figures on a monthly basis. The Consumer Price Index, or CPI, is the main inflation gauge. It measures a basket of goods—food, energy, computers, movies—that consumers purchase on a regular basis. The CPI is used to calculate cost-of-living adjustments and is the main way for policy makers to determine if there's troublesome inflation news. Because energy and food prices can gyrate wildly, a lot of economists focus on the "core" CPI—the CPI with food and energy measures tossed out. This strikes some people as strange, since eating and heating are relatively essential practices, and if the cost of corn is rising or the gas price at the pump is soaring, that seems like inflation to most.

The Department of Commerce also releases the Producer Price Index, or PPI, monthly. This is a measure of wholesale prices—what things cost as companies buy and sell things among themselves. This measure is often watched as a precursor to changes in the CPI. If companies have to pay more, they try to get consumers to pay more for the things they buy. The PPI, however, is not the measure that politicians and pundits refer to when they talk about inflation, they are talking about the CPI.

CONSUMER PRICE INDEX

More than 200 product categories are divided into eight groups that make up the Consumer Price Index:

- Food and beverages (breakfast cereal, milk, coffee, chicken, wine, service meals and snacks)
- Housing (rent of primary residence, owners' equivalent rent, fuel oil, bedroom furniture)
- Apparel (men's shirts and sweaters, women's dresses, jewelry)
- Transportation (new vehicles, airline fares, gasoline, motor vehicle insurance)
- Medical care (prescription drugs and medical supplies, physicians' services, eyeglasses and eye care, hospital services)
- Recreation (televisions, pets and pet products, sports equipment, movie and sports tickets)
- Education and communication (college tuition, postage, telephone services, computer software and accessories)
- Other goods and services (tobacco and smoking products, haircuts and other personal services, funeral expenses)

(Source: U.S. Department of Labor, Bureau of Labor Statistics)

Retail Sales

The Department of Commerce reports total retail sales monthly. Since the U.S. economy depends heavily on consumers, retail sales have become a vital measure of economic strength. These data look at what people have spent money on, from cars to cereal, tallies up the total amount spent and measures that amount against previous months. Weaknesses in the economy can often show up in this data measure. People who have lost their jobs, or worry that they will, start to curtail their purchases, especially of large-ticket items such as cars. Those hesitations drag down the retail sales figures.

Gross Domestic Product

In essence, investors want to know if the economy is growing or shrinking, getting stronger or getting weaker. The gross domestic product, or GDP, is the measure that tells them the answer. The GDP, produced by the Treasury Department, totes up what the economy has done, in terms of growth, each quarter. It's fairly easy to understand. A positive number means the economy is growing; a negative one means it's shrinking. A growth rate of 3% or more is considered robust. Measuring an economy the size of the United States' is no small task. So the government first issues an estimate a few weeks after the quarter ends and then proceeds to revise the figure three times before settling on a final figure, which comes about three months after the end of the quarter.

The GDP figure tells us when we are in a recession. Although growth may be slow and erratic for a period of time, the generally accepted view of a recession is two consecutive quarters of negative GDP measures.

THE FEDERAL RESERVE

The Federal Reserve, or the Fed, plays a vital role in the management of the economy. It also has many other responsibilities, a main one being oversight of the national banking system. The Fed's job is to help maintain an orderly banking system, which is no small task since the banking system is the bloodstream of the economy. If the banking system buckles, we would start to think of soup lines and the Great Depression. Thankfully, that hasn't happened in several decades.

So what exactly is the Fed? The Fed is both part of the government and not part of the government. It's a bit of a hybrid that operates with a government mandate to set important interest rates, issue currency and manage the overall amount of money in the economy. The Fed was created in 1913 to manage the banking system and acts as the U.S. central bank. Other nations have similar institutions.

The Fed is organized across the country as a series of regional banks. The location of the banks reflects the demographics of the early 1900s, rather than the demographics of today. There's a Fed Bank in San Francisco, but not in Los Angeles. There's one in St. Louis, but not in Seattle. There's a Fed Bank in Dallas, but not in bigger Texas cities such as Houston. The presidents of these regional banks sit on the Federal Reserve Board. The chairman of the Federal Reserve Board, who since 1987 has been Alan Greenspan, is among the most powerful and influential players in the U.S. economy.

COUNTRY OR ASSOCIATION	CENTRAL BANK
United Kingdom	Bank of England
Euro-Zone	European Central Bank
Japan	Bank of Japan

The most prominent way the Fed interacts with the markets, investors and the rest of the country is through the setting of short-term interest rates. The Fed, through its Open Market Committee, establishes the federal-funds rate and the discount rate. The fed funds rate is the interest rate banks charge one another for overnight loans. The discount rate, which usually rises and falls in tandem with the fed funds rate,

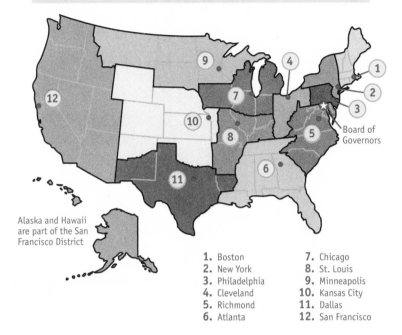

THE TWELVE FEDERAL RESERVE DISTRICTS
(Federal Reserve)

Alaska and Hawaii
are part of the San
Francisco District

Board of
Governors

1. Boston	**7.** Chicago
2. New York	**8.** St. Louis
3. Philadelphia	**9.** Minneapolis
4. Cleveland	**10.** Kansas City
5. Richmond	**11.** Dallas
6. Atlanta	**12.** San Francisco

is the amount the Fed charges banks for overnight loans at its "discount" window. The origins of the term stem from when banks went to the Fed physically to get loans at a so-called teller window. Since lending at the discount window has become rare, the fed funds rate is the one most carefully watched by the markets.

For many years, the Fed operated in an opaque manner, forcing investors to guess what the approximate fed funds rate was. But in the past decade, the Fed has become increasingly open about its operations. It publishes its fed funds rate, it releases minutes from its FOMC meetings and it issues press releases commenting on why it did or did not change short-term rates. The market pays careful attention to the Fed's utterances, because the cost of money—interest rates—plays a vital role in determining the direction of the economy.

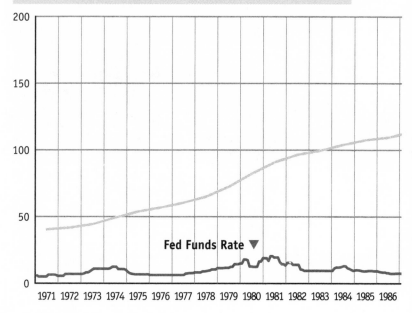

FED FUNDS RATE (INTEREST) AND
CPI (INFLATION) SINCE 1971
(Federal Reserve, Bureau of Labor Statistics)

The Fed is charged with keeping inflation in check. But it also has a legislated duty to keep unemployment low. Sometimes those two goals come into conflict. For instance, if inflation starts to become a problem, as it did in the 1970s (remember those buttons, WIN—Whip Inflation Now—that President Gerald Ford urged people to wear?), the Fed can take drastic action to crush rising prices. In the late 1970s, the Fed, then under Paul Volcker, raised short-term rates to nearly 20%, choking off growth and pushing the economy into a recession in the early 1980s. Rising inflation had sapped purchasing power, making it harder for consumers to make ends meet. That recession slowed the economy and reduced the pricing pressures that had driven inflation to such remarkable heights.

Since 1980, inflation has steadily dropped—called disinflation—and, along with that, interest rates have gone

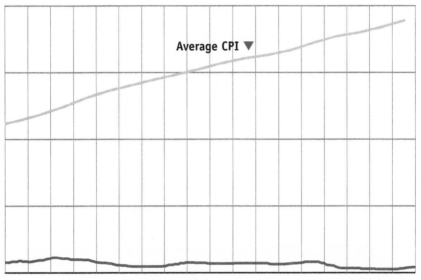

1987 1988 1989 1990 1991 1992 1993 1994 1995 1996 1997 1998 1999 2000 2001 2002 2003 2004

lower. The Fed's short-term rates have fallen from 20% in 1980 to as low as 1% early in this century. By May 2005, the short-term rates have risen to 3%. Longer-term rates, such as home mortgage rates, have dropped from 15% to around 6 to 7% since 1980. And the prime bank lending rate has fallen from 20% in 1980 to as low as 5.5%. The Fed has succeeded in bringing inflation under control, but not without delivering some bitter medicine in the form of higher short-term interest rates that led to some tough recessions, especially in the early 1980s. It is this fear of inflation, and how the Fed might respond to it, that keeps Wall Street watching the economic data closely and musing about how the Fed will react.

On Wall Street, investors say, "Don't fight the Fed." What they mean is that when the Fed is raising rates, stocks aren't likely to do well. Conversely, when the Fed is cutting rates, it's generally better for stocks.

ALAN GREENSPAN

For investors during the past several years, few figures have loomed larger than Alan Greenspan, chairman of the Federal Reserve. While the Fed chief always plays a key role in the markets and the economy, primarily through the management of the nation's money supply, Mr. Greenspan has become something few of his predecessors did: a renowned public figure.

Alan
Greenspan
(WSJ)

Mr. Greenspan has overseen the Federal Reserve since shortly before the 1987 stock market crash, and he's expected to retire at the end of January 2006, when his current term expires. He will leave behind a legacy considered broadly positive, though some economists have debated the efficacy of his policies.

The crash of 1987 provided an early test for Mr. Greenspan, one that most people felt he passed brilliantly. He flooded the system with money and helped ensure that confidence in the banking and financial system didn't collapse. Indeed, despite the crash, which momentarily paralyzed the nation's financial system, the Dow Jones Industrial Average finished 1987 with a small gain and the economy didn't lurch into recession, as many forecasters had feared. Indeed, Mr. Greenspan is widely credited with keeping the U.S. economy moving mostly ahead during his tenure, with brief recessions in the early 1990s and in 2001–2002. It is because of the market and economic success during his tenure that Mr. Greenspan has become so widely known.

For a public figure, however, Mr. Greenspan has a curious speaking style. He often talks in obtuse phrases, giving rise to what some economists call Greenspanspeak. Greenspanspeak rarely reaches clarity, instead offering up convoluted, lengthy sentences that provide Mr. Greenspan with plenty of policy wiggle room. This style may stem from his spotty track record of jawboning. In late 1996, for example, he said the stock market reflected an "irrational exuberance." Such a comment briefly knocked share prices lower, and although they swiftly started climbing again, they didn't peak until early 2000. Another reason for his confusingly structured sentences is that his position is appointed by the president of the United

States. And Mr. Greenspan has pleased several presidents of both parties—Reagan, Bush I, Clinton and Bush II. Sometimes, being a bit vague can be the best way to maintain good relations with the boss.

Critics argue that Mr. Greenspan should have done more to put the brakes on stock market speculation in the late 1990s. But he has maintained that the Fed shouldn't target the prices of assets, such as stocks. He has come in for similar criticism related to the booming real-estate market toward the end of his tenure.

His most controversial policy moves came after the stock market bubble burst. He slashed short-term interest rates to 1% and flooded the system with money, arguing that such radical steps were required to avert a deflationary crisis, in which a vicious spiral of falling prices would lead to reduced growth and failing businesses. Such a scenario has recently gripped Japan and last crippled the United States during the Great Depression. As Mr. Greenspan prepares to retire, the deflationary threat seems to have passed, and short-term interest rates have once again started moving higher.

Perhaps Mr. Greenspan's greatest legacy will be the establishment of price stability, or the reduction of inflationary pressures. During Mr. Greenspan's tenure, inflation as a potential economic bogeyman has diminished greatly. Indeed, confidence in the Federal Reserve's ability to combat inflation has contributed to a remarkable reduction in long-term interest rates, which set borrowing costs for mortgages, credit cards and corporate borrowing. The fall in long-term rates is one reason that home ownership in the United States is at record levels.

THE MONEY SUPPLY

Money-supply figures are important to economists, but investors have paid a dwindling amount of attention to them. But, for economists, monitoring the money supply is essential. Investors should care about the money supply because it plays a role in trying to gauge inflation threats. Too much money supply, or money supply growing too quickly, can lead to inflationary pressures, which erode the value of investments. Tight money supply, or shrinking money supply, can diminish economic growth, which could also erode the value of investments. What is too much, too fast, too little or too tight, however, is the subject of earnest debate among economists.

The Fed oversees and controls the money supply in the system. The basic money-supply gauge is M1, which consists of funds that are readily available for spending, including checking accounts (both those that pay interest and those that don't) and currency. M1 is sometimes broken down into M1-A and M1-B. M1-A is the total of private checking account deposits at commercial banks plus cash in the public hands. M1-B is cash plus checking-type deposits at all financial institutions, including credit unions and savings-and-loan associations.

M2 consists of cash and all private deposits except very large ones left for a specified period of time. It also includes certain short-term assets such as the amounts held in money-market mutual funds. M3 is the total of cash plus all private deposits and certain financial assets, such as money market funds. According to the Federal Reserve, the M1 money supply in February 2005 was $1.366 trillion; the M2 money supply was $6.45 trillion; and the M3 was $9.50 trillion.

What do all the *M*s mean? Money supply is part of the standard equation that determines the rate of inflation. This may sound a bit confusing, but it's really quite simple. The Fed *can* increase the money supply by printing money. But it usually affects the money supply through the purchase and sale of Treasury bonds in the open market. When it buys Treasurys, it pushes more money into the system. When it sells Treasurys, it takes money out of the system. Prudent oversight of the money supply is a key way in which the Fed manages economic growth.

THE WALL STREET JOURNAL
FEDERAL RESERVE TABLES *(WSJ)*

Federal Reserve Data

MONETARY AGGREGATES
(daily average in billions)

	1 WEEK ENDED:	
	Mar. 7	Feb. 28
Money supply (M1) sa	1351.6	1377.4
Money supply (M1) nsa	1333.3	1392.5
Money supply (M2) sa	6451.5	6458.2
Money supply (M2) nsa	6464.8	6408.5
Money supply (M3) sa	9502.9	9526.6
Money supply (M3) nsa	9531.4	9499.9
	4 WEEKS ENDED:	
	Mar. 7	Feb. 7
Money supply (M1) sa	1363.8	1368.2
Money supply (M1) nsa	1354.4	1350.0
Money supply (M2) sa	6451.3	6463.2
Money supply (M2) nsa	6420.7	6392.7
Money supply (M3) sa	9503.7	9502.6
Money supply (M3) nsa	9496.2	9452.9
	MONTH	
	Feb.	Jan.
Money supply (M1) sa	1366.7	1358.5
Money supply (M2) sa	6456.1	6442.2
Money supply (M3) sa	9502.3	9485.3

nsa-Not seasonally adjusted. sa-Seasonally adjusted.

Each Friday *The Wall Street Journal* publishes data from the Federal Reserve on the money supply. The figures break down the aggregate money supply figures (M1, M2 and M3, both seasonally adjusted and non–seasonally adjusted) into weekly comparisons, the last four weeks, and the two most recent months. While the first two measures show a mixed picture in terms of money supply growth, the February and January figures show that money supply is declining, ever so modestly. Money supply declines when the Federal Reserve is seeking to slow the economy down.

FISCAL POLICY

The government controls fiscal policy. Essentially, this is the yin to the Fed's yang. Some economists have great faith in the Fed's powers, and these are often called monetarists. Others favor the power of the government, and these come in two main groups: classical, or Keynesians, and supply-siders, or Lafferites. The classical economists far outnumber the supply-siders, but the supply-siders have some influential allies, such as *The Wall Street Journal* editorial page and a large wing of the Republican Party. To sum up the difference: classicists believe that the government, through taxing and spending, can affect the economy positively; supply-siders prefer that the government get out of the way and let the people drive the economy. In practice, fiscal policy takes a bit from both camps.

Essentially, fiscal policy is how the government uses its budget and what impact that has on the economy. It's a mixture of taxes, regulations, spending, borrowing and politics—such as fighting wars and negotiating trade treaties. All these factors boil down into the fiscal policy.

For investors, the three big elements of fiscal policy are taxes, regulations and spending. Put simply, what we pay in tax, we can't invest. And investing in heavily regulated industries, such as the drug industry, requires investors to understand what the government is doing in terms of setting rules about new products. When Republicans are in power, regulations tend to diminish, and vice versa for Democrats. But that's not always the case. Republican administrations have fathered large government regulatory initiatives, such as the creation of the Environmental Protection Agency under Richard Nixon. And it was a Democratic administration (Clinton) that oversaw vast reductions in Depression-era banking regulations.

MONEY

This is, after all, a guide to money and investing. So what about money? Money makes the world go around, to paraphrase an old saw. But money is also a wonderfully mysterious idea. Think of it: a group of people, most of whom have never met one another, have agreed that a piece of paper is worth something and can be used to acquire goods and services. There's nothing behind the paper other than the collective belief that the piece of paper is worth something. A dollar buys you a cup of coffee in Chicago. Why? Because we've all decided that it works best to believe that piece of paper is good for a cup of coffee.

It wasn't always so. Long ago, before money, or currency, before paper and coins, people traded things: a bushel of wheat for a ceramic bowl, for example. This barter system worked fine, but it had disadvantages. It wasn't practical to lug around bushel baskets of grain all day long. So bartering evolved to using smaller, more transportable objects. Some people used beads. Others used gems. The value of the various trinkets used varied widely, meaning that most transactions still required quite a bit of negotiation.

Gold became a popular currency before the widespread adoption of paper money. In 1091 B.C.E., the Chinese approved the use of gold bars as a form of money. The Roman Empire issued gold coins. In 1284, Vienna introduced the gold ducat, which would be a dominant world currency for almost five centuries.

The transition to paper money moved along an erratic path. China introduced paper money in the ninth century, but its use died out about five hundred years later, when rampant printing of currency led to terrible inflation. When too much currency is printed, the value of each piece of currency declines. As the amount of currency increases, it takes more currency to buy the same thing. China didn't return to paper money for several hundred years.

Paper arrived in the United States in 1690, when colonists in Massachusetts printed notes. For a period of time, paper money in the United States and elsewhere could be converted into something else, usually gold. In other words, if someone gave you five dollars for a cup of coffee, you could take that five dollars and redeem it for gold or some other precious metal. Paper money's convertibility helped provide assurance to those who used the money in transactions that it was worth the number printed on the paper.

Paper money is no longer convertible to gold or silver. Indeed, paper money is worth what it is because the government says that's what it's worth. Rather than the value of paper being set to something such as gold ("the gold standard"), currency systems today are called "fiat" systems. In other words, by fiat, or government order, the currency is simply worth what it is.

SECURITY MEASURES AGAINST COUNTERFEITING
(Bureau of Engraving and Printing)

A. Watermark: Hold the bill up to the light and look for the watermark, or faint image, similar to the large portrait. The watermark is part of the paper itself, and it can be seen from both sides of the note.

B. Security thread: Hold the bill up to the light and look for the security thread, or plastic strip, that is embedded in the paper and runs vertically to the right of the portrait. If you look closely, the words "USA 50" and a small flag are visible along the thread from both sides of the note. This thread glows yellow when held under an ultraviolet light.

C. Color-shifting ink: Look at the number "50" in the lower-right corner on the face of the bill. When you tilt the note up and down, the color-shifting ink changes from copper to green. The color shift is more dramatic in the newly redesigned notes, making it even easier for people to check their money.

D. Microprinting: Because they are so small, microprinted words are hard to replicate. The redesigned $50 note features microprinting on the face of the note in three areas: the words "FIFTY" and "USA," and the numeral "50" can be found in two of the blue stars to the left of the portrait; the word "FIFTY" can be found repeated within both side borders of the note; and the words "THE UNITED STATES OF AMERICA" appear on President Ulysses S. Grant's collar, under his beard.

E. Low-vision feature: The large numeral "50" in the lower right corner on the back of the bill is easy to read.

F. Federal Reserve indicators: A universal seal to the left of the portrait represents the entire Federal Reserve System. A letter and number beneath the left serial number identifies the issuing Federal Reserve Bank.

G. Serial numbers: The unique combination of eleven numbers and letters appears twice on the face of the note. On the new $50 note, the left-hand serial number has shifted slightly to the right, compared with previous designs.

H. Symbols of freedom: New symbols of freedom have been designed on the face of the $50 note to represent images of the American flag. The traditional stars and stripes of the United States flag are printed in blue and red behind the portrait of President Grant. A field of blue stars is located to the left of the portrait, while three red stripes are located to the right of the portrait. A small metallic silver-blue star is located on the lower right side of the portrait. The symbols of freedom will differ for each denomination.

I. Color: The most noticeable difference in the newly designed $50 note is the addition of subtle background colors of blue and red to both sides of the note. Also, small yellow 50s have been printed in the background on the back of the note. The Series

2004 notes mark the first time in modern American history that U.S. cash will include colors other than black and green. Different background colors will be used for the different denominations. This will help everyone to tell denominations apart.

J. Updated portrait and vignette: The oval borders and fine lines surrounding the portrait of President Grant on the face and the U.S. Capitol vignette on the back have been removed. The portrait has been moved up and shoulders have been extended into the border. Additional engraving details have been added to the vignette background.

U.S. MONEY

The U.S. Bureau of Engraving and Printing (BEP) prints the paper currency in the United States, and the U.S. Mint mints the nation's coins.

The BEP prints billions of dollars in paper money, called Federal Reserve notes, each year and delivers them to the Federal Reserve. The notes are produced in Washington, D.C., and Fort Worth, Texas. One of the most important things the BEP does is develop security measures for the nation's currency. Controlling the amount of money in circulation is key to managing the economy, and one means of control is to stamp out counterfeiting.

In recent years, the BEP has taken several anticounterfeiting steps, and as a result our money has changed. Greenbacks, a common slang for dollars, aren't just green anymore. Color has been added to the $10, $20, $50, and $100 bills, and the portraits on the front of the bills are printed off center to make copying the bills more challenging. The color on the bills shifts, the watermark on the bills is difficult to duplicate, and the fine printing creates another obstacle for would-be cheats.

The BEP prints primarily $1 (George Washington), $5 (Abraham Lincoln), $10 (Alexander Hamilton), $20 (Andrew Jackson), $50 (Ulysses S. Grant) and $100 (Benjamin Franklin) bills, with the $100 bill the largest in circulation since 1969.

Nearly half of its bills are $1 bills, and more than 95% of the bills (or reserve notes) it prints each year replace notes already in circulation. The average life span of a dollar bill in

THE FOREFATHERS ON OUR CURRENCY *(WSJ)*

George Washington

Abraham Lincoln

Alexander Hamilton

Andrew Jackson

Ulysses S. Grant

Ben Franklin

THE CIRCULATION OF MONEY

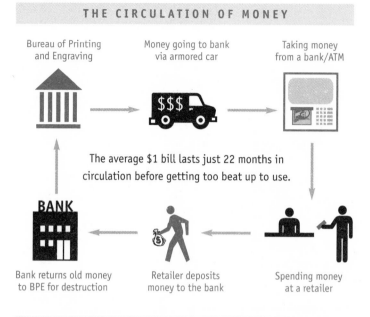

Bureau of Printing and Engraving

Money going to bank via armored car

Taking money from a bank/ATM

The average $1 bill lasts just 22 months in circulation before getting too beat up to use.

BANK

Bank returns old money to BPE for destruction

Retailer deposits money to the bank

Spending money at a retailer

circulation (before it becomes unusable) is roughly 22 months, according to the BEP. A $100 bill is expected to circulate for 8.5 years.

While the $100 note is the largest currently in circulation, in the past $500 (William McKinley), $1,000 (Grover Cleveland), $5,000 (James Madison) and even $10,000 (Salmon P. Chase) notes were printed. (While Messrs. McKinley, Cleveland and Madison were presidents, Mr. Chase was a Treasury secretary under President Lincoln during the Civil War.)

Along with standard notes, the BEP has issued special notes. To commemorate the Bicentennial in 1976, the BEP issued $2 notes with Thomas Jefferson's portrait on the front. Some of them remain in circulation, but most are in the hands of collectors.

The U.S. Mint coins all the lucre that jangles in our pockets. Like the BEP, the Mint delivers its coins to the Federal Reserve for distribution into the system. Along with coins, the Mint oversees the United States' gold and silver assets. The

CURRENCY NO LONGER IN CIRCULATION
(Bureau of Engraving and Printing, U.S. Mint)

A. Two dollar silver certificate ca. 1896

B. Five dollar bill ca. 1869

C. Fifty dollar bill ca. 1880

D. Five hundred dollar bill ca. 1863

E. One dollar bill ca. 1869

F. Two dollar bill from the Chicago Federal Reserve Bank ca. 1918

G. Two dollar bill ca. 1869

H. One hundred dollars in gold coin certificate ca. 1922

I. One hundred thousand dollars in gold certificate ca. 1934 *Photograph & image copyright © 1987, 1997 Howard M. Berlin*

FORT KNOX

How much gold is there in Fort Knox? According to the U.S. Mint, 147.3 million troy ounces. That figure has remained steady for many years, with small bits removed from time to time to test the gold for its purity.

While little gold has left Fort Knox in recent years, there's not as much of the yellow stuff as before. Shortly after establishing the U.S. bullion depositary center at Fort Knox in 1937, the facility had 649.6 million troy ounces of gold in storage.

Fort Knox, while commonly associated with its gold holdings, is also an important Army post. Among other military units, the U.S. Army Armor Center is based in Fort Knox, which is southwest of Louisville, Kentucky.

Fort Knox's gold holdings are in one of the most secure facilities in the world. No visitors are permitted, which has been the case since its founding. Over its history, Fort Knox has not only protected the nation's gold, it has also held items on behalf of other governments, notably the Magna Carta during World War II. The facility, which is managed by the U.S. Mint, also stored the Declaration of Independence and the U.S. Constitution during World War II.

The government also stores gold at other facilities, including the West Point Mint near the U.S. Military Academy, north of New York City. Much of the U.S. silver reserves is stored at West Point, earning it the nickname "the Fort Knox of silver." Like the Fort Knox facility, it was established in 1937. It became an official Mint facility in 1988. And as at its better-known cousin, no visitors are permitted. Other BEP facilities, such as the Denver Mint, can be toured.

Mint produces its coins in Denver, Philadelphia, San Francisco and West Point, New York.

The standard coins are the penny (one cent), nickel (five cents), dime (ten cents), quarter (25 cents), half dollar (50 cents) and dollar (100 cents). Other coins have circulated during the nation's history, including a half penny, from 1793 to 1857, and a twenty-cent piece, from 1875 to 1878.

Today, the standard coins have some twists. The Mint has launched a program to emboss different states' symbols on the back of the quarter over the next several years. By 2008, all fifty states will have their own back side of a quarter. The dollar coin comes in three flavors. The oldest has Dwight D. Eisenhower on the front. More recent vintages have Susan B. Anthony and Sacagawea on the front.

The Mint also produces commemorative coins and special silver, gold and platinum coins for collectors. These coins may accidentally go into circulation. If you see one, grab one, since they are worth more than the face value!

THE RISE OF ELECTRONIC MONEY

While it took some time to move from gold-backed money to "fiat" money, money is going through another major transition: it is disappearing. In 2003, for the first time, U.S. consumers used plastic more than cash to make purchases. People "write" checks on their computer and zap the payments to creditors and merchants. Direct deposits and money transfers are now a matter of keystrokes rather than greenbacks. An entire world of paper money is swiftly being outflanked by credit cards, debit cards and the Internet. Twenty years ago, checks had to be flown around the country to be processed. Today, the processing is all electronic.

Credit and debit cards have become the most popular means of buying and selling. A credit card is backed by a bank and permits a purchaser to use it to buy something. The bank delivers the money, and the credit card user is billed by the bank. The bank charges an interest rate on the outstanding debt the consumer has not paid off and also often adds an annual fee for its service. Credit cards essentially enable consumers to take out a loan on a moment's notice to make a purchase. The consumer can pay the debt off right away or over several

TYPICAL BANK ACCOUNTS AND INTEREST RATES
Source: Bankrate.com

ACCOUNT TYPE	INTEREST RATE (MARCH 2005)
CDs—1 year	2.98%[1]
Checking Account	.30%[2]
Savings Account	.49%[3]
Money Market Account	.71%

1. Deposit must remain in account for one year. Penalties for early withdrawal.
2. Doesn't include fees.
3. Doesn't include fees. Figure is for a passbook savings account.

All figures are national averages as of August 29, 2005, except for savings, which is as of April 13, 2005.

months. Many consumers choose to pay their credit debt off over time, and in 2004 credit card debt held by U.S. consumers topped $830 billion.

Debit cards work similarly, but instead of taking out a loan from the bank, the debit card takes the money out of your bank account. This kind of electronic transfer has become increasingly popular over the past several years, challenging the primacy of credit cards.

Electronic money may eventually mean the elimination of coins and notes. Which would be a shame. There's something nice about rubbing a couple of twenty-dollar bills together or jangling some coins in the pocket. But it is possible that backers of beads probably felt the same way as coin and paper steadily took over their position in the currency game.

BANK ACCOUNTS

Many of us keep our money in the bank. The bank, of course, doesn't keep our actual dollars and cents in the vault; it keeps an electronic record of that money. The bank does keep some cash on hand to satisfy withdrawal demands, but most of our deposits are active elsewhere, usually in the form of loans to people buying homes or cars.

The most basic form of keeping our money in the bank is a savings account. Such an account pays a small amount of interest, and we can deposit and withdraw cash from the account, either at the bank or via an automated teller machine, or ATM.

Many of us have a checking account. This is like a savings account and usually pays some interest on the money deposited. But unlike a savings account, a checking account permits us to write our name on a piece of paper (a check) and give money from our account to a person or company without having to go to the bank physically and get the money. The check is processed electronically, and the money moves from our account to another account, whether our landlord's or a retailer's.

Some people also keep their money in certificates of deposit, or CDs. These are similar to savings accounts, in the sense that we deposit money in the bank and receive interest in return. But a CD has a fixed period of time during which the depositor can't withdraw the money without suffering a penalty. Because the depositor has promised not to take the money out for that period of time, the interest paid on the account is higher than on a savings or checking account. CDs are generally short term in nature, ranging from several months to a few years.

Money market deposit accounts are similar to savings and checking accounts, and many investors use money market accounts as a substitute for checking accounts, though some money market accounts place restrictions on the amount of checks that can be written. These accounts pay a small interest rate.

All of the above accounts are federally insured by the Federal Deposit Insurance Corporation. The FDIC was created by the government in 1933 after a raft of bank failures wiped out many citizens. The FDIC takes in premiums from banks and savings and loans and monitors the health of banks. In return, in most cases the FDIC guarantees accounts of up to $100,000 in the event of bank failure. It's important to note that similar insurance is not provided for other investments, such as mutual funds, stocks and bonds.

THE WALL STREET JOURNAL
CURRENCY TABLES *(WSJ)*

Currencies

Percentage change since April 19, 2004   89.6   ▼ **-0.1**

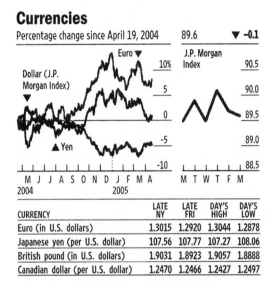

CURRENCY	LATE NY	LATE FRI	DAY'S HIGH	DAY'S LOW
Euro (in U.S. dollars)	1.3015	1.2920	1.3044	1.2878
Japanese yen (per U.S. dollar)	107.56	107.77	107.27	108.06
British pound (in U.S. dollars)	1.9031	1.8923	1.9057	1.8888
Canadian dollar (per U.S. dollar)	1.2470	1.2466	1.2427	1.2497

The Wall Street Journal publishes currency information in several places. Readers can start on page C1, where quotes on the euro, Japanese yen, British pound and Canadian dollar are given in U.S. dollars.

The *Journal* also publishes Key Currency Cross Rates and Exchange Rates. The Key Currency Cross Rates table enables a reader to figure out how much a dollar is worth compared to the euro and vice versa.

TRADING MONEY

Because money is no longer backed by a precious metal, its market value is determined by several other factors. Among them: the strength of the government backing the money; a nation's fiscal and trade policies; the relative flow of capital among nations; and the rate of return, or interest rate, that currency owners can expect.

Trading in the currency markets dwarfs that in other markets. More than $1 trillion in currency moves around the world each day via the currency markets. These markets are essentially the trading in various currencies that occurs through large banks. Dollars buy euros, and yen buy Swiss francs. The currency markets, unlike the bond or stock markets, technically operate all hours, every day. Of course, traders need someone to trade with, so activity on holidays and weekends is very light.

The trading of "free-floating" currencies establishes the exchange rate among those currencies. The market determines how much the dollar is worth compared to the euro, for instance. Governments can take steps to affect the value of their currency, but the market has the final say. A government can purchase massive amounts of its own currency, driving its value higher, but, given the enormous size of the currency markets, this is not considered an always effective strategy. Since traders analyze each government's fiscal health and trade standing, among other matters, the government can best affect the value of its currency with sound policies. Short-term interest rates can also have an impact on the value of one currency against others. If one nation's central bank sets short-term rates at 20% and another nation's central bank sets rates at 2%, people will flock to the 20% return. Usually, the difference isn't quite so stark; the point is that currency speculators analyze what kind of return they will get, as well as a government's fiscal health.

Currency trading is dominated by large players, such as global banks, big hedge funds and institutions. It is not a market that a lot of individual investors play in. But understanding currency rates matters to those traveling abroad as well as to those doing business abroad. Exchange rates affect repatriated profits. If the dollar is weak, U.S. exports can be priced more competitively. If the dollar is strong, a trip to the Bordeaux region of France, for example, is more affordable. Recently, the dollar has been weak. In early 2005, it took $1.30 to buy a euro, the currency of France and eleven other countries. Just a few years ago, about 90 cents would get you a euro.

The Wall Street Journal and the Online Journal have lots of currency tables. The *Journal* also covers the currency markets both online and in each day's paper. The Online Journal has more extensive and more frequently updated currency information at its Markets Data Center, which includes exchange rates, hourly exchange rates, key cross rates, currency futures, currency futures options and world value of the dollar data.

Online Resources

www.moneyfactory.com The site of the Bureau of Engraving and Printing, the printer of paper money in the United States. Includes lots of information, ranging from the history of paper money in the United States to anti-counterfeiting efforts.

www.usmint.gov The Web site of the U.S. Mint, which produces all the coins in the United States, including collectible coins. Provides history, fun facts and information about how coins are made and circulate.

www.federalreserve.gov The Web site of Board of Governors of the Federal Reserve System. This site contains lots of economic data and analysis. It is also a gateway to pages maintained by the twelve Federal Reserve banks, which have their own Web sites with regional economic data and research.

www.bls.gov Home of the Bureau of Labor Statistics, which is part of the Department of Labor. Here you will find all kinds of economic data, including the Consumer Price Index and the unemployment rate.

www.imf.org The International Monetary Fund's Web site. Includes data on the reserves held by global central banks as well as various analytical papers examining the global economy.

www.economy.com A highly informative site providing information about the economy and economic trends.

www.nber.org The National Bureau of Economic Research, a site that includes economic data, analysis and other information.

www.ustreas.gov The Web site of the U.S. Department of the

Treasury, which includes information about currency, coins and financial markets.

Suggested Reading

The Worldly Philosophers: The Lives, Times and Ideas of the Great Economic Thinkers by Robert L. Heilbroner. A look at some great economic thinkers from Adam Smith to John Maynard Keynes.

Secrets of the Temple by William Greider. A detailed look at the Federal Reserve. Is sometimes overly conspiratorial but has lots of good reporting and detail about the Fed and its operations.

Basic Economics: A Citizen's Guide by Thomas Sowell. Aimed at smart people who want to have a better grasp on how the economy works.

Wealth of Nations by Adam Smith. A classic on economic theory that explains much about our current system.

The Communist Manifesto by Karl Marx. Marx's rebuttal to Smith's capitalistic ideas.

The General Theory of Employment, Interest, and Money by John Maynard Keynes. The bible of classical economists.

The Theory of the Leisure Class by Thorstein Veblen. Quirky economics book for the more adventuresome.

Maestro: Alan Greenspan and the American Economy by Bob Woodward. In-depth look at the long-serving Fed chief.

CHAPTER 6

MUTUAL FUNDS

Mutual funds have become the most popular way for investors to participate in the financial markets. They now act as vehicles for retirement planning and saving for a kid's college education and may play a role in how the government manages the social security pension system. From small beginnings early in the twentieth century, mutual funds have become a giant part of the financial landscape.

Essentially, mutual funds are a grouping of individuals (or, in some cases, institutions) who invest their money with a company that manages that pool of money on their behalf. The underlying logic of mutual funds is that it provides stock market diversity without requiring a great deal of cash. An individual would need more than $100,000 to build a diversified portfolio of individual shares. But a mutual fund investor can send $1,000 to Fidelity or Vanguard (or any other fund company) and find herself holding an ownership stake in a number of companies. Essentially, a mutual fund pools the assets of its investors and invests the money on behalf of those investors. Fidelity will take in millions of dollars and buy up stock in IBM or General Motors, and each investor in the mutual fund is, by extension, an investor in those companies.

The rise of mutual funds has given individual investors the chance to participate in the stock market in a way not previously possible. Underscoring that success, even after the bursting of the stock market bubble in 2000, more than half the households in the United States owned stocks, mainly through mutual funds. At the end of 2004, nearly $8 trillion was held in more than 8,000 mutual funds that invest in stocks, bonds and other investments.

STOCK MUTUAL FUNDS

The biggest chunk of the fund industry focuses on stocks, and just under half the assets held by the industry is in stocks. Within that universe, investors have an eye-popping number of options: index funds, growth funds, sector funds and much, much more. Fidelity Investments, one of the biggest mutual fund companies in the world, has about forty different kinds of stock mutual funds focused on the United States. Fidelity gives investors mutual funds that focus on small stocks, mid-sized stocks, dividend-paying stocks, growth funds and value funds. If you've got an investment notion, chances are that Fidelity has a fund that would fit. And not just Fidelity. Other big fund companies, such as Putnam Investments and Janus Investment Professionals, also offer a range of investing choices.

Many investors have become familiar with mutual funds via their 401(k) or other retirement programs, which we'll talk about more in chapter 7. Most such programs provide employees with a menu of fund options that the employee can choose from to build an investment plan. It's always smart to check with a financial adviser or an in-house retirement adviser before deciding how to deploy your retirement savings. Factors such as your age, your anticipated date of retirement and the amount of corporate matching all play a role in mapping out the proper investment strategy.

Index Funds

The largest group of stock mutual funds focus on stock market indexes. The most popular such index funds model themselves on the S&P 500-stock index. As the name implies, that means these funds hold stakes in 500 companies, approximating the makeup of the S&P 500 itself. The largest such fund is the Vanguard 500 Index Fund, but it has many imitators. Similar index funds are modeled on the Russell 2000 index of small-cap stocks, the Dow Jones Wilshire total stock market index and other popular stock market measures. The advantages of an index fund are many. For starters, tracking an index doesn't take as much work as trying to go out and find undiscovered stock gems. In essence, the fund company outsources the research function to S&P or some other indexing outfit. This means that the fees for index funds are the cheapest among mutual funds. For instance, the Vanguard 500 Index Fund has an expense ratio of 0.18% of assets invested. By comparison, the Fidelity Large Cap Stock fund has an expense ratio of 0.78%.

Index funds also provide for diversification. Buying shares in an S&P 500 fund provides an investor with a stake in 500 stocks, which would be tough to do individually unless one had a lot of cash on hand. One common misconception about index funds, however, is that they are somehow "safe" or "safer" than other stock investments. If the stock market has a bad year, index funds won't avoid the suffering. Some investors were surprised by this fact after the stock market bubble burst and the S&P 500 index funds put in three down years. Diversification helps, but it can't provide a guarantee against struggling in tough markets.

Growth Funds

Another broad grouping of mutual funds falls under the category of "growth" funds. These funds, naturally, look for stocks that are growing. The concept of growth can get a little squishy, but many fund managers talk about steady earnings growth, quarter to quarter, as one measure. Growth-oriented fund managers often hunt for stocks with momentum; i.e., they want to buy stocks that are rising and go along for the ride. More aggressive growth managers may find themselves owning some stocks that race ahead for several quarters, but then hit the wall. When these types of stocks have problems, growth managers sprint for the exits. Growth investing tends to be more aggressive than other forms of mutual fund investing. Such funds tend to do well when the economy is moving quickly and badly when the economy is in a funk.

Value Funds

Unlike their growth cousins, value funds tend to hunt for undiscovered or undervalued gems. They are less concerned with momentum or quarter-to-quarter earnings growth. Value-minded investors tend to examine a company's financial statements, aiming to find stocks that have greater worth than the market is giving them. In a basic sense, the value fund manager looks for good companies that are being ignored. Value managers build positions in these companies and wait for the market to appreciate that they've overlooked something. It's a less sexy form of investing than growth investing, but remember that the tortoise won the race with the hare.

Income Funds

These funds have characteristics similar to value funds, in that the managers hunt for stocks of a reasonable price. In addition, they look for stocks that pay a good dividend. Income funds, in the traditional sense, focus on finding yield—another term for dividend payouts.

Small-Cap, Large-Cap, Midcap

Funds are also broken into different market capitalization styles. Market capitalization, often shortened to market cap, is simply the number of shares outstanding multiplied by the share price. So a company with 1 billion shares at a price of $10 has a market cap of $10 billion. As the names imply, small-cap funds focus on smaller stocks, usually stocks with a market cap of under $1 billion. Midcap funds focus on stocks between $1 billion and $10 billion, and large-cap funds focus on everything north of $10 billion. In the never-ending stratification of funds, the caps can blend with the traditional descriptors above. So you may see midcap value funds or small-cap growth funds. One thing fund companies excel in is creating more and more products, especially if a certain sector gets hot. Remember all those Internet funds created in the late 1990s? Not many of them are still around. And most of those that are around have mangled the definition of "Internet" to the point that just about any company could qualify for the fund.

Bond Funds

Along with stocks, mutual funds also invest in bonds. According to the Investment Company Institute, a mutual fund trade organization, more than $1.2 trillion was held in bond funds in 2004, including taxable bonds and municipal bonds. Like their stock cousins, bond funds come in varying shapes and sizes. Dreyfus, a large mutual fund company, has more than two dozen bond fund offerings, including the broad Dreyfus Premier Corporate Bond Fund and the more precise Dreyfus New York Tax Exempt Bond Fund.

Bond funds mirror chapter 3's discussions of different kinds of bonds. Funds may invest in Treasurys, corporate bonds, convertible bonds, junk or high-yield bonds, government agency bonds or municipal bonds. In addition, bond funds have varying durations, some focusing on shorter-term bonds, others on intermediate- or longer-term bonds. Like stock mutual funds, index funds are popular among bond fund investors. Lehman Brothers has some of the most popular indexes on which bond funds base their index investing strategies, including the Lehman Brothers Aggregate Bond Index, a measure that tracks the total U.S. bond market, including Treasurys, government agency debt, and investment-grade corporate debt.

BALANCED FUNDS

Balanced funds are for investors who want both stocks and bonds. The split of assets may vary, but generally, balanced funds have a bit more money invested in stocks than bonds. This kind of fund appeals to investors who are seeking to diversify their holdings, rather than focus on just stocks or just bonds.

MONEY MARKET FUNDS

Some fund investors don't always want to invest all their money in stock or bond funds, or sometimes they can't make up their minds or want to wait before making decisions about newly raised cash. In such cases, assets usually go into a cash-equivalent investment, such as a money market fund. These funds are considered the safest of mutual funds, though no mutual fund is guaranteed as a savings or checking account is. Money market funds are managed to maintain a price of $1 per share, though yields, or interest-rate payments on the money invested, can fluctuate, depending on market conditions. Because of their safe nature, money market funds tend to pay very low yields. During the early part of the twenty-first century, when short-term interest rates fell to 1%, money market funds paid barely more than 1% in interest annually. In early 2005, the Fidelity Spartan Money-Market Fund paid 1.54% in returns over the previous year, which was below the rate of inflation, which stood at about 3%, meaning that money held in the fund was losing value. While the returns aren't awe-inspiring, the stability and safety of money market funds are attractive for investors seeking to diversify away from a stock-heavy portfolio.

GOING OVERSEAS

Mutual funds also provide investors with a chance to invest outside the United States. The two main groups of non-U.S. funds are emerging-markets funds and international funds. Emerging markets funds focus on stocks in developing countries in places such as South America, Asia, Africa and Europe. International funds usually focus on more developed economies, such as western Europe and Japan. Emerging-markets funds are riskier, of course, because bad things can occur in developing nations. For instance, the 1998 Russian financial crisis stung a number of emerging-markets funds. The crisis was triggered by financial problems among Russian banks and the deteriorating Russian fiscal position. The crisis led to sharp drops in stock and bond markets and a flight of capital out of Russia. But with great risk can come great reward. More recently, mining stocks, such as Anglo American in South Africa, have been good performers. A number of financial advisers recommend some exposure to emerging-markets. International diversification has become more important in a globalized world. In 2004, individual U.S. investors poured a record $689 billion into overseas funds.

OTHER FUNDS

Mutual funds have blossomed to cater to nearly every thinkable investing idea. There are funds focused on socially responsible investing; funds that invest only in commodities, such as gold, silver, wheat and oil; funds that position themselves as bearish on the market; funds that invest only in specific sectors of the market. All told, fund investors have an enormous menu to select from. But don't let the proliferation of fund investing ideas become confusing. Work out a plan with a financial adviser, and stick to that plan. Ultimately, a lot of the different funds are driven more by marketing executives than by any real need among investors in the marketplace.

Sometimes taking the basic approach makes more sense than getting overly creative.

INVESTING IN A FUND

So now we have a basic overview of the funds available. How do you go about investing in mutual funds? Apart from setting up an investment strategy, investing in funds requires understanding some basics about how the fund world works, including fees, loads, net asset value and taxes.

The biggest issue for a fund investor is the cost of buying mutual funds, a cost that manifests itself in the form of fees and commissions, or loads. Each fund has an "expense ratio," which is the percentage of your assets it charges each year for handling your money. These fees go to portfolio manager salaries, bookkeeping, printing and sending out statements, trading costs and other administrative expenses. Some expense ratios also include marketing fees, known as 12b-1 fees. The fees range from very small, such as the 0.18% charged by the Vanguard 500 Index fund, to 2% for the more expensive funds. These fees may seem small, but they can add up. Putting $10,000 into a fund with a 2% expense ratio and assuming a 10% annual return would add up to a little more than $3,100 in fees over ten years on an investment that would grow to nearly $21,200. By comparison, the same investment, with the same assumed return, with a 0.18% expense ratio would mean $312 in fees over ten years and an investment that would grow to about $25,400. So fees definitely do matter!

Mutual funds can also have other fees, called loads, which are onetime commissions charged either when you invest in the fund or when you redeem your investment. Front-end loads, paid when you initially invest in a fund, are typically 2% to 5% of the money you invest, though they can run higher. Back-end loads are fees charged when you withdraw, or redeem, money from a mutual fund. Back-end loads can be flat fees or can slide. For instance, some back-end loads go down over time, meaning that early redemptions are costlier than later redemptions. Such a scale is aimed at encouraging you to keep your money with the mutual fund for a longer period of time.

Information about a mutual fund can be found in its prospectus. Since fees can play a big role in how your investment performs, it's important to check the prospectus to find out what kind of fees your mutual fund is charging.

Standard mutual funds are priced once per day, after the market close. (Exchange-traded funds, as noted in the next section, trade throughout the day and therefore are priced throughout the trading day.) This price is the net asset value, essentially a tallying up of all the assets held by the mutual fund divided by the number of investment units in the fund. When you invest in a mutual fund, you are buying a number of units based on the net asset value. For instance, if a fund has a net asset value of 50, a $1,000 investment will get you 20 units.

Mutual funds can also pass various taxes on to the investor, including capital gains taxes and taxes paid to foreign investors. Again, this information is in the fund prospectus. Investing in mutual funds is a great way to invest in a wide array of shares without having a lot of money. But the fees, loads and taxes can vary widely. As an investor, it's smart to examine a fund's prospectus to make sure you know what kind of expenses you face. Unlike a car, the most expensive fund may not necessarily be the best one.

EVALUATING A MUTUAL FUND

Picking the right mutual funds is a lot like selecting the right kinds of stocks to purchase. Among the similar strategic rules of thumb: watch the fees (as mentioned above), diversify your holdings to manage your risk, and don't chase performance.

Let's start with diversification. If you have a 401(k) fund, you probably have a good number of funds to choose from. You don't want to put all your eggs in one basket, so holding a diversified portfolio is important. A smart fund strategy mixes

THE WALL STREET JOURNAL
MUTUAL FUND TABLE (WSJ)

The Wall Street Journal publishes mutual fund tables each day for Nasdaq-published share classes of funds with at least $100 million in assets. The funds are listed alphabetically by family name. Funds can also be tracked by their five-letter symbols, but the *Journal* lists the funds by their fund names.

Here's what the basic headings mean:

FUND	NAV	NET CHG	YTD %RET	3-YR %RET	FUND	NAV	NET CHG	YTD %RET	3-YR %RET
EqIncB	17.13x	-0.02	-2.8	2.3	UltShortBd r	10.03	...	0.4	NS
GISI B t	8.84	0.01	-1.1	4.6	USBI	10.93	...	-1.1	6.1
HiIncBdB t	8.03	0.01	-0.7	9.5	Utility	13.47	0.04	-0.9	5.1
IntSmCoB	26.43	-0.03	2.6	14.1	ValStra	35.43	0.11	-5.3	8.4
KaufmnB p	5.05	0.03	-4.0	7.8	Value	71.41	0.20	0.2	11.3
KaufmnSCB p	19.74	0.16	-4.0	NS	Wrldw	17.91	-0.01	-1.9	6.6
MidGrStB	27.64	0.16	-0.8	5.4	**Fidelity Selects**				
MrkOppB p	13.09	-0.03	0.3	6.3	Banking r	36.60	-0.12	-7.6	5.3
MunHYAdB p	9.82	0.01	1.0	6.0	Biotech r	50.16	0.19	-13.0	-4.2
StrIncB	8.66	0.01	-1.2	9.6	Broker r	52.22	-0.19	-6.5	5.0
USGvtB t	7.71	...	-1.0	3.8	Chem r	70.34	0.25	3.1	16.8
Federated C					Comp r	33.34	-0.01	-5.1	-2.3
AmLdrC	24.38	-0.02	-2.3	1.9	CstHou r	43.17	0.26	-0.9	16.1
CapAppC p	24.03	-0.01	-2.8	0.3	DfAero r	68.11	0.14	4.8	13.2
FedMrkOppC p	13.07	-0.02	0.4	6.3	DevCom r	17.12	0.02	-11.4	3.3
HiIncBdC t	8.03	0.01	-0.7	9.5	Electr r	37.40	...	-1.0	-9.2
KaufmnC t	5.05	0.03	-4.0	7.8	Energy r	37.63	0.11	15.7	16.1
KaufmnSCC p	19.74	0.17	-4.0	NS	EngSvc r	48.03	0.26	12.6	13.5
MaxCapC p	23.60x	-0.04	-3.2	1.1	FinSvc r	108.70	-0.30	-7.2	4.6
StrIncC	8.66	...	-1.2	9.5	Food r	50.52	0.12	-0.3	4.9
Federated F					Gold r	26.06	-0.35	-3.2	13.4
BondFdF r	9.00x	-0.03	-0.9	8.2	Health r	126.87	0.24	-1.0	1.9
CapIncF	7.14x	-0.02	-1.3	0.5	HomeFin r	55.15	-0.28	-12.6	7.3
GISI F r	8.86	0.01	-0.8	5.4	IndMat r	40.50	...	2.0	16.7
MunHYAdF	9.82	0.01	1.1	6.8	Insur r	59.40	-0.24	-3.9	7.9
FedUSGov1-3Y	10.50	...	-0.3	2.2	Leisr r	72.80	0.12	-7.1	6.2
Fidelity Advisor A					MdEqSys	23.06	0.02	-1.5	13.9
BalancA t	15.83	-0.02	-2.5	3.3	MedDel r	46.99	0.33	4.8	18.6
DivGrthA	11.21	0.01	-4.7	-1.0	Multimedia r	42.77	0.06	-5.4	6.6
DivIntlA	18.63	0.03	-0.3	14.2	NatGas r	33.29	0.14	11.7	20.3
EqGrA t	43.46	-0.04	-4.5	-3.0	NatRec r	19.40	0.02	11.9	14.2
EqInA	27.49	-0.03	-1.5	4.8	NetInfra r	2.06	0.01	-12.3	-8.5
FltRateA r	9.99	...	0.9	4.1	Pharm	8.43	0.03	-6.9	-2.9

A. Fund: This is the name of the mutual fund. The fund family is in bold, and the various funds are listed indented below the fund family name.

B. NAV: This is the net asset value, or the price of each unit of the fund. This price is calculated each day after the close of trading.

C. Net Chg: This is the change in the NAV from the previous trading day.

D. YTD%RET: This is the year-to-date performance figure, in percentage terms. It doesn't include loads or redemption fees a fund investor may face. It also assumes reinvestment of all distributions and subtracts the annual expenses.

E. 3-YR%RET: This is the trailing three-year performance, in percentage terms, on an annualized basis.

Investors can get real-time information and historic data about their mutual funds at the Online Journal.

bond funds and stocks funds as well as domestic and overseas exposure. A smart strategy also includes "rebalancing."

Each year, you should look at your mix of funds to make sure they still dovetail with your strategy of diversification. If one strategy has done especially well, it will grow to become an outsized part of your fund portfolio. Each year, rebalancing your funds will help you avoid getting overexposed to a particular portion of the market. In the tech boom of the late 1990s, those who didn't rebalance found themselves in a bad position when tech stocks collapsed in 2000–2001. Rebalancers would have suffered fewer losses and found themselves in a position to handle the downturn better.

The rebalancing act is crucial to avoid a familiar pitfall for fund investors: chasing performance. Each year, newspapers such as *The Wall Street Journal* list the top-performing funds. A lot of investors then plow their money into these top-performing funds. But a useful saw of investing is "Past performance is no guarantee of future performance." Indeed, last year's best-performing fund can quickly become a laggard. Chasing performance is one of the most common fund investing errors. Rebalancing and sticking with your diversification strategy can help avoid this.

A number of investing advocates encourage investors to focus on index funds, rather than actively managed funds. Research data show that actively managed funds have a tough time beating funds managed against an index. In addition, the simplified nature of index, or "passive," investing means that index funds are cheaper.

After settling on a proper strategy for your anticipated needs, picking from the world of funds can be bewildering. Thousands of funds are competing for your attention. A first step when considering a fund is looking at the fund's prospectus. Like an IPO prospectus, a fund prospectus tells you a great deal about what a fund is up to. It contains information about the fund's investment goals, risk posture, fee information, past performance data and amount of assets held.

Another important thing for fund investors to read is the "Statement of Additional Information," or SAI. This is known as "part B" of a fund's registration statement, and if you ask for it, the fund company must send it to you. The SAI provides a lot of detail on the fund's operations, its history and its past performance. In addition, the SAI details tax matters and other issues important to investors. The back cover of a fund's prospectus should tell you how to get the SAI from the fund company.

A fund's name can also help you figure out what the fund is up to in terms of weighing how risky it is. But not always. According to SEC rules, a fund called the ABC Growth Fund must adhere to its name in 80% of its investments. But the other 20% can go into areas that might surprise you. The prospectus or the SAI should give you a good idea about what that other one fifth of the fund is up to, which should help you evaluate the possible risks the fund is taking.

In a fund, size matters. Some successful funds take in increasing amounts of cash, sometimes finding themselves with too much to invest effectively. If a successful fund continues to take in billions of dollars, you might want to find a similar fund with fewer assets on hand. The bigger a fund gets, the harder it is for it to "move the needle" in terms of performance.

Experience also matters. A fund that has performed well for a long time with the same manager is a positive indicator. The name of the manager and his or her tenure is included in the fund's prospectus. It's best to let rookie managers get some seasoning before wading in with them.

Finally, a word on rankings. Morningstar and other outfits provide all kinds of fund rankings. These rankings can provide some basic assistance to the fund investor. Extremely low rated funds are more likely to be clunkers, and highly rated funds can merit a closer look. But investors should be aware that these rankings are based primarily on historical information. And as noted above, past performance is no guarantee of future performance!

THE RISE OF ETFS

Traditional mutual funds are priced once a day, after the close of trading. As previously mentioned, the price of a fund is called its net asset value. Since a fund is priced once a day, that's the only time fund shares are effectively bought and sold. Some fund investors, however, want to be able to buy and sell funds throughout the trading day, rather than just once a day. And the pricing rules for mutual funds can become subject to abuse. In 2003, regulators discovered that some investors, mainly large hedge funds—investment pools that cater to institutional investors and the wealthy—had found ways to take advantage of improper pricing of mutual funds. These traders would dart into and out of the funds to take advantage of the pricing anomalies and make lots of cash. Regulators have issued new rules aimed at cracking down on such abuses.

The trading scandal also made another kind of fund, exchange-traded funds, or ETFs, more popular with investors. Exchange-traded funds are basically mutual funds that trade like stocks. Rather than have their price set once per day like traditional mutual funds, exchange-traded funds have their prices constantly set and reset throughout the trading day. Investors seeking to invest in ETFs purchase the shares on an exchange, such as the American Stock Exchange, rather than directly from the fund company. Most ETFs focus on a specific index, such as the Nasdaq 100 (the 100 biggest Nasdaq stocks) or the iShares Dow Jones US Healthcare Sector Index, and in that way are similar to index mutual funds. ETFs offer flexibility, since the owner of the fund can buy and sell quickly, rather than having to wait for the new postclose once-a-day price set by traditional mutual funds. But investing in ETFs can also be more expensive than investing in mutual funds. Index mutual funds have very low fees, but buying shares in an ETF usually means paying a commission to a broker, which, if the investor isn't a long-term holder of the ETF, can be pricier than investing in a traditional index mutual fund.

THE WALL STREET JOURNAL ETF TABLES (WSJ)

The Wall Street Journal publishes daily data on exchange-traded portfolios, including exchange-traded funds and HOLDRs (Holding Company Deposi-tary Receipts). Here's how to read those tables.

52-WEEK			YLD	VOL		NET
HI	LO	STOCK (DIV)	%	100s	CLOSE	CHG
109.83	97.27	Diamond 2.41e	2.3	58582	105.92	–0.37
76.85	67	PharmaHldrs 1.72e	2.3	3460	73.30	–0.55
102.15	83.80	RetailHldrs 3.97e	3.9	13835	101.45	0.60
2.98	1.97	B2BHldrs .83e	40.3	344	2.06	...
187.09	127.79	BiotchHldrs .04e	...	6917	184.90	–1.04
17.30	13.16	BrdBndHldrs .09e	.6	3099	16.11	–0.10
66.20	52.85	Europe01Hldrs 2.30e	3.6	8	64.20	–0.15
38.36	29.70	IntArchHldrs .22e	.6	15605	36.04	–0.13
72.48	49.15	IntrntHldrs	...	1664	57.25	–0.18
4.82	2.86	IntInfrHldrs	...	688	3.96	–0.09
56.50	50.61	Mkt2000Hldrs 1.71e	3.1	3	54.69	–0.11
142.88	126.25	RegBkHldrs 4.81e	3.5	10917	137.95	–1.27
108	68	OilSvcHldrs .54e	.5	44676	102.25	–0.10
37.20	27.78	SemiConHldrs .18e	.5	119101	36.90	–0.08
40.75	30.43	SftwreHldrs 3.21e	8.8	10947	36.42	–0.33
30.10	25.68	TelecomHldrs 2.10e	7.7	1449	27.32	–0.35
115.22	80.08	UtilHldrs 3.70e	3.3	3180	112.71	–0.12
62.87	51.57	WirlsHldrs 7.13e	12.5	43	57.16	–0.60
44.69	41.04	iShrComexGld	...	176	42.03	–0.04
81.57	54.70	iShrDJUSEn 1.01e	1.3	863	78.20	–0.17
69.82	53.32	iShrDJTA .50e	.8	582	65.35	–0.22
54.50	42.04	iShrDJUSBM .94e	2.0	509	47.85	–0.06
54.75	46.70	iShrDJUSCGds .97e	1.8	237	54.01	–0.13
61.70	50.82	iShrDJUSCSv .18e	.3	188	61.07	–0.03
113.68	98.60	iShrDJUSFin 2.48e	2.3	51	109.77	–1.29
62.50	52.01	iShrDJUSHlth .54e	.9	805	62.05	–0.30
57.24	48.07	iShrDJUSInd .56e	1.0	241	55	–0.15
66.92	49.34	iShrDJUSRE 3.85e	5.9	5568	65.57	0.27
59.71	50.28	iShrDJUSTot 1.16e	2.0	787	59.02	–0.34
79.72	57.74	iShrDJUSUtil 2.32e	3.0	351	78.25	–0.15
98.20	85.85	iShrDJUSFI 2.19e	2.3	134	96.73	–0.94

A. 52-Week Hi Lo: The high and low price for the fund in the trailing fifty-two weeks.

B. Stock (SYM): The name of the fund, often abbreviated. The listings aren't purely alphabetical, as in a standard stock table. Instead, single-fund listings are alphabetical and fund families are listed in groups, similar to the mutual fund tables.

C. Div: The amount of dividend paid, annually, if any.

D. Yld: The dividend divided by the share price produces the dividend yield.

E. Vol 100s: The previous day's trading volume, expressed in 1,000s.

F. Close: The previous day's closing price.

G. Net Chg: The net change in price from the previous day.

BRIEFING BOOKS
THE WALL STREET JOURNAL

COMPANY RESEARCH

QUOTE American Strategic Income Portfolio III Inc. (CSP)

06/01/05 2:55 p.m. EDT NYSE

Go to Stock Charting page

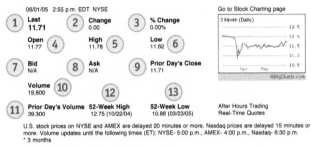

1 Last **11.71**	**2** Change 0.00	**3** % Change 0.00%
Open 11.77 **4**	High 11.78 **5**	Low 11.62 **6**
7 Bid N/A	**8** Ask N/A	**9** Prior Day's Close 11.71
Volume 19,600 **10**	**12**	**13**
11 Prior Day's Volume 39,300	52-Week High 12.75 (10/22/04)	52-Week Low 10.88 (03/23/05)

After Hours Trading
Real-Time Quotes

U.S. stock prices on NYSE and AMEX are delayed 20 minutes or more, Nasdaq prices are delayed 15 minutes or more. Volume updates until the following times (ET): NYSE- 5:00 p.m., AMEX- 4:00 p.m., Nasdaq- 6:30 p.m.
* 3 months

Historical Quotes
Find a Security's closing price on any day after 1/2/1970
(1/2/1970)

Symbol: [ ]   Date: [ ]   [Go]   Help ?

Source: BigCharts

The Online Journal provides real-time and historic information about ETFs and closed-end funds.

1. **LAST:** Most recent share price for the fund.
2. **CHANGE:** Change in price from the previous session's closing price.
3. **% CHANGE:** Percent change in price from the previous session's closing price.
4. **OPEN:** Opening price for that day's trading.
5. **HIGH:** Highest price reached in that day's trading.
6. **LOW:** Lowest price reached in that day's trading.
7. **BID:** Most recent bid price to acquire a share.

8. **ASK:** Most recent asking price to sell a share.
9. **PRIOR DAY'S CLOSE:** Closing price from the previous session.
10. **VOLUME:** Number of shares traded.
11. **PRIOR DAY'S VOLUME:** Number of shares traded in the previous session.
12. **52-WEEK HIGH:** Highest share price in the previous fifty-two weeks.
13. **52-WEEK LOW:** Lowest share price in the previous fifty-two weeks.

Despite being a bit more expensive, ETFs have swiftly attracted a strong following. At the end of 2004, ETFs had $226.21 billion in assets. ETFs, like mutual funds, come in a dizzying variety, ranging across bonds, stocks and sectors, but most are based on an underlying index, like the S&P 500 or the Nasdaq 100.

CLOSED-END FUNDS

Closed-end funds are essentially ETFs, because they trade like stocks. But there are subtle differences. Buyers of closed-end funds have to purchase shares from someone who already owns shares in the fund. "Open-ended" is a term that refers to traditional mutual funds, in the sense that new investors are always welcome to invest in the fund. Rather than being based on an index, closed-end funds are portfolios of securities that are generally picked by a fund manager. These funds tend to trade at prices above or below the net asset value (NAV) of the closed-end fund, depending on how investors view the fund's prospects. Among the biggest closed-end funds are HOLDRS Semiconductor fund and the Calamos Strategic Total Return Fund. Closed-end funds typically have a finite asset base raised at the offering of the fund.

Online Resources

www.ici.org Web site of the Investment Company Institute, the trade group for the mutual fund industry. Includes fund flow data as well as educational information and analysis of the fund industry.

www.fundalarm.com A free, noncommercial Web site run by Roy Weitz. Eclectic, wry and informative.

www.brill.com A mutual fund news and information site.

www.morningstar.com News, information, fund ratings and research tools covering the fund industry.

www.smartmoney.com A sister site to the Online Journal, SmartMoney.com has excellent mutual fund tools and information.

www.moneycentral.com Run by Microsoft; filled with good research tools, news, commentary and information about mutual funds and other investments.

Suggested Reading

Common Sense on Mutual Funds by John C. Bogle. Advice and insight from the man who built Vanguard into a fund industry giant.

How Mutual Funds Work by Albert J. Fredman. A basic guide for investors wanting to know more about how the mammoth fund industry works.

The Great Mutual Fund Trap by Gregory Arthur Baer and Gary Gensler. For those who have been torched in funds, this sobering account can help in the recovery.

Get a Financial Life by Beth Kobliner. A handy guide for younger investors trying to map out a mutual fund investment program.

The Intelligent Asset Allocator by William J. Bernstein. A guide on how to build a portfolio intelligently. Written not by a professional investor but by someone who had to learn from the ground up.

CHAPTER 7

RETIREMENT INVESTING

R*etire rich*. Those two words have sold many books. But retiring rich remains a big challenge. It requires planning and discipline. And in the past twenty-five years, it has meant a great deal more study and work for individuals. Over that time, the United States has steadily moved from a defined-benefit retirement system to a defined-contribution retirement system. Under the defined-benefit plan, workers earned pensions that their companies paid out after retirement. These programs quietly accrued money on an employee's behalf, invested it, and then paid retirees from this pool of money. This kind of program still exists at many companies, but increasingly companies have moved to a defined-contribution program. At the end of 2004, about 42 million Americans had about $1.9 trillion in such retirement accounts, which are called 401(k) accounts after the provision in the tax code that permits them.

Under a defined-contribution program, the company and the employee both contribute money to a retirement account, and the employee can choose how that money will be invested from an array of choices provided by the company. Similar retirement programs have been adopted by the government for its workers. Such programs have the benefit of giving individuals more choice in how their retirement savings are managed.

But sometimes individuals aren't as clever as they should be. As a general rule, a younger worker should have more money invested in stock funds, which have historically provided a higher rate of return. Older workers should have less in stocks and more in bonds, which provide a reliable income stream and are less volatile. Yet in 2003, 38% of 401(k) accounts held by workers in their twenties had no money in stock funds and another 22% had 50% or less, according to a study by the nonprofit Employee Benefit Research Institute and the Investment Company Institute, the mutual fund industry's lobbying arm. Meanwhile, 13% of workers in their sixties were exposing themselves to high risk by putting more than 90% of their money into stocks.

Concern that employees need more guidance has led to one major rule change by the Labor Department, which regulates 401(k) plans. In December 2001, the department gave the green light for investment companies to hire independent advisory firms to manage 401(k) accounts for individual investors. For such guidance, 401(k) account holders pay annual fees that generally range from 0.25% to 0.6% of assets. This comes on top of the fees charged by the stock and bond funds in the 401(k) account.

401(K)

As noted above, an increasing number of individuals are saving for retirement via a 401(k) retirement account. This is sometimes called a "salary reduction" account, because individuals defer a portion of their salary and place it in the 401(k) account. Companies often match a portion of the individual's contribution, and the money in that account, unlike your regular salary, isn't taxed right away. Instead, the tax is deferred until you begin withdrawing money from the account. The advantage is that by not paying taxes up front, you have more money to put to work. In addition, the money earned in the account is tax-deferred until you begin withdrawing from the account. When you do retire, the money you withdraw from the account is taxed at your personal tax rate. Retirees often have less income, and therefore a lower personal tax rate, than when they were working.

A 401(k) plan is usually run by a company (the sponsor) and handled by an administrator, generally a mutual fund company. The company sets various rules for participation, including how much the company will match your own contributions to the plan, if at all. Some companies are generous, matching as much as 50 cents for each dollar you invest, up to a certain limit. Other companies are stingier, and don't offer any matching. In addition, self-employed people can set up their own 401(k) programs, called solo 401(k)s. Solo and regular 401(k)s permit individuals to defer as much as $15,000 of their salary into the retirement account, under 2006 laws.

Unlike a pension plan, a 401(k) is portable, meaning that you can take it with you when you take another job. (You can also leave it where it is, but it's your money, so you get to decide how it's handled.) Since the average American worker switches jobs about eleven times over a lifetime, that means 401(k) investors need to know what to do when making such moves. When you do make a job move, you have various options. As noted, you can take it with you or leave it at the former firm. You can also do a "rollover," which means moving the money into either your new company's plan or into your own Individual Retirement Account (IRA). This transfer usually occurs between the old plan and the new plan or between the old plan and the financial services firm handling the new IRA. But some people opt for an "indirect" rollover. In this case, your old company gives you a check for the money in your account, less a 20% tax withholding in case you decide to keep the money for yourself (more on cashing out shortly). You have sixty days to put the money into a new plan or IRA. If you do so, the tax withholding is returned when you file your taxes. Some people use the "indirect" plan as a short-term loan, but if you don't actually put the money in the new account, you pay the price of cashing out.

Taking the cash out before retirement means paying an early-withdrawal penalty of 10%, along with taxes on the money you cash out. In many cases, the taxes and penalty total half the amount of money in the account. Even with those penalties, about 70% of job movers take the cash, according to the National Association of Securities Dealers. When making a job change, you have thirty days to decide how to handle your 401(k) account. But once you make a move, you can't make another such move until you switch jobs again.

Leaving your money behind at your old company can cause some headaches. Some companies restrict your ability to deploy your assets, and rather than having your retirement accounts in a single place, you have to manage money in two locations: your new company account and the old one. Most financial planners advise you to roll over into your new company's plan, unless the new plan is much worse (fewer investing options, higher fees) than the plan you're leaving.

Rolling over into an IRA gives you more investing flexibility. IRAs, like 401(k)s, are tax-deferred accounts. But unlike 401(k) plans, IRAs permit investors to invest in a wide range of stocks, bonds and mutual funds. We'll dig more into IRAs later in this chapter.

CATCH-UP CONTRIBUTIONS

Under 2006 rules, the maximum annual tax-deferred contribution to 401(k) and similar programs is $15,000. But after you turn 50, the government rules permit so-called catch-up contributions. These bigger chunks of tax-deferred money are aimed at helping people who are closing in on retirement build a bigger nest egg more quickly. Such catch-up contributions, however, aren't always possible. Some 401(k) programs don't permit them, and they are not required to do so. In

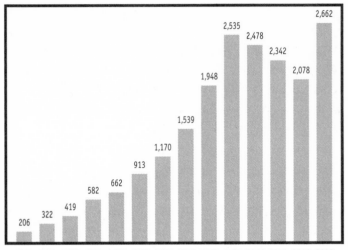

**RETIREMENT INVESTMENTS HELD
IN MUTUAL FUNDS, 1990–2003**
(Investment Company Institute)

Billions of dollars

Year	Value
1990	206
1991	322
1992	419
1993	582
1994	662
1995	913
1996	1,170
1997	1,539
1998	1,948
1999	2,535
2000	2,478
2001	2,342
2002	2,078
2003	2,662

2006, the maximum catch-up contribution, which is in addition to the standard contribution, is $5,000.

BORROWING FROM YOUR 401(K)

It's your money, so if you want to take a loan from yourself, a 401(k) provides that option. The law permits you to borrow as much as $50,000, but no more than half of your account. Most loans are for five years, which is the maximum term allowed, though some plans permit shorter terms and many offer the option to repay the loan earlier than scheduled. If you're taking a loan from your 401(k) to buy a primary residence, the loan term may extend to twenty-five years.

Once you've borrowed the money, you begin repaying the loan back to your account. Under most plans, this is handled by automatic deductions from your paycheck. Some programs permit the repayments to be reinvested immediately. Other plans keep the loan money in a separate place and reinvest it only when the loan is entirely repaid. Being able to put your money back to work right away is important, so you should examine the rules of your program before taking out a loan.

Borrowing from your own account has several advantages. For starters, you are paying yourself, rather than a bank, the interest on the loan. Also, there's no tax penalty on the loan, unless you fail to repay it. Then the loan becomes an early withdrawal with the associated penalties. The downside is that money you withdraw isn't growing in your retirement account. So if there's a big move in the market, you are not going to participate as fully as you would have had you not taken the loan. Also, if you leave your job, under most plans you have ninety days to repay the loan. Failure to repay means early withdrawal, and that means taxes and penalties.

IRAS AND OTHER RETIREMENT ACCOUNTS

Individual Retirement Accounts, or IRAs, are a lot like 401(k) programs. They permit an individual to invest money on a tax-deferred basis. IRAs have wider options than 401(k) programs, permitting investors to dabble in individual stocks, bonds and even collectible coins (as long as they are U.S. coins).

An IRA can be set up at a bank or with another financial services firm, such as a brokerage firm. The government sets the maximum contribution limit, and for most investors that limit is $4,000 a year. If you're over fifty, you can tack on an additional $500 a year. The money that goes into your IRA isn't taxed until it's withdrawn.

Unlike with a 401(k), you can't take out a loan against your IRA.

Roth IRAs are another retirement option. They are a very different beast from the standard IRA and 401(k) programs. Contributions to Roth IRA accounts are taxed, but the withdrawals—if you follow the basic rules—are tax-free. And unlike other retirement accounts, Roth IRAs have no minimum withdrawal requirements or age limits once you retire. Converting to a Roth IRA is an option for people who have an adjusted gross income of less than $100,000.

SEP-IRAs are designed specifically for self-employed people and small-business owners. Such programs permit up to 25% of income, to a maximum of $42,000 in 2006, to be contributed on a tax-deferred basis. The basic rules that govern 401(k)s apply to SEP-IRAs.

OTHER RETIREMENT ACCOUNTS

If you work for a nonprofit or in education, chances are you have something called a 403(b) plan. Such a plan is similar to a 401(k), with some differences. For instance, in such plans, investments are limited to annuities or mutual funds. An employer providing a 403(b) plan may match your tax-deferred contributions, but such matching is more common with 401(k) accounts. Unlike with a 401(k) plan, however, if the employer matches your contribution, vesting is immediate. (Many 401[k] plans require you to work at the company a set period of years before vesting. If you leave the company before the vesting period is complete, the company takes back its matching portion.)

If you work for a state or local government, you are probably saving under a 457 plan. Unlike a 401(k), the money in the 457 account is held in trust for you during your employment with the government. A 457 plan permits more "catch-up" options than a standard 401(k), including contributions of double the allowable limit ($15,000 in 2006) in the three years prior to retirement.

Federal government workers, including the military, are familiar with the Thrift Savings Plan. This plan is similar to 401(k)s, but it offers five investment choices, fewer than many private sector 401(k) plans. The program follows the basic rules of 401(k) plans, and the government has a matching program.

RED FLAGS

Looking out for trouble is important. The Department of Labor cites several possible warning signs that your 401(k) plan could be in difficulty. Among them: investments you didn't authorize, frequent and unexplained changes in the plan administration, late or irregular payments to former employees and inaccurate balance information. If you see warning signs, call the plan administrator. If unsatisfied, you can contact the Labor Department's Employee Benefits Security Administration at (866) 444-3272.

INVESTMENT STRATEGIES

Now you know the basics of retirement investing. What's the smartest strategy? There are two basic issues in retirement investing: how to invest and how to withdraw. We'll deal with investing first.

In setting up an investing strategy, it's wise to talk to a financial planner who can help set up a plan. But there are some basics every retirement investor ought to know. For starters, your age plays a big role in determining how to deploy your assets. When you're younger, you ought to be investing in riskier assets, such as stock funds or funds that focus on investing in developing markets. As you get closer to retirement age, you should lean toward investing in safer assets, such as Treasury bonds, making capital preservation (i.e., saving what you have) a key goal, rather than high-risk investing. An investor in her twenties ought to have about 80% in stocks. An investor in his early fifties should have trimmed that exposure back to somewhere closer to 40% or 50%.

Investors have many choices in 401(k) programs, including stock funds and bond funds. Some funds also provide more exotic options, such as guaranteed investment certificates (GICs), variable annuities and even, in some cases, the opportunity to invest in individual stocks. GICs provide a set guaranteed rate of return and are considered a conservative investment. Variable annuities—contracts guaranteeing a future payment to the investor, usually starting at retirement—pay a return based on the investment strategy of the annuity.

Diversification is also important. Some 401(k) programs contribute company stock rather than cash to match employee contributions. But tying your retirement savings too closely to a single stock is highly risky, as employees of WorldCom and Enron discovered—a number of workers' retirement nest egg was practically wiped out when those companies collapsed.

As you build your retirement investments, it's important to keep track of your 401(k) and its asset allocation. As we discussed in the chapter on mutual funds, if one strategy does particularly well, it may become too large a part of your portfolio. Smart investors rebalance their portfolios each year to maintain the proper distribution among stocks, bonds and cash, based on their investment strategy. Some investors who didn't pay attention during the late-1990s tech boom found themselves highly exposed to that sector when it collapsed in 2000. A rebalancer would have taken gains and redistributed those gains in investments that didn't collapse, ensuring a better overall return. Since markets fluctuate, a rebalancer has a better chance of avoiding large pitfalls in specific sectors.

WITHDRAWING MONEY

This is the tricky part. When you retire, and after you're $59\frac{1}{2}$, you can start taking money out of your 401(k) without facing early withdrawal penalties. You will, however, have to start paying taxes on the money you withdraw. Also, after you turn $70\frac{1}{2}$, you have to begin drawing down money from your 401(k), unless you're still working. If you're still employed, you can postpone withdrawals until the April 1 following your retirement. Once you do retire, or if you're retired and reach $70\frac{1}{2}$, the rules governing tax-deferred accounts require a minimum withdrawal, based on your age and account size. If you don't take out the required minimum, you face penalties of up to 50% on the money you didn't take out. This rule is aimed at making sure the money in tax-deferred accounts eventually is taxed.

Retirees can leave their retirement account with their company after they stop working. This may be the easiest path, but it's not always the best. Some plans convert your investments into an annuity, which pays out a fixed amount each year. Other plans permit systematic withdrawals from the plan. Both these options are convenient. But some plans restrict your ability to move assets around in your retirement account once you stop working. Also, some require you to start withdrawing money right away, and some retirees like to have their tax-deferred accounts grow a bit more before beginning withdrawal. Fees can also be higher than those of an IRA.

Many retirees roll over their account into an IRA. This permits a retiree younger than 70½ to keep making tax-deferred contributions. In addition, you can roll over the account into several IRAs, designating a different beneficiary, such as a spouse or child, for each account.

Other retirees opt for a lifetime annuity. This option isn't widely available, but some plans have it. Under this plan, rather than rolling over into an IRA or engineering a systematic withdrawal program, you convert your 401(k) assets into a lifetime annuity. This annuity comes in two forms, variable and fixed. A variable annuity depends on the investments' performance. A fixed annuity pays out a set amount of money each year. The advantage of annuities is that they assure a retiree that they won't outlive their assets. The downside is that with fixed annuities inflation can eat away at the annuity's returns over time. And a variable annuity payment can rise or fall, depending on investment performance. Also, annuities can have high fees, and once you opt for an annuity, changing your mind is expensive and entails steep penalties.

SOCIAL SECURITY

All American workers who work at least ten years, or are married to someone who has worked at least ten years, receive Social Security benefits when they retire. The benefits vary depending on how much money you or your spouse earns over your lifetime. For instance, a person born in 1967 who makes $125,000 in 2005 would, by the Social Security Administration's rough estimate, receive monthly benefit payments when he or she reaches full retirement of about $2,100 in 2005 dollars. A person earning $40,000 a year would receive about $1,400 in monthly benefits in 2005 dollars when he or she reaches full retirement.

The full retirement age, which is currently 65, is slowly climbing higher due to longer life expectancies and concerns about funding Social Security. For instance, people born in 1960 will not reach full retirement age until they turn 67. Individuals can start taking benefits when they turn 62, but if they start earlier than the full retirement age, the payments are reduced.

Social Security is a pay-as-you-go system, meaning that today's workers are funding today's retirees through taxes. The number of workers supporting each retiree is shrinking. After World War II, the ratio was about sixteen workers to each retiree. Now it is about three to one. That shifting ratio has raised questions about Social Security's future, and some politicians want to make adjustments in the program to maintain its solvency.

Financial planners will tell you that Social Security should be considered a supplemental retirement benefit. That's another way of saying that smart retirement planning relies on managing your retirement investing plan wisely.

Online Resources

www.smartmoney.com Retirement news, information and worksheets.

www.moneycentral.com Microsoft's main finance page includes tools, news and information about retirement planning.

www.aarp.org The American Association of Retired Persons, the major lobbying organization for retired people and those headed that way.

www.nasd.com The National Association of Securities Dealers has a useful 401(k) learning center.

Suggested Reading

Ernst & Young Retirement Planning Guide by Robert J. Garner et al.
401(k)s for Dummies by Ted Benna and Brenda Watson Newmann.
Get a Financial Life by Beth Kobliner.
The Motley Fool Personal Finance Workbook: A Foolproof Guide to Organizing Your Cash and Building Wealth by David Gardner et al.

CHAPTER 8

PRIVATE MONEY

While mutual funds are the realm of everyone from Joe Six-pack to Jane Billionaire, hedge funds are more the purview of the richer crowd. These investing partnerships have soared in popularity over the past decade, with hundreds of such funds popping up all the time. Usually, hedge funds are written about with a broad brush. They are called "secretive" or "fast-moving." They are often associated with short selling, or betting that a stock price will fall. But the hedge fund world has grown so vast that simple descriptors no longer work very well. Some hedge funds certainly operate in the shadows, seeking secretive ways to make money. Many others, however, are rather plain-vanilla outfits. Whatever the case, with more than $1 trillion under management and new funds starting on a nearly daily basis, hedge funds have become a large player in the financial markets.

SOME HEDGE FUND HISTORY

Hedge funds have been around since 1940, when the investment act of that year created an exemption for certain investment vehicles that catered to the wealthy. Traditionally, hedge funds were meant to act as a "hedge," or a form of insurance against unexpected market moves. In order to hedge against a market downturn, these funds would invest in more exotic investments than traditional mutual funds, and they could—and still do—go "short" on stocks or stock indexes. But hedge funds have grown far more complex since their earlier, humbler hedging days. Today, more than eight thousand hedge funds trade everything from stocks to complex debt products.

For many of the past sixty years, hedge funds popped into the popular mind only intermittently, usually when something dramatic happened in the financial markets. For instance, in 1992, George Soros, a big hedge fund manager, "broke" the British pound, making billions of dollars in the process. He bet that the pound would be unable to remain in a certain government-mandated range. The range pegged the pound's value against other currencies within specified exchange rate values. He was right; the British government was wrong. The government abandoned the specified band, and the pound sank sharply. Mr.

George Soros *(WSJ)*

Soros thus made both a large fortune and a name for himself as a hedge fund manager. During the 1997 Asian financial crisis, many governments blamed hedge funds for diabolical actions that led to the crisis. Some countries set up new investing rules to hamper fast-moving funds, such as hedge funds. More recently, hedge funds have been blamed for abusing mutual fund trading rules, a practice that erupted into scandal in 2003.

In the past several years, hedge funds have moved from being a province of the wealthy to include pension funds, university endowments and other large institutions as investors. Also, some funds are, in fact, "funds of funds." These funds of funds pool money from investors both small and large and then funnel that money to a group of hedge funds. This funds-of-funds approach has broadened the reach of hedge funds.

So what exactly are hedge funds? Essentially, they are a good bit like mutual funds, pools of investors' money that a money manager (or team of managers) can direct as he sees fit.

But unlike mutual funds, hedge funds have far fewer regulatory restraints. They don't have to disclose their investment strategy, nor do they have to say much about what they are doing. They can shift on a dime—going short one week, long the following. They can borrow a lot of money to maximize investment bets. In short, hedge funds can do just about anything they want to.

The term "hedge fund" implies that these investment vehicles are a bid for safety; one "hedges" ones bets when one is unsure. Though hedge funds began with this idea in mind, today's hedge funds are often anything but. Many use aggressive strategies, swiftly moving into and out of positions, racing to find the best possible returns anywhere in the marketplace. This aggressiveness can lead to outlandish success—or to spectacular failure. Hedge funds also charge large fees. Management fees are usually 2% of assets (mutual funds are generally cheaper) and 20% of profits. Now, 20% of profits sounds like a pretty big figure. It is. But the difference is that hedge funds aren't paid when they lose money (except for that little management fee, of course), while mutual fund companies are always paid their fees by investors, regardless of performance.

RESOURCES

Getting information on hedge funds isn't easy. Since they are private partnerships, they aren't under any special reporting obligations. Still, a number of the large hedge funds do release information about their holdings. These positions are often a bit out of date, but they do give a sense of what the fund is up to. Also, if a hedge fund acquires more than 5% of a company, it has to notify the SEC of that position, and the position becomes public information.

Some organizations, such as CSFB/Tremont Advisers, track hedge fund performance broadly. Also, some hedge funds have their own Web sites, which include basic information on the fund. One issue facing hedge funds is that they are banned

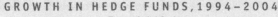

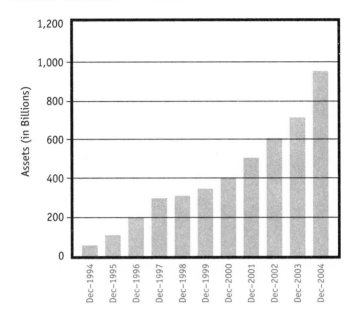

GROWTH IN HEDGE FUNDS, 1994–2004
(Tremont Capital, Inc.)

from advertising under the investment act of 1940. Thus, even setting up a Web site can make a hedge fund nervous about overstepping the rules that provide them with such broad investment freedom.

The Wall Street Journal and the Online Journal carry many stories on the hedge fund industry.

VENTURE CAPITAL

Rich people and institutions, such as pension funds and university endowments, have many different investing options beyond the mutual funds that most of us invest in. Along with hedge funds, rich folks invest in venture capital. In the late 1990s, venture capital became as hot as Arizona in August. Some venture funds, such as CMGI and Internet Capital Group, even began trading as stocks. Even though venture capital became part of the common lingo, most people didn't really know what it meant.

Venture capital is a lot as its name implies, though one is tempted to place "ad" before "venture." These funds, like hedge funds, are pools of money gathered up from institutions and wealthy individuals. But rather than focusing on the public markets, venture funds focus on young, small companies. They take great risks on untested or unproven ideas, and the thesis is that they will get great rewards when the young companies grow into mature, publicly traded stocks. A number of well-known technology companies received early backing from venture capital funds, notably Apple Computer and Google. But not every venture investment turns out as those two did. Indeed, a successful venture fund is a bit like a successful major-league hitter. Batting .300 means you're doing pretty well—in other words, about 70% of venture investments fail. And that's for the good funds.

The venture capital world is most associated with technology investing, and the heart of the U.S. venture community is in Silicon Valley. But other venture hubs can be found around Boston, where biotechnology is a popular field, and in Texas, where successful technology companies such as Dell Computer have helped spur start-ups.

Venture money plays a key role in companies' pre–public market development. Often when a company files to go public, its ownership includes a number of venture capital funds. Here's how a successful venture investment works. Coe LLC, a venture fund, eyes a promising software start-up. The start-up doesn't have a lot of cash, but it has a clever idea and strong management. The founders of Coe need money to bring their idea to the marketplace. So the venture fund buys a stake in the company, say 25%. In order to do so, it determines a value for the company. This valuation process is usually done by getting competing VC firms to bid for an investment. Each bid will include a money amount as well as a valuation of the company. Let's say the winning VC valued Coe LLC at $10 million. So, for $2.5 million, it gets its 25% share. (Such financings are often far more complex, and, because they are done in private, the exact details aren't easily available.) After three years of successful growth, the company decides to go public with an IPO. The investment bankers (remember them?) value the software company at $100 million. That means the venture stake has grown tenfold over three years, to $25 million. Of course, as noted above, a lot of times that 25% becomes zero. It is a high-risk, high-reward game.

PRIVATE EQUITY

Another nonpublic part of the investing firmament is private equity funds. Similar to venture funds, private equity funds gather pools of money from institutions and wealthy individuals. Unlike venture funds, however, private equity funds usually focus on acquiring mature companies or divisions of large companies.

Private equity funds are generally larger than venture funds, and they often use lots of borrowed money to execute transactions. Oftentimes, a private equity fund hunts for assets that are undervalued or fallen on hard times. Or it hunts for divisions that no longer fit the core mission of a particularly far-flung company. Recall how investment bankers love to build up companies, tear them apart and build them up again? Oftentimes in the teardown phase, private equity funds are buyers. In 2002, Diageo, a large liquor conglomerate, found itself trying to figure out what to do with its Burger King unit. Not seeing many synergies between burgers and Bacardi, Diageo sold Burger King to Texas Pacific Group, a private equity firm, for $1.5 billion. Similar to a venture fund, the private equity fund seeks to improve the business and eventually sell it to another large company or take it public with an initial public offering.

Private equity, venture capital and hedge funds all operate in the shadows, not providing a great deal of public information. But they are key players in the investing world. Understanding where private money intersects with the public market helps individual investors better understand how the world of money and investing works.

Online Resources

www.nvca.com Home of the National Venture Capital Association. Contains industry statistics, news, information and analysis.

www.vcinstitute.org An educational site focused on venture capital and private equity investing.

www.privateequityweek.com A Thomson Financial site focused on private equity news.

www.hedgefundcenter.com A site that delivers information on hedge fund investing. Subscription required.

www.hedgeworld.com A site that has hedge fund information and news. Subscription required.

Suggested Reading

When Genius Failed by Roger Lowenstein. An exploration of the collapse of Long-Term Capital Management, a high-flying hedge fund.

Ugly Americans by Ben Mezrich. A look at the role global hedge funds played in the Asian financial crisis of 1997–98.

Running Money: Hedge Fund Honchos, Monster Markets and My Hunt for the Big Score by Andy Kessler. An insider's tale about working at a hedge fund.

Barbarians at the Gate by Bryan Burrough and John Helyar. An examination of the buyout of RJR Nabisco by private equity giant Kohlberg Kravis Roberts.

The Nudist on the Late Shift by Po Bronson. A clever, whimsical look at the world of Silicon Valley, the heart of venture capital investing.

The New New Thing by Michael Lewis. A perusal of Silicon Valley during its Internet-fed heyday.

CHAPTER 9

OPTIONS, FUTURES AND NONTRADITIONAL INVESTMENTS

During the past couple of years, oil prices have become nearly as familiar as the Dow Jones Industrial Average. War in the Middle East, Israeli-Palestinian tensions; often, these international conflicts are viewed through the energy markets. But what really happens in the energy markets? It's not as if a guy were standing there with a few barrels of oil, seeking a buyer. When commentators talk about rising or falling oil prices, they're talking about the price of oil futures.

Now we're in among the back roads, far from the main thoroughfares of stocks, bonds and mutual funds. Futures and options are common investment vehicles, and they are simple forms of an exotic term: derivatives. A derivative is simply a financial product derived from an underlying product. Thus, oil futures are derived from the future arrival of some oil. Options operate a bit differently, but the focus is also on the future. An option gives an investor the right, but not the obligation, to buy something—stocks, bonds, baskets of stocks—at some fixed future date. Futures give an investor the right—*and* the obligation—to buy anything from lumber to pork bellies at some fixed future date.

The entire concept of options and futures can seem daunting. But it's really not so. Take futures. Your neighbor owns an organic farm, and you particularly like his sweet corn. Bob, however, finds himself short of cash after buying his seed in the spring. He says, "Look, why don't I sell you twenty ears of corn for twenty dollars. I'll get it to you by September 1." You recall that his corn was so good last year that he was selling 20 ears for $30. (That's some really excellent corn.) You say, what the heck, you'll give him the $20. The corn's in the ground, and it's not going anywhere. You'll just pray for some good weather. Right there, doing Bob a favor, you've just bought corn futures! The broad futures market works pretty much the same way; it just has quite a few more moving parts.

FUTURES

The earliest futures markets are reckoned to have started in rice-rich Japan in the eighteenth century. Growers wanted a way to make sure they could get a certain price for portions of their harvest each year. Thus, they began selling futures on rice. Brokers emerged to make markets—find buyers and sellers to put together—and the concept of futures investing was born. Today, futures markets cover everything from oil to lumber to pork bellies (bacon). Futures markets focused heavily on commodities for much of their history. But in recent years, financial futures, like futures on the Standard & Poor's 500-stock index, have become increasingly popular. These financial instruments provide investors ways to hedge their positions. Investors use options in the same way, but let's not get ahead of ourselves.

The big U.S. futures markets are in Chicago and New York. At the Chicago Mercantile Exchange (CME) and Chicago Board of Trade (CBOT), heartland agriculture and financial futures dominate. In New York, at the New York Mercantile Exchange

(NYMEX) and the New York Board of Trade (NYBOT) in lower Manhattan, futures in precious metals, oil and some agriculture products trade. There are smaller exchanges, such as the Grain Exchange in Minneapolis and the New York Cocoa Exchange. But most of the action takes place at the CBOT, CME, NYMEX and NYBOT.

Lower trading floor, Chicago Mercantile Exchange

FUTURES TRADING AT THE FOUR BIG MARKETS			
Chicago Mercantile Exchange	Chicago Board of Trade	New York Mercantile Exchange	New York Board of Trade
Frozen pork bellies	Corn futures	Light, sweet oil futures	Coffee futures
Random-length lumber futures	Wheat futures	Heating oil futures	Cocoa futures
Euro foreign exchange futures	Soybean futures	Coal futures	Cotton futures
S&P 500 futures	Fed fund rate futures	Gold futures	NYSE composite futures
NASDAQ 100 futures	Interest rate futures	Silver futures	Frozen concentrated orange juice futures
		Palladium futures	

As in our example, producers, whether they be farmers or oil drillers, use the futures markets to raise cash, hedge positions and increase the predictability of an otherwise unpredictable business. Many participants, however, are not involved in the making or buying of the actual products. These investors buy and sell futures right up until the delivery date. They don't really want to have 1,000 bushels of winter wheat delivered to them, so they seek to exit the market—sell their positions—before the futures come due. However, it has been known to happen that financial players have made mistakes and find themselves trying to dispose of a truckful of pork bellies.

The futures markets have all kinds of colorful language and terms to define futures prices. The two most commonly used are "backwardation" and "contango." Futures prices go out several months, with the near month usually the most actively

THE WALL STREET JOURNAL
FUTURES TABLES (WSJ)

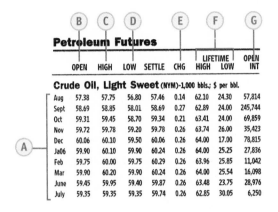

	OPEN	HIGH	LOW	SETTLE	CHG	LIFETIME HIGH	LIFETIME LOW	OPEN INT
Crude Oil, Light Sweet (NYM)-1,000 bbls.; $ per bbl.								
Aug	57.38	57.75	56.80	57.46	0.14	62.10	24.30	57,814
Sept	58.69	58.85	58.01	58.69	0.27	62.89	24.00	245,744
Oct	59.31	59.45	58.70	59.34	0.21	63.41	24.00	69,859
Nov	59.72	59.78	59.20	59.78	0.26	63.74	26.00	35,423
Dec	60.06	60.10	59.50	60.06	0.26	64.00	17.00	78,815
Ja06	59.90	60.10	59.90	60.24	0.26	64.00	25.25	27,836
Feb	59.75	60.00	59.75	60.29	0.26	63.96	25.85	11,042
Mar	59.90	60.20	59.90	60.24	0.26	64.00	25.54	16,098
June	59.45	59.95	59.40	59.87	0.26	63.48	23.75	28,976
July	59.35	59.35	59.35	59.74	0.26	62.85	30.05	6,250

A. Date that the futures become effective. At that date, holders of futures must purchase the commodity associated with the contract. In this case, the table outlines the futures dates for upcoming Crude Oil contracts traded at the New York Mercantile Exchange.

B. Opening price of the future for that particular monthly contract.

C. High price of the futures for that contract during the trading day.

D. Low price of the futures for that contract during the trading day.

E. The change in price from the previous trading session's closing, or settlement price.

F. Lifetime high and low. This figure places the previous day's trading into context, letting the investor know where that contract is priced compared to earlier trading activity.

G. Open interest is a gauge of the amount of trading in a particular contract. Nearer months tend to have a higher level of open interest than months further in the future.

traded. If the prices in the later months are higher than the price of the actively traded contract, the prices are in "contango." If the prices in the later months are lower than the price of the actively traded contract, the prices are in "backwardation." A simple example: If September oil futures are at $40 a barrel and September contracts are the most actively traded contracts, a December price of $45 a barrel would be a contango, while a December price of $35 would be backwardation. Those are two strange and handy words to drop into any investing conversation.

The Wall Street Journal carries tables on most futures in the Money & Investing section. The Online Journal has an extensive array of futures data that is useful for investors interested in futures.

OPTIONS

Options are a bit more complex than futures, but they operate under the same basic principle: What will something be worth at some future date? The big difference between options and futures is that an option gives you the right, but not the obligation, to buy something at a future date. Let's go back to Farmer Bob and his very expensive corn. If you decline the invitation to buy futures on Bob's corn, he offers to sell you the chance to buy twenty ears of corn on September 1 at last year's price of $30. You didn't buy the futures because you have commitment problems. But you think, the weather's been good, and I bet Bob will have more demand for that fantastic corn than he had last year. So the idea of locking in the chance to buy at $30 makes sense. So you say you'll give him $5 now for a right to pay $30 for his corn on September 1. In order for this to make sense, you are probably thinking that his corn will become like gold and sell for at least $36, maybe $40, for twenty ears by the time September 1 rolls around. You have just bought an option on Bob's corn. If the price comes in at $20 for twenty ears, you rip up that option and just buy the corn for $20. You're out $5, but at the time you thought it a risk worth taking.

Most options trading revolves around stocks. And, as is the case with futures, it's an inexpensive way to make some big bets. Unlike with futures, though, your maximum loss is only the amount you initially invest. You aren't forced to buy on the future date—you simply have the right to buy. Let's take a concrete example. Megachip, a semiconductor giant, has had a tough summer. Its profit margins have thinned, and its share price has dropped to $20. But you have a buddy who is a client of Megachip, and he tells you that things are turning around

MARGIN

Buying and selling futures requires an understanding of margin. Margin rules for futures are much looser than margin rules for stocks, as discussed in chapter 2. In buying and selling futures, investors can use large amounts of borrowed money, or margins, to make their bets. This extensive use of borrowed money makes these markets very risky. For instance, it may cost $100 to make a $1,000 bet, but that bet could go down quickly, creating hundreds of dollars in losses. The use of margin makes the idea of trading futures attractive, because it costs so little to get in. And it's tempting to think that just a little investment can turn into a big payoff. But as in life, such a tactic can work in both directions.

Let's take a specific example. You think the price of heating oil, which trades on the New York Mercantile Exchange, is going higher because *The Farmer's Almanac* has predicted a very cold winter in the Northeast. In July, you buy $100,000 worth of December heating oil futures. Because of margin, you have to put up only $5,000 to make this $100,000 bet through your broker. For a time, not much happens. Then in November, after a balmy Thanksgiving and updated forecasts of a frostless winter, heating oil futures collapse. Your December futures have fallen to $55,000 in value. You've managed to lose $45,000. Take away the initial $5,000 invested, and you are down $40,000 to your broker. This may sound like an extreme example, but such scenarios do occur in the futures market, with fortunes made and gained over the course of short periods of time.

and the second half of the year will be great. You look at the September options for Megachip, and you see that you can pay $2 for $20 options. The $2 is called the "premium," which is the amount you need to pay for that right. Owning the "call" option means that on a fixed date in September, you can buy Megachip shares for $20 each. If you think Megachip is headed to $30 during that time frame, this gives you a chance to take advantage of that move without buying the shares themselves. Generally, options work in parcels of 100 shares. Thus, a premium of $2 per share means spending $200 to get options on 100 shares at $20. If Megachip goes to $30, you can exercise the call options, buy the shares at $20 each and sell them at $30 each, making $1,000. You'd make out just as nicely if you had just bought the common stock at $20, but that would've required a lot more money up front. In addition, if Megachip's shares had kept skidding, the common shareholder has to watch in agony as the shares lose value. Instead, if Megachip shares drop rather than rise, the option buyer felt slightly bad when the option expired worthless.

Options investing isn't for everyone. It is complex and requires a good understanding of math and risk. Most everyone in the options market is a full-time professional trader. If you're investing as a sideline—for your retirement, for instance—you are playing a part-time game dominated by full-time sharks. That's something to consider before telling your spouse over breakfast about a get-rich-quick scheme in the options market you heard about on the radio.

Four times a year, options on stock index futures, stock index options and stock options all expire on the same day, and traders call those days "triple-witching" sessions. The four days are usually the third Friday of March, June, September and December. In recent years, single-stock futures also expire that day, and that has led some to adopt the term "quadruple-witching" session. Volume, inevitably, is heavy, as various contracts are fulfilled on the day of expiration, and trading on triple-witching days can be volatile.

PUTS AND CALLS

The option trade concerning Megachip is a "call" trade. Such an option means you have a call on that stock when the option expiration date arrives. Calls are bullish bets. But an investor could also buy a put, which is a negative bet on a stock. Let's go back to the Megachip example. Let's say Megachip is at $20, but your buddy who is a customer says the company's situation is getting worse and worse. Products are arriving late, and employees' morale isn't good. He sees little hope for a turnaround, despite rosy projections on Wall Street. You're not sure how much you trust your buddy, but you want to make a bearish bet on Megachip. So you buy the $20 put options, which are priced at $1. Again, since these are 100-share parcels, that's $100. A put option gives you the right, but not the obligation, to sell 100 shares of Megachip at $20. If you think Megachip is headed to $15, you are locking in a gain.

Along with buying puts and calls, you can also sell, or "write," puts and calls. This is a trickier proposition, because unlike the buyer, the seller does have an obligation to take the other side of the trade if the buyer exercises the option. When you sell, or "write," options, you are doing the inverse of what the buyer is doing. So a buyer of calls is bullish; a writer of calls is bearish. The same works for puts, where a buyer of puts is bearish and a writer of puts is bullish.

Here's how writing works. Take the Megachip example again; you have written the call that the investor has bought to buy Megachip shares at $20. As the writer, you get the premium. If the premium on the $20 call option is $2 a share, you receive $200, since the option is attached to a parcel of 100 shares. Now, as the writer of a call, you are anticipating that the option will expire worthless. In other words, on the expiration date, Megachip shares will be trading below the strike price of $20, making the call options nonsensical. But if Megachip rises, you will have to sell 100 shares to the call buyer for $20 a share. If you've done no planning ahead, you will have to go into the open market, find 100 shares and buy them, eating the difference in price between the open-market price and the option price. The inverse scenario works for put writers.

One strategy often aimed at individual investors by various financial sales folks is "writing covered calls." In this strategy, you write calls on stock that you already own. As the writer, you get the premium. Since you own the stock, you can pay off the option should it expire in the money. Of course, if it's a particularly good stock, having to sell it earlier than you want to can be an unfortunate turn of events. Overly aggressive covered-call writers can write themselves out of their entire portfolio of shares.

OTHER KINDS OF OPTIONS

While standard stock options expire on a monthly basis and are generally not bought more than a year in advance of expiration, options and options on futures and long-term options also abound. Here's a brief summary of the different kinds of options.

LONG-TERM OPTIONS

These options come in several forms and give the investor a chance to buy an option deeper into the future. Among these instruments, Long-Term Equity Anticipation Securities, or LEAPS, are perhaps the best known. LEAPS can expire more than two years into the future. And, like options, LEAPS can act as calls or puts on a particular stock.

INDEX OPTIONS

These options behave like stock options, but they are based on an underlying index, such as the S&P 500. These options expire monthly and quarterly.

FUTURES OPTIONS

These options are based on an underlying future contract, and they behave like options, meaning the buyer has the right but not the obligation to buy or sell. This can get tricky, because the underlying instrument, the futures, are an obligation to buy the futures.

THE WALL STREET JOURNAL OPTIONS TABLES *(WSJ)*

The Wall Street Journal publishes extensive options information at the On-line Journal. The options data is part of a large amount of free market data that is available to online readers for free at www.wsj.com/free.

LISTED OPTIONS QUOTATIONS
Friday, July 29, 2005

OPTION/STRIKE		EXP	-CALL-		-PUT-	
			VOL	LAST	VOL	LAST
ADC Tel	22.50	Sep	10	4	826	0.30
26.14	25	Sep	27	2.15	1,020	1
A M R	14	Aug	617	.60	70	0.55
AT&T	22.50	Jan	209	.10	714	3
AbtLab	17.50	Sep	1,122	.75	4	1.25
Abgenix	10	Aug	2,325	.75	35	0.35
10.37	12.50	Jan	1,010	1.55	210	3.40
Activisn o	16.88	Aug	2,003	3.50	...	...
Activisn	17.50	Aug	1,241	2.80	250	0.05
Activisn o	18.75	Aug	1,197	1.55	33	0.15
AdobeS	30	Aug	1,890	.60	223	0.90
AdvMOpt	35	Oct	4,400	7.10	...	...
41.57	45	Oct	2,990	.90	2,990	4.30
A M D	18	Aug	1	2.45	540	0.05
20.08	19	Aug	265	1.40	972	0.15
20.08	20	Aug	497	.55	8,003	0.45
20.08	20	Jan	2	2.25	542	1.85
AdvNeurm	45	Aug	9	5.40	1,037	0.20
50.04	50	Aug	6	1.60	687	1.65
Aetna	75	Aug	155	3.55	707	1
77.40	80	Aug	3,163	1	51	3.50
AffCmpS	50	Aug	2,924	1.60	903	1.30
Affymet	40	Sep	...	...	599	0.40
46.69	50	Aug	701	.50	848	3.50
Alcoa	35	Jan	1,013	.15	...	...
Alkerm	15	Feb	516	2.60	...	...
AllegTch	30	Aug	1,179	.70	20	1.35
AlliData	40	Dec	...	...	583	1.90
Alltel	65	Jan	2,000	3.90	...	...
66.50	70	Jan	2,154	1.55	...	...
AlphaNRs	30	Aug	824	.45	11	1.50
Altria	60	Dec	...	...	1,180	1.45
66.96	65	Aug	833	2.40	2,592	0.25
66.96	65	Sep	2,718	3.20	2,604	1.15
66.96	70	Aug	4,549	.15	12	2.30
66.96	70	Sep	3,376	.75	35	3.70
66.96	75	Sep	784	.15	...	...

A. **Option/Strike.** The name of the company stock that the option pertains to and the strike price of that option. The strike price is the level at which the option holder has the right, but not the obligation, to purchase or sell the stock that the option pertains to.

B. **Expiration of the option.** Options expire monthly.

C. **Call volume and last trade.** The call option gives the option holder the right, but not the obligation, to purchase shares at the option strike price when the option hits its expiration date.

D. **Put volume and last trade.** The put option gives the option holder the right, but not the obligation, to sell shares at the option strike price when the option hits its expiration date.

NONTRADITIONAL INVESTMENTS

Most investing revolves around stocks and bonds, often through mutual funds. More adventurous investors can explore the world of futures and options. And richer people have hedge funds as a different kind of investment vehicle.

But in the wake of the stock market bubble in the late 1990s, investors have turned to a variety of arenas in the hunt for investment returns. Investors, like other parts of society, go through their own fads. For a time, anything dot-com seemed a ticket to riches. More recently, real estate has seemed like the next sure thing. Over time, investing in a diversified portfolio of stocks and bonds, usually through mutual funds, has proved the smartest strategy. But it's worth exploring some of the other places in which people like to put their money.

COLLECTIBLES

The rise of eBay and other online auction sites has made collectibles far easier to trade. Time was, folks would go out antiquing in the countryside, hunting for trinkets of hidden value. This still goes on, but many people have migrated their aging valuables onto the Internet in search of prospective buyers. And since more valuable trinkets are easily obtained, more and more people have decided to invest in collectibles.

Investing in collectibles can be a welcome distraction from the world of stocks, bonds and mutual funds. For starters, you have something to hold in your hand and admire. In the post-bubble era, the psychic income from investments has become more important to people who watched their stocks evaporate into thin air.

But many collectibles have their own risks. Regulators are fewer, markets are wilder, and authenticity is elusive. Even in Israel, where authenticating items from the biblical age is a rigorous discipline, counterfeiters can flourish.

If you're acquiring collectibles away from reputable auction houses, such as Sotheby's, Christie's or Swann, you should seek out as much information as you can about ownership history of the collectible. Getting snookered isn't any fun, and remember: If it's too good to be true, it probably is.

ART

The art market has provided remarkable returns for collectors with a sharp eye for promising young artists or for those lucky (and rich) enough to spot which old works will become wildly popular. The high-end art market, which operates primarily through auction houses like Sotheby's and Christie's, caters to a small, elite group. Most of those folks probably aren't reading this book. But there is a world of art accessible to more regular folks. And collecting fine art provides an investor with not only a possible investment return, but also the thrill of having some original art in the home.

Art collecting, like investing in stocks and bonds, requires that you do the appropriate research to determine authenticity, quality and market value of specific types of art. A number of books on the art of collecting art can prove useful in this endeavor.

USEFUL ART-COLLECTING BOOKS

Collecting Art: A Journal to Get You Started by Glen Helfand

Discovering Art: A User's Guide to the World of Collecting by Jeanne Frank

History of Art, Revised by Anthony F. Janson

Design of the 20th Century by Charlotte Fiell and Peter Fiell

COINS AND STAMPS

Collecting coins has been popular for centuries. In the United States, the American Numismatic Society (www.amnumsoc.org) acts as the chief arbiter for the coin-mad world. Rare coins are fun to own, and building a coin collection has kept many a youngster busy. But coins are not often great investments, barring the very rare coins and coins that are made of precious metals. For instance, a gold coin would trade in conjunction with gold prices. And while the price of gold enjoyed a boomlet in 2004, it remains far below the highs reached in the early 1980s. The same can be said for silver coins.

Stamps are also a popular collectible. The American Philatelic Society (www.stamps.org) is the main organization that gathers stamp collectors together. Like coin collecting, stamp collecting has more entertainment value ("Hey, have a look at my stamp collection") than investment value. Still, as with coins, enthusiasts can build a portfolio that will become valuable over time. Unlike coins, however, stamps don't contain precious metal that can help with valuation.

MISCELLANY

Collectibles include a wide range of other items. Among them: baseball cards, cartoon cels and mementos from past important events, such as old presidential campaign buttons. Some of these items can become very valuable: a 1909 Honus Wagner T206 Tobacco baseball card sold for more than $1 million in 2000. Not bad for an old baseball card! But most such collectibles rarely rise to such lofty heights. And collectibles, with rare exceptions, can see wild swings in value. Again, collectibles, in most cases, aren't sound investment strategy. But they can provide some pleasure, and you can leave your big bound book of stamps to your children and grandchildren. And if they keep it in the family, your great-great-great-great-great-granddaughter can leave the highly valuable antique collection to the American Philatelic Society for stamp collectors to admire in the ages to come.

The Wall Street Journal provides extensive tables on options. And the Online Journal has an even broader array of tables.

Online Resources

www.cme.com Web site of the Chicago Mercantile Exchange, which trades everything from pork bellies to S&P 500 futures. Quotes and product information.

www.cbot.com The Chicago Board of Trade, where wheat, corn and soybeans trade. Quotes and product information.

www.nymex.com The New York Mercantile Exchange, home of light, sweet crude oil, heating oil, gold and silver. Quotes and product information.

www.nybot.com The New York Board of Trade, where cocoa, coffee and frozen concentrated OJ trades. Quotes and product information.

www.cboe.com The Chicago Board Options Exchange, a large options exchange, which has a nifty educational area called the Options Institute. Quotes and product information.

www.cftc.gov The chief commodity regulator, the Commodity Futures Trading Commission. Consumer protection information, educational information and other regulatory news.

www.futuresindustry.org The Futures Industry Association, the trade group representing the futures markets.

www.optionscentral.com The Options Industry Council, trade group for the options industry.

www.weather.com Don't laugh. If you're serious about corn or wheat, even heating oil, knowing the weather is key!

Suggested Reading

Getting Started in Options by Michael C. Thomsett. Good beginner's guide that helps demystify options investing.

Getting Started in Futures by Todd Lofton. Good beginner's guide that helps demystify futures investing.

The Four Biggest Mistakes in Option Trading by Jay Kaeppel. A concise look at common mistakes made by options investors.

Hot Commodities by Jim Rogers. Sometimes a bit over the top, but a good read and highly educational for those curious about futures investing.

The Power of Gold by Peter L. Bernstein. A thorough history of a commodity that everyone knows: gold.

The Prize by Daniel Yergin. An epic book about the history of crude oil and its role in the world, both economically and politically.

CHAPTER 10

Real-
Estate
Investing

During the first part of the new century, real estate en-joyed a tremendous run. Unusually low interest rates made mortgages more affordable. And investors stung by the stock market collapse in 2000 hankered for more tangible things to invest in, such as a home. Initially, these gains came from the appreciation in the values of primary residences. But as homeowners watched their homes shoot up in value, they began looking elsewhere for real-estate investments.

In 2005, economists were locked in an intense debate about whether or not real estate had become a "bubble," meaning that prices had soared to unsustainable levels. In a "bubble," like the bubble in Internet stocks, prices ultimately collapse. Few economists expect that housing prices will collapse, but the heady growth of the first five years of the new century will be hard to maintain. Moreover, other signs of "bubble" behavior are prevalent. "Get rich in real estate" schemes, for example, abound. Search for "real estate" on Google, and find the many hucksters trying to tell you how to spend nothing to make millions in real estate. Remember, if it's too good to be true, it probably is.

But investing in real estate is a key part of any investor's financial planning. For most of us, our homes are a big part of our net worth. And as we grow older, we build equity in our homes that can help to fund our children's college or our own retirement. In this chapter, we'll take a look at investing in our homes, second homes, income properties and real-estate investment trusts.

OUR HOMES

Psychologists say that buying a house and getting married are two of the most stressful things in life. The reason buying a home is so intense is that it usually costs a lot of money. For instance, someone making $50,000 a year might reasonably purchase a home that costs $300,000. Compared to the salary, that's a lot of cash. But buying a home (unless you've just inherited a fortune from Daddy) doesn't mean plunking down $300,000. Instead, most home buyers put down a down payment, usually 10% to 20%, and then take out a mortgage on the remainder. So in our example, that means a $30,000 payment and a $270,000 mortgage. That mortgage is then paid off over an extended period, usually thirty years, in a process called amortization. Spreading the $270,000 out over a long period of time makes such a purchase possible.

Owning a home comes with a lot of tax advantages, something that renting doesn't have. For instance, interest paid on mortgage is tax-deductible. And in some cases, home improvements can provide tax advantages. Selling a home also has some tax advantages. If you are single and have lived in your primary residence for two years, the first $250,000 of profits from the home sale are tax-free. If you're married, the exemption is $500,000. And you can take that tax advantage once every two years. If you buy and sell more frequently than that, the tax rules are much more complex and you'd be wise to check in with an accountant. While some critics complain that individuals have

DOW JONES INDUSTRIAL AVERAGE VS. DOW JONES REIT COMPOSITE INDEX . 2000–2005 *(WSJ)*

While stocks have ambled higher, REIT stocks have soared.

Dow Jones Industrial Average

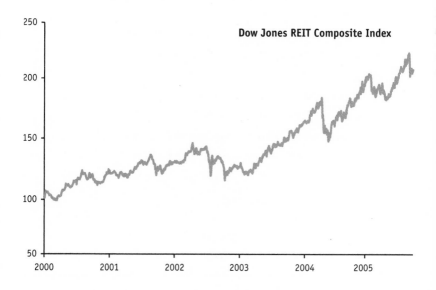

Dow Jones REIT Composite Index

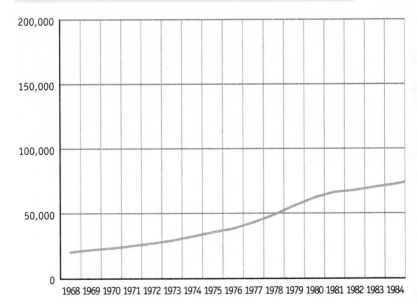

MEDIAN SALES PRICE OF EXISTING SINGLE-FAMILY HOMES
(National Association of Realtors)

started "day-trading" homes, the tax laws make such "flipping" challenging.

Buying a home in a hot market can be unnerving. Real estate in places such as Silicon Valley and Los Angeles seems to have gotten insanely expensive. A general rule of thumb is that even in rich markets, if you plan to live in the residence for ten years, it makes more sense to buy than to rent. But the real-estate market in some places has gotten so intense that some real-estate investors are questioning that old rule of thumb.

SECOND HOMES

A growing number of people have decided to invest in second homes rather than putting more money into stocks or bonds. A lot of times, these second homes double as vacation homes. For instance, in Minnesota, a lot of families have a home in the Twin Cities and also a cabin "up north" to which they can escape in the summer. In Chicago, a second home might be in

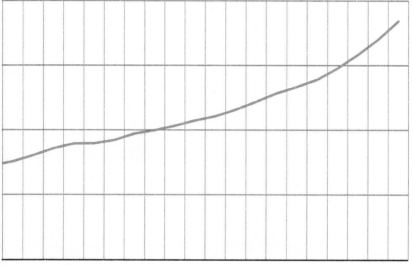

1985 1986 1987 1988 1989 1990 1991 1992 1993 1994 1995 1996 1997 1998 1999 2000 2001 2002 2003 2004

Florida or Arizona, where people like to go when the Windy City gets very cold. A second home may be a simple lakeside nonwinterized bungalow or a condominium by a golf course.

Investors have some options about optimizing the purchase of a second home. They can use the second home as a personal property, in which case the interest payments are tax-deductible. Under the tax code, taxpayers itemizing deductions can claim mortgage interest payment deductions on the first $1 million of debt incurred for the purchase of a first or second home. To qualify as a second home, an owner must use the second home for more than fourteen days per year.

The other option is to rent the second home when you're not using it. If you rent for fewer than fourteen days, you can still qualify for the personal home deduction. If you rent for more than fourteen days, the tax treatments change, because now your second home is considered an investment property. Expenses such as mortgage interest and maintenance are divided between personal and investment use, proportional to

FINANCING

When interest rates are falling, a homeowner can refinance her home and reduce her mortgage rate. Since rates fell from 2000 to 2005, many people went through the process of refinancing. When refinancing is done, the home is reappraised. If the reappraised value is higher than the original home value, meaning that your equity in the home has increased, refinancing can provide the chance to cash in on some of that gain. Rather

AVERAGE MORTGAGE RATE, 1995–2004 (WSJ)

the number of days of rental use and actual use. The expenses counted as investment are deductible; the portion allocated for personal use, including mortgage interest, is not deductible, because an investment property is not considered a personal second home.

than simply reducing the monthly payment, a cash-out refinancing can en-able the homeowner to take some of the increased equity in cash rather than in a reduction of the monthly payment. Refinancing isn't free, so a homeowner needs to calculate whether interest rates have fallen enough for refinancing to make sense. In addition, some mortgages have a penalty for prepayment. In a refinancing, you're essentially paying off the old mortgage with a new one, so look carefully at your mortgage for prepay-ment clauses before doing a refinancing.

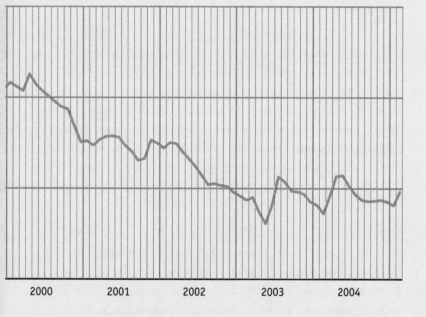

Tax benefits are a key element of home ownership, whether of a first or second home. Consulting with a tax specialist is the best way to approach the purchase of any real estate, primarily because state and local taxes vary across the country.

INCOME PROPERTIES

Some real-estate mavens aren't satisfied with just a couple of homes. Instead, they want to buy something grander: income property. This can be as simple as a home to rent out, or more complex, such as an apartment complex.

Investing in income property is riskier than buying a second home, because rather than having a place to visit on the weekends, an income property is purchased to deliver, well, income. A two-family home, called a "duplex" in some parts of the country, may sound easy to rent and maintain. But if one unit is empty, 50% of your rental income isn't coming in that month. And that rental income is usually aimed at paying off a mortgage used to purchase the income property. Having a 100-unit building makes it less likely that you'll face a 50% vacancy rate, but even a 10% vacancy rate means you are trying to rent out ten units, which can take a lot of time. Investing in income property sounds glamorous, especially when you run the numbers with full vacancy rates and no turnover. But pipes break, people move out and the roof sometimes needs replacing. The landlord of an income property has to deal with all these headaches. Landlords who have a lot of money can hire other people to handle these things, but most of us investing in real estate don't start with such full pockets.

Valuing an income property is more complex than valuing a residence. When you buy a residence, you are calculating your ability to pay a mortgage out of your own earnings. When you buy an income property, you're calculating how the income (rents) will help pay the mortgage.

So how to value an income property? An income property has an annual net operating income, or NOI. This is a figure of rental income less anticipated vacancies, maintenance and other expenses, not including interest payments or other debt related to the property. Most investors divide the NOI by something called the "cap rate" to come up with the proper value for one apartment in a complex. The cap rate relates to the expected annual rate of return on the property, and most income property buyers recommend using a cap rate of 9% (0.09) or 10% (0.10) when evaluating a property. So a property with an NOI of $100,000 and a cap rate of 9% would have a value of $1.1 million. This kind of simple calculation isn't perfect, but in a real-estate market that is increasingly frantic, doing even simple math can help you understand if you're overpaying for a property. Like investing in stocks, investing in real estate works best when you don't overpay. Cap rates vary depending on all kinds of local variants, such as the proximity of good schools, safety and local economic growth.

Local knowledge is an important factor in real-estate investing, especially when it comes to income properties. For instance, some communities have strong tenant laws that can make eviction difficult. Local knowledge can also help you spot undervalued properties. Many states and localities have real-estate organizations that provide information and guidance to income property investors. If you're thinking of going down the income property path, it'd be wise to join such a group.

REITS

Investing in income properties is expensive and potentially time-consuming. Buying a second home can also be too much to chew. Many of us are doing our best just to keep up with the mortgage payments on our own residence, let alone think about a second home or an apartment complex. But that doesn't mean investing in real estate isn't possible. In recent years, one of the hottest parts of the stock market has been among real-estate investment trusts. In 2004, REITs (pronounced "reets," like beets), were the best-performing mutual funds sector in the United States, gaining 32%, according to Lipper, a data-tracking firm.

REITs trade like stocks. They pay good dividends and provide for capital appreciation (a rising share price). Best of all, instead of having to take out a $1 million mortgage, a REIT investor can spend as little as a few dollars to acquire a share in a REIT and get a piece of the real-estate action.

REITs generally own and manage income-producing commercial real-estate properties. There are shopping mall REITs, hospital REITs and apartment REITs, among others. The reason REITs pay handsome dividends is that they are required to pay their shareholders 90% of their taxable income in the form of dividends. While the average stock pays a dividend yield of about 2% per year, REITS pay between 6% and 8% a year, on average.

There are about 180 REITs trading in the United States, according to the National Association of Real Estate Investment Trusts (NAREIT). These REITs have assets valued at more than $375 billion.

Not all REITs are terrific, and in a difficult real-estate market, REITs suffer, too. As a rule of thumb, when interest rates move higher, REITs become a less attractive investment option. That's because higher long-term rates mean an investor can get returns from safer Treasury bonds that begin to rival the riskier REIT dividend payouts. In 2005, with ten-year Treasurys paying 4.5%, REITs with dividends of 7% and 8% still look attractive. An important caveat about REIT dividends: unlike stock dividends, which are taxed at 15%, most REIT dividends are taxed as regular income.

For most of us, REIT investing is easiest via publicly traded REITs or REIT-focused mutual funds. Another simple way to invest in REITs is via exchange-traded REIT funds or closed-end REIT funds. There are also nontraded REITs in the private market, but publicly traded REITs are better for the average investor. Publicly traded REITs follow the same disclosure and corporate governance rules that apply to other stocks, and the public market provides for greater transparency, making it easier for an investor to do his or her homework.

Online Resources

www.nareit.com Web site of the trade group representing real estate investment trusts. Lots of data and basic information for investors interested in REITs.

www.realtor.org Web site of the National Association of Realtors. Includes recent government actions and other data that can assist the real-estate investor.

http://realestate.yahoo.com Lots of basic information for renters, landlords and real-estate investors.

www.smartmoney.com Includes mortgage calculators and other tools for real-estate investors.

Suggested Reading

Dictionary of Real Estate Terms by Barron's Financial Guides.
The McGraw-Hill 36-Hour Real Estate Investment Course by Jack Cummings.
The Beginner's Guide to Real Estate Investing by Gary W. Eldred.
What No One Ever Tells You About Investing in Real Estate by Robert J. Hill.

CONCLUSION

In this book we have tried to provide you with a solid under-pinning for understanding the world of markets, money and investing. Learning these basics has hopefully erased a fear of finance and, at the same time, enabled you to participate in discussions about such topics. But, more important, it should help give you the confidence required to take charge of your money and investing life.

And that is key, because your financial future is increas-ingly up to you. Retirement plans are moving more toward 401(k) programs and away from pensions that others manage on your behalf. Investing and saving for your children's col-lege education is more important than ever. Even self-directed health-care savings and investing programs are on the rise.

In addition, whether you like it or not, financial markets play a huge role in our everyday life. Mortgage rates flow from the yield on the ten-year Treasury bond. Interest rates paid on certificates of deposit stem from short-term rates set by the Federal Reserve. The stock market can tell us how healthy a company or the broader economy is. The bond market offers signals on the inflation outlook. Not convinced? Spend a day tallying up the business interactions you have. Buying a news-paper. Booking a flight. Filling the gas tank. Buying a stock. You may find it surprising how much of your life is intertwined with the world of money and investing.

And, as you know now, it's not eye-glazingly dull. Financial markets produce winners, losers and great drama—every day. Discovering a great investment opportunity is like finding out a closely held secret. Learning how the complex, global economy works can be exciting: Products in Target come from China, India, Germany and Texas, and food in our grocery stores arrives from places like Japan and Latin America, as well as from Iowa and California. All around us, the world hums with interesting economic tales.

But it's important to realize that this book is just a starting point. Things move fast, and that means educating yourself is an adventure that keeps racing ahead. Each chapter in this book provides books of interest that can help you learn more. Also, each chapter features important Internet resources for your future use. Don't let this book be the last stop in your investment education. Continue to learn and discover, and by doing so, you will be better positioned to prepare for your financial future.

GLOSSARY

American depositary receipt (ADR) A stocklike security that allows companies outside the United States to list their stock in the United States. Foreign companies also list under American depositary shares, or ADSs.

Annual meeting A meeting of a public company's shareholders once a year to vote on various corporate proposals.

Annuity A contract sold by a life insurance company guaranteeing a future payment to the investor, usually starting at retirement. With a fixed annuity, the payments are in regular installments. With a variable annuity, the payments depend on the value of the underlying investments.

Asset-backed securities Securities backed by collateral such as credit-card receivables or auto loans.

Assets Everything a company or individual owns or is owed.

Backwardation In commodity futures trading, when the future month prices are lower than the current or near-term prices.

Balance sheet A listing of assets, liabilities and net worth, showing the financial position of a company at a specific time.

Basic shares Sometimes called the primary figure; refers to the shares outstanding. (As opposed to diluted, which refers to all potential shares outstanding.)

Basis point In bond-market jargon, one basis point equals one-hundredth of a percentage point, except in quotations, where percentage points are used instead: 50 basis points equal 0.5 percentage point.

Bearer bond A bond for which the owner's name is not registered on the books of the issuing company. Interest and principal are thus payable to whoever holds the bond.

Bearer stock A stock certificate that is not registered in anyone's name. Such stock's shares are negotiable without endorsement and transferable by delivery.

Bear market A market in which the value of securities—stocks or bonds, for example—is generally declining.

Bid price and asked price In the securities business, the bid price is what the prospective buyer is willing to pay, and the asked price, or offer price, is what a prospective seller is willing to accept. In real estate, the prospective buyer similarly makes a bid at a given price, and a prospective seller sets an asking price.

Big Board The New York Stock Exchange (NYSE).

Blue-chip stocks Stocks of companies known for their long-established record of earning profits and paying dividends, including the stocks in the Dow Jones Industrial Average.

Bond A general term for debt instruments.

Bond rating Bonds receive a rating based on the issuer's ability to repay the bond. Such ratings apply to companies and governments that issue debt.

Broker An employee of a brokerage firm who handles transactions. The most common is a stockbroker, who often handles the investment accounts of individual investors.

Brokerage The handling of transactions, usually through arranging buyers and sellers for stocks, bonds and even companies.

Brokerage firm A firm that brokers transactions. Brokerage firms are also referred to as *securities companies, investment banks* or *Wall Street firms.*

Bull market A market in which the value of securities—stocks or bonds, for example—is generally rising.

Buyback (n.), buy back (v.) Terms referring to a company's repurchase of stock, usually on the open market.

Capital The money, equipment or property owned or used in business by a person or corporation.

Cash flow Usually defined as earnings plus depreciation allowances and other charges.

Central bank A bank having the responsibility for controlling a country's monetary policy.

Chicago Board of Trade The main U.S. exchange for trading certain financial and commodity derivatives, including Treasury bonds, grains and the Dow Jones Industrial Average index futures.

Chicago Board Options Exchange One of the nation's main stock options markets.

Chicago Mercantile Exchange (CME) A futures market, it trades meat, livestock and currency futures, as well as S&P 500 index futures. Sometimes called "the Merc."

Circuit breakers A tool utilized by the New York Stock Exchange to control dramatic market drops; when trading reaches a circuit breaker, it is halted.

Commercial paper Short-term obligations used by industrial or finance companies to obtain cash.

Commodity In a market sense, a product of mining or agriculture before it has undergone extensive processing; in a general sense, anything that is bought or sold.

Commodity futures Contracts to buy or sell given amounts of individual commodities at given prices within specified periods.

Common stock When other classes of stock are outstanding, the holders of common stock are the last to receive dividends and the last to receive payments if the corporation is dissolved. The company may raise or lower dividends on common stock as the company's earnings rise or fall.

Consumer price index (CPI) A statistical measure of the average of prices of a specified set of goods and services purchased by wage earners in urban areas.

Contango In commodity future trading, when future-month prices are higher than current or near-term prices.

Convertible bond A bond carrying the stipulation that it may be exchanged for a specific amount of stock in the company that issued it.

Cost of living The amount of money needed to pay taxes and to buy the goods and services deemed necessary to make up a given standard of living, taking into account changes that may occur in tastes and buying patterns.

Coupon A slip of paper attached to a bond that the bondholder clips at specified times and returns to the issuer for payment of the interest due.

Crash In the stock market, a precipitate decline in prices, usually accompanied by a sharp decline in economic activity.

Dealer Dealers, as opposed to brokers, act as principals in transactions, buying and selling for their own accounts.

Debt In the context of the securities markets, bonds, notes, mortgages and other debt instruments, or forms of paper showing amounts owed.

Deflation A decline in the general level of prices for goods and services. It is the opposite of inflation. Disinflation, by comparison, is the slowing of price increases.

Depression A steep decline in economic performance.

Derivative A financial contract whose value is designed to track the return on stocks, bonds, currencies or some other benchmark.

Diluted shares All potential shares outstanding of a company's stock.

Discount A security that is selling at a price lower than a comparable or benchmark security.

Discount rate The rate of interest charged by the Federal Reserve on loans it makes to banks and other depository institutions. The discount rate has an influence on the rates the institutions then charge their customers.

Discount window A system the Federal Reserve uses to lend reserves to commercial banks.

Disposable personal income The income a person retains after deductions for income taxes, Social Security taxes, property taxes and other payments such as fines and penalties to various levels of government.

Dividend A payment distributed on a per-share basis to stockholders as a return on their investment, usually on a quarterly, semiannual or annual basis. A stock dividend is usually expressed as a percentage.

Dollar-cost averaging The systematic purchasing of fixed dollar amounts of securities, rather than fixed numbers of shares, at regular intervals. A given amount of money thus buys more shares when the price is low and fewer shares when the price is high.

Dow Jones Industrial Average The stock market indicator comprising thirty of the leading issues; administered by the editors of *The Wall Street Journal*.

Duration In the debt securities market, the average number of years required to receive the interest and principal from a bond or portfolio of bonds. The cash flows are discounted to present value based on current interest rates. Longer durations have greater sensitivity to interest rate changes.

Dutch auction So called because, as in flower auctions in the Netherlands, the sellers set the prices they will accept. Traditionally, the prices are lowered until the sellers sell all the flowers they want to. In the U.S. corporate world, the highest price within a present range necessary to acquire all the shares the company wants becomes the purchase price for all the shares.

Earnings per share Obtained by dividing the number of common shares outstanding into the amount left after dividends have been paid on any preferred stock.

Electronic communications network (ECN) A screen-based order-matching system through which individuals and institutions can trade securities directly without a market maker or floor specialist as intermediary. The largest is the Instinet Group, which trades primarily Nasdaq stocks. Nasdaq agreed to acquire Instinet in Spring 2005.

Emerging markets Economies that are making a transition to market economics from state control or shelter.

Employee Stock Ownership Plan (ESOP) A plan that provides tax advantages when companies give shares to their employees. Under such a plan, a trust is created, and banks make loans to the trust to buy the company's stock. As the company makes payments to the trust to retire the debt, the trust allocates the stock to employees.

Employment report The Labor Department's employment report, usually released on the first Friday of the month, is considered the first official look at U.S. economic activity in the preceding month.

Equity When used in a financial sense, the value of property beyond the amount that is owed on it. In the context of the securities markets, the stock-ownership interest of shareholders. A stockholder's equity in a corporation is the value of the shares he holds. A homeowner's equity is the difference between the value of the house and the amount of the unpaid mortgage.

Euro The common currency for twelve of the European Union nations.

Eurodollars U.S. dollars deposited in banks outside the United States. The term refers only to the location of deposit. In all other ways, Eurodollars are no different from dollars deposited in the United States. They are also known as *offshore dollars,* or, if they are deposited in Asia, as *Asian dollars.*

Ex-dividend Stocks are usually traded ex-dividend, or without the declared dividend, four trading days before the stock-of-record date that determines which holders will receive the dividend. Stock trades on the ex-dividend date are generally at lower prices, reflecting the absence of the dividend rights.

Exercise In options trading, the conversion of an option into a position in the underlying future, security or commodity to which that option applies.

Federal funds Money in excess of what the Federal Reserve says a bank must have on hand to back up deposits. The excess may be lent overnight to other banks that need more cash on hand to meet reserve requirements. The interest rate on these loans, which is regulated by the Federal Reserve's Open Market Committee through the purchase and sale of Treasury bills, is the federal-funds rate.

Federal Open Market Committee The policy-making arm of the Federal Reserve.

Federal Reserve System, Federal Reserve Board The *Federal Reserve System,* established in 1913, is the central banking system of the United States. The *Federal Reserve Board,* located in Washington, D.C., governs the Federal Reserve System.

Fiscal policy, monetary policy *Fiscal policy* involves government taxation and spending. *Monetary policy* involves central banks' interest rates or minimum reserve requirements.

Fiscal year The twelve-month period that a corporation or a governmental body uses for bookkeeping purposes. Fiscal years are expressed according to when the year ends: the year ending March 31, 2002, for example, was fiscal 2002. The federal government's fiscal year runs from October 1 to September 30. When the entity's fiscal year is the January–December calendar year, the term "fiscal" isn't necessary.

Fixed-income investment A bond or other security that pays a fixed rate of return or a preferred stock that pays a fixed dividend.

Float In banking, the time between the deposit of a check in a bank and the availability of the funds to the depositor. In securities matters, the number of shares of a company that are outstanding and available for trading by the public.

401(k) The employer-sponsored salary-deferral plan that allows employees to contribute a portion of their gross salary to a savings plan or company profit-sharing plan. Substantial tax penalties are applied if the funds aren't kept in the plan until the employee reaches age 59½, retires or leaves the company.

Global Depositary Receipts They are similar to American Depositary Receipts, which allow companies outside the United States to list their stock in the United States. Global Depositary Receipts allow companies in the United States, Europe, Asia and Latin America to list their stock in various markets around the world. Companies in emerging markets such as India, China and Brazil are the prime issuers of GDRs.

Government debt The total amount of obligations owed by a government.

Government deficit The annual shortfall between revenue and expenses.

Gross domestic product The total value of goods and services produced in a nation. GDP has replaced gross national product as the Commerce Department's main measure of U.S. economic output.

Hedge fund A lightly regulated private investment partnership that invests across all manner of global financial markets and can "hedge" its positions by betting against the market. Invested in largely by wealthy individuals and institutions, hedge funds often use leverage and derivatives to maximize their bets.

Hedging In commerce, the buying or selling of a product or a security to offset a possible loss from price changes on a future corresponding purchase or sale.

Index fund A mutual fund that seeks to produce the same return that investors would get if they owned all the stocks in a particular stock index, such as the Dow Jones Industrial Average.

Inflation A sustained rise in prices.

Initial public offering (IPO) Used to take a company public, allowing investors to buy the company's stock.

Junk bond The jargon term applies to a high-yield corporate or municipal bond that rating agencies consider speculative. Such bonds typically offer higher yields and involve higher risk than bonds with investment-grade ratings. If junk bonds are rated at all, they are rated below triple-B by Standard & Poor's and below Baa by Moody's.

Leveraged buyout The purchase of a company by a small group of investors, financed largely by debt. Ultimately, the group's borrowings are repaid with funds generated by the acquired company's operations or the sale of its assets.

Liabilities Claims against a corporation or other entity, including accounts payable, wages and salaries due to be paid, dividends declared payable, taxes payable and obligations such as bonds, debentures and bank loans.

Limit order A request by an investor that his or her broker purchase or sell shares of a stock at a specific price, rather than at the prevailing market price.

Liquidation The process of converting assets, such as shares of stock, into cash. When a company is liquidated in a bankruptcy or other action, the cash obtained is used to repay debt, first to holders of bonds and preferred stock. Any remaining cash is distributed to holders of common stock.

Liquidity The ability of an asset to be bought or sold quickly and in large volume without substantially affecting its price. Checking accounts, money market mutual funds and Treasury bills are considered liquid assets.

Lots Groups of 100 shares.

Margin In securities trading, the amount of cash a buyer must put up in borrowing from a broker. If the margin requirement set by the Federal Reserve Board is 50%, that is the percentage of the purchase price the buyer must put up; he may borrow the rest. A margin call for additional margin results if the value of the securities declines.

Market capitalization, market cap The stock market value of a traded company. Market cap is calculated by multiplying a company's share price by the number of shares it has.

Market maker On the Nasdaq Stock Market, market makers are authorized to buy and sell a certain security. While the NYSE has a single specialist referee a single stock, the Nasdaq has multiple market makers overseeing the trades of a single stock.

Maturity In the securities market, the time at which a debt instrument is due and payable. A bond due to mature on July 1, 2020, will return the holder's principal and final interest payment on that date.

Money market The market in which short-term debt instruments are issued and traded. This includes Treasury bills, commercial paper and bankers' acceptances.

Money supply The total stock of money in the economy, consisting primarily of currency in circulation and deposits in savings and checking accounts. Too much money in relation to the output of goods tends to push interest rates down and push prices and inflation up; too little money tends to push interest rates up, lower prices and output and cause unemployment and excess plant capacity.

Municipal bond A bond issued by a state, county, city, town, village, possession or territory, or a bond issued by an agency or authority set up by one of these governmental units.

Mutual fund A securities portfolio managed by an investment company to provide investors with diversification. Also called an *open-end investment fund,* it continually sells and redeems shares at prices based on the asset value of the fund's portfolio. So-called *load funds* are offered through brokers, with their fees added. *No-load funds* are offered directly to individual investors.

National Association of Securities Dealers (NASD) Based in Washington, D.C., the agency is responsible for the operation and regulation of the Nasdaq securities market. The NASD Regulation Inc. (NASDR) subsidiary of the NASD regulates the activities of broker-dealers who trade Nasdaq stocks. NASDR also regulates the sale of mutual funds, direct-participation programs and variable annuities.

New York Board of Trade Formed in 1998 by the merger of the Coffee, Sugar & Cocoa Exchange and the New York Cotton Exchange.

New York Mercantile Exchange (Nymex) A center for trading oil, gas, electricity, platinum and palladium futures and options. Trading includes contracts for heating oil, gasoline and light, sweet crude oil.

New York Stock Exchange (NYSE) The oldest stock exchange in the United States, founded in 1792. Also known as the *Big Board.*

Odd lot An amount of stock not divisible by 100 shares; usually fewer than 100 shares.

Offering price The price at which new issues of stock are marketed to the public.

Option In the securities business, a contract that gives the holders the right, but not the obligation, to buy or sell a set amount of securities or commodities at a set level.

Over-the-counter stock Technically, any stock not listed and traded on an organized exchange or on Nasdaq. But Nasdaq stocks are colloquially called over-the-counter stocks.

Premium A security that is selling at a price higher than that of a comparable or benchmark security.

Price/earnings ratio Calculated by dividing the price of a stock by its annual earnings per share. The *trailing P/E ratio* uses the reported earnings for the previous 12 months, and the *forward P/E ratio* uses analysts' forecasts for earnings over the next 12 months. The P/E ratio is also known as a stock's *multiple.*

Prime rate The interest rate used by banks as a reference point for a wide range of loans to medium-size and small businesses, as well as for some types of loans to individuals. Also known as the *base rate of interest.*

Prospectus A formal document outlining the financial and other information necessary for investors to consider purchasing a new security. The prospectus details the issuing company's financial statements, its business history, a description of its officers and the current status of outstanding litigation.

Real-estate investment trust (REIT) A company that buys, sells and operates land properties.

Recession A downturn in economic activity. Informally, the rule of thumb is that a recession begins after two consecutive quarters of decline in a nation's gross domestic product. The National Bureau of Economic Research makes the formal declaration.

Recovery In a business cycle, the period after a downturn or recession when economic activity picks up and the gross domestic product grows, leading into the expansion phase of the cycle, or levels above those prevailing before the recession.

Redemption In bond trading, a transaction in which the issuer calls in the bond issue and returns the principal amount to the investor. In some cases, the issuer must pay a premium for calling in a bond before its maturity date.

Registered bond A registered bond is recorded in the name of the holder on the books of the issuer or the issuer's registrar and can be transferred to another owner only when endorsed by the registered owner.

Reserve requirement The proportion of their customers' deposits that commercial banks must keep in cash or on deposit with the Federal Reserve System, by order of the Federal Reserve Board, to protect the deposits.

Resistance level In securities trading, the price level at which a rising market is turned back downward. Resistance levels usually are seen as selling opportunities. If a rising market passes a resistance level, it often becomes a *support level.*

Return on investment A percentage obtained by dividing the company's assets into its net income.

Revenue The amount of money a company takes in, including sales, rents, royalties and interest earned. The figure doesn't normally include excise taxes and sales taxes collected for the government.

Reverse stock split By reducing the number of shares held by the public, a company making a reverse stock split increases the per-share price of the stock. Companies frequently use reverse splits to enable their stock price to meet minimum regulatory listing requirements for the stock price.

Revolving credit A line of credit that may be used repeatedly up to a specified total, with periodic full or partial repayments.

Russell 1000 and 2000 Published by the Frank Russell Company, the indexes are measures of the stock-price performance of companies. The Russell 1000 includes the 1,000 largest-capitalization companies, including those in the S&P 500. The Russell 2000, which is more widely followed, comprises the next 2,000 companies after those included in the Russell 1000.

Sales The amount of money a company receives for the goods and services it sells.

Same-store sales Expressed as a percentage gain or decline, representing only the changes in sales at the stores currently in operation that were also operating a year earlier (or sometimes longer before that, depending on a company's definition).

Sector fund A mutual fund that invests in a single industry sector, such as biotechnology, gold or the Internet.

Securities Reference term for a financial asset, such as stocks or bonds.

Securities and Exchange Commission The government agency that enforces securities laws and sets disclosure standards for publicly traded securities, including mutual funds.

Short When investors bet against a stock, bond or other security, they go "short." Investors who go short borrow and then sell the security, intending to repay the loan by purchasing the security at a future, lower price.

Specialist On the stock exchanges, an exchange member designated to maintain a fair and orderly market in a specified stock.

Spread In securities trading, the difference between prices linked closely by market patterns or market trading strategy. In fixed-income securities, the yield differential between two comparable securities or investment instruments.

Stock split A company splits its stock for several reasons, the result being more shares outstanding. A two-for-one stock split means that the number of shares outstanding has doubled. Companies also can execute a "reverse" stock split. In that case, the number of shares outstanding diminishes. A company that does a one-for-two reverse stock split then has half as many shares outstanding.

Stop order In securities markets, an order to a broker to buy or sell a security when the market price reaches a given level.

Strike price The price at which an option contract allows the underlying instrument to be bought or sold; also known as the *exercise price*.

Support level In securities trading, the price level at which a falling market turns back upward. Support levels are usually seen as buying opportunities.

Triple witching The term is applied to the times each quarter when index options, index futures and stock options all expire in the same

Thursday–Friday period. Triple witchings can cause stock-market volatility on the Fridays involved, as stocks are bought or sold to offset expiring options positions. Double witchings occur when index and stock options expire together.

Underwriter In the insurance business, an entity that assumes risk for a fee. In securities markets, an underwriting firm or syndicate is one that agrees to purchase a new bond or stock offering from the issuer, for resale.

Unemployment rate As compiled by the Labor Department, the percentage of people in the work force who are looking for jobs, adjusted for seasonal variations.

Unlisted stocks These formerly were considered to be those not listed on a formal exchange. Now if the stocks are carried on the NASD's Automated Quotation Service, they are termed Nasdaq stocks, or NASD-listed stocks. Only shares listed on the so-called pink sheets and not on the Nasdaq tables are considered to be unlisted.

Venture capitalist Someone who invests a pool of money in businesses in exchange for a role in running the businesses and obtaining a share of the profits.

Wall Street Not just a street in Manhattan, Wall Street is shorthand for the securities business. Sometimes referred to as "the Street."

Wilshire 5000 The broadest U.S. stock index, covering all Nasdaq Stock Market stocks and all stocks traded on the New York and American stock exchanges.

Yield The annual rate of return on an investment, as paid in dividends or interest.

Zero-coupon bonds Bonds that pay no interest but are issued at a deep discount. Investors' gains come from the difference between the discounted purchase price and the face value received at maturity.

ACKNOWLEDGMENTS

I have many people to thank in the crafting of this book. First of all, the Money & Investing staff at *The Wall Street Journal*. A group of smart, dedicated and hardworking reporters and editors, they brilliantly bring to life the complex and arcane world of Wall Street and investing. A special thanks to Phil Kuntz, Michael Siconolfi and Dan Hertzberg, all of whom helped make this book possible.

Roe D'Angelo, Ken Wells and Steve Adler convinced me to take on this project, though at times I doubted their wisdom in the matter.

Raymund Flandez did heroic work in pulling together graphics, data and other important information in this book.

Shana Drehs, who probably had more fun editing books on hockey heroes of yore, was patient—and painstaking—in keeping this book on track. I thank her and her colleagues at Crown for making this book as good as it can be.

Chris McCullough and *The Wall Street Journal* Market Data Group provided quick and helpful answers to my many questions.

Finally, a word of thanks to the many market professionals that I've come to know over the years. People such as Jim Griffin, R. Byron Wien and Arthur Gray Jr. have helped me learn a great deal about the complex and fascinating world of economics, investing and markets. For a liberal arts student who studied American history of the antebellum South, my education in these areas has come through talks with people like Jim, Byron and Arthur and the reading of the many books they have recommended to me.

INDEX

ABOUT THE AUTHOR

DAVE KANSAS is editor of *The Wall Street Journal*'s Money & Investing section. He oversees coverage of Wall Street, banking, markets, investing and personal finance. In addition, he occasionally writes stories for the *Journal* and is a guest on radio and television programs, commenting on the financial markets and investing.

Mr. Kansas rejoined the *Journal* in December 2001 as deputy managing editor of The Wall Street Journal Online at WSJ .com. He served in that role until February 2003, at which time he was named acting money and investing editor. In December 2003, Mr. Kansas was appointed to his current position of money and investing editor. Prior to rejoining the *Journal,* Mr. Kansas was editor in chief of TheStreet.com and served on the company's board of directors.

Mr. Kansas originally joined the *Journal*'s New York bureau in September 1991 after completing a summer internship on the *Journal*'s monitor desk. He became a reporter on the spot news desk in October 1992 and began reporting and writing for the "Abreast of the Market" column in the Money & Investing section in August 1994. In December of that year, he became the primary writer of the section's "Markets" column, covering the New York Stock Exchange.

In 1987, Mr. Kansas began his journalism career as an engineer and a reporter at the NBC Radio Network. He later worked for *Newsday* as a reporter.

In January 2001, Mr. Kansas's book *TheStreet.com Guide to Investing in the Internet Era* was published by Doubleday and was an Amazon number 1 seller. A paperback edition was published in January 2002.

Born in St. Paul, Minnesota, Mr. Kansas attended Macalester College in St. Paul and received a bachelor's degree in history from Columbia University in New York. He remains a die-hard Minnesota sports fan and is a Minnesota Wild season-ticket holder.

He lives in New York City.

Also Available from

THE WALL STREET JOURNAL

The Wall Street Journal Complete Personal Finance Guidebook is an easy-to-understand primer on personal finance. With chapters on banking, investing, borrowing, insurance, 401(k)s, and taxes, this practical book offers truly useful suggestions for how to make the right decisions in the present and how to best plan for the future.

0-307-33600-X, $14.95 paper (Canada: $21.00)

The Wall Street Journal Personal Finance Workbook guides you through the world of personal finance, making it quick and easy to organize your cash, keep your finances in order, and build wealth. Complete with a series of worksheets, charts, and step-by-step instructions, this is an essential companion to *The Wall Street Journal Complete Personal Finance Guidebook.*

0-307-33601-8, $13.95 paper (Canada: $21.00)

The Wall Street Journal Guide to the Business of Life

Become an instant expert in the things that really matter—this fact-filled guide covers travel, health, entertaining, real estate, technology, and more.

1-4000-8159-9, $27.50 hardcover (Canada: $39.95)

The Wall Street Journal Identity Theft Guidebook

Learn to combat identity theft and protect yourself against it.

978-0-307-33853-2, $13.95 paper (Canada: $17.95)
Available wherever books are sold.

It's going to be a great year....

I took a deep breath outside the door to Yearbook class and then sauntered—yes, I actually sauntered—into the room, doing my best imitation of calm, confident me. I was totally nervous. I had butterflies in my brain. But it was good nervous, excited nervous. I was one of the chosen people.

Have you ever had the feeling that you were destined for greatness? Not that you would ever admit that to anybody. But have you ever heard the all-in-your-head voice telling you that you're special, that the whole reason you're even on the planet is not just to annoy and bankrupt your parents, that it's also to do something unique and totally amazing?

I had that feeling as I sauntered into Yearbook on the first day of sophomore year. The soundtrack in my head was indie groovy and super danceable—and that was even before I saw Eric Sobel.

OTHER BOOKS YOU MAY ENJOY

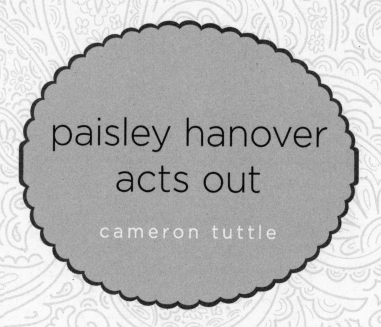

paisley hanover
acts out

cameron tuttle

illustrations by Alli Arnold

speak
An Imprint of Penguin Group (USA) Inc.

For Barbara, one of the cool moms—Un of a Kind,
UnFinished, UnForgettable

SPEAK

Published by the Penguin Group

Penguin Group (USA) Inc., 345 Hudson Street, New York, New York 10014, U.S.A.

Penguin Group (Canada), 90 Eglinton Avenue East, Suite 700, Toronto, Ontario, Canada M4P 2Y3
(a division of Pearson Penguin Canada Inc.)

Penguin Books Ltd, 80 Strand, London WC2R 0RL, England

Penguin Ireland, 25 St Stephen's Green, Dublin 2, Ireland (a division of Penguin Books Ltd)

Penguin Group (Australia), 250 Camberwell Road, Camberwell, Victoria 3124, Australia
(a division of Pearson Australia Group Pty Ltd)

Penguin Books India Pvt Ltd, 11 Community Centre, Panchsheel Park, New Delhi - 110 017, India

Penguin Group (NZ), 67 Apollo Drive, Rosedale, North Shore 0632, New Zealand
(a division of Pearson New Zealand Ltd)

Penguin Books (South Africa) (Pty) Ltd, 24 Sturdee Avenue,
Rosebank, Johannesburg 2196, South Africa

Registered Offices: Penguin Books Ltd, 80 Strand, London WC2R 0RL, England

First published in the United States of America by Dial Books,
a member of Penguin Group (USA) Inc., 2008
Published by Speak, an imprint of Penguin Group (USA) Inc., 2010

1 3 5 7 9 10 8 6 4 2

Text copyright © Cameron Tuttle, 2008
Illustrations copyright © Alli Arnold, 2008
All rights reserved

CIP DATA IS AVAILABLE

Speak ISBN 978-0-14-241561-0

Art by Alli Arnold
Designed by Jasmin Rubero

Printed in the United States of America

chapter one

I took a deep breath outside the door to Yearbook class and then sauntered—yes, I actually sauntered—into the room, doing my best imitation of calm, confident me. I was totally nervous. I had butterflies in my brain. But it was good nervous, excited nervous. I was one of the chosen people.

Have you ever had the feeling that you were destined for greatness? Not that you would ever admit that to anybody. But have you ever heard the all-in-your-head voice telling you that you're special, that the whole reason you're even on the planet is not just to annoy and bankrupt your parents, that it's also to do something unique and totally amazing?

I had that feeling as I sauntered into Yearbook on the first day of sophomore year. The soundtrack in my head was indie groovy and super danceable—and that was even before I saw Eric Sobel.

There he was, fiddling with the settings on his camera.

No way. Eric Sobel in Yearbook? Using my awesome power of deductive reasoning, I figured he was a staff photographer this year. Eric Sobel, the star of varsity soccer—*varsity*—sitting here in Yearbook. I was at the championship soccer game last year, when he was just a freshman, and he scored not one but two goals in overtime. We won the game, and when they gave him the MVP trophy, his eyes got all watery, and he almost cried. I could tell. I had binoculars.

There's something irresistible about a guy who cares enough about something—even if it's soccer—to almost cry.

And just seeing him sitting there in Yearbook cranked the volume on my internal sound system way up. I pictured us studying together after school at Freddie's Pizza, leaning close over our homework, whispering dreamy words like *sine* and *cosine* and *tangent*. He'd laugh, and I'd lovingly push his dirty-blond bangs out of his eyes. Then he'd smile at me all sweet, and tenderly wipe a small piece of tomato-y pepperoni off my cheek.

I knew immediately that this year was going to be the best year of my life.

Then I walked into the side of a desk.

Ugh, embarrassing. OMG. I was such a high school cliché, and it was only third period.

"Take a seat, people," said the Yearbook advisor, Ms. Madrigal. She was perched on a stool behind the podium, starting to take attendance. I turned around in a full circle looking around for an empty seat. But every desk was taken. So I made my way over to the far side of the room and hopped up on the windowsill. Public school budgets—there are never enough desks for everyone.

I hadn't thought of Eric Sobel as a Yearbook type. But I

figured there were a lot of things I didn't know about him—yet. The classroom was filled with student leaders and arty-smarty types, cool brains, people who obviously had intelligent, informed opinions about things like hybrid cars and the best cafeteria food at Ivy League schools, people who went to foreign films on a Friday night and drank too much coffee on purpose. I was in heaven. I was going to learn so much from these people—but more importantly, my seven-point plan was falling perfectly into place.

See, I have this killer seven-point, college-application action plan. It's not like I'm totally neurotic or uptight or anything. I'm just very practical. I've got to have it all worked out if I'm going to be Yearbook editor senior year. I've mapped out the things I need to accomplish over the next three years so I can have a sick college application and lots of options for schools. Life is all about options, right? At least that's what my mom keeps telling me. I want options.

My seven-point action plan is not just about getting straight A's or being the best at soccer or joining Yearbook or running for sophomore class vice president. That would be insanely stupid and boring. My plan is to distinguish myself as a highly motivated, unique individual with quirky, creative habits, diverse goals, and quality personal values.

How did that sound? Did you buy it? Did it sound real? I don't want to lay it on too thick—just thick enough to stick in the acceptance pile at the admissions offices.

I checked out the other sophomores in class, assessing my

competition for Yearbook editor senior year. Yearbook is mostly seniors and juniors with only a handful of sophomores. You have to submit a writing sample and an application to even be considered for the class. Right now, my sophomore competition was Dwight Cashel, a brainiac, but so squeaky clean that he's kind of uptight and annoying. No one would want him to be editor. Then there was Bentley Jones—not only super smart but also a superior human being with so many different talents it pretty much made you sick. I couldn't imagine her wanting to be Yearbook editor when she could be playing the sax in the jazz honor band *and* running the anchor lap for the mile relay team at State *and* choreographing and starring in the spring modern dance show. Eric Sobel? No, he was way too shy to want to be editor. It had to be me. I could so feel it.

Ms. Madrigal had stopped talking. She poked at the air with her index finger, counting each student. "That's strange," she said. "Whose name *didn't* I call?"

I looked around the room a little confused, and cautiously raised my hand. And then you'll never guess who else did—Candy Esposito. What was Candy Esposito doing in Yearbook?! She already controlled all the popular categories at school. Wasn't that enough?

"And you are?" asked Ms. Madrigal, looking at me.

"Paisley Hanover."

"Oh, right. Hanover? Hmmm . . . " She scanned her attendance list, shaking her head. "Candy, I don't see you on my list either. Well." She looked around the room with an embarrassed grin. "This is a little awkward, ladies. It seems that this class is over-enrolled by one student. Normally that wouldn't be a problem, but this is an application and invitation only class. If I let both of you in, that wouldn't be fair to the many other students who applied."

A fizzy wad of nervousness ricocheted around my stomach. Was my seven-point master plan already about to collapse into a wimpy, wobbly six-point plan? Eric Sobel looked over at me and kind of smiled. Or did he wince? Oh God, I think he winced.

Ms. Madrigal called the main office on the phone by the door and tried to sort things out. While she talked, Candy Esposito shot me an excited can-you-believe-this? expression, like we were suddenly bonded by this disaster and the best of friends. I gave her an I'm-so-excited-and-confused! look right back. I mean, she's Candy Esposito. What else could I do? I struggled to hear what Ms. Madrigal was saying, but everyone was being extremely selfish by yakking away.

"Okay people," Ms. Madrigal said as she hung up the phone. "Listen up! Paisley and Candy," she said, giving each of us this intense look, "you both submitted excellent writing samples. But apparently there was some clerical error." She swept her gaze around the room. "Now, I could make an arbitrary decision here, but I have a much better idea." As she spoke, she weaved her way between the desks trying to make a personal, Oprah-ish connection with everyone. "Being a member of *The Highlander* staff requires collaboration. It requires teamwork, probably more than any other class at this school. It also demands the ability to work under pressure, often on a deadline with not nearly enough time to do your best work but having to deliver your best work anyway."

A few seniors laughed. "Don't remind me," said this year's editor, Max Chapin. He was probably going to Stanford.

"There is a space for either Candy or Paisley—but not for both, I am sorry to say." Ms. Madrigal actually looked sorry, which made me feel kind of hopeful. Candy already had enough wins. "But I don't think this should be my decision," she said with a glint in her eye. "I think it should be *your* decision." She paused, looking around the room.

Oh no. Oh please no.

"Are you in? Are you with me, people?"

The room erupted in hoots and cheers. Oh no, no, no. This was not good. My fizzy wad of nervousness morphed into a bubbling blob of nausea.

"Candy, Paisley, come on up to the front. You've got a quick assignment. I want each of you to come up with a headline that best describes you and your personality."

What?! Clearly, Ms. Madrigal had been watching way too many episodes of *Survivor*. Everyone groaned, except for all of the people who laughed nervously, including me.

"Think pithy, think clever," she continued. "Don't be shy, be precise. Have fun with it. And then, in a well-crafted sentence or two, summarize the unique talents and skills that you, and only you, would bring to the Yearbook staff. Then we'll take an anonymous vote. The person with more votes gets the last spot in this class. The other person gets to take Drama instead."

Drama?! No way! I am not getting stuck in Drama with the socially disabled and hair-impaired. I felt my nose break into a sweat.

Candy Esposito is not only a junior and a varsity volleyball and track star, she's super cute and super popular, and the worst part—she's super nice! Everyone likes her, everyone! She's impossibly pretty with these pouty lips and a cute, perfect nose that look like they were sculpted by like Michelangelo. And she has this little scar under her right eye that's beautiful like body art and somehow makes her even more unique. And she has sparkly brown eyes, and dimples, and long shiny hair the color of sun-kissed honey. (I know that because certain girls are always trying to get their hair to be the color of hers, and the closest color in a box is called sun-kissed honey.) And if that wasn't horrible enough for me, her father used to be a professional base-ball player and now owns a bunch of Burger Kings, so Candy's always treating her friends to free Whoppers and inviting them to games where they get to sit in her family's box seats.

I looked around the room searching for allies I could count on. Bentley Jones stared at me, shaking her head. She looked really sorry for me. And she *likes* me.

I'm doomed. I'm so totally doomed. How did my seven-point plan turn into a razor-sharp seven-point weapon that's about to obliterate me in front of my peers?! I blinked my eyes trying to focus. Get it together, Paisley. You can do it. You can do it!

I realized that if I had any hope of beating Candy Esposito, I would have to swing big and knock one out of the park. My headline would have to dazzle and delight with unexpected wit and genuine confidence. My well-crafted argument would need to seal the deal, letting everyone know how dedicated I was, how much fun I could be, how much I loved hard work and words of all sizes.

I can do this. I can do this, right? Yes! I *can* do this! What does my terminally positive Dad always say? "Visualize success!"

Candy came over to me and shook my hand. "Good luck, Paisley. I know you'll do great." She had this big smile on her face. God, why did she have to be so *nice*? After that, I didn't have any trouble visualizing success. Unfortunately it was Candy's.

"Okay ladies. Remember, have fun with this. You've got three minutes—"

Three minutes?! Now I know why Ms. Madrigal has a reputation for sadistic, subversive forms of student torture.

"—starting right now."

My butt puckered. I flipped past the doodles of Eric Sobel to a blank page in my notebook. I stared at it. Headline, headline, clever headline describing me. Headline, headline, three-minute deadline? Lifeline! Help! Okay, okay, stay calm. Breathe. Breathe. I looked up in a bug-eyed panic just as Eric Sobel snapped a few pictures.

Oh great.

I started scribbling frantically.

Paisley Hanover—
Something clever
Something clever
Something <u>cleverer</u>
Anything!
Welcome to Never Clever Land
Clever is Crazy Being Polite
Paisley Hanover—Crazy in Polite Ways
Ugh.
Brainy Babe
Quirky Turkey
Strange but True
Hope on a Rope
Dork on a Fork
Fun for All, All for Fun!
A Punny, Funny Friend
Funny Weird
Funny Ha Ha
Funny Weird <u>and</u> Funny Ha Ha
More Laughs than a . . .
More Fun than a Barrel of Sophomores
Sophomore of the Good Stuff
Sophomore of a Good Thing
Paisley—Not Just Those Sperm-Shaped Thingies

Help. Help! Brain freeze. Can't think. Can't think! Dear Universe, please help me think! I should get up and walk out of here right now.

I looked over at Candy. She was slowly tapping her pen against her naturally soft, pink lips. I could tell she was thinking of something really amusing just from the look on her face. OMG! She's cracking herself up. Crap! Focus. Focus. You can do it! Candy doesn't love words as much as you love words. She loves everyone and everyone loves her, but that is not the same as being a good writer. Right? Focus!

Focused on Fun
Focused, Fun, Fabulous!
Little Miss Funshine
Freckles and Funshine
Freckles Are Fun
One of a Kind
Fun of a Kind
Fun of a Kind Girl
Fun for Your Life
Tickled Think
The Sizzle _and_ the Steak
Functional _and_ Fashionable
Smart, Stylish, and . . . totally stupid!
Shigoogley!
What?
Irony. Irony. Try irony.
Paisley Hanover—I Should Have Overslept!

That's good. That's kind of funny.
No, not so funny.
Paisley Hanover—Write On!
Will Write for Clothes
I'm Dying Here!
Not as Popular as Candy
Will Write for Candy
I'd Vote for Candy

"Okay, time's up!" called Ms. Madrigal as if that was good thing. I looked up in a panic.

If only I'd known then what I know now, I definitely would have thought of Sidebra* and Panties, and I would have owned the whole situation with total supreme confidence. But then this would be a very different story.

"Who wants to go first?" Ms. Madrigal asked, looking from me to Candy.

"Paisley does," said Candy all cheery and nice. Thanks a not, Candy.

I wish I couldn't remember exactly what happened

*SIDEBRA

Okay, I should probably just explain this right now. No, that's not a typo—that's a sidebra. I admit it was a typo the first time. I'm kind of a bad typer. But I've learned that sometimes it pays not to use spell-check or look in the mirror before leaving the house. I mean, some of your best stuff can come from your quote-unquote mis-takes. Trust me. I know. It's called a happy accident.

So, what *is* a sidebra? No, it's not for women with three boobs. And it's not like an under-arm-holster-purse-thingie. Although that would be kind of cool. I should doodle that one. Anyway, no, a sidebra is actually one of my best happy accidents. It's one of the weird things I'm known for at school. But that's all I'm going to say for now.

next. I mean, isn't your brain supposed to be your friend and protect you from the pain of horrible trauma by forgetting it? My brain is definitely not my friend.

I don't know why I chose the headline I did. It just jumped out at me from the list. And then it popped out of my mouth. I do know that I believed in it at the time. It was sort of clever (I thought) and informative (I guess), and it seemed like me (whoever that is).

There I was, standing in front of the class, clutching my notebook, looking around the room at all of these dying-to-judge-me faces. I tried to visualize success. But all I could visualize was pain. I could feel it in the air. I could feel my pain, I could feel everyone else's pain, and I could feel everyone else feeling my pain. Stop. You can do this. *You can do this!* cheered my all-in-your-head, personal rah-rah. Believe it. Just believe it. Sell it to the back of the room! Then I set my notebook down on the podium and went for it.

I jumped out toward the class like some demented clown. "Paisley Hanover—*Fun* of a Kind Girl!" And then I punctuated my headline with some bizarre manic gesture that could only be described as spastic jazz hands.

A camera snapped like crazy. People laughed. A lot of people laughed, actually, including Ms. Madrigal and Candy. For a second, I thought it would work. I really thought I could win. Some people even took notes when I read my well-crafted supporting sentences.

But I was no match for the tantalizing possibilities of

"Sweet, Nutty, Mouth-Watering Candy" delivered with Candy Esposito's irresistible blend of cute and confidence. And when she mentioned free Whoppers, onion rings, and golden-brown french fries on every work weekend? It was all over.

How embarrassing. How—ugh! What an idiot. I never had a chance against someone as popular as Candy Esposito. What was I thinking? Everything was over—the assignment, our little competition, the vote, my love connection with Eric Sobel, my shot at being Yearbook editor, my seven-point master plan, my hopes of getting into the college of my dreams, and the best year of my life.

And it was *still* only third period.

chapter two

I must have been having an out-of-body experience as I trudged down the hall to Drama. I was repeatedly and mercilessly scuffing the heels of my new suede boots along the concrete. I would *never* do that to new boots if I were actually inside my own body.

Why? Why? WHY did I have to act like such a weirdo at that exact moment? If only I had gone with my second choice, "Paisley Hanover—I'd vote for Candy!"

How could I possibly end up in Drama and not Year-book? I'd been planning and prepping and—and I didn't even have anything in *common* with Drama geeks! There was no way I could spend an entire year in third period with a bunch of weird-ass freakazoids.

I texted Jen.

OMG Humili8d! ES saw it! Must di.

Suddenly, Drama class actually seemed like the ideal place for me to go and quietly die. I mean, no one would know me there. I grabbed the cool metal handle, pulled open the door, and made my not-so-grand entrance into Drama.

Mr. Eggertson was standing in front of the stage, talking in this booming theatrical voice. Everyone turned and stared at me. Everyone. I stopped.

"New student?" asked Mr. Eggertson.

I nodded, holding up the yellow registration slip that I had just picked up in the office.

"Grab a seat."

Wow. The room was completely filled with Pleasant Hill High extras. Who were these people? Did they even go to my school? Wow. What weirdness—weird bodies, weird hair, weird clothes, weird hats. It was like I just walked into Weirdos "R" Us. Perfect. I should fit right in.

I slumped down in the nearest chair and tugged at a loose brown thread in my skirt, pretending I wasn't eyeing every other person in the room. Mr. Eggertson was going on about the origins of theater in ancient Greece and somewhere else really old. He had short dark hair and looked more like a dancer than a teacher, really muscular and lean.

I tried not to move my head while I checked out the other kids. This one girl—at least I think it was a girl—was wearing an orange and yellow knit elf hat with big earflaps, and it was like eighty degrees out. Next to her was Mime Guy. He had this blond Afro and was wearing a long black cape and a battered top hat. He might as well have worn a sign that said "Please Beat the Crap Out of Me."

I casually looked to the left. Teddy Baedeker, aka Special Ted, was sitting straight up in his chair staring at me. Teddy is a learning-disabled kid who's been in the class ahead of mine since forever. He's always been sweet and really harmless, but now he's sweet and really horny and gets boners in class all the time. Like right now, he sat up even straighter in his chair and nervously scratched his you-know-what.

I quickly looked away.

I prayed to Our Lady of Perpetual Boners for protection. She's this secret patron saint that Jen and I made up last year. Jen is Catholic, so she knows all about praying to saints and stuff. I closed my eyes. *Please, please, please, don't let me be sitting anywhere near Teddy Baedeker when he pitches his next pants tent. Thank you. Amen.*

When I opened my eyes, I saw a few kids I actually recognized. That weird retro lesbian Cate Maduro held her phone in her lap speed-texting someone. She looked over at me, then back to her phone. What's up with her freaky fifties hairdo? That bright red lipstick? Those pointy-toed Keds? Was she living in a time warp?

SIDEBRA

Why do guys scratch their little friend all the time—in public?! Do they think they're invisible? Do they think no one notices? Do they not even care? They should care. It's disgusting. And frankly, I'd rather not be reminded that some guys even have one. But if they can't help doing it, there should at least be some universal sign to warn innocent bystanders. You know, like those baseball hand signals—ear tug, right elbow pat, double nose wipe, left elbow pat, everyone look away now!

Cate and I kind of used to be friends when we sat next to each other in seventh-grade Spanish. We got A's all year and got in trouble all the time, always moving crazy Señora Pillsbury's glasses or hiding all of her chalk or setting her clock radio to go off really loud in the middle of class. But we had totally different friends and never really talked outside of class. And now, I don't know. Last year she got all retro and weird and next thing you know she was making out with some girl at an after-game dance and telling everyone she was a lesbian.

I looked around again, still trying not to move my head. Way off to the side, Mandy Mindel, this shy girl who plucks out all of her eyelashes, was slumped in a chair looking even more lost than usual. Whenever I see her, I always wonder about her parents. I wonder if they named her Mandy thinking it would become this cute, popular girl name. But instead Mandy Mindel ended up being shorthand for a painfully shy and lonely nervous wreck. I always thought her parents must be bummed.

Then I spotted Jean Merrill sitting with one long, gangly leg crossed over the other. She was looking all granny-chic wearing this little cardigan over a vintage polka-dot blouse with these wrinkly linen wide-leg floods and what looked like orthopedic dancing shoes. I couldn't decide if the shoes were thrift-shop cool or just tragic. Wow. She's got to be over six feet tall now. No wonder she can't find pants that fit.

I still felt bad about accidentally on purpose calling her String Bean Merrill over the loudspeaker at the eighth-grade dance because she had grown like a foot and a half that year. My mom, who unfortunately now is best buds with her mom, told me that Jean had to see a shrink because of it. I guess "Bean" kind of stuck. So now when I see her, I always go out of my way to be extra nice to her.

I gave her a short wave, trying to play it cool. She rolled her eyes and turned away, then leaned over and whispered something to a couple of Library Girls sitting next to her. They all kept turning and looking at me, laughing their glasses off.

So much for Drama being a place to go and quietly die. I had to get out of this class. This couldn't be good for my sanity or my popularity.

Mr. Eggertson was drawing something on this big white board, so I tried to appear interested and engaged.

But just then, the door behind me squeaked open. I turned. Clint Bedard.

He quickly slid into the chair right next to mine and sniffled hard. Mr. Eggertson didn't even look. What was Clint Bedard doing in Drama? I would've expected him to take an elective like Bomb-Making or Car-Jacking—something, you know, career-related.

I looked down at his hands. I think you can tell a lot about a guy from his hands. They were almost elegant, like artist hands, with long slender fingers and dirty fingernails. Maybe he worked as a mechanic after school? He had this woven black rope brace-let around one wrist and two chunky silver rings on his index fingers.

I should probably tell you that I don't know Clint Bedard, even though he's in my grade, but I know his reputation. He's the kind of guy who freaks out most dads and turns on cer-tain moms. Can I say that? Oh well, I did. Anyway, last year, he set the school roof on fire shooting bottle rockets, and all classes were canceled for three days. He has this hair, this sexy dark thick hair that's always messy and sticking up, like some hot senior babe has been running her hands through it in the backseat of a car. I always thought he was bad news and kind of felt sorry for him. But that was before he was sitting right next to me, close enough that I could smell his hair product. Hair product? That's weird. I expected him to smell like cigarettes or Taco Bell.

He kicked both feet out and leaned back in his chair, folding his arms behind his head. Nice biker boots. I inched my chair away from him a little so I could get a better look without being totally obvious. He had this amazingly detailed tattoo on his upper arm. What was that? It looked like some crazy maniac sticking out his tongue. He caught me staring at him and flashed this naughty, flirty grin—and *what was that?*

I tried not to laugh as I scribbled in my notebook.

Dude, you've got glittery lip gloss on.

I held my notebook out in front of him and tapped my finger on the page. He took my pen and started writing.

Watermelon. Wanna taste?

Before I could even think, he grabbed the notebook again and wrote:

Who's that?

He drew an arrow pointing to—OMG! A doodle of Eric Sobel kicking a heart-shaped soccer ball.

I calmly pulled my notebook back, closed it, and looked back at Mr. Eggertson. I pretended to concentrate, but I was pretty much dying inside.

Mr. Eggertson pointed up above the front of the stage. "The proscenium arch serves as a window through which the audience views the actors on the stage." He paused and looked around the room. "Am I losing you?"

Silence.

"Okay, everybody up! On your feet. Shake out your arms. Shake out your legs. Good. So, what is acting?"

"Faking it," Cate Maduro yelled out. A few people laughed.

"That's part of it. What else?"

"Performing on stage!"

"Playing a role and memorizing lines!"

"Good, what else?"

"Pretending to be someone you're not!"

"That's high school!" shouted Jean Merrill, cracking herself up and everyone else too, including me.

"Okay, okay," said Mr. Eggertson. "Acting is all of those things. But more than anything else, acting is *reacting*. Being present in the moment and really paying attention to what the other person is saying and doing. Let's try an exercise. Partner up with someone you would never normally speak to."

I glanced around the room. Well, that would be about everybody. I took a few steps toward Jean Merrill. "Partners?"

She looked at me skeptically, twirling a long piece of blond hair over and around her index finger. "Yeah, fine. Whatever."

Mr. Eggertson went on. "I want you to be as honest as you

can be in a short, spontaneous conversation. Talk about anything, but keep it real. Pay attention to the words, intonation, *and* body language. Don't act—*react*. And begin!"

She just stood there staring at me, looking slightly disgusted.

"So, um," I started. "How was your summer, Jean?"

"Look. Just call me Bean, okay? Everyone else does now. Thanks to you."

"Oh. Okay." I nodded. Was she still mad at me? Yup, pretty sure she was. I tried to win her over. "Cute shoes."

"Thanks." She pushed her glasses up with the back of her hand. "But don't call me String Bean, Bean Stalk, Bean Stalker, or Beano. Got it?"

"Got it."

"And whatever you do, don't call me anything over a loudspeaker or I will stab you in the eye with a dull number two pencil." She laughed. "God, I crack myself up."

"And switch!" Mr. Eggertson had a deep voice like some TV announcer. "New partners. No friends!"

Believe it or not, I felt really relieved when skinny Charlie Dodd ran up to me and wiped his forehead with the bottom of his maroon XXL polo shirt. Charlie and I aren't really friends, but I know him from carpool. He's kinda nerdy and used to wear only polo shirts tucked in. He had them in like a million different colors. Then last year, he switched to XXL polo shirts, untucked. So, I guess now he's like Gangsta Nerdy or something. I never thought I'd be so happy to see him.

"And begin!"

"Thanks, Charlie."

"Charles, please," he said in this British actorly way. "It's my stage name."

"I didn't know you were into Drama."

"Yeah, I want to expand my nerd rep in new, exciting ways. You can only go so far with Chess Club and the French horn."

I laughed. "How come you're not this funny in carpool?" I asked.

"I am. You ignore me." He said it like it was no big deal.

I almost blurted out, "No, I don't!" That would be reacting, right? But I decided to take an insane risk and actually be honest. "I do? Sorry." I really meant it.

"And stop! Find a new partner, please!"

"No worries," said Charlie before walking off.

Whenever anyone says "No worries," I get the distinct feeling I should be worrying. I stood there trying to think. Do I ignore him? I don't think so. I just never notice him much because I'm always half-asleep or listening to my iPod or doodling in my notebook—I have a little doodling obsession—or cramming for a test or texting someone. Is that the same thing as ignoring him? I decided to have a real conversation with Charlie in carpool at least once a week. Then I turned around, hoping to find Clint Bedard, and smacked right into—

"And begin!"

Oh crap. Cate Maduro was standing right in front of me with her hands on her hips.

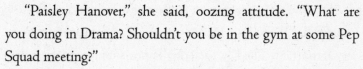

"Paisley Hanover," she said, oozing attitude. "What are you doing in Drama? Shouldn't you be in the gym at some Pep Squad meeting?"

Oooh, she was nasty. And Pep Squad? What a cliché. I looked at her like I was beyond bored. Her skin was even paler than usual against her bright red lipstick, and her dark hair curled around one side of her face like a question mark. She was wearing these tight, way-out-of-style pants with a high cinched waist.

I tried to stare her down. But she had these crazy blue eyes that shot through you like demonic lasers. Must be colored contacts. So I went with Plan B—sneak attack.

"So, are you like really a lesbian now?"

She didn't look the least bit flustered as she leaned into my face and whispered, "Who wants to know?" Her breath smelled like spearmint Tic Tacs. I didn't even flinch. I was a little sorry I had gone there, but I was not about to be intimidated by some sketchy social misfit. I stared right back.

"Everyone. People can't stop talking about you."

"Really? What people?"

"What do you think we talk about at Pep Squad meetings?" For an instant, Cate Maduro looked terrified, then she laughed at me in that nice-try way.

"And stop! Okay, grab a seat! What did you notice?" Mr. Eggertson asked. Everyone just sat there. "Come on, people. What was consistently happening in all three conversations?"

I raised my hand. "Most people say the opposite of what they really mean?"

"Exactly!" Mr. Eggertson smiled and even looked a little impressed. "Which is why body language and intonation are so very important. The key to acting is not simply understanding the words—it's understanding the emotions *behind* the words." He paused. "I want you all to keep this in mind, because in a week or so, I'll be assigning you a partner and a scene. The two of you will be rehearsing every day for two weeks, after which you will perform your scenes for our fall drama night production, *Acting Out.*"

Muffled groans and twitters from around the room. I felt my lungs drop into my stomach.

"*Acting Out* is open to the public to make sure that we have a good-sized audience." Mr. E. paused. "And always great fun."

Yikes! I hoped none of my friends found out. Just then my phone vibrated. I pulled it out fast. A text from Jen. Finally.

r bench @ mrng brk. BIG NWS!

I texted her right back.

Me 2! c u

Cool. Our munch bunch was on.

I turned around to find everyone suddenly lying on the floor. What had I missed? I got down and stretched out awkwardly.

"Now breathe," Mr. Eggertson was saying. Everyone started making these strange humming and vibrating sounds. "This is how we warm up and tune up our instruments," he said. Apparently, that's what you call your body when you're an actor—your quote-unquote instrument.

"Continue exhaling, people!"

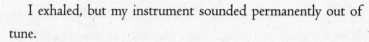

I exhaled, but my instrument sounded permanently out of tune.

What could Jen's big news be? Maybe she got the inside scoop on Cindy Kutcher's new boobs? Maybe Bodie dumped her? A girl can dream, can't she?

"Keep it steady," Mr. Eggertson called out. "Now slowly raise the pitch until you can feel the vibration in your nose and the front of your face like a mask of sound."

Someone made a big fart noise. Everyone laughed, even me. Then the whole room began to swell with the hum of vibrating noses and faces. It sounded like a giant mosquito.

"Perfection, people! You are all going to be famous!" Mr. Eggertson shouted. "I can hear it in your noses."

When we finally stood up, Mr. Eggertson divided the class into two groups, and we did this lame trust exercise, where one by one, everybody had to stand on the edge of the stage and fall backward into the arms of the other students. You had to trust that the group below would work together to catch you and not let you hit the floor and crack your head open. If you asked me, it was a lot to ask on the first day of school.

But weirdly, it wasn't. There was this chill acid jazz playing from Mr. E.'s iPod. The windows were open, and you could get a whiff of that sweet green smell coming from the cut grass in front of the school. The room felt warm in the morning sun and kind of cozy. I was starting to think I could get used to Drama.

Fortunately, I was in the catching group first. Some people had to be coaxed. But most people just leaned back and went for it. The more people trusted you, the more you really didn't want to let anyone down, the more you wanted to catch everyone safely and lower them gently to the floor, even the fat kids. Especially the fat kids. And everyone really did work together. It was kind of amazing.

I was having this warm and fuzzy, people-are-beautiful moment, and then Clint Bedard took a diving leap into the crowd like it was a mosh pit. He would've broken his neck if he hadn't landed right on top of me. A bunch of us ended up in a pile on the floor groaning and laughing.

And then, without even getting off of me, Clint said in the most innocent voice, "Air male delivery for Paisley Hanover." He laughed. I laughed. What else could I do? I had to do something. Then we all laughed so hard that someone farted for real. And no. It wasn't me.

Mr. Eggertson was royally pissed. "That's one, Mr. Bedard. Two gets you a fast pass to the vice principal's office. Three and you're out of here." Clint flashed his flirty little grin at me. He seemed quite pleased with himself.

We all regrouped in front of the stage in our human catcher's mitt formation to finish up the trust exercise. Bean Merrill went next. All six feet of her—light as a tall, skinny feather. Then Teddy Baedeker went. I was shocked. The way people gently caught him and slowly lowered him to the floor, you would have thought he was the secret lovechild of our star quarterback and homecoming queen—not Special Ted, the weirdest kid in school. It was really cool. Really.

Then it was my turn. So I'm up there, standing on the stage with my back to the crowd, wondering if everyone can see up my skirt, but I'm also feeling full of trust and like cotton-candy luv fuzz. Then people started saying super encouraging stuff like "Come on Paisley, we've got you." "Relax!" "Just let go, lean back, and trust." So I did.

But just as I was beginning to fall backward, someone shouted, "Nice butt, you rah-rah!" And then people started to catch me, and for a second I thought everything was going to be fine. But then someone pinched me in the butt. Hard. And I yelped because it really hurt and I squirmed to get away. And then people started laughing. And then they basically dropped me. On my hip.

"Whoops!"

"Are you okay?"

"Sorry, Paisley."

"Bummer."

I lay there staring at the floor, waiting for the pain in my hip to subside, trying to ignore the shidiots still laughing at me.

"Hey, people, that is no way to build trust!" Mr. Eggertson shouted.

You can see little faces in the pattern on the linoleum floor tiles. There's a blockhead boxer with a flattened nose, a sleeping lady with long swirling hair, and a smirking, baby cupid angel. You can see little faces in the linoleum until your eyes start to water and fill up with tears.

No. I will NOT cry.

"Paisley?" asked Mr. Eggertson, kneeling down next to me. "Are you all right? Do you need to go to the nurse's office?"

"Fine. I'm fine!" I jumped up really fast and walked it off, rubbing my hip with the heel of my palm. I kept staring out the windows. I didn't want to see anyone, and I didn't want anyone to see me.

Bean Merrill touched my shoulder like she was tagging me it. "You okay?"

"Yeah. Fine. Whatever." I picked up my backpack and limped out of class. I so wasn't fine. But it wasn't my hip that was really hurting.

chapter three

When I limped out of Drama, I was so in my own tortured head that I actually walked right past Yearbook just as class was letting out. It was the last place on the planet I wanted to be, and that was before Bentley Jones, Dwight Cashel, and Eric Sobel, the three lucky smarty sophomores who had gotten into Yearbook instead of me, bounded into the hall, bursting with superior college-application energy.

I wanted to strangle them. Instead, I ducked into the sticky bun line.

Every day at morning break, Jen, Amy, Carreyn, and I always shared a sticky bun. It was a tradition. Today it was my job to wade through the lines and pick out the biggest one with the most sugary goo on top. I struggled upstream from the cafeteria toward sophomore hall, my hip still throbbing, protecting the sticky bun with my life—if anything could cheer me up, it was sugar with friends.

We had all agreed to meet at my locker to download about morning classes. I couldn't wait to vent about my tragic life to Jen. I spotted Amy and Carreyn straddling the bench in front of my locker, reserving our prime location. I ducked under the hall railing and cut across the lawn where sophomores were grouped together in little conversational pods.

I should probably tell you a little about my school so you can picture it. Where I live, it never gets super cold. Like maybe it's snowed once and that was totally freaky. We basically have an outdoor campus. It's not like one big tall building. It's a bunch of one-story buildings in rows with covered hallways in between. There's a huge parking lot in front of the school and then once you get past the main offices and the main quad and the cafeteria, there's senior hall, junior hall, sophomore hall, and then freshman hall stuck out in the boonies near the band room. Does that make sense? Maybe I'll just draw a picture.

"Hey Paisley," said Charlie Dodd, waving at me sort of sympathetically. I waved back. I hoped I didn't see anyone else from Drama out here. A few other kids said hi too. I smiled and waved, but I kept walking—limping—maneuvering my way through the pods.

SIDEBRA

Yes, I know it's about time I addressed my weird name. Paisley. Paisley Hanover. And don't even bother. I've heard them all—Pains Me, Parsley, Spazley, Lazy Paisley, Crazy Paisley, Crazily Paisiley, Paislini, Paislini Bikini, Paisley Poo, Pays Late, Never Pays, Paised & Confused, blah, blah, blah. But it's been my name for my whole life, so it seems totally normal to me. And no, I wasn't named after that fabric with the sperm-shaped thingies on it. I was named after Paisley, Scotland, this town where my mom's family used to live like a million and two years ago. I've never been there, but I've checked it out online. I was kind of bummed to read that Paisley the town actually *was* named after the fabric with the sperm-shaped thingies on it. But I wasn't. Remember that. You'll be quizzed later.

"Hi Pais!" Amy and Carreyn called out at the exact same time.

Amy is tall and pretty with straight brown hair and big eyes and a really big personality. And she also has what Mom calls big bones. So she's literally been on a diet since the sixth grade. All that dieting and she still has big bones. She's usually super funny, but she can also be a little crabby, probably because she's constantly hungry. I don't know why she's so hard on herself. Well, actually I do. Her mom is sort of an uptight starvoholic perfectionist freak. She even makes *me* feel nervous. Anyway, we're always telling Amy that her body is great, that there's nothing wrong with it, but it's hard to convince her.

Carreyn eats enough for both of them but somehow stays way skinny. I guess she has a super fast metabolism, which is a blessing considering the incredibly bad perm she just got. Carreyn isn't the cutest face-wise, but she has a good bod. And she's always working it. "Go with your strengths," she says. "Go with your strengths." Her hair is the color of sun-kissed honey (told you) and she has big white teeth and a huge goofy smile that makes you want to smile with her. Sometimes Carreyn can be a little insecure about her looks. Actually, a lot insecure. But I admire her creativity and fierce determination to look better. Really, I do. She's always trying different things and she's truly fearless in the beauty and self-improvement department.

"Hi, guys," I called back.

"Oh my gag," Carreyn whispered. "Have you seen Cindy Kutcher's new boobs?"

"No thank you," I said. "But I heard all about them. Nice birthday present from your parents."

"Can you say impending back surgery?" Amy asked.

"That's so awful." Just the thought of it made me cringe. "Hey, have you seen Jen?"

"Nope," said Amy. "I'll bet she's with Bodie."

I looked around. "What? She just texted me and said she'd meet us here."

"Paisley, take a relaxative! If she said she's coming, she's coming. Cute outfit," said Carreyn, nodding with approval.

"Thanks." I dropped my backpack and casually posed. Then winced. Who wanted a hip fracture the first day of school? But my outfit was pretty cute. I was wearing this short lime green and brown mod patterned skirt and this super cute clingy brown top with a scoop neck that was tight but not slutty tight. And, of course, my new chocolate brown suede boots.

"I didn't know we were wearing boots today," Carreyn whined, looking confused and a little deflated. She had on satin ballet flats and quickly pulled her feet under the bench and out of view.

"We're not wearing boots. I am."

Amy looked down at her size eleven feet jammed into her size ten ballet flats and shook her head. "I can't believe I fell for this. I don't even like ballet flats. On me, they look like ballet *fats!*"

"Amy, stop. You're not fat," I said, poking her in the rib cage.

"But if you're *feeling* fat, can I have your quarter of the sticky bun?" Carreyn asked.

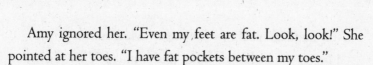

Amy ignored her. "Even my feet are fat. Look, look!" She pointed at her toes. "I have fat pockets between my toes."

"Amy!" I said, exasperated. "You're starting to sound like you have fat pockets in your brain."

Amy got all serious. "Is that possible?"

"Oh my God!" I had to change the subject. "You'll never guess what happened to me this morning."

"Is it a guy? Did someone ask you out?" asked Carreyn, flapping her hands in front of her.

"Was it Teddy Baedeker?" said Amy, trying to look sincere.

Carreyn laughed and a chunk of half-chewed sticky bun flew out of her mouth.

"Uh, no," I said. Poor Teddy Baedeker.

"Well, Eric Sobel sort of looked at me in Yearbook," I said slowly, not wanting to disappoint, and not really wanting to confess the horrid details.

Their eyes got kind of big and they both sighed, "Wow."

"Yeah. Wow." I plopped down between them on the bench. But you know, why ruin three people's mornings with my sad story? So I leaned in. "Amazingly, he's even hotter than last year," I whispered, as if delivering insider info. "His hair is a little longer, a little shaggier, and sexy. And . . . " I paused for dramatic effect. "He's taller."

They both stared at me like they were having a personal moment with the new and improved Eric Sobel.

Finally Carreyn whimpered, "It's not fair. He's already too gorgeous."

Amy nodded, nibbling on a grape. "More please."

"He just looked at me and kinda smiled! There isn't any more." I looked at Carreyn and then Amy. "Yet!" I giggled, hoping it didn't sound forced, knowing I was completely deluded.

My chances with Eric Sobel were, like, nonexistent. The most we had in common was being on the same page of the school newspaper at the end of freshman year for that stupid Spring Superlatives thing. Eric Sobel was "Best Dressed." And I was "Best Laugh." Unfortunately it's because I've kind of developed a reputation for laughing so hard I sometimes pee a little in my pants. Some people, especially really hilarious people, won't let me ride in their car anymore. Okay, not really. But that was the joke for a while last year.

Now I checked down the hall in both directions. "Where is Jen?"

"I guess she *is* with Bodie." Amy shrugged and took a sip of Diet Coke.

"She's got Bodie on the brain twenty-four/seven." I pulled off a little piece of sticky bun. "It's so strange for her."

Jen first started hanging out with Bodie at Bigwood, this swanky athletic club that looks like a big ski lodge, where they both worked over the summer. After Bodie broke up with Candy Esposito, he started flirting with Jen like every day while she was folding towels. She loved it. And I was excited for her. At first.

"Well, if you ask me," Carreyn said, "she's been acting beau-coup bizarro ever since Hutch's pool party."

"It started way before that, like when they moved into that little house," I said.

Carreyn and Amy nodded. I knew they were picturing Jen's new house because they had these pained, slightly grossed-out looks on their faces.

Jen's parents were getting divorced, so they had to sell their house at the beginning of the summer. It was depressing enough that her parents were splitting up, but you should have seen where Jen and her mom and her little brother were living now. It was this tiny little house down behind the Save Mart—and they were *renting*. Her dad moved into some apartment in the next town over to be closer to the girlfriend he supposedly didn't have. What a creep. Jen had seen them together at least twice, and the girlfriend was way younger. Gross.

"Hey, Pains Me!"

Hilarious. I've never heard that one before.

Peter Hutchison strutted over. Oh great. Hutch is this big obnoxious loudmouth jock. The sad thing—he's supposedly one of the smart ones. Unfortunately, he's friends with everyone I'm friends with, so I have to tolerate him. Hutch was wearing his black and gold letterman's jacket, as always. His freshman year he lettered in football and basketball, even though he sat on the bench the entire basketball season. He never went anywhere without that jacket.

I rolled my eyes. "Hi, Hutch. New jacket?"

Amy and Carreyn laughed.

"You miss me?" He tried to put his arm around my shoulder, but I stood up and spun out of reach.

"Yes, I missed you," I said sweetly. "What's your name again?"

Hutch laughed way too hard. "You also missed a sick party at my house, know what I'm saying?"

"Really? You had a party? When?" Of course I was invited, so I knew about the stupid party, but I was at a spa retreat with my grandmother over Labor Day weekend—I totally love my Grambo, but there are some things about a grandmother it's just better not to see.

"Like you didn't hear about it. Right," he said.

Charlie Dodd walked toward us down the hall sipping a smoothie and listening to his iPod, probably some Gangsta Nerdy tune. In one smooth athletic move, Hutch stripped the ear buds from Charlie's ears, swiped the cup from his hand, ripped the straw and lid off the cup, and swung the smoothie up to his mouth.

Charlie just stood there.

Hutch slammed it down in about three chugs, then wiped his hand across his mouth. "Thanks, little dude." Hutch handed the empty cup back to Charlie.

Charlie had experienced this type of respect for most of his life and took it like a man—a smart and scrawny man. "My pleasure." He smiled. "Can I get you anything else? Breakfast is the most important meal of the day."

"Thanks, I'm good."

"I really hope the Fem Boost doesn't make your man-boobs bigger." Charlie clutched his backpack like a football and bolted down the hall.

"You little rectal wart!" Hutch took off after him, blasting his way through the mid-morning crowd.

"What a moron," I said, watching Hutch chase Charlie down the hall.

"Really? I think Charlie's looking kinda cute this year," said Carreyn, sounding a little crushed out.

"Gross!" said Amy.

"I meant that Hutch is the moron," I said.

Carreyn was suddenly all freaked out. "Amy, I was totally kidding!" She laughed in her semi-manic way. "God, I can't believe you thought I was serious. Charlie Dodd's gross!"

"*Hutch* is gross," I said. "What a skeezer buttcap." I sat down on the bench in front of my locker and checked my phone for messages from Jen. Nothing. I texted her.

Wat up? Whr r u?

"So what happened at that party?" I asked Amy and Carreyn. "Jen's definitely withholding details, but I can't figure out why."

"I don't know." Carreyn popped the last piece of sticky bun into her mouth. "But it was a lot of fun in the hot tub."

"Fun?" asked Amy. "It looked like a varsity grope-fest to me."

"Don't be such a B with an itch! They're great guys." Carreyn wiped sugar slime off her upper lip. "If you'd fit into your new bathing suit, I'm sure you would've been sitting there right next to Jen."

"Actually, no. I wouldn't," Amy snapped. "I don't just let any guy grab my butt the way you do."

Carreyn's mouth dropped open and her hands fell to her hips. "What are you saying? Are you calling me a slut?"

Fortunately, just then the warning bell for fourth period rang. Amy gave Carreyn a you-would-know look and walked off to her next class before I had to break up a brat fight.

Jen texted me back.

w/ BoD

sorry. c u @ lunch

Unbelievable. I would never blow off my best friend for some guy on the first day of school. Would I? No. I would not.

Well, okay, Bodie isn't just some guy. He's a junior. He's Bodie Jones, star running back. Bodie Jones, power forward and awesome three-point shooter. Bodie Jones, all-state sprinter. Bodie Jones, brother of Bentley, herself a superior human being. And, on top of all that, he's a really great guy—funny, cute, nice, and extremely well groomed. He volunteers at the local nursing home, he's willing to be hypnotized and make a fool of himself at school assemblies. He's Bodie Jones, total A-lister. I slowly turned the combination lock and opened my locker. I hate Bodie Jones.

I don't know if your school is like this, but at our school, popularity works a lot like celebrities in Hollywood. There's the A-list, the B-list, the C-list, the D-list, and the indie darlings. And then there's everyone else. The extras.

Basically, I've always been a B-lister. There was the year I had to wear headgear, which dropped me to the C-list, but that was a long time ago. Then last year, something truly amazing happened. I became a B+-lister. I had never been so popular, and it felt awesome. It was this weird lucky bunch of things that all came together.

First, I have red hair, which not everyone goes for. But I grew it longer over the summer before ninth grade, and that definitely helped. And my brother Parker was a senior and really cool in an indie darling way, which gave me an all-access pass to some parties and stuff that most freshmen would never even know about. And then the other lucky thing that happened—Jen got boobs. Huge, round, full, bounce-when-you-run boobs. And every guy in school started noticing her and wanting to find out who she was. And since I'm her best friend, a lot of those guys started talking to me. So I suddenly had tons of face time with older cute

SIDEBRA

A-list: Varsity Jocks (guys), Varsity Poms (cheerleaders), BPs (beautiful people), Yearbook editor, and student body officers. (Only juniors and seniors allowed!)
B-list: Freshman and sophomore Jocks, Poms, BPs. Cool kids who just moved here. Stars of boys' teams. Sporty, cute stars of girls' teams. JV Poms. Anyone dating an A-lister.
C-list: Uncool kids with really nice cars, brains who unexpectedly got really cute or surprisingly good bods, baton twirlers, and leads in school plays.
D-list: Mathletes, AV Guys, Library Girls. Clueless kids who try way too hard to be popular and always end up making total fools of themselves (i.e., people only know their names because they're idiots).
Indie Darlings: Kids with special skills or weird talents. Like Tracy Monroe, our very own Olympic swimmer, or Clint Bedard, our very own arsonist. (Everyone likes an indie darling at least for a week. They have crossover appeal because they do whatever they want and they're good at it.)
Extras: Everyone else.

guys and I didn't even have to flirt or fake-laugh at any dumb jokes.

But then something happened. Her parents' divorce, this party at Hutch's . . . I don't know. It's like, where did Jen go? Literally.

Ugh. Could this day get any worse?

I jerked open my locker and grabbed my American History textbook. As I pulled it out, a folded-up piece of paper flew out of my locker and landed on the ground between my boots. I picked it up.

FRECKLES ARE SEXY

OMG! What?! I casually looked around to see if anyone was watching me. It had to be a joke. No one thinks freckles are sexy. Do they . . . ?

Who?

chapter four

I cut fourth period. I wasn't planning to. It just kind of happened.

As I walked down the hall, I studied the note for clues—all capital letters written in black ink on plain notebook paper. Not much to go on. But that's weird—all the E's looked like backward 3's.

The hall was starting to get crowded. I looked up, and there they were again! What was it with these three? Were they all best buds now?! Bentley Jones, Dwight Cashel, and Eric Sobel had turned the corner and were headed in my direction, talking and laughing like the world were made of lollipops and midgets. I waited for them to hook arms and skip down the hallway singing *Follow the Yellow Brick Road! Follow the Yellow Brick Road! Follow, follow, follow, follow, follow the Yellow Brick Road!*

I wanted to sic my flying monkeys on them. Crap. No time. I walked backward and turned into the library.

They were supposed to pass by, and then I was going to go straight to American History. But they didn't. They stopped right in front of the library, and then all three turned to see

"Sweet, Nutty, Mouth-Watering" Candy Esposito come bopping down the hall. And then they followed me right into the library! I mean, what?!

I lunged behind the magazine rack to scope out an escape route. While I was hiding, I noticed a flyer on the bulletin board announcing that sign-up sheets for class officers would be posted in the main hall. I made a mental note. Thank God Candy Esposito was a junior and couldn't run against me for vice president.

When the coast was clear, I made a beeline for the back wall, bent double as if I were looking for something—only really, *really* fast. I wasn't in the mood to hear Candy Esposito go on and on with fake modesty about how she really didn't deserve to win the Yearbook spot, but when you're so well liked and have so many friends, people always just vote for you.

I hid behind the thick reference volumes and spied on them through the shelves. They were standing across the room, talking to who I guessed was the new librarian, but it was hard to see. They were probably introducing themselves as the next generation of Yearbook Royalty. Ergh. I was about to make a break for the door, when the final bell rang.

Oh no! I collapsed against the back wall. When I'd asked if this day could get worse, I wasn't looking for a sarcastic answer.

Parker had warned me about Mr. Yamaguchi, my American History teacher. It was better to break your own leg than show up late to his class. I looked around for the thickest reference book I could find, inched it off the shelf, and let it drop directly onto my foot. Silent library scream!!!! It hurt like crazy, but

sadly, nothing broke. That's the downside of nice boots. So . . .
I just kind of . . . didn't go to fourth period.

I made myself comfortable, hiding in the reference section,
and started reading about beetles. Did you know that there are
more species of beetles than plants? There are over like 350,000
species of beetles, not counting the unnamed ones. And they're
surprisingly well accessorized.

That's when I heard Candy Esposito's voice coming from the
other side of the reference shelf.

"Hi, so are you almost done with the computer?" she asked.

I peeked through the encyclopedias. Candy was talking to
this junior girl, kind of a C-lister, not totally unpopular but
definitely *not* a pop.

"No."

"Are you sure?" Candy asked, smiling. "Because I *really* need
to use it, you know, like right now."

"Why don't you ask one of them?" The girl pointed down
the row. Dwight Cashel and Bentley Jones were sitting at the
other computers, probably researching papers that wouldn't even
be assigned until next year.

"Well, I could, but I know them and I know they're working
on really important stuff."

Holy shiitake mushrooms! Did Candy actually just *say*
that—and with a huge smile on her face?!

The girl didn't say anything back. I mean, what could she
say? She just looked up at Candy and then down at the key-
board. I couldn't see her face, but I watched her shoulders sink

down. She saved and closed her file, then got up and walked away.

"Thanks!" Candy waved, all super sweet.

That was . . . gross. And I thought Candy was supposed to be one of the *nice* ones.

I turned back to my book on beetles and wondered if the cute popular beetles took advantage of C-list beetles, but I couldn't find anything. I was totally absorbed in the feeding habits of tiger beetles when she found me.

"Are you researching a particular species of beetle? Can I help?" an unfamiliar voice asked.

I looked up, I'm sure with a painfully guilty face. "Uh, no. Thanks. I'm okay."

"Hi. I'm Ms. Whitaker, the new librarian."

Librarian? I'd heard of Ms. Whit, but she did *not* look like a librarian. She looked like some brainy babe hipster. She wore these cool chunky glasses and a bunch of bright-colored bangle bracelets and this beaded necklace and . . . Whoa. She had a tattoo. A librarian with a tattoo? Is that even allowed?

"Hi." I went back to my beetles and concentrated very hard, hoping she would respect my appreciation for arthropod knowledge and move on.

"I love beetles too. See?" She held up a clear hunk hanging from her necklace. There was a big green shimmering beetle frozen in resin. "*Cotinis mutabilis*, a fig-eater beetle."

I wrinkled my nose and leaned in to examine it. "Wow. That's really . . . dead."

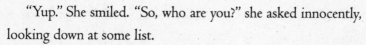

"Yup." She smiled. "So, who are you?" she asked innocently, looking down at some list.

Uh-oh. "Paisley? Paisley Hanover?"

She ran a finger over her eyebrow a few times. She had these wild blue-green eyes. "I don't see you on my list for study hall."

Busted! I didn't have the energy to make up some elaborate story, so I went with the truth.

And guess what? Ms. Whit was pretty cool. She even laughed when I mentioned Mr. Yamaguchi.

"Yeah. I've met him. You don't want to start the year on his bad side."

She let me hang out in the library for the rest of fourth period, just this once, as long as I agreed to come to her "Real Research in the Digital Age" lunch seminar next week and bring friends.

"Yeah, sure," I said. That was easy. Ms. Whit was definitely my kind of librarian.

There were rumors about the faculty at Pleasant Hill as well as the students. Mr. Eggertson had been a truly talented actor with a real agent and everything, and then his wife had gotten pregnant with twins, and he'd been teaching full-time ever since. Our vice principal, Mr. Canfield, was secretly gay, but don't tell his 300-pound wife or their two kids. Mr. Yamaguchi was a big-shot corporate lawyer who burned out and started teaching because he thought it would be relaxed and far more rewarding. Now he was more unrelaxed and burned out than ever. Our head custodian had actually gone to Pleasant Hill High. And foxy Señor Abbott's wife was a Bolivian heiress.

But one of the best rumors revolved around Ms. Whitaker, the new librarian. Someone had heard that she was a radical socialist, and while certain people at our school liked to throw that term around, no one (other than Toby and Kobe Bach-Avery, whose parents really were socialists) really had any idea what being a socialist actually meant—i.e., no iPhone, no Xbox, no cable TV.

My mom told me that Ms. Whit wasn't a radical socialist—she was a radical social*ite*. Her family owned the county's big newspaper and, apparently, she walked away from millions simply to piss off her snooty parents. When I first heard this, true or not, I immediately liked Ms. Whit. I had never thought of anyone over thirty as even having parents, at least not having parents enough that you would want to piss them off. And then to find out she had a tattoo? Like I said, my kind of librarian.

I stealthily maneuvered my way around the library, acting all I-Spy, trying to avoid the Yearbook Royalty. As I inched along the side windows, I glanced outside—and there was my locker.

Hmmm. What a perfect place to set up a stakeout. Maybe I could catch a glimpse of my locker stalker in action.

Then I made a break for the magazine lounge and hid behind a *National Geographic*, which is not that easy to do, considering its size. I looked up just as Eric Sobel sat down next to me on the couch, picked up a *Sports Illustrated*, and conspicuously held it up in front of his face just like me.

"Hey," he whispered from behind the magazine. "Hey you, behind the herd of endangered elephants."

I peeked at him from behind my magazine, trying to hide my face from Candy, who had just reached right past me for this week's *The Economist* and then returned to her computer.

Was Eric Sobel talking to me?

"Check this out." Eric surreptitiously slid a neon yellow flyer in my direction. "It might work for you. Instead of Yearbook."

Yes, Eric Sobel was talking to me!

I tried to concentrate on the headline. *The Fly is Open!* Wait. Was he serious? I looked back at him. He had the most intense green eyes and dark, dark, long lashes.

"I shot some photos for them last year," he whispered. "Not Yearbook-related, but still. It's a wacked out but fun crew."

I took the flyer from him and skimmed it. I could hardly believe he was talking to me, let alone making suggestions for electives.

The Fly is Open!
for business this year

Despite senseless draconian budget cuts,
The Fly is still in business.
Come to a lunch meeting to learn how
you can join our new all-volunteer staff
and discover the many joys of journalism—
long hours, no pay, great parties.
We need writers, editors, field reporters, columnists,
photographers & coffee sherpas.

No experience or scruples required.

WHERE: Room 107

WHEN: Friday @ noon

You can kill the budget
but you can't silence the pen...
or the computer...
or the website...or whatever.

I looked at him kind of amazed. He was trying to help me. He was seriously trying to help me. "Thanks," I whispered.

"Sure." He slowly lifted his magazine to cover his face.

I shoved the flyer into my bag. He's got to like me, right? I mean, not necessarily *like me* like me, but at least like me as a friend. I mean, maybe not as a weekend friend, but as a school friend, right? God, I sounded like a needy gooberish girl. I was not going to think about him or wonder about him or obsess about him or fantasize about him until he gave me a sign. I looked over at him.

Nothing.

Ergh.

Some of you may think that a school library is the center of the boring universe. And the only reason to go there is to avoid people or read magazines for free or take a nap where it's air-conditioned.

All I'll say is this: What ended up going down in our library was definitely *not* boring. But that's all you get. For now.

chapter five

Finally the bell for lunch rang. I leaned against the window, waiting for the library to clear out, and spied on my locker. Nothing unusual. And then the crush of loud, rowdy, hungry kids surged into the hallway, blocking my view.

And there was Clint Bedard, walking across the grass. I started to go, but something made me turn back and watch him for a second. He was long and lean and moved with this easy, relaxed rhythm. Clearly, he had his own internal sound system too. And it was good. As he walked down the steps and away from all the yelling, chasing, obnoxious sophomorons, I wondered where he was going and what was playing on the soundtrack in his head. I barely remembered him from last year. Maybe now I'd be seeing him everywhere, like a new vocabulary word.

I could see Amy and Carreyn already parked on our bench. And there was Jen standing with them. Yay! I looked inside the little pocket in my bag to make sure I still had my freckles love letter. There it was. I threw my bag over my shoulder and headed out.

But by the time I got to our bench, Jen was gone. I checked down the hall in both directions. "Where did she go?"

"Oh, it's very sad." Amy shook her head and took a sip of Diet Coke.

Carreyn nodded. "We weren't sure how to tell you. We've lost her again."

"What? No."

"Yup." Amy looked disappointed, for real. "She left us. She's in the main quad eating lunch with Bodie. Sorry."

"But we agreed to meet right here!" I pulled out my phone as if waving around proof would change anything. "What did she say? Is she mad at me or something?"

"I don't think so," said Amy.

"She seemed fine to me," Carreyn added.

"I'm going down there."

"Where?" asked Carreyn. "To the quad?" Her eyes bulged.

I nodded.

"No way," said Amy. "Are you sure you want to do that?"

The main quad at lunch is kind of scary. There are benches on all four sides, and there's a huge bronze statue of our mascot, The Pleasant Hill Hornet, right in the middle surrounded by this low round brick wall that everyone sits on. At lunch and break, the main quad is packed with Jocks and Poms and BPs. You pretty much have to be a junior or a senior, or dating a junior or a senior, or insanely confident, to hang out there.

At the beginning of every year, there's always some poor clueless freshman who's stupid enough to walk across the quad, gets chased down and duct-taped to the bronze hornet, and then crowned with a brown paper lunch bag. My brother Parker told me about this girl a few years ago who was running across the quad at lunch carrying her flute case, when she wiped out in her clogs and went flying. She landed splat on the bricks surrounded by her books and her lunch and her open flute case. Everyone just laughed at her. He said she never got over it and ended up transferring to another school. Isn't that awful?

And I could relate. I used to play flute. I chose it because it was the smallest instrument and the case would be really easy to carry to school. But I had to give it up because I kept hyperventilating and passing out whenever I practiced. Anyway, when Parker told me that story, it really freaked me out, and I had this dream that it was me wiping out in the quad, only it wasn't a flute, it was a tuba, and I was totally naked—except for the tuba. Aren't crazy anxiety dreams the best? By the way, I look really good in a tuba.

I couldn't believe Jen was eating lunch in the main quad on the first day of school. I mean, we were

SIDEBRA

I admit that a big bronze hornet with its four front legs up, like a boxer in fighting position, is totally ridiculous. The bronze hornet was donated to Pleasant Hill High a few years ago by alumnus Monty Montego. According to anyone who remembers him, in high school Monty was a total dweeb with bad teeth and greasy, already-thinning hair. Now he's a local celebrity—the anchor guy on Evening News 7—and has big, blinding white teeth and a thick, expensive head of hair. He not only donated the statue, he did a three-part on-air story about the design, forging, and installation of the big bronze hornet so we'd all know exactly how much he'd spent.

Weight of the hornet:
approximately 3,500 lbs.
Height of the hornet: 93"
(that's almost eight feet!)
Cost of the hornet: $50,000
Supplying the quad with a monstrous, self-congratulatory bug: Priceless.

definitely popular, but only B+-list popular. Either Jen had a death wish, or she and Bodie were even tighter than I thought.

Jen's been my best friend since she moved here from Michigan in fifth grade. And we've eaten lunch together every single day, except for that month in sixth grade when we were in lunch suspension for faking a screaming, hair-pulling girl-fight during recess in front of a substitute yard monitor. We got in big trouble, but it was worth it.

Different friends have cycled in and out of our lunch bunch every year. But Jen and I have always stuck together—until today. I was starting to get a really bad feeling about this thing with Bodie. The old flat-chested Jen would never do anything like this. I pulled my phone out of my bag to see if she had called or texted. Nope.

I stuffed most of my sandwich back into the Ziploc bag. I wasn't feeling very hungry anymore. Actually, I was feeling pretty sucky. Maybe she had a good reason for blowing me off. Maybe something had happened. But I definitely wasn't going to risk going into the quad. I just wanted to scope it out from a safe distance.

If you stand in the main hall, you can look out the windows past some bushes and get a perfect view into the quad. I tried to act casual, like I was just early for sixth period and not like I was spying on my best friend.

Wow. There she was, right near the hornet, standing in a small group with Bodie and Candy Esposito and a few other juniors, looking all fabulous and popular. Jen was laughing and obviously in on whatever joke Bodie was telling.

I leaned against a pole, pulled out my phone, and hit Jen's speed dial. I was going to tell her that she was looking totally popular and BP. I looked back out the window. I wanted to see the expression on her face when I said it. It took a few seconds for her phone to ring. I couldn't help smiling as I watched her dig into her tote bag. She pulled it out, checked the caller ID, and then dropped the phone back into her bag.

I'm sorry, what?

I quickly hung up and watched her say something and laugh and fake hit Bodie on the arm in this girlie flirtatious way. Candy Esposito suddenly got all animated and talky and then—no she *didn't*—started waving her hands around in a crazy, manic gesture.

Spastic jazz hands.

What? No. No! A few people laughed. Then Bodie spastic jazzed her back, adding some fancy footwork and turning it into a bad *High School Musical* dance move. Everyone burst into hysterics. My so-called best friend Jen was actually bent over, gasping with laughter. I just stood there, mortified. I was already feeling totally loserish. But being ignored, gossiped about, and laughed at all at once was threatening to put me over the edge. And wasn't Bodie supposed to be one of the nice ones? Wait. Why did I suddenly feel like I was having déjà vu?

How could this day have gone so wrong?! I turned away and sunk down onto the shiny linoleum floor. It felt cool and smooth against my palms, and oddly comforting. I greeted the faces in the linoleum. Hello blockhead boxer with a flattened nose. Hello sleeping lady with long, swirling hair. This was the only thing that felt right so far about my first day of school.

"Repugnant."

I looked up. Charlie Dodd was standing in front of me, shaking his head.

"Repugnant?" I repeated.

"I didn't want to say anything at morning break with all your friends around. But yeah. What happened to you in Drama class. Repugnant."

Huh? I must have been staring at him with a this-does-not-compute expression.

"PSAT vocab word. Offensive. Repulsive. Disgusting. You studied for the PSATs over the summer, right?"

"No."

"Really? Wow, Paisley. You're way behind." He turned and walked up the hall, the tail of his XXL polo shirt flapping like a dress.

Normally, I wouldn't even care what Charlie Dodd thought. But Charlie is a total brain and he knows what he's talking about when it comes to grades and tests and all things nerd. Plus, after our "conversation" in Drama, I was trying to take Charlie Dodd more seriously.

Repugnant. Repugnant. I sighed. It was the first day of school and I was already way behind, on top of being a total weird-ass freakazoid loser. I was pretty sure I wouldn't have any trouble remembering the word repugnant, though, since it perfectly described my first day of sophomore year.

chapter six

And things only got worse. For the rest of the afternoon, I prayed that this was just some twisted first-day-of-school anxiety dream and that soon I'd wake up and laugh about it as I went off to live my fabulous sophomore life. Of course, the only dream part was that I *had* a fabulous sophomore life.

As the last bell rang, my phone started buzzing. Another text from Jen.

Grls lkr rm. 3:15 Rly!

I texted back.

ok c u

In the locker room, I pulled my hair back into a ponytail and sat down on a bench to lace up my cleats. Still no sign of Jen. Carreyn had transformed her wild permed hair into two poofy pigtails. I watched her tie a black ribbon around one and a yellow ribbon around the other. Whatever Carreyn lacked in skills on the field, she more than made up for in school spirit.

"We're so gonna be late," said Amy to her own reflection as she quickly applied lip gloss and passed it to Carreyn. Amy believed that if you look your best on the field, then you'll definitely play your best. Carreyn had a whole different take. Who cares if you aren't that good if you look good doing it, which explained her short shorts and tight tank top. Carreyn is the only one of the four of us who wasn't a starter, but she still made practice every single day. She hated to be out of the loop.

It was already 3:25. If we weren't dressed and on the field by 3:30, we'd have to run a lap for every minute we were late. Coach Sykes loved to torture us. She pretended to hate us and told us we were all spoiled rich kids, which we weren't. Most of us were actually middle-class kids, and only some of us were *really* spoiled. But when we scrimmaged, she thought it was hilarious to divide our team into two groups, the Haves and the Have A Lots. We pretended to hate her back. But I knew her hard-ass routine was all an act. She loved us—at least she did right after we won the district championship last year.

"I'm gonna go," said Carreyn apologetically. "I don't want to get in trouble."

"Me too," added Amy. "I'm feeling too bloated to run extra laps. And I cannot deal with Coach Psycho today."

They both looked at me, waiting to see if I was coming.

"I'll wait for Jen," I said, slamming my locker shut and hooking the lock through the latch. "I want to hear her big news. We'll run late laps together."

"You're such a good friend, Paisley," said Carreyn. "See you out there!" Her pigtails bounced like little pom-poms as she trotted out the door after Amy.

I really wanted to tell Jen about the horrors of Yearbook and Drama, and I especially wanted to show her my

FRECKLES ARE SEXY note and see who she thought could've written it. I loved Amy and Carreyn, but I knew if I showed the note to them, everyone would find out about it and I'd probably never get another secret note—or I'd start getting stupid copycat notes like PICKLES ARE SEXY. No thanks.

I tightened and retied my laces and looked at the clock. I washed my hands, splashed water on my face, and looked at the clock. I did a few quad stretches and looked at the clock. It was already 3:34. By the time I got out to the field, I was already looking at five late laps. Where was she? It was bad enough that Jen was late herself on the first day of practice. But making me late too? Coach Psycho was going to kill us—we were supposed to be team leaders.

I'd wait three more minutes.

I waited five and then stopped for a drink on my way out the door. I was slurping the cord of water arcing over the drinking fountain when I heard footsteps running outside and a familiar laugh.

"Hey Pais!" Jen shouted like she had just won the lottery. She ran through the open locker room doors and gave me a quick hug. "Sorreee! Sorry I'm so late."

"No big. Cute tote."

"Marc Jacobs. Roger bought it for me. Can you believe it?" Roger is her scummy, cheatin' dad.

"That's awesome," I said, thinking it was a total waste of money and a pathetic attempt to buy Jen's approval. Too bad Roger didn't want to buy *my* approval. She didn't seem mad at me, though. Everything seemed normal. Except her cheeks were really flushed, and she had tiny beads of sweat across her nose and a few hairs stuck in her lip gloss.

She ran her pinky along one cheek to free the hairs and tucked a few white-blond strands behind one ear. "I had to move Bodie's car for him." She shook her head, giggling. "I could not get it into gear."

I frowned at her. "What are you now, like his personal assistant?"

"No." She stepped back. "I'm his *girlfriend*, Paisley," she said in this really condescending voice. "That's what girlfriends do."

I rolled my eyes. "Thanks. I'm not some noob. Hurry up and change. I waited for you, and now we're both late."

"What is your problem?"

"*My* problem? You blew me off at morning break. You blew me off at lunch! Then you told me to meet you here before practice for some big news. Now you're so late, we'll both be running laps until dark!"

"Enough with the bitch-me-out, okay?"

I just glared at her. You've got to be kidding me.

"All right, sorry about break and lunch." She so didn't mean it. "I said I'd be there, then I changed my mind. I wanted to hang with Bodie."

"Obviously," I said coldly. "So is that your *big* news? That you just want to hang with Bodie? Come on, hurry up and change."

"Well . . . " Jen had this strange look on her face. She turned her back to me and started digging through her fab designer tote. "Don't be mad, okay?" She hesitated. "But I'm not going to practice."

"What?"

She looked up and shot me a quick glance in the mirror, then looked away. "Sorry. But I've decided I'm not gonna play soccer this year."

I stood there for a second. I should probably explain that Jen is one of our best forwards. She can shoot with her left and her right foot better than I can. She has awesome ball skills and she's really fast. And the best part, we know each other so well, it's like we can read each other's mind on the field. I never would have scored all those goals last season without her.

She *had* to be kidding.

"Right." I nodded with a fake smile. But then—wait. Where was her soccer bag? I suddenly had a nasty feeling in my stomach.

"Paisley, I'm serious!" She turned around. "I've been thinking about it for a couple weeks . . . But I decided for sure today. I'm gonna try out for cheerleading instead."

I laughed, like really laughed.

"What is so funny? God!" She threw down her fists and stomped her stacked-heel boot. "No one takes me seriously anymore!"

I stopped laughing. OMG. She *was* serious.

"Jen, why would you want to jump up and down on the sidelines cheering for the stars of some other team when you can *be* the star of our team?"

"I don't expect you to understand."

"Why not?"

"Well, you can't see! I'm just not that into soccer anymore. Sorry, but you'll just have to accept that we're growing in really different directions."

I laughed again. Was she for real?

"You know, you shouldn't laugh. When I make cheerleader, I'll be mucho popularo. And guess what? You probably will be too."

"And that's all you think I want?"

She dropped her head and gave me her duh look.

"What if you don't make cheerleader?" I asked.

"I'll make cheerleader. Bodie's on it. He's tight with the Varsity Poms and asked a couple of them to teach me the routine before tryouts next Tuesday." She smiled like this was the greatest thing.

"Jen, I don't get you. Are you like Bodie's little doll now?"

"Paisley, he loves me, really loves me, and I love him, and I want to spend as much time with him as possible. What are you, like jealous?"

"Jealous?! Ever since you started hanging out with him, you've been all . . . " I shook my head, trying to figure out what to say that wouldn't insult her.

"Bored with you?"

I wanted to explode. I couldn't believe this! I blinked my eyes and took a deep breath. "Jen, sometimes I— Right now I just— Ugh! I just really can't stand you right now." So much for not insulting her.

"Oh Paisley, you are *so* back-in-the-day. Grow up."

chapter seven

"Wait. She actually used those words? Mucho popularo?" asked Amy with disgust.

"Yep."

Amy and Carreyn and I were doing this passing drill where you start in a triangle and have to chase your own pass. We kept passing and running and passing and running farther and farther from the other groups so no one could hear our conversation.

"I don't know," said Carreyn, passing the ball to me. "I think we could use a Pom in our group. It might be fun."

"Don't you get it?" I blasted the ball back to Carreyn. "If Jen makes cheerleader and becomes a Pom, she won't *be* in our group anymore."

"Oh, right."

"Think she'd really do that?" asked Amy. "Just drop us?"

"She's not thinking about us. She's thinking about Bodie. This whole cheerleader thing is all about Bodie. She would never quit soccer for *cheerleading* if it weren't for him. And if she makes it, even if she wanted to stay friends with us, think her new Pom BFFs would let her hang with us? Think not."

Amy trapped the ball with her foot. "Pais? How come you

didn't know about this?" she asked sincerely, which was weird for Amy. "I mean, you're her best friend." She kicked the ball to me just as Coach Sykes blew her whistle. I stood there wondering the same thing and watched the ball roll past me.

"I've seen one-legged sixth graders with better ball skills!" Coach Sykes barked. "I am not here to babysit a bunch of gossip girls every afternoon. If you're not here to work your little stingers off, then go to the mall tomorrow and don't bother coming to practice." She threw her hands on her hips, looking around to see if she had scared us even a little. "Okay, let's hear it, ladies!"

We all ran together into a big swarm of black and yellow pinnies and cheered like Kool-Aid-drinking freaks. "Buzz! Sting! Win! Go, Lady Hornets!"

Coach Sykes clapped and hooted. "Yeah! That's what I like to hear!" Then she turned to me. Her eyes were filled with faux hatred. I tried not to laugh. "Parsley, where's your evil twin Jen Sweetland?"

I knew where the evil Jen was. I had just talked to her. What I didn't know was where the good Jen had gone—the one who used to make me laugh, the one with the smart mouth and kooky antics. I couldn't tell Coach Sykes the truth about Jen. She would totally freak. And besides, I was still hoping to talk Jen out of cheerleading. "Cramps," I told her. "Really bad cramps."

"That's no excuse!" she barked. "Women have been menstruating since the beginning of time. Life must go on, ladies. It's still survival of the fittest, which reminds me." She pointed her finger in my face and yelled, "Give me fourteen laps now. Fourteen!" She glared at me. "Remember, I'll be watching you even when I'm home with my feet up on the couch drinking a cold beverage and watching *Extra*."

I started running my late laps as everyone else cleared off the field.

Three down, eleven to go. The girls' field was now empty except for me.

Pais? How come you didn't know about this? How come? How come? How come?

Why *didn't* I know Jen was going to do this? It's true. I *should* have known. I was her best friend. At least I used to be.

I kept running, and more and more questions I couldn't answer filled my brain. Why did I care if someone thought I was a rah-rah and dropped me on my butt? Why did I care what Jen did? Jen *wanted* to be a Hornette. Why did I care what anyone thought at all? And why did I keep thinking about Clint Bedard? Maybe I *was* jealous of Bodie? Maybe I *was* jealous of Jen? And why did I always do what I was supposed to do? Coach Sykes

SIDEBRA

Our cheerleaders were officially called the Hornettes—the delicate, feminine version of the Hornets, named decades ago in a far more innocent time when no one would make the obvious association and start calling them the Hos, which of course everyone did now. As a popularity power cluster, our cheerleaders were the Poms, but behind their backs, everyone but their closest friends called them the Ho'nettes—the Hos for short. And not just because they were totally obnoxious about flaunting their popularity and lording it over everyone else, but also because they had really hot uniforms and a reputation for being as easy as pie.

But Jen wasn't easy. I knew her. So why would she want to be now?

wasn't watching me. No one was watching me. I was running double-digit late laps on the honor system like an idiot.

But the really impossible question was why Jen would even *want* to be a rah-rah Hornette. Was it really worth it, just to be more popular?

I stopped running at nine laps, walked a little, and then collapsed on the ground. Who cared if I got in trouble? The grass felt cool against my sweaty cheek. I lay there trying to catch my breath. My lungs burned along with everything else in my body. It was September but it still smelled like summer and still felt warm even though the sun was about to drop behind the roof of the library. I kind of wanted to cry, but I was too tired and too mad.

All the other girls were long gone, but the boys' team was scrimmaging on the next field over. I closed my eyes and got lost in the sounds of their scrimmage.

"Time! Got time!"

Thump.

"On your back!"

Thump! Thud.

"Hey!"

Whistle.

"Down the line!"

Thump. Thump.

"Gotcha back!"

Then a long triple whistle and a few celebratory whoops, followed by the sounds of guys talking and then clearing the field.

After a while, I lifted my head and turned to cool my other cheek on the grass. I watched a few guys practicing corner kicks.

I closed my eyes again and imagined that I was invisible. I had a feeling that this could be my new favorite hobby, and I was determined to get really good at it. Finally, it was quiet, so quiet I could hear my heart pounding through the ground.

And then I heard the hard thump of a soccer cleat against a ball and the satisfying slap of a ball hitting the back of the net. I opened one eye. Some guy was standing alone on the next field. His hair was damp with sweat and his shirt was drenched. It was Eric Sobel.

With one eye I watched him line up a bunch of soccer balls at different points across the top of the penalty box. He stepped back and attacked each ball. Left foot, right foot, left foot, right. He blasted each ball into the back of the net, leaning over the ball and following through every time, just like I know I'm supposed to do. He was incredibly focused and serious until he nailed the last ball into the left corner of the net.

"Goooooooooooooooal!" he yelled like that lunatic South American soccer announcer, running around in a circle. And then he pulled off his shirt and threw it into the air and did this goofy little dance.

Wow. I had seen pictures of him on Facebook, but he never looked like this.

He jogged toward the goal to retrieve the balls. Just as he got there, he jumped up, grabbed the cross bar with both hands, and did fifteen pull-ups. I know, I counted, which was why I couldn't be bothered to breathe.

Eric Sobel is much more than gorgeous. He's gorgelicous. I knew he had good legs. All soccer players do. But his torso was . . . amazing. It was like he had grown so much over the summer that his smooth tan skin barely fit his body anymore, like his skin had been shrink-wrapped over this perfect male anatomy. He could have been on the cover of one of those catalogs that are supposedly selling casual clothes but are really selling shirtless boys at the mall. I wanted to lick Eric Sobel's chest. OMG, did I just say that? OMG, I so did.

I closed my eyes and smiled. This serendipitous sight had quite possibly saved my entire day. Maybe everything was going to be okay. Or maybe not. But even if I got dropped on my head tomorrow in Drama and died a humiliating, horrible high school death without a single real friend, I'd die happy with that image of a shirtless Eric Sobel in my brain.

Eric collected the balls in a yellow mesh bag, reached down to grab his sweaty shirt off the grass, and started walking in my direction. OMG, *he was walking in my direction!* What should I do? What should I *do*?! I couldn't get up now because I'd look totally stalkerish. Maybe if I just didn't move and prayed that the sun was in his eyes and that he was having some deep soccer thought, he wouldn't even notice me. I put my head down, closed my eyes, and held my breath. I could hear his footsteps getting closer and closer.

"Hey," he said. I opened one eye and he did the cool-guy head nod.

"Hey," I squeaked, not moving an inch.

"You okay?" he asked without stopping.

"Uh, yeah. I'm just . . . listening, to the earth. I want to be a good friend to the earth and good friends are good listeners, right? And this spot right here"—I pointed at the ground— "this is a really good spot. To listen." I took a deep breath. Oh my God. I was ridiculous!

Eric stopped and nodded slowly, like he was actually trying to understand me. "Okay, cool. I'll try that spot sometime." He smiled and pushed his sweaty bangs off his forehead.

As I watched him walk away, I did the silent all-in-your-head shriek. *Aaaaaaaaaaaaah!* I wanted my whole body to melt like hot wax through the grass, into the ground, and drip down into the core of the earth because . . . the earth is my friend.

Aaaaaaaaaaaaah!

chapter eight

Before you meet my parents, I want to tell you a little about my town, which is technically a city but feels more like a town, a small town. It seems like everyone either knows everybody else or knows about everybody else. My mom says that in our town, gossip is currency. So even if you don't have the biggest house or the nicest car, or even a car at all, you can still feel rich if you have good dirt on someone.

I guess our town is a lot like other suburban towns outside a big city. Except it has a pretty embarrassing name, so I'm not even going to tell you what it is. Yep. It's that embarrassing. Let's just say that if you passed the sign for our town on the freeway, you'd either think that it was the most beautiful place on earth or the name of a cult. Sometimes it feels like both.

Anyway, we've pretty much got all the things we need. And anything we don't have, like a real mall or a multiplex theater, is in the next town over. But not a lot happens in our town at night. You can pretty much lie down in the middle of our main drag after 10:00 on a school night and not be in any danger of getting flattened. I know. I've done it. One night, Jen and I stretched out in the street for over an hour and counted eleven shooting stars.

If you turn off the main drag at the bank and go about three miles up this long winding road, you'll eventually pass our old elementary school, Charlie Dodd's house, and Jen's old house on the way to my house, which is where I was headed now.

I dropped my soccer bag and my book bag and my muddy cleats on the kitchen floor and opened the refrigerator.

"Hey Pais! How'd it go today?" My dad was standing in front of the kitchen table wearing his dorky neon yellow running vest and doing his usual stretches while he skimmed the *Wall Street Journal*. He's way into multitasking.

"It sucked." I looked around for something to drink.

"Are we being ironic?" He switched feet and started another quad stretch. "Is sucked a good thing this year?"

I pulled my head out of the fridge just long enough to roll my eyes at him and then went back to my search. "We're out of sparkling water," I grumbled.

"It couldn't have been that bad." He switched legs. "Could it?"

I filled him in on a few highlights of my day, which were actually all low points. (No, I didn't mention Eric Sobel's shrink-wrapped, lickable torso. He's my dad!)

"What you need, Paisley, is a shot from Doctor Positivo!" He pretended to give me an injection in my shoulder. I ignored him. It's one of his usual routines. "A little positivo potion will kill off those negative thought germs."

"I don't have negative thoughts, Dad. I had a sucky day. Okay?"

My dad is all about having a super positive attitude. He actually believes that that's the solution to everything. Obviously, he's way too old to remember what it's really like to be a teenager. But it's impossible for me to argue with him about it. He works really hard and he's always doing these big real estate deals, he's always running marathons, so he's in really good shape, and he's always annoyingly happy.

And then there's my mom.

"Hello, my lovelies!" My mother entered the kitchen as if she were walking onstage for her cabaret act. Only she was wearing very big sunglasses and a very small white tennis dress. Thank God she's been using that self-tanning lotion on her thighs. "Was everyone's day as delicious as mine?" She didn't wait for a response. "We won!"

I closed the refrigerator door, hopped up onto the counter, and started pulling at a piece of string cheese.

Mom did this little dance move around the kitchen island, giving me a quick hug as she passed by, then she danced her way over to Dad and kissed him hard on the lips. Do I really need to see this? No.

"Mmm. An oaky Chardonnay," said my dad, licking his lips.

"We stopped for a celebratory glass of wine after our match. Did I say glass? I meant bottle. We clobbered them!" She looked over at me. "Shoulders back, Sweet P! You're slouching."

I sat up straight and stuck out my poor excuse for boobs.

"That's it," she cheered. "Back rest, no chest. Spine straight, chest great!" She gave my ponytail a love squeeze and started rubbing the back of my neck. It felt really good. I didn't move, hoping she wouldn't notice she was doing it and would keep going while she talked. "And they must have been at least ten years younger than we are. *And*—get this—they had all of this fabulous matching crapola. You'd think they were sponsored by Nike. But we were awesome!" she said, swatting the air with an imaginary two-handed backhand. "We really were. We played like Venus and Serena on Advil."

My dad laughed. "Congrats, babe. Let's go out to dinner and keep celebrating. What do you say, Pais?"

"Okay," I mumbled.

"I'm only doing six, so I'll be back in"—he checked his running watch—"forty-four minutes."

Only six miles? See what I mean about his annoyingly positive attitude? He ran through the kitchen and right out the back door.

I waved at no one. "Bye, Dad."

"Hon, how was your first day?" Mom asked.

"Good." I didn't even hesitate. "It was really good." I just smiled and slid down off the counter.

"Oh, I'm so proud of you. I want to hear all about it at dinner." She grabbed me and gave me a hug and a kiss on the cheek. I leaned back, trying to pull away. "Mo-om!"

She started tickling me. "Admit it! Admit it, you love me!" My mom laughed.

"Mo-om!" Okay, I was laughing a little. "Get away. You are so weird." Finally, I broke free and picked my stuff up, lugged it upstairs, and took a long, environmentally unfriendly shower.

That's pretty much what it's like at my house. We're all busy, doing our own thing. And as long as we all act like everything is going great, then everything goes great. Does that make sense?

After dinner, I went upstairs to do my homework and some cyber-stalking. I had to push my cat Dyson off of my laptop again. He's gotten in the habit of curling up and sleeping on it all the time, I guess because it's warm.

Dyson jumped up on my lap and settled in, power-purring while I stayed up late on Facebook. I studied Jen's profile, reading through her list of friends and—OMG! I wasn't a Favorite Friend anymore! What?! When did that happen?

I followed her trail of faves to Bodie's page, Candy Esposito's, Amy's, Carreyn's, Hutch's. There was a zoomed-in photo of Jen and Bodie making out on Hutch's page. It had to be from that party last weekend. They really *did* hook up. Wow. And how. It was like graphic. Actually, there were a lot of kissing photos on Hutch's page. Weird. Also, a bunch of shots of Jen with Bratty Sasshole #1 and Bratty Sasshole #2, laughing with their

SIDEBRA

No, I didn't name him Dyson. When I adopted him at the SPCA, Dyson was the name on his cage, and I was dumb enough to think that really was his name. But then my brother Parker told me that the SPCA people just make up the strangest names they can think of and he was probably named after a vacuum cleaner. I didn't believe him. But I went back a few days later, and saw three cats named Eureka, Hoover, and Electrolux. Oh well. It was too late. He was already Dyson to me.

mouths wide-open and looking pretty drunk. Classy. When did Jen get so tight with the Sassholes? They were total A-list McMeanies.

I should explain that Bratty Sasshole #1 and Bratty Sasshole #2 is my personal shorthand for these two nasty Varsity Hornettes. Here's all you need to know: They're juniors in Bodie's group, so they're total pops, and they're super tight with Candy Esposito, and they're basically joined at the hip. They talk alike, dress alike, and act alike, and if BS1 didn't have dark hair, and BS2 didn't have blond hair, I probably couldn't tell them apart. I don't know if anyone really likes them or if everyone's just afraid of them and *pretends* to like them. But you definitely don't want to get on their bad side. They will crush you. And they will do it with a smile.

My attention snapped back to Jen's profile. Wow, somebody definitely had it out for her. There were some truly nasty anonymous things posted in her Honesty Box. *Careful girlie, you're drinking your own cool-aid!* What does that even mean? *You think you're so hot—but you're snot.* I said nasty, I didn't say original. *Better watch your cute little backside, Sweetland.* Okay, that sounded ominous. I had no idea who wrote these things. And no—it wasn't me. Like I would ever.

That night I slept outside by the pool. I wanted to feel like it was still summer when everything really *was* good, when Jen and I hung out almost every day, and sophomore year was nothing but a happy fantasy, something to shop for and plan for and dream about. I scrunched down in my sleeping bag and stretched back on the chaise longue so I could look up at the stars, the same stars that Jen and I had stared at all summer.

It was a really clear night. The jumbo crickets were chirping like crazy. Schirp-schirp, schirp-schirp, schirp-schirp. That sound filled the whole sky. It hung from every tree branch, every telephone wire, the edge of every roof. Schirp-schirp, schirp-schirp, schirp-schirp. I don't know why, but it gave me a really good feeling.

I watched for shooting stars and tried to imagine what Jen's life was like since her parents split. Maybe that would explain why she was acting so un-Jen-like.

Her dad is a certifiable creep who cheated on her mom and now doesn't seem to care about anyone but himself. Her mom is going back to work selling real estate, so she's studying for some big test all the time. And—this is weird—she got her eyes done over the summer. It was spooky seeing her with two black eyes, like someone had beaten her up. Jen was totally freaked out and she practically lived at our house for a few weeks. Her mom said it's an investment in their future and that she needed the surgery so she could keep her eyes on the prize.

I don't know. If my family were having a major meltdown, maybe I'd be getting super drunk at parties and clinging to my new boyfriend like my life depended on him too. I should ask Jen's mom what she thinks is going on. I love Jen's mom. She is definitely one of the cool moms and always says brutally honest, funny things like, "It takes a very small man to drive a truck that big" or "Gossip is the opium for the asses" or "If you ever find yourself, Roger, I hope it's nowhere near me."

I think she'd be honest with me if I asked her about Jen. But my mom says not to bug her. She thinks Jen's mom is having a midlife crisis because her husband has replaced her with a younger, thinner version of herself. My mom has a theory for everything—

Shooting star!

—but what is a midlife crisis, anyway? Maybe *I'm* having a midlife crisis. Maybe my neurotic self is really, really mature for its age. Or maybe I'm actually halfway through my life and I'll be dead when I'm 30. That would mean I only have . . . I closed my eyes . . . 5,475 days left, that's . . . 131,400 hours, of which . . . 43,800 I'll probably be asleep. So I might only have . . . 87,600 hours left to get stuff done. Yeah, I did that all in my head.

But wow. 87,600 hours. I'd better get going. I have a lot to do.

chapter nine

I woke up early, so early that the sky was still violet-blue. That's one of the things I love about sleeping outside—I never need an alarm. I just lay there, all cozy in my sleeping bag, and listened. A few birds were chit-chatting away, a car started, and sprinklers danced back and forth across somebody's lawn. The air tasted cool and crisp and sweet. Considering yesterday's hellishness, I felt great.

And I decided that I was going to feel great all day—no matter what happened. I swiped a handful of morning air and closed my fist tight, holding my secret stash of positivity particles. Okay, a little lame maybe. But I'm my father's daughter.

After rolling up my sleeping bag, I went inside and up to my room, turned on some music, and assessed the outfit situation. I wanted to feel confident but casual and definitely not be trying too hard. Jeans, sandals, and this cute little top with hand-stitched detailing on the neck and sleeves. Perfect.

In carpool, I made a point of sitting next to Charlie Dodd so we could have a real, meaningful conversation. I looked around the minivan. Most kids were listening to music, trying to sleep, or staring out the window in a catatonic stupor.

"So Charlie, I was wondering. What's your opinion of *The Fly*?" I asked, doodling a cartoon fly in my notebook.

He looked at me kind of weird. "Button fly or zipper fly?"

"No! Our school newspaper, *The Fly*?" I pulled the flyer Eric Sobel had given me out of my bag and showed it to him. "I might go to this meeting."

Charlie read through it and shrugged. "The editors seem genuinely iconoclastic, but their product is fairly bourgeois. Are you thinking of joining the staff?"

"Maybe."

He nodded. "School newspaper always looks good on college apps. And if it's not a real class, then maybe you can sign up but not have to do anything."

"I'd kinda like to do something, actually. I thought I was going to be in Yearbook, but . . . " I didn't want to finish my sentence.

"Yeah, I heard about that headline slam in Yearbook yesterday. Bummer."

"*You* heard? How did *you* find out?"

"Dwight Cashel wrote about it in his blog. He's in love with Candy Esposito."

I sighed and looked out the window.

Mr. Eggerston didn't waste any time in Drama. Thank God. People had been lobbing weird, sympathetic looks at me since the moment I walked in—except for Clint Bedard. He stared at me with this knowing smile. I just had no idea what it was he knew.

"Okay, people! This is what's called an open-scene exercise,"

Mr. Eggertson called out. He stood on the stage waving a stack of index cards. "These words don't actually mean anything. Each of you has to *give* them meaning through your delivery, through your intonation, through your instrument. It's not merely about *saying* the words, it's about communicating the subtext." He slapped his palm with the stack of cards. "And if you don't know what that means, look it up or ask someone who does know. Okay, people, partner up!"

Everyone scrambled, searching for a partner that they liked or could at least stand to look at.

I dropped my notebook on my chair and turned to Bean Merrill, who had been right next to me. "Bean? Wanna . . . "

"Um, nothing personal, but . . . " She pointed with her head toward this genius AV geek, one of the few tall guys in the room, and then smiled conspiratorially and loped off in his direction. I had to smile too.

I quickly looked around for Charlie Dodd. But he was already talking to Clint Bedard. Who happened to be looking really good today. Stop it!

I looked to the left and then to the right in what I hoped was not an obvious panic. Oh no. The only two people left were Teddy Baedeker and Cate Maduro. Crap.

Cate glanced at Teddy, then back at me. She shook her head, not even trying to hide her disgust at being stuck with me, and walked slowly in my direction. She was wearing this little pearl choker and tight sweater set—oh, and a beauty mark. Whatever. Teddy ran a hand through his short, overly gelled hair, scrunched up his nose, and nodded. He was used to this.

Cate was a few feet away from me when she abruptly turned a hard right and threw out her arms. "Teddy!" she exclaimed, like she was greeting a dear old friend. "Howdy, partner."

What a freakin' psycho.

"Okay Paisley," said Mr. Eggertson. "You're with me. Up here. We'll demonstrate."

I glared at Cate as I walked by. What was her problem?

I hopped up onto the stage, and Mr. E. handed me an index card. It said: *Shake before opening. Naturally and artificially flavored. Triggers sudden slim-down of as much as seven pounds.* Oh crap. This was going to be hard.

Mr. E. leaned over and whispered in my ear, "I just called off our engagement. Got it?"

I nodded.

I took a few seconds and thought hard about the time my old cat Scamper got hit by a car and I buried him in the backyard in a cardboard TiVo box. Then I looked up at Mr. E. with real tears in my eyes.

"Shake before opening." I trembled, obviously in pain. And then I pleaded, "Naturally?"

He looked at me and shrugged. "Was the staff."

"And artificially flavored." My lower lip quivered. I was amazed. "Triggers? Sudden slim-down?" I started to cry for real. I had no idea where this was coming from.

He looked really, really sad and took my hand. "Respectful, supportive, and . . . "

I pulled my hand away and touched my heart. "Of as much as seven pounds," I whispered, and turned away.

"And scene!" yelled Mr. E. The class clapped, like *really* clapped.

Cate Maduro just stared at me coldly with her arms crossed. But Bean flashed me a big goofy smile with an I'm-impressed! nod.

"Okay, people! What was going on in the scene?"

"Breaking up!"

"He dumped her!"

"He broke her heart!"

"Yes, exactly, all those things. Any questions? Okay!" Then Mr. E. turned to me. "Nice work, Paisley." He seemed genuinely impressed. I kinda was too.

At lunch, I was headed to my locker when I passed Bodie and some Varsity Jocks in the hallway. It made me think of those photos I'd seen on Facebook the other night. Something strange definitely happened at that party. But what? And why wasn't anyone spilling? I was lost in my own head space until I heard Amy's booming laugh.

Jen and Amy were standing in front of my locker giggling about something. I was partly relieved but mostly annoyed to see Jen hanging out with us at lunch again. I was still spinning on what she'd said yesterday. It's not like I was just going to *forget* about it, you know? But she couldn't have meant all that . . . Could she?

I slipped into perky girl character and put a smile on my

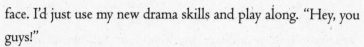

face. I'd just use my new drama skills and play along. "Hey, you guys!"

"Hey Paisley!" they said together. Then they both waved at me doing the exact same manic hand gesture that I had done in Yearbook. I stopped cold and watched them burst into hysterics.

"Thanks a not, you guys!" I was really pissed.

"What?" asked Amy. "We're just rippin' on you."

But Jen was still rippin' *into* me. "It's way adorable, really," she added acidly, then smiled and did the spastic jazz hands wave to Carreyn, who was bouncing down the hallway toward us. Of course, she spastic jazzed right back with her big goofy grin.

"It's not adorable!" I fumed. "It's embarrassing! Does everyone on the planet know what happened to me in Yearbook? Ugh, stupid spastic jazz hands!" I was so flustered, it took me like three tries to get my locker combination right.

"Spastic jazz hands?" Jen asked snarkily, one eyebrow cocked.

"Yes! The whole thing was totally humiliating," I said, ignoring her taunting.

"That's not what Candy said." Jen acted all in-the-know. "She told me you were awfully cute and funny and then, when you did your *spastic jazz hands*, it was hilarious. I think it's Candy's new favorite dance move."

The three of them all started bouncing their hips and doing the move with cheerleader enthusiasm, chanting, "Spastic jazz hands! Spastic jazz hands! Spastic jazz hands!"

I slammed my locker door shut.

Then all of a sudden, Jen went into full-blown-freaky-cheerleading mode. "Come on, Paisley! Don't be mad! It's really funny! Don't feel sad!" she yelled, then high-kicked and dropped into the splits.

I stared at her. Had she completely lost her mind? She raised her arms above her head. Oh no. *Again?* I turned and stomped off down the hall before I could find out.

She cheered after me. "Roll on, Paisley! You're our girl! Just relax or you might hurl!"

"*Hurl?*" I heard Amy ask.

"Whatever," Jen replied. "I was improvising. *You* find something that rhymes with girl."

I tried to stay positive, I really did. But Candy Esposito not only took my spot in Yearbook, she also took my positivity stash. That girl was so greedy! I just wanted to get as far away from my hilarious friends as possible. If I did a big loop around the whole campus, by the time I got to the tennis courts near the band room, maybe lunch would be over and I'd be calm enough not to want to kill my friends.

Spastic jazz hands . . . Spastic jazz hands?! Where did that even come from? It's not like that move is part of my usual repertoire. If only I had calmly and casually said, "Paisley Hanover—I'd vote for Candy," like I didn't even really care about Yearbook, like I understood the popularity equation and had a firm grasp on irony instead of just my desperation. Why? Why? WHY?

"Paisley?"

I stopped my all-in-your-head self-torture and looked around. Mandy Mindel was actually talking—talking to *me*. She leaned against the wall near the double doors that opened onto the front lawn, looking like she might collapse if the wall weren't there.

"Hi, um. I was . . . um. I was wondering if you were, if you were going out, out to the front lawn?" she asked, obviously in psychic pain.

The front lawn is where the Drama geeks and other freaks gather at lunch, where no one can see them doing whatever they do.

"I wasn't planning to."

She nodded. "Oh, okay, never mind. Sorry."

"Why? Are you going out there?"

"Well." She scratched her nose really hard, pushing it around with the back of her finger. It looked like it was made of rubber and might pop off her face.

Mandy wears glasses all the time, which is lucky because it helps hide the fact that she had no eyelashes. I tried really hard to look at her eyeballs and not her eyelids.

"Do you want to go out there?" I asked.

"Well." She blinked nervously. "Only if you do. I mean, if you did, I would. I would walk with you if you . . . if you wanted."

Wow. For a second I had a sense of someone else's constant high school hell. Suddenly spastic jazz hands didn't seem like such a global crisis.

"Yeah, you know. I do want to eat lunch on the front lawn. Come on." I pushed open one of the doors. "Thanks for walking with me."

She didn't say a word as she followed me out into the bright noon sunlight.

It took a few seconds for my eyes to adjust. Wow. There were lunch pods for the Pleasant Hill extras too. Who knew? There was a cluster of junior and senior Drama Queens, some AV Guys and YouTubers passed around a video camera, a few NILs stretched out in couples feeding each other. Gross. NILs are what we call nerds in love, two fugly social misfits who somehow found each other and fell in love, or at least in lust. The Goths were gathered in the shade under the tree. A bunch of Emos were lying on the grass too depressed to eat.

I turned to Mandy. "Come on." We slowly weaved our way through the various groups. Mime Guy in the cape was playing Scrabble with some other Drama dweebs and the uncool foreign exchange students. Teddy Baedeker was juggling two oranges and an iPhone. Hold the phone—he wasn't bad.

Mandy dropped to her knees and inched over into their group. I kept walking, taking it all in, and then I spotted Bean Merrill and Charlie Dodd sitting with Cate Maduro and a few Library Girls near the school sign.

"Yo, Paisley!" said Charlie, waving me over.

Cate Maduro looked up at me and then fell back on her hands. "Oh my God, it's everyone's favorite rah-rah." She was

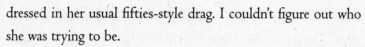

dressed in her usual fifties-style drag. I couldn't figure out who she was trying to be.

"Hey Paisley," said Bean, looking sort of curiously at me. "Sit down."

I plopped down next to Bean and crossed my legs on the fringes of their pod and dug into my lunch.

"Are you lost, Paisley?" asked Cate Maduro.

"Just ignore me, okay?"

"That's easy."

I ignored her.

Bean pointed toward my feet. "Sweet sandals."

"Thanks." I slowly unwrapped my sandwich—smoked turkey with sun-dried tomatoes and arugula on a baguette. I made it myself. "So, are you guys nervous about doing our first scene?" I took a bite and looked around the circle.

"I'm not," said Bean. "As long as I don't get Mandy Mindel or Special Ted as my scene partner."

"Oh, I hope he's *my* partner," said Cate Maduro all seductive. "I'll bet he's an amazing kisser."

Everyone laughed.

"That's disgusting," said LG Wong. She's the queen of the Library Girls and a total goody-goody. Most people think LG stands for Library Girl, and now it kind of does. But it really stands for Lydia Georgette. No wonder she goes by LG. Anyway, she plays classical piano and at least three other instruments, gets straight A's, and reads so much she has to

carry all of her books around in one of those rolling suit-
cases. The weird thing, she has this cool chopped-out anime-
girl haircut.

"I hope I get Clint Bedard," said Bean with a smirk. "Have
you seen him lately? He's lookin' hot in a lost boy kinda way."

"I know," I agreed. "Where was he last year?"

"Probably in jail!" said Charlie.

"What, are you jealous?" I asked.

He scoffed. "Highly unlikely. Why would I be jealous of
some brainless, subordinate lowlife?"

Cate dropped her head and peered at Charlie over her cat-eye
sunglasses. "Because he's hot."

"So's a pile of dog crap. And I'm not jealous of that."

"Charlie!" Cate pretended to be shocked. "You are so
cute when you're mad. Did he beat you up? Or just steal your
lunch?"

"I'm not mad," he said, sucking hard on the straw sticking
out of his juice box. "I'm more . . . " He turned and looked
right at Bean. "Disappointed."

"What?" she asked, all exasperated. "Don't be such a nerdathon."

LG Wong jumped in to change the subject.

"So, Paisley, what's it like being one of the chosen people at
PH?" She looked at me as she cleaned her glasses. Then she put
them back on. "I've always wanted to know."

"Leave her alone," said Bean.

"No, I want to hear this," said Cate Maduro. "Does it hurt

your head being so popular? Does the pressure just make you want to kill yourself?"

Charlie Dodd chimed in. "She's not *that* popular."

"She's A-list, total insider," said LG to Charlie. "I'm serious. I really want to know what it's like."

"Hello? I'm sitting right here. I can't believe you guys. You're totally clueless if you think I'm A-list popular," I said. I was trying to stay positive and bond. "No one is *that* popular. At least I'm not. I really relate to you guys," I said earnestly. "I don't always say the right thing or wear the right thing."

Silence.

Okay, that didn't come out right. "What I mean is, everyone at this school struggles to fit in. Even me. Especially me."

They all laughed, except for Charlie, who just stared at me like I was insane.

"Yeah right," said Cate Maduro. "Oh no, who do I sit with today? The Poms or the BPs?" They laughed again.

"Or the Sporties or the Perfect Girls?" said LG, throwing her hand over her forehead like some cartoon damsel in distress. "Gosh, it's so darn confusing being popular."

"Do I go out with the varsity football star on Friday night," said Charlie, acting all girlie, "or the varsity soccer star?"

"Or maybe I'll be really generous and go out with both!" added Cate Maduro, all cheerleader perky. Everybody thought that one was hilarious. The Library Girls couldn't stop laughing. All their glasses almost fell off.

I just sat there feeling depressed. For some reason, I didn't expect the unpopulars to be so nasty too. At least the populars *pretended* to be nice to each other—sometimes. I looked away. Mandy Mindel and Teddy Baedeker were laughing at Mime Guy pulling himself across the grass with an invisible rope. Why did I even come out here?

I started to pack up my lunch. "Well, you'll be happy to know you're just as nasty as the most popular people at this school."

"Come on, Paisley," Charlie groaned. "We're just raggin' on you."

"Whatever."

"Well," said Cate, sitting up and tucking her legs under her, "you'll be happy to know you're just as vain as the least popular people at this school."

I couldn't believe Cate actually said that right to my face. I glanced around the circle with this is-she-for-real? look. Charlie and Bean seemed a little uncomfortable.

"So, um, Cate, why do you hate me so much? I mean, what did I ever do to you?"

She shrugged, suddenly acting all blasé. "I don't hate you, Paisley. You're just . . . *so* Pleasant Hill."

I glared at her. "What is *that* supposed to mean?"

"Oh my God!" Bean reached over and grabbed something out of my bag. "*The Fly* meeting. I totally forgot!" She jumped up, waving the neon yellow flyer, and grabbed my hand. "Come on, Paisley, we're gonna be late."

She pulled me up and we ran across the lawn toward the

door. We didn't stop running until we were inside the main hallway.

"That was totally weird," she said to herself, shaking her head. She opened the flyer she was clutching in her hand and started reading.

"Thanks, Bean." That *was* weird. I tried to think of what I could've done or said to Cate Maduro. Nothing. I haven't even talked to her since seventh grade.

Bean looked up from the flyer, all innocent. "For what? I really wanted to go to the meeting. Room 107. Come on." She took off up the hall.

I stood there for a second, trying to understand what had just happened. And then I chased after her. I figured if Yearbook wasn't in the cards for me this year, then I might as well check out our school's tacky, unprestigious alternative, *Fly Paper*, aka *The Fly*: "All the news that sticks to print."

chapter ten

The meeting was already going on when Bean and I walked into room 107. Everyone turned and stared. Why is everyone always staring at me these days? Someone handed each of us an issue from last year, and we slipped into seats in the back row.

Miriam Goldfarb was sitting on a desk in the front row talking. She had smarty arty glasses, dark curly hair, and a nasally voice.

"And you won't be the only ones volunteering to produce our un"—she dropped her head and gazed over her glasses at the room filled with people as if she were seeing us for the first time—"our un-award-winning news rag, *Fly Paper*, affectionately known as *The Fly*."

She spoke in this strange singsongy rhythm, pausing like she didn't know what she was going to say next, although she obviously did. Miriam Goldfarb was the editor of *The Fly* and a total brain.

"Our new librarian, Ms. Whitaker, has kindly offered to volunteer"—pause—"her time as our faculty advisor."

"Hello," said Ms. Whitaker, waving. A few people clapped.

"Thanks to the prevalent football fascist mentality here at Pleasant Hill High— Gooooo Hornets!" Miriam yelled. "*The Fly* is no longer an accredited class. It's a *club!*"

A wave of boos followed. The room was a bizarre mix of kids from all four grades. I couldn't get a read on how to describe them or how they all happened to end up in this room for this meeting. But they all had a lot to say.

"Journalism—not jingoism!" someone shouted.

"Hey, when's the first party?"

"It'll be a cold day in Pleasant Hell before the pen is silenced!" yelled Logan Adler.

Then some guy playing the bongos started drumming and chanting, "*The Fly* will never die. Nev-er die, nev-er die, nev-er die," and everyone joined in.

I scrunched down low in my chair and hugged my backpack. What was I doing here?

"Okay! Okay!" Miriam raised her arms and her nasal voice. The crowd immediately quieted down. "Just because we don't have a budget doesn't mean we won't have fun!" Miriam continued. "We'll be doing a lot of"—pause—"fundraising throughout the year, like bake sales and car washes, and of course begging our parents." She cackled. "As you know, *The Fly* parties are legendary." Everyone cheered like maniacs. "So we'll start charging non-staff to get in." Miriam looked around the room, smiling like a proud parent. "*The Fly* may be the ugly, obnoxious, unloved, uncoordinated, unpopular stepchild here at Pleasant Hill High, but we are the *only* newspaper this school has—and our voice will be heard!"

More cheers and bongo drumming. The "nev-er die" chant started up again.

"Miriam, may I add something?" called Ms. Whitaker over the noise.

"Of course. Please do." The room quieted down.

"We have a huge challenge this year, no doubt, but it's worth it to keep the paper alive. Yes, *The Fly* is our only school newspaper, which means it's the only school publication to reach people on a regular basis. That means *your* words can reach people—and that's power!" You could tell she was getting really into it. "Each one of you has the opportunity not only to report the news here at school, but also to inform people about global issues, inspire readers, and get them thinking about new ideas. If you decide to get involved and write for *The Fly*, which I hope you will, that power is yours."

"Hear, hear, Ms. Whitaker! Hear, hear!"

Miriam Goldfarb was a weirdo. No wonder they killed the budget, with her as the editor. But still, there was something about her . . . It was like she didn't go to our school every day. She just went to her life.

While Miriam talked on, I flipped through the issue from last year. There was a cute photo of Charlie Dodd blowing a gigantic bubble out of his French horn at some carwash for new band uniforms. And something about Bodie Jones catching air and dunking the ball at the buzzer to win the game. I kept flipping. *The Fly* was filled with sports scores and photos with bad punny captions, hard-hitting stories about trash in the quad, fluffy profiles on standout faculty members and students, and controversial op-ed pieces intended to pad college admissions packages more than change minds. One op-ed headline read: "Can't We All Just Not Get Along?" Hilarious. By Miriam Goldfarb. That figures.

This year, with no budget, *The Fly* would probably be even worse.

"As you know, I am the editor, and that"—Miriam gestured grandly toward the back of the room—"adorable dumb blond is my assistant"—she paused again—"editor Logan Adler."

Logan walked up to the podium, smiling like a giddy beauty pageant finalist, and waved to the group as if he'd just been crowned rather than insulted. "Thanks, Mim"—he air-kissed her sweetly—"for that flattering introduction. You are far too kind." He wore a black T-shirt that said DUMBE BLONDE across the front.

Bean reached for my notebook, flipped to a blank page, and scribbled something. Then passed it back to me under my desk.

They're a couple! ♥♡

I looked at her, hoping for visual confirmation. She gave me a knowing nod. All I could think was, thank

SIDEBRA

Even though she was a senior and he was a junior, and she was nasal-neurotic brainy, and he was adorable-funny brainy, somehow Miriam and Logan *were* a couple. They went to journalism camp over the summer and fell madly in love in the fact-checking seminar. He wrote a really funny piece about it on his blog.

Oh, and he's not really blond. He bleached his hair the week before school to protest the big cut in our school district's arts budget. And now he was starting a protest group called the Dumbe Blondes. Their mission: to attend all varsity games and school events and cheer like ditzy idiots, showing district administrators the future of Pleasant Hill High if all the cool arts classes were cut. Signs with grammatical errors and misspelled words were emphatically encouraged.

God they found each other. I held my notebook on my lap under the desk and wrote, How do you know?

Bean grabbed it and scribbled another note, then passed it back to me.

Read his blog. It's hilarious!

Logan Adler flipped open his notebook and looked down at the podium. "Okay, let's get down to business." Then he looked up with a big love-crazy grin. "By the way, ignore her. She's off her meds and she's about to be accepted early-admission to Yale, so she's obnoxious as hell."

As I doodled his T-shirt design in my notebook, Logan read off a bunch of jobs that needed to be filled—writers, editors, photographers, production supervisors, columnists, reporters in the field, party planners—with a brief description of each job.

"Sign-up sheets are here." He pointed to the front row. "And hey, regardless of whether or not you join *The Fly*, I hope you'll *all* join the Dumbe Blondes!"

There were a few beauty-pageant-quality shrieks of joy. I guess some people were already in the club.

SIDEBRA continued

FYI: You don't need blond hair to be a Dumbe Blonde. You just have to be an authority-questioning, arts-loving activist.
PS FYI: Dumbe is misspelled on purpose. You know, it's like satire? Because so many people mix up blonde and blond or never even bother to learn the difference? So anyone who spells dumb with an "e" is even *dumber* than a dumb blonde. Get it?
PPS FYI: *Blond* is an adjective, as in "She has unnaturally curly blond hair."
Blonde is a noun, as in "He had a morbid fear of beautiful, tall blondes."

And I'm pretty sure blonde is only used to describe a female with blond hair. Are you confused yet? Just remember: Blonde with an "e" is always for she.

And Blondie is not a person—it's a band.

"You'll not only get one of these snazzy T-shirts for a mere ten dollars"—Miriam slowly waved her hand up and down his side like a game show prize girl—"you'll also get the satisfaction of driving the administration bonkers!"

More cheers and squeals of blondish joy.

"And if we make enough noise this year, we can save electives like Art, Band, and Drama from extinction."

Wait. Drama? They were maybe going to cut Drama?

"Remember kids, protesting is good, clean fun!"

The room rumbled to life as everyone started talking and moving toward the sign-up sheets.

"What do you think? Wanna sign up for something?" Bean asked me.

"Um, I don't know." I didn't want to hurt her feelings if she was totally into it. "It could be fun. But I'm pretty busy with soccer and stuff." I hesitated. "Did you know Drama was in trouble?" I asked her.

"No, but it figures. They want to fry anything remotely creative."

I chewed a cuticle but didn't say anything.

Bean didn't seem to care if I wanted to sign up for *The Fly*. She did. So she signed up to be a field reporter for Drama. Then she joined the Dumbe Blondes. And you know what? So did I. It was only ten bucks. And I got a snazzy T-shirt. Bean looked at me sort of surprised. I didn't blame her. I was surprising *myself* today. And guess who bought a shirt right after me? Ms. Whit!

On our way back to our lockers, Bean and I were holding

up our T-shirts, acting all goofy and ditzy like the dumbest of the Dumbe Blondes, cracking each other up. Bean started doing these funny, idiotic cheerleading moves. I joined in, doing the moves I'd seen Jen practicing earlier.

Then I looked down the hall and froze. Jen and Carreyn were standing there, staring at me coldly.

"Oh, *that's* really nice, Paisley." Jen said my name like it tasted bad.

"What?"

"What are you trying to say, that we're dumb?"

OMG! This was getting insane. "Jen," I said slowly, "it's *not. About. You.* It's the name of a protest group we just joined. God, not everything is about you."

Jen stared at me all bug-eyed. Carreyn lifted her chin and crossed her arms, adjusting her nearly identical, cheapo version of Jen's designer tote bag.

Bean looked from them to me, me to them. "Excuse me?" Bean waved. "Excuse me? Not sure if you noticed, but I'm blond too?"

Carreyn and Amy glanced at her like they couldn't care less, then turned back to me.

"Oh, so then I guess you're saying *all* blondes are dumb." With that awesome comeback, Jen turned and stalked off in the opposite direction.

"Yeah," Carreyn said, stink-eyeing us, then following Jen down the hall.

I sighed. Unbelievable.

"I really like your friends." Bean smiled sweetly.

chapter eleven

I called a powwow. I had to. Before this thing with Jen spiraled totally out of control and took Amy and Carreyn with it, we needed to talk—all four of us, face-to-face, and definitely not at school. Maybe if we had a pool powwow, everyone would remember how much fun we had over the summer. Maybe we could get it back.

So the four of us agreed to meet at Amy's house on Saturday afternoon for a pig-out party and a heart-to-heart. Or so I thought.

I was a little late because I had to ride my bike and it was super hot that day. When I got there, Amy was stretched out on her huge pink bed, flipping through a magazine, drinking a Diet Coke, and eating cookies and edamame, this strange Japanese diet food she was all into. Carreyn was on the carpet in the splits position, bouncing away her muscles or tendons or whatever, along with her self-respect.

See, Carreyn had gotten the brilliant idea of trying out for cheerleading too. I admired her enthusiasm, but sometimes she could be such a clone. I mean, what would Carreyn even do if she didn't have someone else to imitate? As I walked in, she was trying to enlist Amy—again.

"Come on, Amers," Carreyn begged. "We'll have so much fun. If we make it, we can all cheer together at the opening game next Friday and then go to the dance with all the Poms!"

"No way." Amy held up a hand without taking her eyes off her magazine. "I'd rather be on YouTube dancing topless than be a cheerleader. Oh, my bad! That is being a cheerleader." She looked up and guffawed.

"That only happened once!" Carreyn sounded all insulted. "Pleeeease? We really need girls like you for the base of the pyramid."

Amy gave her the smack-down look, and Carreyn shut up.

"Jen's not here yet?" I asked, wiping my face with the sleeve of my T-shirt.

Amy and Carreyn looked at each other.

"Nope. Not yet," Carreyn said. "I think she had to go by her house or something." Carreyn reached for a brush on the bedside table and began frantically brushing her hair. She had been trying to brush out that crazy perm all week. Now her hair just looked frizzy and damaged like she stuck her finger in a light socket every night before bed.

Amy shrugged. "Or she's probably late 'cause she's talking with Bodie."

Carreyn paused her hairbrush attack. "Like if she's with Bodie, they'll really be talking? Think not."

"Ugh, Bodie! I am so sick of Bodie!" I kicked off my shoes and pulled off my sweaty Peds and flung them on the carpet. "I'm boiling. Let's go swimming."

Carreyn looked at Amy before saying, "No, let's wait here for her. I'm sure she'll be here soon."

I flopped down across the foot of Amy's bed on her pink angora throw blanket, reached for a pink frosted animal cookie with sprinkles, and took a bite. Being in Amy's room was like being inside a big poof of cotton candy. Everything was pink and soft and fluffy. She even had a pink aromatherapy candle that *smelled* like cotton candy. Not what you'd expect from a big girl with a big voice and a monster goal kick.

"How come you're so sick of Bodie?" Carreyn asked. Amy didn't even look up from painting her toenails—guess what color?

"I don't know." I took another bite of the cookie and thought about it. "It's not him, really, it's just . . . He's changed everything."

"Yeah," Carreyn agreed. "Think he's changed Jen?"

"Duh. Big-time."

"Yeah. I think she's changed too," Amy agreed.

"Do you think she's conceited now?" Carreyn asked. Amy looked up from her toes to see what I would say.

"No." I shook my head. "It's not that."

"You have to admit, though, she's gotten a little conceited," said Carreyn. Amy looked back at her toes.

"It's something else," I said. "I don't know. I just wish she'd talk about it. She's like totally ignoring me."

"Selfish?" asked Carreyn. "You must think she's being selfish, right?" She nodded.

"I don't know. Not really."

"Not at all?" Carreyn asked.

"Well, I guess a little." I sighed. "But I think it's more like she's confused. Like she's trying to be someone else but has no idea who. I think her parents' divorce has really messed her up. And Bodie, he's someone she can cling to."

"So you're saying she's clingy?" asked Carreyn.

"Static clingy." I shook my head. "This isn't the Jen I know."

"Maybe Body Snatchers got her and turned her into a zombie?" Carreyn asked with big eyes.

"Invasion of the *Bodie* snatchers!" Amy added. We all laughed—Amy laughed so hard Diet Coke came out her nose. She pinched the tip—"Burning, burning"—and then wiped it over and over with the back of her hand.

"Well maybe, in a way, that *is* kinda what happened," I said, reaching for another cookie. "I think she hooked up with Bodie at that pool party and now it's like she can't think for herself."

"No way? They *hooked up* hooked up?" asked Carreyn. "They weren't even together then. You think she's become a slut?" She shoved a fistful of popcorn into her mouth.

"I hope not," I said. "But she's definitely been really different since that party. I don't know . . . I'm not sure I really trust Bodie. I know he's supposed to be a great guy and all. But what if he's just using Jen? He's definitely the kind of guy who can get away with that."

"*What?!*" a voice screamed from under Amy's bed.

Oh my God. What was that? I sat straight up. I looked from

Amy to Carreyn and then down at the floor. What the . . . ?
Jen was scrambling out from underneath the bed like an angry
crab.

"You think I'm messed up and clingy?!" she yelled at me,
red-faced and spitting mad.

"What?" I looked at her and then quickly at Amy and Carreyn again. I sat up on my knees. "No!" I said, breaking into a
fresh sweat. "I didn't say that! I just—"

"And that Bodie's just *using* me?!"

"No! Jen, what are— Why are you—"

And then I stopped.

I was having this long, slow, horrible realization. My pulse
pounded in my ears. I looked from Jen to Amy to Carreyn. And
then I lost it.

"Oh my God. I can't believe you guys!" I felt a huge lump in
my throat. "I can't believe you!" I jumped off the bed. "What
is your problem?! God, you're supposed to be my *friends!*" I
stood there in the middle of Amy's bedroom. And no one said
a word.

Then Carreyn started to laugh. "Come on, Pais. We're just
kidding. Whatever."

"Whatever?!" I screamed and threw a cookie at the wall as
hard as I could.

Jen just glared at me, blinking away tears. Amy wouldn't even
look at me.

I so didn't want to—I willed myself not to—but I totally
started to cry. My best friends had set me up. There was nothing

left to say. I threw open Amy's bedroom door so hard it smashed against her dresser. I ran down the hall and out the front door. Then I jumped on my bike and pedaled as hard as I could.

I was crushed. And then I was mad. And then I was totally crushed. And then I was unbelievably, raging mad. Was that all Jen's idea? Or did Carreyn plan it to get on Jen's good side so she'd be totally in with her and I'd be totally out? And why did Amy go along with it? I replayed the conversation in my head, and then burst into tears all over again.

I was pedaling so furiously with my head down and crying like the Bionic pissed-off Woman that I didn't even see the storm drain. Before I knew what was happening, my bike suddenly stopped cold. I went flying over the handlebars, doing this perfect slow-mo backflip for, like, ever.

Thud.

I landed really hard on the pavement and skidded to a stop on my shoulder just off the road. I blinked my eyes a few times. I couldn't move. I couldn't breathe. Was I dead? No, unfortunately. I lay there on the hot dirt sputtering, gasping for air, waiting for my lungs to come unpuckered. And I had this rich flash fantasy of Jen and Amy and Carreyn sobbing at my standing-room-only funeral and feeling beyond horribly guilty for the rest of their miserable lives.

No such luck. My lungs came unglued. I sucked in air. And I finally caught my breath. It smelled nasty over here, like some animal had been hit by a car and was decomposing in the dry grass a few feet away.

I stood up slowly. Ow. And brushed some of the dust and gravel off. Ow. My back hurt, my shoulder hurt. And my bare feet were burning up! Ow! Ow! Ow! I hopped from foot to foot trying to pull my bike out of the storm drain. I finally wrestled it free. But the front wheel was totally mangled and bent. And the tire was flat. I had to make a run for some shaded dirt under a big bush. I hopped from foot to foot in the tiny patch of shade. Why why WHY did I leave my shoes and phone at Amy's house? I ran back to my bike, picked it up, and started the wobbly push toward the shade of a pathetic little tree. Ow. Ow! OW! I spotted a mailbox down on the other side of the road and ran for it.

By the time I hopped and hobbled to the top of the drive-way, I felt like I'd been dancing on red-hot coals. The driveway opened up into this big flat area in front of a huge modern house. I dropped my bike and sprinted for a tree by the lush green lawn, howling all the way.

I was bent over panting and sweating like a pig when I heard the front door open. I looked up. Oh God. Oh God, no.

Cate Maduro was standing in the doorway.

chapter twelve

There she was, wearing flip-flops, sweatpants, and a tank top. And looking surprisingly normal.

"What are you doing here?" I blurted out, as if she were barefoot and sweating in *my* driveway.

She casually put one hand on her hip. "I live here. What are you doing here?"

I wiped the sweat out of my eyes and checked the soles of my feet for blisters. "Can I use your phone?" I asked.

Cate looked at me like I was insane.

"Please?"

She followed the you're-insane look with one of her you-pathetic-loser head shakes.

"Never mind." I turned around and tiptoed to the edge of the lawn psyching myself up for my red-hot coal dance, take two.

"Wait."

I turned around. She pointed to my shoulder. "You're all bloody," she said.

I looked over my right shoulder. Blood had seeped through my white T-shirt. It looked kind of like the shape of a pork chop. "Yeah, I wiped out in a storm drain and flipped over the handlebars."

"Really? I always wanted to see someone do that." She stepped back inside and waved me toward the door. "Come on."

I left my crippled bike on the lawn and followed her into the house. "Wow." I stared up, gaping at this giant wall of glass. The living room dropped down a few steps and there was a round fireplace suspended from the ceiling in the middle of the room. "This house is intense. It's like something you'd see in a magazine."

"What, did you think I lived in a double-wide?"

"No. I . . . I just, I don't know." I followed her into the kitchen. It was huge and spotless. I decided to keep my mouth shut.

She handed me the phone and watched me call my mom's cell. I left a message with the address. "She's probably still at Yogilates. It's her new thing."

Cate leaned back against their big stainless steel Sub-Zero fridge and crossed her arms. We stared at each other. This was bad. I looked away.

"It won't be long," I sputtered like an idiot. "I hope."

It was really bad, beyond awkward bad. And then the strangest thing happened.

We both started laughing.

A little at first, and then more, and soon we were both bent over with these big sloppy rolling laughs, the kind that make your cheeks hurt and your eyes water. I thought I was going to pee.

Finally, I stopped and sighed. "Do you have a bike I could borrow?"

She burst into hysterics again. "No."

I tried not to laugh. "Are your parents here? Maybe one of them could drive me home?"

"They're at work." She laughed even more. "They just love to work." She slowly stopped laughing.

"Oh." I stood there. It was awkward again. "Should I wait outside?"

She didn't answer. But she did fill a glass with cold water from the fridge door and pushed the glass down the counter in my direction. Then she handed me a wet paper towel folded neatly into quarters.

I reached over my shoulder and carefully blotted my pork chop stain. "Ow."

"Let me see," she said. I tried not to watch as she lifted the bloody T-shirt flap away from my oozing, shredded skin and peeked at it. "Ew," she said, pulling her head back and making this grossed-out face.

"What?"

"It's got gravel in it."

Cate has her very own bathroom and it's extremely cush. She filled the bathtub with a few inches of cold water so I could soak my scorched feet, and then we sat on the side of the tub while she plucked out pieces of gravel with tweezers. I felt a little weird taking my shirt off in front of her, so I held a bath towel to my chest. She acted like it was no big deal. She just sterilized Mr. Tweezerman and went to work like she performed roadkill surgery every day. And it was the weirdest thing . . . I actually told her everything that had happened at Amy's house.

"I never liked those girls," she said like she wasn't the least bit surprised. Plink! She dropped another tiny rock into this mod glass soap dish.

"They're not usually like that. Really. Ow!" I flinched and pulled away.

"Sorry." She gently blotted. "Maybe not to you."

I didn't say anything and tried to remember a time when Jen or Amy or Carreyn had even talked to Cate Maduro. I couldn't think of anything, but maybe I hadn't been with them. Were my friends all turning into a bunch of mean girls? Or had they always been like that and I never noticed? Was *I* like that?

I wanted to ask Cate, but I didn't have the guts. And besides, she had pointy tweezers in her hand, and I was half-naked.

"Popularity is poison," she said. Plink!

"Come on, you wouldn't say that if you were popular." Whoops. That just slipped out. But Cate surprised me.

"I wouldn't *want* to be popular at Pleasant Hell," she said.

I was quiet. Was she just saying that because she was bitter? Or was she for real? I stared at my puffy pink feet in the water. Wait. Was *I* for real? I had been doing so many bizarre things over the last couple days because of Jen. Trying to avoid her, trying to act like everything was fine, trying to act like I didn't care or miss her when I did and I do. And Jen was doing bizarre things so Bodie would like her more. And Carreyn was trying to be just like Jen so any guy would like her at all. And Amy was just going along with it all. Were *any* of us for real?

Cate spread a glob of antibiotic ointment over my scrape. "Muy gooey, chica!" We both laughed. It was one of the dumb things she used to say in Spanish class, and it turned into one of those all-purpose sayings that could mean anything we wanted it to, depending on how you said it. I had forgotten about that.

Then she taped a big square gauze thingie over it. "Here. You can have these." She handed me the box of gauze squares. "I haven't used them since I got my scorpion tattoo last year." Scorpion tattoo? Oh, right. I'd almost forgotten that she was the McNasty who loved to sting me. It's amazing how different people can be away from school. "Did you know that some scorpion species reproduce without mating?"

"Nope." I shook my head. "How . . . convenient."

"Wanna stay for dinner? LG is coming over. I rented *Heathers*."

Whoa. I couldn't believe she'd just asked me to stay for dinner. "You're good friends with LG Wong?"

I heard my mom's car honk outside.

"Yeah. She's nothing like she seems at school. LG's got the best goody-goody schoolgirl act of anyone I know."

Schoolgirl act? "I can't tonight. We're . . . " What? What were we doing? "We're having a family dinner. My brother's home from college." Why did I just lie?

My mom honked again. I turned and hobbled toward the front door.

"Here." She kicked off her flip-flops. "Wear these."

"Really? Thanks." I slipped them on. "And thanks for the clean shirt and, you know, everything."

She nodded. "See ya." She almost looked sad.

I think we were both wondering the exact same thing as I got into the car. What would it be like on Monday when we saw each other? Would we be any different? Or would we act the same as always, like we had absolutely nothing in common? One girl pretending she hated everyone, and the other girl pretending she liked everyone. Just because that's what everyone expected.

chapter thirteen

When I got home, I went up to my room and closed the door even though I knew my mom was dying to interrogate me and squeeze out every juicy detail of my tragic day. Dyson was curled up on my laptop as usual. I picked him up, carried him over to the bed and snuggled with him, feeling like he was the only friend in the world that I could trust.

Why is it that someone like Cate would be so much nicer to me than my own quote-unquote friends?

I listened to Dyson's power-purr and tried to make sense of what had happened at Amy's. What could Jen have said to them to make them do that to me? I was convinced now that it *had* to have come down from Jen. But why?

I must have fallen into a deep emotional coma, because I woke up in my clothes on Sunday morning. My shoulder ached like crazy. And then a wave of dread swept over me as it all came flooding back. I wasn't getting up today. No way. Finally around 1:00, my mom knocked gently on my door.

"Hey, can I come in?" she asked. "I brought you waffles since you were sound asleep by dinnertime last night."

Okay, that was so not fair. I love waffles.

"Thanks." I sat up in bed, and Mom propped me up with a few pillows. Then I started inhaling my waffles.

Mom hovered at the foot of my bed and watched me eat. "Pais, what's wrong?"

"Nothing."

She just looked at me. Why can they just stare at you and make you break? What is that?

"Jen hates me," I blurted. My mouth was full, but the floodgates had opened. I gave my mom the short but full-strength-agonizing version of the story.

"Oh, honey, she doesn't hate you. She's going through a difficult, painful time now. Scoot over." She sat down next to me on the bed and gave me a big hug, and I actually let her.

"It was awful, Mom," I said into her shoulder.

"Honey, there are so many things in life that you can't control, like what other people do, or say, or feel," she said, stroking my hair. "All you can do is try to control how *you* feel about it."

"Well, I'm mad!"

"I know you are. I don't blame you. And I'm not saying that you shouldn't feel your feelings. But Jen may not be able to handle all of your anger and disappointment right now. I'll bet she really needs you to be a friend."

"I've tried to be her friend!"

"Hey, why don't you write her a letter, a letter that you're never going to send, where you get to express all of your feelings—your anger, hurt, frustration, jealousy, disappointment, whatever. I guarantee that you'll feel much better. It always works for me."

"Mom, I'm not jealous."

"Okay. I was just making suggestions."

I figured it couldn't hurt.

Dear Jen,

Let me introduce myself since you may not remember me. My name is Paisley Hanover. I'm your friggin' best friend for the past five years!!! Remember? What is going on with you?! God, you just seem like a totally different person these days. And can I just say, the new you is NOT an improvement. You're selfish, you're insecure, you're nasty, you're fake, and you're obviously pretending to be someone you're not just because of Bodie and your new wanna-be "fab" friends. Gag! Barf! Puke in a purse! What happened at that pool party?! And who am *I* supposed to talk to now? We used to

I wasn't even finished venting and I was already feeling so much better. When I came back from the bathroom, Dyson was settling down on my laptop again. "You crazy kitty," I said in my cat voice as I lifted him off the keypad.

I sat down, ready to finish my vicious letter, and stared at an empty screen. OMG. It was gone! I clicked around trying to find it. Oh no oh no oh no. I clicked desperately, hoping it was saved as a draft or something. Finally, I clicked SENT MAIL.

Oh no.

Oh crap.

Oh puke in a purse.

chapter fourteen

When I saw her at school the next morning, Jen refused to talk to me, except to say, "I'm not talking to you." She gave me the wave-off and looked the other way. Like I even *wanted* to talk to her. I mean, really—*she* was mad at *me*? Ergh!

"I'm not talking to you either," Carreyn snarled.

I waved, like, see ya, and watched her follow Jen down the hall.

Amy just looked at me like I was an idiot. "Let me get this straight." She hoisted her hands onto her hips. "You wrote a vicious hateful vent letter in an *e-mail* with Jen's address in the To line, and your *cat* accidentally sent it?"

I nodded. Even I had a hard time believing it when she said it like that. But whatever! Amy had gone right along with Jen's nasty plan. I was about to call her out, when—

"How come your cat never e-mails *me*?" she asked.

I wasn't sure if I was allowed to laugh, but I did anyway. So did she. Then she straightened her face. "Obviously, I'm not talking to you *or* your cat." And she stormed off like a soap opera actress, making a goofy face at me over her shoulder. At least Amy wasn't completely bonkers.

I walked into Drama not knowing what to expect from Cate Maduro. I tried to make eye contact with her, but she ignored me. Figures. Just as the bell for third period rang, Bean came rushing over to me with a big smile on her face. She was wearing her Dumbe Blonde T-shirt.

"I got you something at the thrift store."

"You did?"

She handed me a crumpled brown paper bag. I looked inside and pulled out a western-style shirt with this wild faded paisley pattern and square pearl snaps.

"Paisley. Get it?" Bean laughed like a total goofhead.

"Thanks, Bean. I love it." And I meant it.

She smiled even bigger. "It's kinda worn and a little frayed on the edges, but that's what makes it cool."

"Yeah. Thanks." I put it on right over my top. "It fits perfectly."

We sat down next to each other and she started telling me all about her favorite thrift store that you have to take a bus and then walk about ten blocks to get to but it's always worth it. I told her I wanted to check it out. And I meant it.

"Okay people, chairs in a circle. Everybody now!" Mr. E. directed our lumpy blob of chairs into a tight perfect circle. Everyone pretty much sat next to their friends, which meant that I was in between Bean and Charlie.

"This is a concentration exercise. And it's one of my favorites. I think you'll quickly see why." As Mr. E. talked, he walked around the circle, pulling a guy out of one chair and making him swap places with a girl on the other side of the circle. He kept doing this until he had completely reorganized our careful seating. I looked around nervously.

"This exercise is designed to challenge your focus, so you'll really have to concentrate not to break character." He reached for my arm and directed me to switch seats with Svend, our one cool, totally pierced foreign exchange student, sitting between Cate Maduro and Clint Bedard. I didn't look at her, so I don't even know if she was still ignoring me. Clint smiled, raising his eyebrows and patting the seat next to him.

"If you maintain your concentration, each of you will get to be the Responder and then the Asker. If you break concentration at any point, you're out of the circle. Okay, here's how it works. The Asker says, 'Smile and tell me that you love me.' The Responder says, 'You know I love you, honey, but I just can't smile.'"

Some people groaned, but a lot of people just giggled nervously. Yes, I was one of the nervous gigglers.

"You must *commit* to the words. You get three chances to ask the other person to smile and three chances to respond—and *not* smile. You can use your body, within reason, whether you're the Asker or the Responder. You can touch the other person in a respectful PG-13 way, as long as it's in line with your objective. Any inappropriate touching"—he looked straight at Clint Bedard—"will get you a fast pass to the vice principal's office. Any questions?"

"Can I go to the nurse? I'm suddenly feeling ill," said Cate Maduro, all sweet and innocent.

More nervous laughter.

"No. Any other questions?"

You could feel the tension in the room expand as everyone realized who was sitting next to them.

"I want to see all of you committing to your objective. Choose a type of love—romantic, grandparent, best friend, teammate—and commit to it. I'll be paying close attention to everyone. And you *will* be graded." He paused. "One other thing. Your performance in this exercise will directly affect who I partner you with for your *Acting Out* scene study."

More groans.

"Okay." Mr. E. spun around the room with his arm pointing out at the circle. He landed on Mandy Mindel. "Mandy, show us how it's done."

Her eyes got really big behind her glasses. She took a deep breath, turned to Teddy Baedeker sitting next to her, and, like a nervous robot, said, "Smile and tell me that you love me."

Teddy Baedeker turned bright red and burst into hysterics.

"Ted, you're out!"

They both looked incredibly relieved.

I watched the tension move around the circle like slow, tortured knots of electric current. People tried different techniques—aloof, flirty, demanding, pleading, sweet, parental—with varying results and varying degrees of blushing, sweating, and uncontrollable nervous laughter. Most people stayed in their own safe physical space, and most people didn't stay in the circle.

And then Bean did something daring.

When it was her turn to be the Asker, she plopped right down in Svend's lap, casually crossed one long, lean leg over the other, and then threw her arms playfully around his neck like she was his girlfriend and did this all the time. "Smile and tell me that you love me," said Bean with total confidence. It worked. Svend was out like that. Then she scooted behind Charlie and started giving him a back rub. He responded and didn't smile. He didn't smile again. And then Bean started massaging up the back of his scalp in an innocent, hair-salon kind of way. His head sort of rolled back a little, his mouth fell open, and his eyes glazed over. When she asked for the third time, her mouth was just inches behind his left ear. He tried to answer, but nothing came out of his mouth.

"I'm out," he said in a high squeaky voice.

It got closer and closer to me. I had no idea what I was going to do except probably make a total fool of myself. Clint Bedard was about to say the love word to me. Guys like Clint Bedard do not say the love word to girls like me. They say the love word to bad girls, girls who smoke and drink, girls with tattoos, smokin' hot bodies, and no curfew.

Clint Bedard turned and faced me. Gulp. He sat back in his chair all relaxed and cocky, and flashed that naughty, flirty grin. "Smile. And tell me that you love me."

I was so nervous it was easy for me not to smile. "You know I love you, honey, but I just can't smile," I flatlined.

He leaned toward me and put on this sweet puppy-dog face, which was funny because he looked anything but sweet. He whimpered like a cute little puppy dog too. "Smile and tell me that you love me." He whimpered again.

I didn't feel at all sorry for him. But he almost got me. Almost. "You know I love you, honey," I said earnestly. "But I just can't smile." I shrugged, feeling this strange surge of energy.

He sat there for a second like he was stumped and then he scooted over. He was practically sitting in my chair. He slowly reached up toward my face. OMG! And stroked the side of my cheek. I felt the hairs on the back of my neck stand straight up. And I could feel myself turning bright red. A few people laughed and hooted. He reached up and ran his fingers down the side of my neck and down my necklace to my collarbone. More people hooted. My heart was racing—I could hear it pounding in my ears, but I didn't break concentration.

He looked me in the eyes. "Smile and . . . " He said it like he really, really wanted it. He gently tucked a few strands of my hair behind one ear and leaned into me. I was frozen. He smelled kind of sweaty but good sweaty, almost spicy. And then he whispered, "Tell me that you love me."

I got the chills from his breath in my ear. It shot down my spine and ended up melting in a warm pool somewhere below my belt. Whoa. I looked down at the floor, afraid to say a word. He touched my jaw, gently turning my face toward him so I had to look him straight in the eye. I must have had an out-of-body experience, because I don't even remember saying, "You know I love you, honey, but I just can't smile." All I know is that everyone was cheering and clapping and hooting.

Even Mr. E. was clapping. Clint was out. Wow. Maybe I *could* be good at this. I turned and faced Cate Maduro, actually glad to have anyone else to look at, even her. Concentrate. Concentrate. I pretended that she was my best friend and that my life depended on her smiling.

"Smile and tell me that you love me," I pleaded.

She didn't hesitate. "You know I love you, honey, but I just can't smile," she answered, ice cold.

She had her tough-as-nails thing turned up to full volume. So I figured the nicer I was, the more likely I would be to freak her out and break her. I turned my chair so it was facing hers and reached out for both of her hands and held them, really held them, imagining that I was her favorite grandma. I tried to make my eyes gentle and really loving. "Smile and tell me that you love me," I said.

She pulled away from me and shook her head. "You know I love you, honey, but I just can't smile."

I wasn't sure what to try next. But I was into this exercise and I was determined—determined to make her smile and determined to prove to these people that even a rah-rah like me deserves to be in Drama. Oh, what the hell. She doesn't like me anyway.

I reached out both of my hands and cupped her face like I could almost kiss her. Her skin felt really soft. People started hooting and whistling and making obnoxious catcalls. But I didn't budge. It just made me focus harder. I looked in her eyes, shifting from one to the other, searching for her deepest, darkest secret—that sweet, funny girl who had been so nice to me the other day. Then as plainly and as honestly as I could, I said, "Smile and tell me that you love me."

I saw this flash of fear or something crazy in her eyes. Then it was gone. She blinked a few times. She swallowed hard. Then in this small voice she said, "You know, you know I . . . " Then she pulled back and laughed like she was totally embarrassed. "Damn!"

"Cate, you're out!"

The room erupted with more cheers and claps and way more nervous laughter. Yes! I stood up and took a quick bow, then sat back in my chair feeling this giddy rush.

I was a drama queen rock star! I got her! I totally got her. I dared her to ever mess with me again. Or ignore me. Wow. Was I good at this? Maybe I was. Who knew I could concentrate like that? Who knew I could be weirder than the professional full-time weirdos? Ha! I smiled, thinking no one really knew me—not even me.

I looked around the circle, trying not to smile. And then I looked at Bean. We both cracked up. There were only seven of us left out of over thirty. Bean, five hard-core, weird-ass freaka-zoids, and me—Paisley Hanover, everyone's favorite rah-rah.

chapter fifteen

I was riding high until I realized it was morning break. No way was I going go buddy it up with Carreyn and Amy and Jen—assuming Jen even bothered to show.

So I decided to spend morning break in the library, coming off my Drama high—and staking out my locker. I'd figured last week's note was a fluke since I hadn't gotten another. But then right after Drama, I opened my locker and a *second note* was lying on my bio book. I grabbed it.

HOT 4 YOU!

Seriously, was this a joke?! And if it wasn't, then who? Who? WHO was hot 4 me?! Same handwriting. Same plain notebook paper. I looked around at the emptying hallway. Hmm. One thing was for sure—I wasn't telling Jen about this. No way was I telling her my secrets if she wasn't telling me any of hers. If she wasn't even *talking* to me.

When I got to the library, mostly I watched my locker from a seat by the window, but I also watched Clint Bedard, who was sitting at one of the computers. I know, Clint Bedard? In the *library*? He was slowly hunting and pecking. I wish I had the guts to go over there, sit on his lap, and whisper *Smile and tell me that you love me.* Suddenly he looked up, right at me.

"Red, you spying on me?"

I blushed big-time. Oh, perfect. No one had ever called me Red. I couldn't decide if I loved it or hated it. But my ears must have liked it. I could feel them burning. "No," I answered like it was the dumbest question in the world.

"Think you were." He grinned and raised his eyebrows.

"Think not." I turned away and looked out the window again, praying for my face to unblush immediately. Amy was sitting on our bench, watching Jen and Carreyn practice their cheerleading moves on the grass and looking extremely bored. Carreyn suddenly threw her arms out and popped some kid right in the chin. His smoothie went flying. Amy and Carreyn laughed hysterically while Jen went over and helped wipe down the kid. I smiled, feeling a little sad. That was the Jen I knew. I guess she was still in there somewhere.

"Hey Red? Check this out." Clint waved me over. "You're on YouTube."

I looked at him and rolled my eyes. "Okay."

"I'm serious. You've got your own music video." He smirked. I ignored him. "Says you're a fun of a kind girl, but I guess it's wrong."

"What?!" I ran over to the computer. "Show me!"

Clint hit the REPLAY button. I covered my mouth with my hands and almost had a heart attack. It was ME, well parts of me, doing a spastic jazz hands dance along with—and this was maybe the worst part—*me* doing this mortifyingly bad "Paisley Hanover: *Fun* of a Kind Girl" rap! I dropped into a chair, staring at the computer screen. Then I laid my head slowly on the table.

I knew who'd done it. Eric Sobel. It had to be. He was the only one who'd had a camera in Yearbook. Oh God. He must have videotaped me with his cell phone too. I started softly banging my head against the table. But why? WHY would he do this to me?

"Cool effects." Clint nodded. "The editing really pulls it together."

I lifted my head and glared at him.

"Wanna see it again?"

"No," I said coldly. Why had I wasted a single thought on Eric Sobel?

Of course I saw it again basically everywhere I went. Walking down the hall, Cate Maduro didn't waste a moment. "Hi, Paisley!" She jumped out and spastic jazzed me. "You crazy *fun* of a kind girl!" she said with a wink as she walked past.

Mr. Yamaguchi spastic jazzed our whole class when he announced a pop quiz in American History. Ugh. He was one of those teachers who tried so hard to be cool. I was embarrassed, but I was totally embarrassed for *him*.

At soccer practice, the whole defensive line spastic jazzed me when I was dribbling toward the goal. I ignored them, kept dribbling, and blasted the ball into the back of the net.

After practice, I ran a few extra laps. I didn't want to have to talk to Amy—about Jen or jazz hands or anything.

I was lost in my head space thinking about this stuff. Then I caught sight of Eric Sobel out of the corner of my eye. He ran halfway onto the girls' field, chasing a ball. When he saw me, he smiled and did his head-nod thing. Unbelievable. What a buttcap. I didn't smile back. I didn't wave. I didn't nod. I just kept running.

What did he expect?

chapter sixteen

When I walked past Jen the next day at morning break, she didn't say a word. She just stared at me as I walked by, then suddenly spastic jazzed me with this freaky-meanie smile, and then sunk into the splits. Jen was no Favorite Friend of mine either. But I wasn't going to let her know. So I served it right back to her.

"Hi, Jen!" I spastic jazzed her with a big, crap-eating smile. "You ready for cheerleading tryouts today?" I called cheerfully as I walked by. Carreyn and Amy were coming up from the other direction and— What?! I stopped dead, staring. "Oh my God, Carreyn! What happened?" I ran over to them.

The one—maybe the only—good thing about being in a fight with Jen was that I didn't have to deal with *cheerleading*. Jen and Carreyn were so caught up in their fantasy of impending fabulosity that it was dangerous to be anywhere near them— unless you liked getting backhanded in the face or your phone kicked out of your hand.

But this? I didn't even know what to say. The whole cheer- leading thing had fried Carreyn's brain, and the evidence was right here. Carreyn looked—she looked . . . Well, she looked like a giant baked bean. What, had she slept all night in a tanning bed?

"She's been hiding in the bathroom all morning," said Amy. "Give her a break."

"What happened?" Jen asked, genuinely concerned. That was refreshing at least.

Turns out, Carreyn knew it was a stretch (ha-ha) for her to make cheerleader, even JV. So she came up with a secret weapon—body bronzing foam. The night before, she'd applied smooth, long strokes of foam all over her taut little bod, once, maybe twice, okay, three times—just to be sure. She was convinced that her body, bronzed to perfection, would make her stand out to the judges.

Cut to this morning: Surprise! Total disaster. She even pretended to be sick so she wouldn't have to come to school, but her mom forced her.

So now she was sort of standing behind Amy, with her permed hair brushed forward to cover her face. She was wearing a longsleeve turtleneck and jeans.

"Aren't you hot?" I asked, rubbing her back.

Carreyn just turned and glared at me, then looked around furtively. "I'm going back to the bathroom," she whispered, and took off through the crowd, head down.

Okay, so maybe that didn't help.

When the bell rang for lunch, Carreyn was still holed up in the handicapped stall, refusing to come out, much less try out. She texted Amy asking for a burrito, and then Amy texted me:

Crryn stl in toilet. Hlp! Pls?

I knocked on the bathroom door, and guess who opened it? Jen. I didn't want to be in the same room with her, much less in the same handicapped *bathroom*. But I wasn't some nasty sasshole, so I put my feelings temporarily on ice.

"But Carreyn, you've worked so hard. You have to," Amy was saying.

Silence.

I walked over. "You've learned all the moves," I tried, not knowing what else to say. "And . . . and you *rock!*" I looked from Amy to Jen, and shrugged. God, what was I supposed to say? Jen didn't have to stare at me like that.

"Carreyn, the Hornettes need you," said Jen. "They need your confidence and your school spirit, and your smile."

"Really?" Carreyn asked feebly.

"Really!" we answered. Jen looked at her watch. Tryouts started at 12:15.

"I still want to try out, I do. But I . . . I'm a little . . . I really need your support, you guys, okay?" she asked from inside the stall.

"Okay," we all said. Carreyn pushed open the stall door and stepped out like a proud Hornette, her frizzy, permed head held high.

"How do I look?" she asked, smiling uncertainly.

She looked like a giant baked bean covered in toothpaste and wearing a skimpy cheerleading outfit.

"Great!" I said. "You look great! How'd you do that?"

"You can hardly even tell," said Amy, who obviously hadn't been taking Drama.

"What *is* that?" Jen asked, touching Carreyn's skin.

"A little zinc oxide mixed with lotion. I had it in my purse."

"It works." Amy nodded. "It totally works."

"And your hair looks fab," said Jen.

Carreyn beamed.

Whew. Crisis averted. Right?

Wrong.

No one was allowed to watch the tryouts except for the judges and all the girls competing for a spot on the cheerleading squad. But Amy really wanted to see it for some bizzaro reason. I allowed myself to be dragged along—not out of camaraderie, I told myself, but out of morbid curiosity.

Amy and I pulled two empty garbage cans over behind the back of the small gym where the tryouts were happening and tipped them on their sides. We pushed the cans against the wall and climbed up. It smelled a little funky, but we had a perfect view through the open windows.

Carreyn did an awesome job. She kept her wrists straight and her shoulders down and she never stopped smiling. You could tell she believed in herself 115 percent. She didn't make it to the final round, but she sure stood out to the judges.

Jen stood out too. When she stepped into the middle of the gym with the other girls in her group, she was glowing with confidence. Really. Glowing. I rooted for her a little. I mean, what would you do? I didn't want her to *fail*. But oh yuck. Two of the cheerleading judges were her new best girls, BS1 and BS2. I watched distractedly as BS1 demonstrated the series of moves and then strung them together into a short routine.

BS2 punched a button on the sound system, stepped back, and yelled, "Ready? O-kay!" The music blared.

Jen's group started doing the routine, and Jen was doing all of these fabulous cheerleader moves with perfect form—except that they weren't the right ones. She bumped into a girl next to her, who bumped into the girl next to her. They both turned around and scowled at her.

BS2 turned off the music. "Okay. Okay! We'll show you again! *Watch* this time!"

BS1 demonstrated the routine again. "Kick left, step right, hips, punch it left, kick right, turn, low V, shake it, shimmy, turn, daggers, spastic jazz left, snap it, clean it up, spastic jazz right, snap it, clean it up, and splits!"

Wait. What?! Spastic jazz?!

Jen looked around, confused.

"Spastic jazz?!" I gasped out loud. "Oh my God! I can't believe . . . they *stole my move!*"

"I thought you hated that," said Amy.

"I did! I *do*. But still, they shouldn't steal my embarrassing move for their stupid cheerleading routine!"

The music blared again. Jen's group began the routine. At first she seemed to be okay. But then she started screwing up. And the more she screwed up, the worse it got, until you could tell she was totally freaked.

Amy and I looked at each other. What was up with Jen?

She was looking to the left and looking to the right, trying to get back in step. But I could see she was losing it. And then when I was finally like, Oh my God, I can't watch, Jen just stopped. She stood there, glaring at the judges' table. The music blared on around her. Her face was bright red. A couple girls bumped into her and shot her dirty looks. Finally, she took a few steps toward the judges' table and yelled something. She threw her hands down, then turned and ran out the back door of the gym.

Amy and I looked at each other, then ran around to the front of the gym to find her.

"Jen!" I yelled. She was running toward the playing fields. "Wait!"

She finally stopped and sat down in the middle of the field, her shoulders shaking. Amy and I caught up. And suddenly, I realized I didn't even know what to say to her. "Are you okay?" I asked lamely.

She glared at me. "No! God, I'm such an idiot!" She was crying, but she was more pissed than anything. "How could I have been so *stupid?*"

"What do you mean? I thought you looked really good," said Amy, trying to be positive.

Jen didn't even hear her. "They set me up. They *set me up!* Those skinny little brats taught me the wrong routine—on purpose!"

OMG. "But . . . That's so . . . Why would they do that?" I honestly didn't get why they would turn on her.

"What, are they jealous?" Amy asked.

"They're not jealous. They're *vicious,*" Jen spat. "Candy's dying to get back together with Bodie. It's so obvious." She scrubbed the tears off her cheeks with the back of a hand. "She calls him and texts and hangs on him all the time when I'm not around and—and—and I'm gonna kill them. I'm gonna kill them!" Then she balled up her fists and sort of punched the ground, turning bright red again. It was scary.

Amy and I looked at each other.

Then suddenly Jen got all calm and Zen.

Carreyn ran up to us, panting. "What happened? What happened?!"

We all ignored her. "No." Jen exhaled slowly and softly. "Blowing roses. Blowing roses. That's exactly what they want. Bodie can't stand jealous girl drama." Jen smiled serenely. "Somehow, I've got to get *Bodie* to do it."

Jen had totally lost it. And I guess the expression on my face must have said as much. Because Jen looked at me and like, *exploded.*

"What? *What?!* God, you are so . . . " Jen scrambled to her feet. Her face was red and wet and all twisted up. "Just get away from me, Paisley! Go *away!* You're always telling me how I'm doing it wrong. You're always trying to make me feel like crap! I'm sick of it! I'm sick of you!" She looked from me to Amy to Carreyn, who were standing there totally stunned. And then she took off.

I was shocked. I felt this electric current like zap through me and make my head prickle. I looked at Amy and Carreyn. "Where did that come from?" I asked no one in particular.

"Where do you *think?*" Carreyn snapped.

I really didn't know. And frankly, I was starting not to care.

chapter seventeen

There was a lot of avoiding going on that week. I was avoiding evil YouTuber Eric Sobel. Jen and Carreyn were avoiding me. Jen was also avoiding BS1 and BS2 and all of the other McNasty Poms. And, the big news—Bodie was avoiding Jen, and had been for a few days. Amy's cat sent me a text telling me all about it. Jen was totally freaking because she didn't know why. He said it was just because of the football game that night against our biggest rivals, the Cougars. But Jen wasn't so sure and she was getting all insecure and worried that Bodie was about to dump her.

Today was Friday and the first home football game and the first of the Pleasant Hill High insane pregame rallies, where the entire student body crammed into the gym and cheered like some crazy cult.

I spent lunch in the library, as I had for the last three days, trying not to get all pathetic about having to go to the rally by myself. Our rallies are not the kind of thing you want to endure alone.

I waited outside the gym for as long as possible, and even

thought about hiding behind the portable classrooms and not going at all. But I didn't want to get in trouble. I admit it. God, I hated being such a goody-goody.

Mr. Canfield, our vice principal, was closing the doors to the gym and pointed at me. "Hurry up, Paisley. You don't want to miss this."

Actually, I did.

Inside, the gym was a mob scene. The bleachers were packed with kids wearing black and yellow, and the band was already playing a sloppy version of "We Are the Champions." I looked around for someone I knew—anyone. Behind the band, a small group of anti-establishmentors were wearing Dumbe Blonde T-shirts. I so wished I had the guts to go sit with them and be a screaming, arts-loving activist. But so far, I'd only had guts enough to wear my Dumbe Blonde T-shirt to bed. How terribly lame.

The Dumbe Blondes were completely ignored by the popular kids in our class who were all huddled in one section of the bleachers, rocking together left and then right, in time—kind of—to the music. Jen, Amy, and Carreyn were right in the middle of them, which was kind of weird considering Jen's nightmarish cheerleading tryout. I looked around again. I had no idea where to go. I started to panic.

And then I saw Bean and Cate Maduro and some of the other kids from Drama sitting over to one side. Bean waved in my direction, so I headed toward them. All I knew was that I didn't want to be standing on the gym floor when the Ho'nettes paraded out. I was cutting across the gym floor when someone suddenly grabbed my hand.

"Come on, Red. We're gonna get trampled by cheerleaders!" Clint pulled me over to the bleachers and carved a path up to where Bean and Cate were sitting. "Little room, please!" He wedged in next to Cate, who sort of looked at me and nodded, and I squeezed in just as the action started.

"And now, give it up for Pleasant Hill High's award-winning Spirit Squad!" a voice boomed over the loud speakers.

"Do they give awards for drinking spirits now?" Cate asked, all doe-eyed and dopey. "Hurray?" I watched them all laugh.

The band started playing another off-tempo song and the baton twirlers high-kicked their way out into the middle of the floor wearing basically sequin-covered bathing suits. Everyone went wild, screaming and whistling.

"Nice butt-cheek action." Bean whistled like a guy. "Hello! Welcome to wedgies!" she shouted all counter-girl cheerful. We all laughed.

Clint flashed his bad-boy grin. "Can it ever be wrong to rock in a thong?" Then he yelled at the twirlers, "Be sure to butt-floss after every meal!"

"Ew!"

"Gross!"

"That's disgusting!"

We all cracked up.

The Spirit Squad did their routine with only two baton

drops, so they seemed pretty happy. I looked for Jen and Amy and Carreyn, but I couldn't see them from where I was sitting. I wondered if they even missed me, if they even noticed I wasn't sitting with them. And then I realized something. I didn't care. I was squished in between Clint Bedard and Cate Maduro, and I was fine. Actually, I was feeling even better than fine.

Then the Ho'nettes trotted out all bouncing with energy and holding their huge poofy pom-poms high. They stood in formation in the middle of the gym floor, dropped their heads, and froze. The whole gym fell silent. BS1 and BS2 were front and center. Then the band launched into a jazzy, semi-sultry tune, and one by one, the Hornettes came to life with electric smiles as if each of them had been poked by a cattle prod.

Everyone screamed. *Everyone.* It was insane. Cate Maduro did a fake school spirit shriek, pretending to be a lunatic like everyone else. She and Bean and LG Wong kept bursting into hysterics. Clint whistled, and it practically burst my eardrum. Then Bean tapped me on the shoulder and did this crazy teen girl scream and pretended to faint from excitement. I was laughing, this giddy, goofy feeling about to overwhelm me. But then I made myself stop because I didn't want to pee right there next to Clint Bedard.

We all started swaying to the right and swaying to the left with the music. Even though we were sort of making fun of the whole scene, we were having a great time. It had never occurred to me before that this was everyone's school, and everyone's band, and everyone's football team, and that the unpopular kids rooted for the same team as the popular kids, even if their school spirit was spiked with irony.

"Hey!" Bean smacked me in the shoulder. "That's *your* move. Cool!"

The Hornettes were doing spastic jazz hands as they kicked around in a circle and crumpled into a bud of butts. Everybody cheered.

I wanted to feel pissed, but I was kind of amazed. My weirdest, most embarrassing moment of high school life had been incorporated into Pleasant Hill High pop culture. I didn't know what to think of that.

The loudspeaker crackled and popped. "And now it's time to meet the men we're all cheering for, Pleasant Hill High's varsity squad!"

The bleachers erupted in cheers and screams and squeals as the guys ran out of the locker room wearing their jerseys and ran around the gym until they had circled the floor a few times. Most of the guys on the team seemed totally pumped, but Eric Sobel looked mortified to be out there. I almost felt bad for him. Almost.

When Coach Cave started introducing the first-string players by name, Clint leaned over and whispered, "Going to the game?"

His breath on my ear gave me that same strange tingly feeling up and down my spine. I pulled back, a little startled, and nodded.

He leaned in and whispered again, "Going to the dance?"

I pulled away again and looked at him. Was he *trying* to do this to me? Could he *tell* he was doing this to me? I nodded again. *Why* was he doing this to me?

Then he whispered, "Good. Dance with me." He flashed his flirty bad-boy grin.

Oh God. My face went red, and I quickly turned away, staring down at the far end of the gym. I don't know if his lip really touched my ear or if I just imagined it. But it sure seemed like it did. And if his lip really did touch my ear, did he do it on purpose or did it just happen because maybe the guy next to him leaned to the left and pushed him a little? I pretended to be extremely interested in the names of all our linebackers. Next time I looked over at Clint, he was gone, threading his way through the bleachers and out the door.

I turned back to watch the players, but I wasn't watching at all. I was thinking about Clint Bedard. Oh God, why was I thinking about Clint Bedard? He was a total flirt. He probably would've asked Mandy Mindel the same thing if she had been sitting next to him.

I tried to concentrate on Coach Cave's raspy voice. "Number thirty-seven, star wide receiver, Peter Hutchison!" Hutch ran into the middle of the circle, and everyone cheered. "Caught the game-winning catch last season. No pressure, Hutch!" People laughed and hooted. "Number twelve, All-Conference running back two years in a row, the one and only Bodie Jones!"

Bodie took a few steps out into the circle and smiled, a little shy, and then waved. The whole gym went nuts, cheering, and stomping, yelling, "Bodie! Bodie! Bodie!"

Some girl shrieked, "I love you, Bodie!" He got all embarrassed and went back to his spot in the circle. I wondered how Jen must feel sitting there knowing that she had to share him with the entire student body. Or maybe not, if he was still avoiding her.

The rally wrapped up with a "We've got spirit! Yes we do! We've got spirit! How 'bout you?!" cheering competition between the north and south sides of the gym. It was a tie because as Coach Cave said, "There are no losers at Pleasant Hill High!"

Ha. That was a good one.

Everyone cleared out of the bleachers and spilled into the courtyard next to the gym, mingling in their little groups. I wasn't sure where to go, so I stayed with Cate and Bean.

"That was scary," said Cate, holding her head. "I've got to get deprogrammed immediately before I do something insane like go to a football game."

"Hey Paisley, we're going thrifting this afternoon. Wanna come?" asked Bean.

"I can't. I've got soccer."

"Oh right, go team!" Cate made a fist and punched the air.

"Maybe next time," I said, and meant it.

"Right," said Cate, not sounding all that convinced, but looking like maybe she could be.

"Pains me! Show me some love!" Before I saw him coming, Hutch had picked me up off the ground and was spinning me around.

"Put me down! Put me down!"

"You're no fun," he said, setting me on the ground and pretending to mope.

I looked around for Cate and Bean, but they were already gone.

chapter eighteen

By the time the game rolled around, Jen still wasn't
talking to me, and every time I saw Carreyn, she would fling
these weird verbal darts at me. Bizarre stuff like, "Betrayal is a
cruel, cruel friend," as if she was quoting off the back of a trashy
romance novel.

Amy kept her distance, but at least she was sill making goofy
faces at me from afar.

The Dumbe Blondes were sitting together at one end of
the bleachers cheering like maniacs and holding signs like
GO TEEM GO! and HOMERUN! and GO FOR THE
GOLE!

I sat with Bean and Charlie Dodd. It was a really close
game—Bodie scored two touchdowns, Hutch caught a bunch of
passes, and Eric Sobel kicked the winning field goal, which totally
depressed me because now every girl in school would be crushing
on him—as much as I hated to admit that I even cared.

After the game, tons of people were hanging out in front
of the gym, waiting to get into the dance. I was standing there
goofing with Bean and Charlie when Amy walked up, dragging
Carreyn behind her.

"Hey," Amy said to Bean and Charlie, giving me a wacko smile.

"Hey," Bean said back. Carreyn looked totally uncomfortable, like there were at least a million other places she'd rather be.

And then Charlie said, "Hi, Carreyn. Are you going to the dance?"

"Maybe," she said, trying not to smile. Then she whipped her head around and squinted at me. "Paisley, why was *the bottle-rocket bomber* holding your hand at the rally?"

"Clint Bedard?" Charlie asked. "You were holding hands with Clint Bedard?"

I shrugged and smiled. "I wasn't holding hands with him exactly. He's just a guy I know from Drama class."

"He's kinda hot," Amy said.

"He is," said Bean.

"He is," I agreed.

Charlie rolled his eyes. Carreyn looked at us like we'd taken a big hit of helium and were speaking some strange foreign language.

Just then, Jen came running up. "Hey guys!" she said to Carreyn and Amy, giving Bean and Charlie a bizarre look. She grabbed my arm and pulled me away from the pack.

Oh, sure, Jen, just act like everything's fine, like you haven't been giving me the icy elbow all week.

"Look, I know this is going to sound weird," she said, "but just roll with me, okay?" So I did. I rolled my *eyes.* "Bodie and some friends are having a little pre-party before the dance out by the baseball field," she whispered. "I don't want to go alone."

No way. Was she serious? Was she asking *me*? She hadn't talked to me in like three days! And *this* was the first thing out of her mouth?! But all I said was, "Gosh, Jen, you don't have to go alone. Why don't you ask your best buds Carreyn and Amy?"

"You know." She hesitated. "The party's not for everyone. It's kind of *exclusive*."

"Oh, really? Well I'm kind of exclusive too. I don't hang out with people who treat me like crap." I stared at her, waiting. I was sick of being in this stupid fight, but I wasn't about to just totally cave.

She looked over at Carreyn and Amy, then back to me. "Sorry, Pais," she said, twisting her hands. For a second, I caught a glimpse of the real Jen. Or was it the *old* Jen? "Pleeease? I really want you to be there," she begged. "We haven't had any real qual time lately."

"Yeah, I wonder why." I shook my head.

Qual time? I started that one. I turned back to the group, still standing there awkwardly and looking everywhere but at each other. "Hey you guys, go ahead and go in. I'll catch up with you." They all looked so relieved. Carreyn and Amy went one way, Charlie and Bean went the other.

"Thanks, Pais. It'll be fun. Come on!"

Jen dragged me down a dark hallway behind the boys' locker

room and back around behind the pool, then out toward the trees near the baseball field. I could hear people talking and laughing, a few loud *Shhhhh*'s, someone reminding everyone to be quiet.

"Who's gonna be there?" I asked, totally unenthusiastically.

"Bodie's group. You know, guys from the team. I'll bet Eric Sobel will be there." She gave me an I-know-you-like-him smile.

Carreyn and Amy must have dished about my big "encounter" with Eric last week in Yearbook. But honestly? Whatever. I refused to crush on someone who'd uploaded that thing on YouTube, no matter how hard it was to *not* crush on him.

Jen stopped a little ways away from the group and pulled some lip gloss out of her purse. "Yeah. And a few junior and senior girls, some BPs, maybe even a few Poms. Here, try this color. It's yummy." She handed me the lip gloss.

Oh, now I got it. I was her backup in case any of the Varsity Poms got ugly with her again. And the worst thing was, I couldn't decide if I felt proud that she'd asked me or pissed, like I was only worth being a friend when she needed something from me. Actually, you know what? I *could* decide. I was pissed.

"Why do you even *want* to hang out with those nasty Poms after what they did to you?" I asked.

"I don't!" She sounded really frustrated. "Look, Paisley, you don't know *everything* about me anymore."

What did *that* mean?

"Sometimes you have to do things . . ." She sighed. "I *don't* like them, but they're Bodie's friends. So if I want to be with him, then I have to put up with them."

I had a bad feeling about this, but we were approaching the group. I couldn't just leave now. I'd look like a noob. Maybe it wouldn't be so bad, I tried to convince myself. Maybe I'd find the guts to confront Eric Sobel . . . or . . . or something.

There were about fifteen guys and girls standing in the shadow of the trees. It was too dark to see who all was there. But I saw a few guys wearing letterman jackets and two or three Ho'nettes, still in their foxy little uniforms. I could hear paper rustling, beer cans opening, guys talking in low voices, and lots of giggling.

"Hi, Jen." It was Bratty Sasshole #1 acting all fake friendly. She turned to me. "Well hello, Paisley Hanover. What a special treat. Hey, how's your brother?"

I was surprised that BS1 was talking to me. And that she even knew my name. "He's good." I sounded a little confused, like I wasn't sure I had a brother or didn't know what good actually meant.

"Your brother's such a cutie," said Bratty Sasshole #2. "I miss him *and* his fake ID. Be sure to tell him I say hi and buy. He'll know what that means." She laughed. I laughed too, even though I had no idea what she was talking about—and didn't want to.

"So," said BS1, sizing me up. "You're hanging with us now, huh?"

I looked at Jen. But I couldn't see her face in the shadows. Some girl handed her a bottle of what looked like peach schnapps. Jen took a sip.

"Tonight I am. I guess."

"By the way," BS1 said, half smiling, "I *loved* your YouTube video."

Was she serious?

"Big loved it," echoed BS2.

All the girls around me erupted in catty laughter. Of course she wasn't serious. What was I thinking?

"Dude! You're up again!" yelled Bodie, tossing a beer to Hutch.

He caught it with one hand, cracked it open, and chugged the whole thing. Then he let out this long disgusting burp. "Ahh. The sweet taste of victory!" The guys cheered and hooted. Then Hutch crushed the can in one hand and threw it out into the field. "Sobel, you're the man! You're the man! That kick was sick!" He picked Eric up in this big bear hug and lifted him off the ground.

"Okay," said Eric. "Thanks, man. Thanks. Enough." Hutch just laughed and dropped him to the ground.

Bodie kept tossing beers to everyone. "Gentlemen, down your beverages. Doors close at ten. And always remember, an empty beer can is an open container, but a crushed beer can is recycling." Everyone laughed.

Some BP girl passed the bottle of peach schnapps to BS1. She took a huge gulp, coughed a little, then passed the bottle to me.

"No thanks. I—" I hesitated for a second. "I'm so stuffed. I ate like two corn dogs at the game." OMG. What a dorkasaurus.

"Oh, you don't drink?" she cooed at me like I was a two-year-old. "That is *so* cute."

Jen looked alarmed. "Be cool," she hissed. "Anyone want a beer?" She walked away toward Bodie and the cooler.

Fortunately Candy Esposito came up to me right then. "Paisley, hey. How's Drama? I still feel really bad about that. I wish we both could've won."

"Drama's pretty fun. Not what I expected at all. How's Yearbook?"

"Kinda boring, actually. And a lot of work." She took a sip of her beer. "And Ms. Madrigal? She's evil. I was late to class a couple of times and she made me stand in a trash can like I was a piece of garbage. Can you believe that?"

"No way!" said BS2 with genuine horror.

"Way." Candy nodded grimly.

"Totally unacceptable," said BS1. "My parents would've so written a letter to get her fired."

"Done," said Candy smugly. "The letter part, at least."

So this is what the cool kids talked about on Friday night. Wow. I shoved both hands into my jeans so no one would be tempted to pass me a beer. Bodie had his arm around Jen and his hand in the back pocket of her tight jeans. I guess he wasn't avoiding her anymore—at least he wasn't avoiding her butt. So much for our qual time. I looked around for Eric Sobel. He had walked off to the side and was watching a couple of rowdy guys reenact the big plays of the game.

What the hell, I decided. I couldn't possibly embarrass myself any more than I already had this week. I took a deep breath and walked over.

"Hey," I said, trying not to squeak.

"Hey."

I waited a few seconds. "How's soccer?"

"Good." He nodded, looking a little uncomfortable. "How's the . . . the listening spot?"

I groaned and laughed, totally embarrassed. "I don't know where that came from. Too many head balls during practice."

He was laughing too, but in a nice sort of way.

"No. It was cool. It was . . . different." He laughed again.

"That's a generous way of describing it." We laughed a little more and then just stood there feeling weird. He took a sip of beer and stared at the ground.

You know, I wanted to ask, *why did you make that stupid video of me?* or maybe *Will you look for me at the dance?* But all I could squeak out was, "Well, great game tonight." Then I started to walk off.

"Hey," he said softly. I turned around.

He looked nervous, and awkwardly jammed his hands into his front pockets. "Look, um. Yours was better. In Yearbook. Your headline."

"What? Really?"

"Really."

"Wait, are you—? You're not just—" I stopped and pulled myself together. "Really?"

"Really." He nodded like he actually meant it. "Really."

"Thanks." I got all shy for a second. And then I got pissed. "Then why'd you post that completely humiliating video of me on YouTube?"

"I . . . I . . . Sorry. I didn't mean . . . It wasn't supposed to be humiliating. I didn't think people would—I didn't think—I didn't think anyone would even see it. It was supposed to be an homage."

A what? I had no idea what *homage* meant, but it sounded pretty good and kind of exotic and even a little bit sexy. So I played along. I'd look it up later. "An homage?"

"Yeah," he said, smiling kinda shy.

I smiled. God, I was such a goober. "Well, all right then. Apology accepted."

"Cool."

He took a few steps toward me, and my heart started to race. Where was this going? He looked down at his feet, then he tried to look into my eyes, but his bangs were in the way, so he flipped his hair and slowly, slowly leaned toward me, tilting his head just a bit. I couldn't move. Our lips were just inches away. OMG. Was this really happening? I closed my eyes and held my breath—

Actually no. It wasn't. It was just another flash fantasy. I admit it. But it was a really, really, really good one. Don't you think?

Okay, so here's what really happened. No, we didn't kiss or anything, but it was still our first beautiful moment together. And guess who ruined it? Candy Esposito. And to be fair, BS1 and BS2. They all came running over, yelling, "Eric! Eric! Can we get your autograph? We just love you! We love you!" They seemed more than a little buzzed.

Eric was so embarrassed, he didn't say a word. He just laughed nervously and took the black Sharpie that Candy was waving at him. Then all three girls lifted their tops enough so we could see their hard, flat, tan stomachs and screamed, "Sign me! Sign me!" What total McSleazy Skankmeisters. They kept giggling in a way that made me embarrassed to be a girl.

Eric took a few steps back, shaking his head.

"Dude, are you crazy?" Hutch pushed Eric back toward the girls. "There are perks that come with playing football, know what I'm saying? And these are three of 'em."

I turned and walked away. I couldn't watch Eric scribbling on their stomachs as they squealed with ecstasy. How could I compete with that? What was I *talking* about? I didn't *want* to compete with that. Fine. So, if that's what he was into, then whatever. No thanks. Even if he did like me—which of course he didn't.

But I couldn't help looking back over my shoulder.

Hutch was jumping up and down next to Candy Esposito holding his shirt up too, flashing his big hairy belly at Eric. "Sign me! Sign me!" he yelled. Eric seemed to have gotten over his discomfort. Now he was just signing away, one tan belly after another. And everyone but me was laughing.

chapter nineteen

Our fun little pre-party wound down fast after that. Most people decided to head over to the dance. I could hear the muffled booming drums and shrill electric guitar in the distance. Jen was walking with Bodie a few feet ahead of me, so I had plenty of qual time to wonder what other ridiculous things she would do or say to keep Bodie happy.

I wanted to kick her in the butt as hard as I could. Lucky for her, Bodie's hand was still wedged in her back pocket. Now that he was back to acting like her butt barnacle, she was back to *ignoring* me! Why did I set myself up for this?

At least Candy Esposito was being nice, and I was trying to be nice to her even though she was all over Eric Sobel, telling funny stories and hanging on his arm. All I could do was stare at him—but not too obviously, I hoped—from a distance and pretend not to care. Twice he smiled back at me over her shoulder like the two of us were in on some Candy Esposito joke. Twice.

Bratty Sasshole #1 and Bratty Sasshole #2 were leading the charge down the hall when BS1 stopped suddenly and reached out both hands to slow the crowd. "Oh my God! Look!" she blurted in a breathy whisper. She pointed ahead into the shadows. "Two NILs holding hands."

I peeked past BS1's head. There were Teddy Baedeker and Mandy Mindel, sitting together on a bench.

Uh-oh.

"Ooooh," gushed BS2. "I just *love* NILs. They're *so* cute."

"*So* cute," echoed Jen, nodding like a brainless bobblehead.

I looked at Jen like she was a total moron. She saw my face and mouthed "What?" all annoyed, like I was the one who had just said something cheerleader idiotic. I shook my head. I wanted to get out of there.

Now Hutch pushed his way up to the front of the group. "Special Ted! What up, dude?" Hutch was obviously drunk. "Hey, is this your new babe?"

Teddy giggled nervously, wiping his palms on his pants. He looked at Mandy, then back to Hutch. "I don't know."

"Wow, she's *pretty*," said some varsity jerk, stroking Mandy's head like a dog. "Woof! Woof!" People laughed. I guess a lot of people were drunk. Or just regular shidiots.

Mandy twisted away from his hand and stared straight at the ground. "Just leave us alone," she whispered. Then she glanced around for a few seconds with those sad, freaky-looking eyes.

"Hutch, let it go, man. Let's go," said Eric.

"Come on, we're just being friendly, dude."

"You think?" said Eric, sounding annoyed. He looked around the group and I swear he was looking right at me when he said,

"Who wants to hit the dance?" He walked off down the hall. I started to follow, but Candy Esposito chased after him and grabbed his hand. I stopped. She was really starting to bring out the homicidal maniac in me.

Hutch yelled out, "Ted and I are buds! Right, bro?" He hung his arm around Teddy's shoulders and leaned into him. "Right, buddy?"

"Right." Teddy nodded.

Just like that, Hutch managed to get Teddy's wallet out of his back pocket. He waved it in the air above Teddy's head.

"Hutch, give it!" Teddy squealed.

"Dude, hope you're packing!" He flipped open the wallet and dug through it. "No way." He paused, looking Teddy in the eye. "Ted, man, you gotta be prepared for some action."

Mandy looked mortified.

"Hutch, come on," Teddy whined.

I couldn't believe this was happening. I was getting that sick, swishy feeling in my stomach. What were we all doing, just standing around watching like it was some kind of spectator sport?

"Hey!" I said to no one in particular. But it came out as a squeak. Jen turned and shot me a nasty glare.

One of the varsity jerks grabbed Mandy's purse and held it in the air. "They in your purse, bald eyes?" He tossed it to Bodie.

"Oh yeah. Bet she's holding! She's a smart girl." Bodie laughed and everyone laughed with him.

"No," cried Mandy. She looked around and caught my eye, then stared right at me.

"Hey! Come on, you guys!" I yelled. BS1 and BS2 turned around, cocked their heads, and stared at me like I was insane. I glared right back. I looked around for Eric Sobel, but didn't see him.

Hutch and all the other idiots started tossing Mandy's purse back and forth while Teddy jumped around between them, yelling, "Give it! Give it!"

Mandy stood there clenching her fists, tears streaming down her cheeks.

"Aw, Mandy, don't get all emo," Hutch taunted. "Your mascara will run. Oh wait! I forgot—you don't have eyelashes!"

Everyone, even Jen, howled at that one. It was disgusting. I started to back away from the group.

"Give it!" Teddy shrieked. "Give it back!"

"You scream like a little girl!" Hutch yelled.

"You're the girl, Hutch!" Teddy yelled back. "You're the one always looking at me in the locker room." He laughed feebly.

"What did you say, you sick freak?!" He took a swing at Teddy, totally missed, and almost fell over.

I kept backing away and backing away. And then I just turned around and took off. I wish I could say I was going to get help, but the truth is, I was just going. When I rounded the corner of the music building, I stopped. But I could hear it all through my breathing. The flap, flap, flap of Teddy's feet as he ran down the hall. Hutch chasing after him, yelling. The other varsity jerks cheering him on. And then an even bigger roar from the crowd as Hutch tackled Teddy, and Teddy squealing like a wounded animal, and the crowd just laughing and cheering.

"Hold his legs! Hold his legs!" some guy yelled. Then more scuffling and shouting. And then the thick heavy thud of Teddy falling hard against the cement.

I peeked around the corner. Teddy lay there in a crumpled pile, moaning while they pulled off his shoes and stripped off his pants.

"Nice skid marks, dude!"

More laughter.

"He shoots, he scores!" Hutch yelled as he did a hook shot and sent Teddy's balled-up pants flying up onto the roof of the covered hallway. I turned away and leaned against the lockers. A wave of nausea rolled over me. I put my hands on my knees. I could feel my pulse in my forehead. The hoots and laughter faded down the hallway. I stood there for a second, bent over, trying to think what to do, listening to Mandy quietly crying, and then I realized that it was Teddy.

So what did I do? I ran. I ran and ran and ran until I had to stop because I couldn't really see. I wiped my eyes and my nose with the back of my hands as I walked through the empty halls, trying to stay out of the light. I didn't even know exactly why I was crying. I ended up on the far side of the parking lot, nowhere near the gym, trying to fight back the urge to throw up.

I found a pole, a cold metal pole, to lean against and tried to look normal, like everything was just fine. But my head was swimming. From a safe distance, I watched people going into the gym in couples and small groups of look-alikes. What happened back there? I didn't want to think about it, but I couldn't stop. I kept replaying it over and over in my mind, trying to make sense of it, but there was no sense. What a bunch of shidiots. What a bunch of cruel morons. How could I have just stood there? How could I be so truly pathetic?

I pulled my cell phone out and called my mom. I was done.

"NQA Shuttle." I sighed. "I need a pickup. I'm at school."

My mom had no idea what I was talking about.

"Mom," I said, "it's me. N-Q-A, remember? The shuttle?"

Nothing.

I sighed, totally frustrated. "Mom, I need a ride home, no questions asked. Yes, right now."

I leaned there, waiting for my ride, absently watching the doors to the gym from across the parking lot. The music sounded pretty good. I so wished I hadn't gone with Jen to that stupid party. It was almost ten o'clock, and the doors were about to close. Just then, a motorcycle pulled up and screeched to stop. A guy and a girl hopped off, laughing as they took off their helmets.

My heart sank.

It was Clint Bedard and Cate Maduro. They danced like crazed teens for a few seconds next to his motor-

SIDEBAR

My parents have a lot of creative parenting ideas, like the Pick-Your-Own-Punishment Plan and the NQA Shuttle. You can call at any time of the day or night if you need a safe ride home for whatever reason. No Questions Asked. Period. Of course, I had never actually called for an NQA Shuttle pickup before. But still, you'd think my mom would have at least *remembered* what I was talking about.

cycle, then ran for the gym. I couldn't help smiling. Their idea of Friday night fun actually seemed fun. I so wished I was running into the dance with them.

Five minutes later, my mom pulled up. I could see Mrs. Merrill, Bean's mom, waving enthusiastically from the passenger seat. Great. Her window was rolled down and she shouted, "Paisley, you rock!" clenching her fist as much as anyone with long nails and a French manicure can. "I just want you to know how much I respect you and your good choices!" She was looking all gushy and weird.

"Thanks, Mrs. Merrill." What was she *talking* about? What good choices?

Before I could get into the car, Mom had jumped out and rushed around the back to hug me. She grabbed me by both shoulders. "Honey, are you all right? Are you hurt?"

"No. I'm fine."

"Have you been drinking?"

"What? No."

She leaned toward me, stared into my eyes, and whispered, "Are you on drugs?"

I rolled my eyes. "Mo-om. No! What happened to no questions asked?"

"Oh, honey. I'm so proud of you." She hugged me again. "And I'm so relieved. Would you mind driving home? I'd feel much better if you did. I really wasn't expecting to be the designated driver tonight."

"Vivienne? She doesn't even have her license."

"She has her permit. Right? You don't mind, Pais, do you, honey?"

Mind? Why would I possibly mind? I mean, why need your parent when you can *be* your parent. I got into the driver's seat and fastened my seat belt. "I thought tonight was book club night," I said, checking my rearview mirror twice, hands at ten and two.

"It is." Mom giggled.

"We're reading Hemingway," said Mrs. Merrill. "Love him. So spare, so masculine. But I always get a raging hangover when I read him." They both dissolved into giggles.

I hit the left turn signal, checked my mirrors again, and inched out into the lane of the parking lot. In case you're wondering, no, this wasn't the first time I'd had to drive, permit or no permit. What a perfect ending to a perfect night—driving my slightly buzzed mom and her friend home.

Mom reached over the backseat and stroked my hair in that the-wine-really-loves-me way. "Pais, what happened tonight?"

"Nothing."

"Nothing that you want to talk about or nothing that you don't want to talk about?"

I didn't answer.

"Did Jen go to the dance?"

I sighed. "N! Q! A!"

"Right, right. NQA, NQA. You let me know if you want to talk, okay?"

Mrs. Merrill wagged her head back and forth. "This is such a beautiful family moment."

Oh God. She looked like she was about to cry.

I turned up the radio. I just wanted to go home and go to sleep, for like the rest of my life.

chapter twenty

I **went straight to bed** and curled up in a tight ball under my comforter. But I kept hearing Teddy's high-pitched shriek. And I couldn't get Mandy's eyes out of my head. She never said a word, but it was like she was asking me to do something. I tossed and turned and tossed and turned, feeling like scum. Like bottom-of-a-Dumpster scum.

I finally got up and flipped open my computer. I started typing. And no, it wasn't hate mail to Jen, for a change.

> Guess what, people? We do have losers at PH
> High. And most of them are wearing football
> jerseys and cheerleading uniforms. Why is it
> so cool to be cruel? Everyone down the social
> food chain gets eaten by the bigger fool and
> everyone else just watches and laughs. Why?
> Why?! WHY?!

I sat back in my chair, read it over, and then deleted it. My bedroom was dark except for the glow from the monitor.

What was I doing? I should just go to sleep. But my brain wouldn't shut off . . .

I got back in bed and opened up my notebook. I stared at the blank page, holding my pen. But I had no idea what to write.

Why *did* everyone try so hard to be popular? Why did we all compete in the brat-race? And why was it so cool to be cruel? Lately, I realized, I liked the *un*popular people at my school a lot more than the popular people. Most of the pops acted like nasty, brainless clones. At least the unpops had the guts to have their own style . . .

Oh, man.

That was it.

I sat up in bed and started scribbling frantically. I was totally on to something. I jumped out of bed and plopped down in front of my computer and started speed-typing. I typed and typed and edited and typed and edited and rewrote and rewrote and rewrote. This was a lot more fun than writing a vicious vent letter that I could never send. My whole body felt charged up. As I read what I had written one more time, I noticed the sky was getting light.

And then I was done.

Should I send it?

I went to the Pleasant Hill High homepage and linked to *The Fly* website. I found the submissions link, then cut and pasted my essay into the window. I sat back and thought for a minute. Then I clicked to the bottom of the page and deleted "Paisley

Hanover" and typed "Miss UnPleasant." I smiled. I hit SUBMIT.

I didn't think anyone would ever read it. And honestly? I didn't care. Just writing it made me feel like I had scored the game-winning goal.

And then I fell right to sleep.

If only I'd known.

chapter twenty-one

On Monday morning, I was so dreading Drama class. I got there early and parked my butt on a windowsill at the far side of the room. I watched the door, but Teddy Baedeker never showed up. Mandy wandered in looking at the floor. She looked different somehow, smaller almost, like all of her pockets were filled with huge, heavy rocks.

I tried to imagine what it was like to be her, to be that shy, or anxious, or freaked out by life or whatever it was every single day. I mean, how did she even make it to school? And then I had this totally unexpected weird feeling. All at once, I suddenly admired her—Mandy Mindel had more guts than anyone in the whole school.

Bean loped over to me. "My mom won't shut up about you," she said. "It's so annoying. I'm afraid she's gonna make us go on a mother-daughter double date!"

I laughed. "That would be so hilarious. Oh my God, wouldn't it?"

"Really?"

"Sure, it'd be fun," I said.

"Okay, I'll tell her." She walked off and I was left with my dark thoughts.

I had to say something to Mandy. So when Mr. Eggertson said, "Partner up, people!" I ran straight for her. She just stood there, not saying a word. Unfortunately, it was a mirror exercise, so it was like looking at my shy, anxious, no-eyelash self.

We stood a couple feet apart, tracing each other's hand and leg movements. Her eyes looked puffy, like she'd been crying a lot. But the more I looked at her up close, the more I was starting to get used to the no-eyelashes part. It was just Mandy. That's who she was. That's how she looked. It was different, but it didn't seem all that weird anymore. I took a deep breath.

"Last Friday . . . " I whispered, and trailed off. She didn't say anything, but her eyes got really intense. "I—I'm so sorry about what happened, Mandy," I finally managed to get out. She focused in on me hard, the skin on her forehead pinching. But she didn't say anything. "And I'm so, so, *so* sorry I didn't do anything to stop it."

She froze. Her eyes started to water. "You should be so, so, *so* sorry," she said, gritting her teeth.

I was stunned.

And then she whispered, "Why?"

I got a big lump in my throat.

"And change partners!" Mr. Eggertson called out.

I don't even remember who my partners were during the next exercises. *Why. Why?* I don't know. Why does anyone do anything? Why does anyone do nothing? I don't know. I don't know!

I slumped down in my chair. Mr. E. was saying something about our big scene study coming up. I couldn't stop thinking about Mandy and Teddy, and how the biggest loser was probably me.

Me. Me. Me. Wait. What?

"Clint and Paisley," Mr. Eggertson said again.

Clint and Paisley. Clint and Paisley. OMG. WHAT?! Scene partners? Clint and *me?*

I tried my best to look cool and at the same time totally bored, like I couldn't care less, like I was even a little disappointed to get stuck with Clint Bedard as my *Acting Out* partner. But working together every day for two weeks? Blocking out an entire scene, staring purposefully into each other's eyes, speaking real words in complete sentences to each other? My heart was pounding in that way you read about in books but never seems to happen in real life. Why was I such an über goober?

I glanced at Bean sitting next to me. She reached up to push her long bangs out of her face and behind her hand shot me this you-are-*so*-totally-lucky look. I tried not to smile.

And then I didn't have to try, because my gaze shifted beyond Bean to Mandy Mindel. I'd totally forgotten about her. She was sitting across the room, rigid, her arms folded across her chest, staring down at her lap. It was like she wanted to squeeze herself into a little dot and disappear.

Mr. Eggertson handed me photocopied pages of the script for our scene. I pulled my eyes away from Mandy and—OMG. It was from *Taming of the Shrew.* Shakespeare. Yikes! I casually looked over at Clint. He was staring right at me with this odd expression on his face, like he was playing around with something sweet in his mouth. Oh God. I quickly looked down at my script.

Shakespeare? Why did Mr. E. have to give us *Shakespeare?*

I hadn't ever read *Taming of the Shrew,* so I had no idea what our scene was about. I speed-scanned it for clues. Okay, I play someone named Kate or Katherine. He plays Pinocchio? No wait, Petruchio and he's, he's . . . No. He's *wooing* me? To be his *wife?!* I suddenly felt a little warm inside.

Mr. E. continued going down the list of partners and passing out their assigned scenes. Some people groaned, some people laughed. I kept reading.

To tell you the truth, I couldn't understand everything, but it seemed pretty intriguing. Something about a wasp and a stinger and . . . a tongue! Whose tongue? Yikes—that's actually a line in the scene! I swallowed hard. The words were making less and less sense as I read. All I could get was I think he's a fool, but he says he's a gentleman, and I . . . I hit him? Then he's . . . Oh. Oh God. He's holding me—trying to *contain my rage.* And then I hit him *again.* I had to stop reading and look away because I was blushing big-time. I gazed out the window in a daze.

It was a lovers' quarrel. I had no idea that Shakespeare could be so exciting.

Thank you, God. Thank you, Mr. E. Thank you, Universe.

Thank you, William Shakespeare. Thank you, Candy Esposito, for getting the last spot in Yearbook.

I took a very slow, very deep breath. The leafy pattern in the tree outside magically morphed into a profile of Clint Bedard. I imagined the two of us onstage performing our scene, wearing fab Elizabethan costumes. Clint spouted something flirtatious and delicious and Shakespeare-ish that somehow I could understand. I smacked him, and he took me in his arms, then I smacked him again, and we kissed while I pretend-struggled to pull away.

"Hell-*ooh*." Bean tapped me on the thigh. "Hell-*ooh*? Earth to Paisley."

"Paisley. Paisley Hanover!"

What. What? Mr. Eggertson was waving a white slip of paper at me. "Your presence is requested in Mr. Canfield's office. Now."

"Ooooh!" The geek chorus hooted and jeered.

"Is somebody getting Canned?" Clint Bedard teased.

"You would know," I shot back all snarky as I calmly gathered up my stuff. "I'll tell Canfield you say hi." I waved to Bean and Cate and walked out the door, as if I got called to the vice principal's office all the time.

I never really got in trouble, so it didn't even occur to me that I could *be* in trouble. If I had stopped to think about it, though, I would have been worried. Way worried.

chapter twenty-two

On the way to Canfield's office, it hit me. Mandy and Teddy. Ergh! How could I be so clueless? But what did Canfield want with *me?* My stomach fizzed nervously.

There's this line of yellow plastic chairs outside Mr. Canfield's office. I sat in the one closest to his door, which was closed. I could hear voices inside but I couldn't hear what they were saying. All I could think of was Mandy sitting in Drama like a clenched fist—and me so caught up in my own head space. I tried to distract myself by reading all of the stuff carved and scratched into the plastic.

I've got a detention headache
Bite me, fish lips
Squeal & Die!
Time to deface the music

And my personal favorite:
SUSPENSION IS FOR BRIDGES
I wrote that one in my notebook.

Of course, I would never deface school property, but who doesn't love a little public self-expression, especially in times of crisis?

After waiting a while longer, my belly went from fizz to gurgle. So I closed my eyes and said a little mantra in my head. *I didn't do anything. I am innocent. I didn't do anything. I am innocent. I didn't do anything.* But then it occurred to me—that was the whole problem. I didn't *do* anything. I didn't do anything wrong, but I didn't do anything right. I definitely didn't do anything to help Mandy and Teddy.

That's it. I was going to tell the truth. Did I really care if Hutch or Jen or any of the other pops or cheerleaders never spoke to me again? So what if Mandy Mindel became my best and only friend, and I ended up going to the prom with her and Teddy Baedeker because no one else would have anything to do with me?

Okay wait. Maybe I did I care. Let me think this through.

I mean, the damage was already done, right? I couldn't turn back time. I couldn't unhurt Mandy's feelings, I couldn't bring back Teddy's pants. If I ratted on Hutch and the other varsity jerks, then I'd just be causing more pain for a lot more people, including me. Right?

Ugh, what a pathetic, disgusting, lame rationalization. I was going to tell the truth. I *had* to tell the truth. Yes. I would definitely tell the truth.

I dropped my head between my knees to stretch out my lower back and get some blood flowing to my brain. That's when I noticed a bright clean copy of *The Fly* under my chair. OMG. It must have just come out! I wonder if they printed my . . . No. That was crazy. I reached for it. But they might have. They could have. What if they . . . No, of course not.

I stared at it for a second. Then I grabbed it and frantically started flipping the pages.

Just then, Mr. Canfield's office door swung open. I popped up out of my seat and dropped *The Fly* on my chair. I brushed invisible fuzz off the front of my jeans.

"Yes sir, I understand," some guy was saying to Canfield. I leaned over a few inches, just far enough to see into his office. OMG. Eric Sobel was standing just inside the door. He pushed his bangs out of his eyes and clenched his jaw muscle a few times. Oh, he's even cuter when he's in trouble. Ugh, I'm so gross.

"You know where honesty comes from, Eric?" asked Mr. Canfield. "Honor. And you've got it. But get it right next time. I don't want to see you in here again."

"Thank you. I will," he answered, throwing his backpack over one shoulder. I leaned against the wall next to the door and held my breath.

Eric stepped through the door, saw me, and paused for a split second. As he passed by, inches from my face, he stared me straight in the eyes and lifted his index finger to his lips. Then he walked out the door.

Wait! What did that mean? Don't say anything? Don't tell the truth? If I did say something, *whisper?* How could he do this to me? I watched him walk away. And no, he didn't look back. Was he really telling me to stay quiet? That had to be it. I couldn't believe it . . . Could Eric Sobel really sink this low?

"Well, well, well, Paisley Hanover," said Mr. Canfield, zapping me back to reality. He welcomed me into his office with a big fish-lipped smile. "I never thought I'd have to call you in for something like this."

I'd never been in Mr. Canfield's office, but I had heard plenty of stories. Over in the corner was the old glass phone booth, affectionately known as the Fink Tank, where he made students who wouldn't cough up a confession sit for hours and "wait for a call from your conscience."

"Sit down and make yourself comfortable." He sat on the front of his desk and leaned back, crossing his arms so his biceps would look as big as possible. Gross. "We might be here for a while," he said.

"Do I need a lawyer?" I chuckled nervously, only half kidding.

"No, Paisley. Just the courage to tell the truth."

"Okay." I smiled, sinking into a chair that was about three inches lower than normal—on purpose, I'm sure. "No problem," I said, crossing my arms over my gurgling belly. I leaned back and jerked suddenly as the chair wobbled. Canfield had probably sawed off half an inch from one of the back legs to keep the presumed guilty off balance, so they'd fink faster.

"Good. Guess who I got a call from this morning."

I don't know. Your conscience? I didn't say it. I should have.

"Mandy Mindel's parents, on speaker phone. And they were not happy," he said.

He waited. I waited. Was I supposed to say something? "Well, it's so hard to be happy these days. I mean, the world is in such a distressed state," I offered.

"Don't get smart with me, young lady. I know you were there Friday night."

I put on my trying-to-remember face while I quickly ran through my options. Lie. Say nothing. Say, "I don't recall," which always seemed to work on Court TV or for people testifying to Congress. Or tell the truth and be iced out for the rest of my life by my so-called friends and the most popular people in school. Miss UnPleasant wouldn't care, but I still did. Much as I hated to admit it.

"Friday night?" I asked vaguely.

"Don't even bother. I've seen every evasion in the book." He pointed his finger in my face. "I know what happened Friday night. I know *everything* that happens on this campus." He leaned into my face, flaring his hairy nostrils.

And then something weird happened. I looked at Canfield's smug, bullying face, and any desire I had to tell the truth went, like, *poof!* I wasn't going to give him the satisfaction.

"Really?" I asked, all pleasant. "Well, then why are you asking me, Mr. Canfield?"

He cocked an eyebrow at me. After a short pause, he said, "You know where honesty comes from, Paisley?"

Jeez! What was that? Page thirty-two from the lame vice principal's handbook? I thought for a second, then looked at him sincerely. "Honor?" I asked.

He looked surprised for a second. Then he walked around his desk, dropped into his chair, and leaned back. The springs squeaked and pinged under his weight. "That's right," he said. "Honor. And if you have any, Paisley, you'll tell me exactly what happened to Mandy Mindel after the football game on Friday night."

"After the game . . . ?" I felt a fizzy wad of nausea rise, remembering Teddy lying there. I willed it down.

"Yes," Canfield said slowly. "After . . . the . . . game." He leaned across his desk, looking at me like I was some kind of mutant life form.

I didn't know what to do, or who to do it for. I only knew I wasn't doing anything for Canfield.

"I don't know what happened to Mandy," I said, looking him in the eye. Even as I said it, I wanted to grab the words out of the air and shove them back in my mouth. But I didn't. "After the game, I started feeling really gross. I think it was the corn dogs. So I called my mom, and she came and picked me up. We drove home and I puked a few times and then I went to bed. I didn't even go to the dance. You can call her if you want." I reached into my bag and offered him my cell phone.

He smacked his big fish lips together and stared hard at me. "So you don't know Mandy Mindel?"

"Sure, I know her from Drama." I calmly uncrossed one leg and crossed the other. The non-breathable vinyl seat cushion was making my butt sweat. "But I didn't see anything. Maybe she's mistaking me for someone else." Sorry Mandy. "She wears glasses, doesn't she?"

"And you don't know anything about an angry mob?

I sat up straight. "An angry mob? At school? What happened?"

Wow. I think I missed my calling as a bad kid. I was really good at this.

Canfield told me that Mandy Mindel's parents had reported the whole ugly incident. But Mandy could only identify two people in the angry mob by name—her secret crush, Eric Sobel, and her new friend from Drama, me. Mandy wasn't wearing her glasses Friday night and apparently, without her glasses, all nasty popular girls and big jocky idiots look pretty much the same. Glasses or no glasses, I tended to agree with her. But Mandy couldn't ID anyone, and Teddy Baedeker wasn't talking. Clearly, he wanted to live.

I sat there, trying to think things through. So Mandy only named Eric and me. Eric had left before things got really nasty. But maybe someone told him what went down? If Eric knew and didn't tell Canfield what really happened, and I did, then Eric would totally know it was me who narced, and he'd probably never talk to me again.

Wait. Did I even *care* if he ever talked to me again? Ugh. *What did Eric say to Canfield?!*

I just shook my head. "The cruelty among teenagers today is shocking." I sighed. At least that part was true.

"You got that right. It spreads like a disease. Makes me want to crush those little maggots with my bare hands." Canfield had this crazy look on his face. "Now even good kids like Eric Sobel are getting sucked into this crap."

Eric Sobel? But he wasn't even *there* when it got ugly. He left. What was going on?

Canfield mashed his fish lips together. "Well, Paisley, I know you've got a lot of friends, so if you hear anything about this incident, anything at all, please let me know."

I nodded, wondering, *did* I have any real friends?

I left Canfield's office with a sour stomach and an aching brain. As I walked down the hall, my crazy vigilante courage wore off. I'd had my chance to stand up for Mandy and Teddy. And I hadn't—again. And why? Because . . . because I couldn't stand Mr. Canfield? Because I had a crush on some shidiot guy? How horribly, hideously lame.

I wandered into the main quad in a daze. It was still third period. No one was there. It was empty and safe. I sat down on the low brick wall around the bronze hornet and dropped my head into my hands. It felt painfully heavy. The sun beat down on me.

Then my phone rang. Unknown caller. I answered it anyway.

"Hello?"

"Hi, this is your conscience calling." It was Eric Sobel. I suddenly felt exhausted.

"I'm not sure I have a conscience anymore."

"What'd you say?"

"I'm not sure I have a conscience anymore."

"No. What'd you say to Canfield?"

"Nothing. I didn't tell him anything."

There was a long silence.

"You sure?"

"Yes, I'm sure."

"Cool. Thanks."

Another silence.

"So." I hesitated. "So what do we do now?"

"Nothing. Don't say anything else. No matter what, okay?"

"Okay. But what did you—"

"Sorry, I gotta go." And he hung up.

I shook my head. I couldn't believe I'd gotten sucked into this. Now I was just as guilty as the rest of them.

chapter twenty-three

The bell rang for morning break and snapped me back to reality. There was no way I wanted to be in the quad when the jocks and pops flooded in. Unfortunately, there was no escaping them, as I was about to find out.

I speed-walked back to sophomore hall. Amy was already parked on our bench, sipping her breakfast—a delicious, nutritious Diet Coke. I waved to her and quickly opened my locker.

I was shoving my books inside just as Carreyn rushed over like last week's stream of verbal darts had never happened. She almost dropped a huge Cindy-Kutcher-boob-sized sticky bun, she was so excited. "Did you hear about Eric Sobel? Suspended for a week!"

A tightly folded note fell to the ground in front of me. Uh-oh. I stepped on it before anyone could see. Wait. What did Carreyn just say? Did I hear that right?

"No way!" Amy exclaimed.

"Way." Carreyn nodded ominously.

I turned around. "Why? For what?" I asked, feeling the blood drain from my face.

"I dunno—yet. It's all very hush-hush. But something defi-

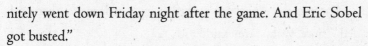

nitely went down Friday night after the game. And Eric Sobel
got busted."

I dropped a pen on purpose so I could bend down to pick up
the pen *and* my latest locker stalker note, which I casually slipped
into the pocket of my hoodie sweatshirt.

It took a second for this Eric news to sink in. Then—oh
no. Oh crap! He must think I squealed! I wasn't sure how I was
supposed to feel about Eric Sobel anymore, but . . . but I knew I
didn't want him to think I'd narced on him to Canfield. I pulled
out my phone.

we nd 2 tlk

I hit SEND, and then I had another horrifying realization. Did
this mean I would be suspended too?! I was telling myself to
stay calm, when I looked up and saw Jen and Bodie walking up
to our bench like they wandered into sophomore hall together
every day. Ergh!

"Hi guys," said Jen all chipper. Amy and Carreyn were ogling
Bodie like he was some kind of rock star. I so wasn't buying it
anymore.

"Hey, Paisley." Bodie nodded, working his smile magic.
"How you doing?"

"Hey, Bodie," I said with a chill. Frankly, I wasn't at all sure
how I was doing, but Bodie wasn't going to charm me with that
smile.

"Hey, can we steal Paisley from you?" Bodie asked Amy and
Carreyn.

"We need some personal qual time," Jen added.

Carreyn and Amy both looked at me a little weird, then nodded. "Sure, yeah," Amy said.

"Come on, Pais." Jen grabbed my hand.

I shook it free. "You know, no thanks, Jen. The last time I fell for that? Not so fun."

"Pais, this is different." She looked at me really seriously. "We just need to ask you something. Two minutes. I promise."

It had better be some sort of apology—maybe for getting me dragged into Canfield's office? Had she heard about that? I nodded reluctantly. "Okay. Two minutes. That's it."

As we walked off, I turned back to Amy and Carreyn and mouthed "Qual time," rolling my eyes.

We headed away from sophomore hall and toward freshman hall. And guess where we ended up? On the exact same bench where Mandy Mindel and Teddy Baedeker had been holding hands. Jen and I sat down while Bodie leaned against the lockers across the hall, watching us.

Jen turned to me and got all serious. "You know you can't say anything to Canfield or anyone, right? Promise me you won't."

"I *didn't* say anything."

"And you won't, right?"

I looked at Bodie. "Why?"

"No reason. I just need to know you won't," she said.

"Someone already did," I pointed out. "I mean, Eric got suspended."

There was a pause. Then Jen and Bodie looked at me like I was some clueless noob and laughed.

"No one narced," Jen finally said.

I must have looked as confused as I felt.

"Eric took the fall. He told Canfield *he* threw Special Ted's pants on the roof, and he wouldn't name anyone else. I thought you knew. God, I love that guy. He's a total stud hero."

Wait. What? "Eric Sobel took the fall? *Eric?* He wasn't even there. He left!"

"I know. Isn't that cool? When he gets back from suspension, I'm going to give him a big kiss."

"Better not, Sweetland." Bodie grabbed her around the waist, and they both laughed. Ha ha ha.

I sat there not even believing this. Why?! Why would he take the blame for those guys? Oh . . . At least that explained the whole finger-to-the-lips thing. Ergh! He was such a moron.

"And you guys think this is okay?"

"What?" Jen asked, pulling away from Bodie. "Yeah, it's better than okay."

"No. No, it's not. It's totally shady."

Jen looked a little concerned. I glanced at Bodie, who had suddenly taken an intense interest in his shoes. I couldn't believe these two.

Jen grabbed my arm. "Paisley, you can't say *anything*. You promised."

"I didn't promise."

"Hey, Red." I looked up. Clint Bedard was striding toward us. "What're you doing out here in Siberia? Missed you at the dance," he said suggestively.

"Hey, Clint." I smiled, pretending everything was fine. He missed me at the dance? "Just having a little private *qual time* with my best girl." I patted Jen on the leg.

Jen gave him a half wave, then shot me a why-are-you-talking-to-*him*? look.

Clint noticed Bodie and stopped. "Hey, Bodie Jones, some game. Two grind-up-the-middle, humiliate-the-defense TDs. Right on." Clint nodded at him.

"Thanks, man," Bodie said, looking surprised. "Didn't realize you were into football."

Jen and I sat there, speechless. People don't normally just walk up to Bodie and start chatting. I loved it.

"You serious, dude? Yeah. It's the last form of sanctioned tribal warfare."

Bodie laughed. "Yeah, I guess."

"See you, partner." Clint pointed at me and walked off down the hall.

My phone buzzed.

listnin spot 6:30 wear ur cleats

Normally this would have made me melt. But now? Argh! I flipped my phone shut.

"Red? Partner?" Jen wrinkled her nose. "Why is the bottle-rocket bomber even talking to you?"

I stood up. I was so ready to get out of there. "We're doing a scene together in Drama, that's why. Is that okay with you?"

"Oh," she said, making this pukey face.

I rolled my eyes. How old was she, like five? Cate Maduro

was right. Popularity *is* poison. It was turning Jen into a mean Bratty Sasshole. "Wait," I said, imitating her brattitude. "Why am I even talking to *you*?" God, I should have just told Canfield everything in the first place, hairy nostrils or not.

"Wait." Jen grabbed my arm. "Where are you going?"

"Canfield's office."

"Paisley, hey! I admit it was really bad judgment. But don't make it worse. I'd appreciate it," Bodie said. He did not look happy.

Jen grabbed my arm again. "Paisley, come on! Show some school spirit. We can't lose Hutch and Bodie and the other guys for the next game."

"School *spirit*?" I pulled away, looking from Jen to Bodie and back to Jen. "Are you Pleasant Hill *high*?"

I turned and walked off down the hall, shaking my head. That was it. I was done with her. I was done with all of them. I was going back to Canfield's office. And I was going to tell the truth.

chapter twenty-four

I burst into Canfield's office without even knocking.

"Good to see you again, Paisley," Mr. Canfield said, hardly looking surprised. "Please, have a seat."

I dropped down into the wobbly Fink Fast chair. Canfield raised his eyebrows, waiting.

I tried to seem composed. "Look, it wasn't Eric Sobel," I blurted. So much for composed. "He wasn't even there Friday night. I mean, he was there but he left. It was Peter Hutchison and some of the other varsity football players."

"Really?" Mr. Canfield leaned back in his chair with a big fish-lipped grin on his face. "I thought you weren't there. Didn't you tell me you and your corn dogs went home early?"

Oh, crap. "Well, I . . . I did. Yes. But that was before I knew Eric Sobel would get suspended for what Hutch did."

Canfield laughed like a barking seal.

"What? I'm serious," I said.

He sat up in his chair and played with a pen, tapping it on the padded corner of the desk blotter. "You'd better be serious— you're making some very serious accusations, Paisley Hanover."

"I realize that. I wouldn't say it if it weren't true."

He leaned back in his chair and put his arm behind his head like he was watching a football game on TV. "Now, if you'd said it was Clint Bedard or rather someone with a history of pants-snatching and other delinquency, no problem. But I have a *very* hard time believing that Peter Hutchison, a fine student, a star player, and a team leader, would be involved in this."

"I *saw* him." I sat up as tall as I could in the Fink Fast chair. "I *saw* Hutch strip off Teddy's pants and throw them onto the roof like he was shooting a basketball."

"Really?" Canfield looked like he was fighting back a smile, then pinched his nose and sniffled. "I'm also having a very hard time believing *you*."

What? It had never occurred to me that Canfield wouldn't believe me. I mean, I always tell the truth! Except sometimes when I don't, which is very, very rare and only for extremely good reasons.

"Well, you either lied to me before or you're lying to me now." He smiled. "So either way, you're really not a credible witness, now, are you, Paisley?"

"I am! I am. I'm telling the truth now. I . . . I didn't before because—look, Eric Sobel is totally innocent! I'm just trying to make things right."

Canfield folded his arms and swiveled back and forth in his chair. "Do you have any evidence? Cell phone photo? Video clip? Will anyone corroborate your story?"

I sighed. "No, no, no, and probably not."

"That's what I thought." He stood up and leaned over his desk. "Next time you try to malign another student's reputation, young lady, I suggest you consider how it will reflect on *your* reputation."

"Mr. Canfield, I am *not* my reputation," I said as politely as possible. "And I'm pretty sure you can't *malign* someone if you're telling the truth about them."

He *laughed* at me. Can you believe it? Canfield was such a condescending pig. And obviously not particularly bright. There was no way I was going to let him shut me down.

"Maybe we should look it up," I said, smiling.

He leaned into my face, hairy nostrils flaring. "Don't you dare mouth off to me unless you want to get suspended too."

Okay, so maybe there was one way to shut me down. Still, I had an idea.

I got out of there as fast as I could. Fine student? Star player? Team leader? Hutch was a jerk, plain and simple. Obviously, Canfield wouldn't have asked for evidence if I had named someone who wasn't a star football player, someone like Clint Bedard. God, even the faculty at this school were desperate for the popular kids' approval. Pathetic.

But I wasn't done. No way. In fact, I was just getting started. I marched out of Canfield's office and straight into the quad. It was almost the end of morning break now, and the quad looked a lot different than it had a half hour ago. It was packed with pops. I stopped after a few steps as a wave of adrenaline surged through me.

There they were—Jen and Bodie, the varsity jerks, Candy Esposito, BS1 and BS2, and Hutch, laughing and smiling and talking. Good thing Hutch looked in high spirits, because I was about to bring him down.

chapter twenty-five

I stood motionless in one corner of the quad, psyching myself up. Where was the soundtrack in my head when I needed it? I concentrated hard, summoning some personal power music. Yeah, there it was. My brain-speakers cranked. I started across the quad doing my baddest power strut.

"Hey! Nice hip action, Hanover!" someone yelled.

Everyone in the entire quad stopped talking and turned to stare at me. Well, not really. But it felt that way. Jen looked terrified. Bodie frowned. Candy looked like she was trying not to explode with laughter.

I kept walking.

"Peter Hutchison?" I yelled, just a few feet away.

He turned around, looking startled. "Jesus Christ! You sound like my mother."

"Eric Sobel got suspended!" I totally got in his face, only, because he's so tall, it was more like in his chest. "He got suspended for the disgusting crap *you* pulled on Friday night!"

Everyone in the group took a step back like they were afraid my rage would splatter on them. Then someone started giggling.

"Oooh, watch out, Hutch!"

Hutch laughed it off. "Yeah, it sucks about Sobel." He fake sighed, shaking his head.

I was horrified. "Is that the best you can do?"

"Oh, wait. You *are* my mother."

Bodie and a few other varsity jerks laughed.

"What is so funny?" I asked, looking around.

"Paisley, please," said Jen. "You're embarrassing yourself."

"*I'm* embarrassing myself? What, like you did when your super cool shidiot friends tortured those kids, and you and everybody just stood around laughing because you're all too cool to care?"

Silence.

BS1 cocked her hip. "Whatever. It was kinda funny."

"You know, *you* were there too, Paisley," said Candy Esposito, pointing her manicured finger at me.

"Yeah, but I was *not* laughing." Okay, I know. I didn't do anything to stop it either. I know that! But I wasn't . . . I wasn't *like* these people. I turned to glare at BS1. "And FYI—it was *not* funny."

Hutch stepped between us. "Paisley, is it that time of the month for you? Because if it is, I can understand why you're so irritable. But I'm pretty sure there's a pill for that now."

"Why don't you grow a pair, Hutch! Go tell Canfield what really happened!"

"Ooooh!"

"Eric Sobel shouldn't have to take the fall for you," I said.

"He didn't *have* to, Pains Me, he *wanted* to. It was his idea." Hutch shrugged, shaking his head. "Whatever. He's fine. No school, watching soccer all day. Sobel's lovin' it."

It hadn't occurred to me that Eric might have volunteered for this. I stood there, all of a sudden unsure. Should I defend my point? Or just run for the middle of the quad like a naked girl wearing a tuba? If Eric volunteered, did I even have a point to defend? Oh, he was such an idiot!

"Why don't you go find some other stupid cause to fight for, Hanover?" Hutch walked off laughing. Jen was staring at me like I had absolutely zero comprehension of reality. Bodie and Candy were trying not to laugh. Too hard.

"Fine, maybe I will!" I called lamely.

"This is hilarious. Have you guys seen this?" BS2 had her nose buried in *The Fly*.

Oh, God. *The Fly!*

She held up the page. "'How to Be UnPopular'? Yeah right," she snickered. "Like anyone would *want* to know how."

Suddenly, it was like listening through the wrong end of a telescope—everyone sounded tiny and far away . . . In my wildest weirdest flash fantasies, I honestly never thought my essay would be printed in the school paper. I thought maybe Miriam Goldfarb and Logan Adler would get a good laugh, but . . .

BS1 leaned in and glanced at the headline, then snorted. "Who cares?" She pushed the newspaper down. "Wanna split a burrito?"

I casually strolled off the quad, and then broke into a full-out sprint as soon as I was in the main hall. I found a stack of newspapers outside the main office, grabbed one, and slipped out the doors to the front lawn. But I didn't get the chance to read the Miss UnPleasant essay because I kept hearing bursts of laughter and snippets of conversations—

"UnPop Culture?"

"Love it!"

"Kiss anyone who's different!"

"Hilarious."

OMG. OMG! OMG!!! Uns were reading Miss Unpleasant's essay!

I walked casually out onto the grass and roamed aimlessly through the various pods of unpops, trying to overhear what people were saying.

"Big kiss, class dismissed!"

"That's perfect!"

"It's about time."

"Adopt-a-Pop! It even rhymes!"

"Who do you think she is?"

"Cate Maduro?"

"But what the hell is a *sidebra*? You think this Miss UnPleasant chick has three boobs or something?"

What? *Three boobs?* I skimmed Miss UnPleasant's column. Whoops. Typo! I meant side*bar*. But I immediately liked sidebra much better. It has a sassy swing to it.

Whoa. *Tons* of Uns were reading Miss UnPleasant's essay— and laughing and talking and quoting it and . . .

This was amazing.

This was so freakin' *cool*.

This was riding the fast train to fabulosity.

HOW TO BE
UnPOPULAR

Okay, people—listen up! Let's all move our chairs into a circle. Welcome to the first day of UnPop Culture, Pleasant Hill High's sick new social studies class. Please note: This class will be graded on a slippery slope, just like life.

Okay, who wants to share first?

Me! Me! Me! (Surprise! I'm the teacher *and* a student!)

Can I just say, I absolutely *love* Pleasant Hill High more than life itself, but I feel so, so, *so* sorry for the Pops at PH. The Jocks, the Poms, the BPs—all these poor rah-rahs are living a too-cruel-for-school nightmare.

Why? Because they're trapped in a no-fun house of mirrors where all they can see is their own reflection. Poor, poor Pops. How boring it must be! No variety pack and no imagination. All those shiny, happy, zit-free freaks talk alike, walk alike, dress alike, think alike— oh wait, you're not allowed to think when you're popular. Silly me.

Tragically, the Pops don't get to explore the free world or enjoy the fun fringe benefits of being an outsider. They don't get to frolic in the freedom that comes with being ignored and invisible. They don't get to know anyone with strange ideas, strange clothes, or strange secret obsessions.

Instead, the big boys brag by stripping the pants off the helpless—then pitching those pants onto the school roof. So brave, so strong! And the mean girls set up their sweet "friend" for a cheerleading choke by teaching her the wrong routine. So cool, so classy!

Worst of all, when you're a Pop, there's no place to go but down. Uh-oh. Do I hear the

SIDEBRA

Gosh, It's *Really* Hard Being Popular!

Don't think the Populars need your help? Read on, people!
It's painful being popular.
Things You Get to Do When You're . . .

POPULAR	**UNPOPULAR**
Pretend to be invincible	Pretend to be invisible
Get a fake ID	Get a real identity
Act like everyone else	Act out!
Dis anyone who's different	Kiss anyone who's different
Hide your real feelings every day	Hide your real feelings every day
Stress! Everyone's watching you— even though they aren't	Relax! *No one's* watching you— even though they are

sound of a cracking mirrored floor? Oh well, never mind. Have to go to Pep Squad practice!

It breaks my heart (really!) when I see the Pops gossiping in the halls or puking up lunch in the girls' bathroom or spitting on nerds outside a school dance. Poor little Pops. They don't stand a chance in the real world. They have no real skills and (whoops!) they peaked way too early.

But I'm determined to change all that! I believe that everyone at PH deserves the chance to be UnPopular—even the meanest, shallowest, cutest, best-dressed, and most entitled. Yes, I'm here to help.

Every underprivileged Pop can learn how to be UnPopular in just four easy steps:

1. Own a brain and know how to use it.
2. Have the guts to stand up for yourself and what you believe in, especially when everyone else is acting like a total moron.
3. Be weird—make weird friends, do weird things, wear weird things, say weird things, date weird things.
4. Be yourself. (OMG! Is that allowed? What will everyone think?!)

Okay, people! Here's your homework assignment:

If you're one of the fortunate UnPops at Pleasant Hill High, please reach out to one of the needy students and adopt a Pop. Be sure to keep a picture of your adopted Pop in your locker or on your phone to remind you of their pathetic rah-rah daily existence. By sharing your mental wealth with a Pop, someone less fortu-nate than you will have at least three well-balanced thoughts a day. Hooray!

And maybe, if we're lucky, one day Pleasant Hill won't feel like Pleasant Hell.

Big kiss, class dismissed!
Miss UnPleasant

chapter twenty-six

At practice, I was brutal. Slide tackling everyone. Winning every loose ball, elbowing, bumping, grunting. I
was so pumped after seeing my words in print *and* seeing all the
UnPops so into it, I even scored three goals in our scrimmage—
without Jen. Coach Sykes loved me.

We did our moronic Lady Hornets cheer, and then everyone
else trotted off toward the girls' locker room. I headed over to
my sweatshirt on the side of the field.

"So who do you think wrote it?" Amy asked me, wiping the
sweat off her forehead with her sleeve.

"I have no clue." I shrugged. "Someone very angry and deeply
tortured."

"Well, that could be anyone at this school." Amy smiled.

"It was probably some Pop trying to be deep. Maybe the Bratty
Sassholes put their airheads together." We howled at that one.

Amy kicked a ball toward the locker room and chased after
it. "Pais, you coming?"

"Gonna run a few laps. Go ahead."

"You're crazy, but okay. See you later."

I waved and pulled on my sweatshirt. The fields were clearing out, but I didn't see Eric Sobel anywhere, so I started jogging. I only ran one lap and then I walked over to one of the goals and waited there for a while, doing stretches against the goalpost. He probably wasn't coming. I wandered toward the middle of the field and my best guess for the listening spot and flopped down on the grass.

I always see faces in the clouds. Always. No matter how I'm feeling, I can find a cloud face that mirrors mine. There it was. I growled up at a fierce face in the sky. "Errrghh."

This whole Miss UnPleasant thing was, like, wow. I had never imagined that anyone would even *read* what I wrote, much less care enough to quote Miss UnPleasant. The UnPops seemed to love her. The Pops were . . . well, they were the Pops.

I slid my hands into my pockets and felt the locker stalker note. I'd forgotten all about it. A thrill went through me as I carefully unfolded it like I was unwrapping a precious gift.

WANT TO KISS YOU ALL OVER

I kind of gasped. Really. OMG. OMG! I felt tingly. This was getting serious—and we hadn't even gone on a single date yet!

"Hey!" Eric Sobel jogged up, wearing a backpack.

"Hey." I quickly folded up the note and stashed it in my pocket.

"Sorry. Running five miles from my house takes longer than I thought." He was dripping with sweat. I hoped he wouldn't take his shirt off. I didn't think I could handle it. He unzipped his backpack and dropped a soccer ball on the ground. "Come on."

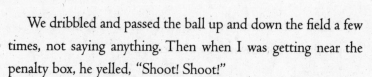

We dribbled and passed the ball up and down the field a few times, not saying anything. Then when I was getting near the penalty box, he yelled, "Shoot! Shoot!"

I touched the ball one more time and kicked it as hard as I could, keeping my head down and my body over the ball.

"Gooooooooooal!" he yelled, running into the back of the net to get the ball.

What a goober, what a totally adorable goober. Stop it!

"Nice shot! Upper left corner. Perfect placement," he said.

I laughed. "Thanks. I was aiming for upper right."

"Yeah, I bet." He juggled the ball with his feet as we walked toward the middle of the field, keeping it alive for about thirty kicks. Finally, he caught the ball in his hands. "Last one to the listening spot is a—"

"Double-wide buttcap!" I yelled.

He laughed and took off running.

"Hey!" I sprinted after him.

He slid to a stop. "I win!"

"Wrong spot!" I ran past him and slid down at a different spot. "I win!"

"Really?" He put his ear to the ground and listened. "Nothing. Well, I guess you would know because the earth is *your* friend."

I laughed like a total dork.

He log rolled over to me and stopped a few feet away. We both just lay there looking up at the sky.

"Dragon!" I pointed up at a cloud.

"Yeah." He rolled over on his elbows. "I heard you gave Hutch the smack-down today. He texted me."

I cringed.

"I see why you did it. I mean, I get it. But . . . yeah, it's kind of . . . embarrassing."

I looked at him. I knew what he meant. But it wasn't really about him, I realized.

"I don't need you to stick up for me, okay?" he said.

"Okay. Sorry. I was . . ." I turned back to the sky. "I wasn't really sticking up for you. It was more like I was trying to take Hutch down. Even though he basically laughed at me."

There was an awkward pause. "So, um . . ." Eric finally said. "You wanted to talk?"

Oh God. I suddenly realized—when I sent him that text, I thought that *he* thought that *I* had squealed on him. But now . . . what *did* we need to talk about? I sighed and rubbed my forehead.

"What?"

"Nothing. I just . . . Well, why *did* you tell Canfield that you did it?"

"Oh man." He rolled onto his back.

"Really. I don't get it. Why?"

He didn't say anything.

I rolled onto one elbow. "Why would you cover for them?" He plucked a piece of grass and bit the soft white end. "It's like you think it's okay, what they did. Or that you're trying to protect them." He closed his eyes and chewed on the grass. We lay there in silence for what seemed like minutes. I sighed. No response. Okay, I was starting to get pissed. I sat up. "Hell-*ooh?* Eric?"

"What do you want me to say?" He sat up too. "I was busted! And no one else was, except for you. I don't know—it seemed like the right thing to do."

"I was there! If you had seen what really happened that night, you would *not* have taken credit for it. It was ugly. Hutch is such an unbelievable jerk."

"He's not a jerk. Well, yeah, he is a jerk sometimes, but he can't help it. He doesn't mean to be."

"Why are you even friends with those morons?"

"Who am I supposed to be friends with? The debate team?" he snapped.

I didn't say anything. Maybe Eric Sobel was more like me than I'd realized.

He lay back down. "And I *don't* think it's okay. But getting half the first-string suspended for the next game wouldn't fix the problem."

I sat there hugging my knees.

"Giant rat eating a cat." He pointed up at the clouds.

"Where?" I lay back onto the grass.

"Two o'clock."

"Looks like the social food chain at our school."

He laughed. "Yeah."

The colors in the sky were beginning to change from blue to pinks and violets as the fading sun hit the edges of the clouds.

I studied Eric's profile, watching his jaw muscle clench and unclench. He has cute little ears with attached lobes. I couldn't hear anything but my heart pounding and Eric calmly breathing. Why do I always say the wrong thing? I closed my eyes, wishing again that I could just melt into the center of the earth.

"Did you read *The Fly* today?" he asked. I tried not to squirm. "I read it online. There was this column, 'How to Be UnPopular.'"

"Really?" I lay there waiting to be slammed. I didn't care about the other Pops, but I wasn't so sure I wanted to hear Eric Sobel rip me to bits.

"It was pretty cool. You should check it out."

What?!

He rolled onto his elbow, facing me. His other hand was on the grass, about half an inch away from mine. "Do you ever wish you were unpopular? So you could fly under the radar and just do your own thing and not have everyone watching everything you do all the time—or have to sign anyone's stomach?"

OMG. I love this guy. "Yeah, sometimes." I rolled onto my back. Staring into his intense green eyes was freaking me out. "I hate it when people ask me to sign their stomachs."

He laughed and flicked my arm. "You know what I mean." Even though it seemed highly unlikely, I was getting the feeling that Eric maybe liked me—*liked me* liked me. But I couldn't be sure because he never did anything or said anything. Shy guys . . . ugh!

We were quiet for a long time. But I think the earth was giving me special powers, because I suddenly felt fearless.

"So, are you and Candy Esposito like a thing now?"

"What? No way. She doesn't like me. She just hangs on me to make Bodie jealous."

I popped back up on my elbow. "Really?"

"Oh yeah. She's dying to get back together with him. Don't tell Jen. Candy's not my type anyway."

"I thought she was everybody's type." I brushed the grass in front of me with the palm of my hand, trying to decide if I should ask what I really wanted to know. Would it make me seem totally desperate? Or maybe I'd seem refreshingly direct and confident? Or maybe I'd seem refreshingly desperate. Oh, what the hell. "So, who is your type?"

He looked at me. "I dunno." Then he closed his eyes and smiled like he was embarrassed or thinking of some inside joke. "Someone cool, someone doing her own thing, someone bad-ass like that Miss UnPleasant chick."

"What?"

What?! OMG. That's *me*—or at least a part of me. He likes part of me?! He thinks I'm bad-ass? He thinks I'm cool? I had to try very hard to be cool at that moment.

"Wait, the snarky girl who wrote that UnPopular thing?"

"Yeah, she just seems . . . funny and smart and . . . " He scratched his eyebrow, thinking. "She calls people on the BS that everyone else at this school ignores," he said, turning to look at me.

I smiled. "Some geeky guy in computer lab probably wrote it." I poked him in the arm.

"Nah. It's got a lot of chick energy. She's probably some edgy indie babe who just moved here, *or* some geeky computer guy with a lot of chick energy." We both laughed. "But I'm gonna figure it out."

"Figure what out?"

"Who wrote it, who she really is."

Oh, wait. Of course. He doesn't *like me* like me. He likes my made-up character! "How are you gonna do that?"

"Access *The Fly's* web log somehow and track the IP address of the computer she used to send the column. Shouldn't be too hard."

Holy crap! "They can do that?"

He nodded. "Hey, are you going to the carnival thing next weekend?" he asked.

"The Walnut Festival?"

He nodded again.

"Yeah, I was planning to go. Wouldn't want to miss the festival of nuts."

"Cool. Maybe I'll see you there?"

And he didn't say that like a statement. *Maybe I'll see you there.* It was a question. *Maybe I'll see you there?* You know, like an invitation.

"Sure." I smiled.

OMG. Could Eric Sobel be my locker stalker?

chapter twenty-seven

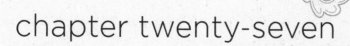On the way to school the next day, I was busy doodling a very detailed rendering of the Fink Fast chair in my notebook when Charlie Dodd turned to me with this really serious look on his face. "Can I talk to you about something?"

He looked like he was in pain. "What? Are you okay? Do you have cancer? Genital herpes?" We had just learned all about STDs in Health.

"No! I just have a question." The sleeping-braces-kid next to him slowly fell over onto Charlie's shoulder. Charlie pushed him back toward the window. "I'm giving you permission to be honest, brutally honest." He looked at me with this tortured expression and then finally whispered, "Am I popular or unpopular?"

I couldn't help laughing.

"What? What's so funny? I'm serious!"

"Nothing. Sorry. I just wasn't expecting that." I tried not to laugh.

"It's not funny! I really need to know because some people think I'm popular, you know like super-geeks and Library Girls, but other people would most likely call me unpopular. So?"

He paused, looking like his whole life depended on my answer. "Which am I?"

He just told me to be brutally honest but still, I didn't want to insult him.

"You are . . . You're . . . " What was the right nice-person answer? I didn't know.

"Just be honest. *Please?*"

"Charlie, you're like in your own category. It's not popular or unpopular, it's . . . it's like *neo*-popular. You can exist in both worlds happily and thrive."

"No! I don't want to be popular. I don't want to be popular of any kind. I can't peak too early. I'll never get into Princeton if I am perceived as peaking too early!"

Sleeping-braces-kid woke up and looked around the mini-van. "What? What?"

"Go back to sleep," said Charlie. "This is all just a minivan nightmare."

Charlie kept talking and I pretended to listen while I doodled, but I was really thinking. It was so weird. After the Miss UnPleasant column, two people in the last twenty-four hours had told me they would rather be unpopular than popular. Their reasons were totally different, but still. Maybe there was something to this whole UnPop Culture thing.

"Hey, are you gonna run for class office?" Charlie asked.

"What? Why?"

"The sign-up sheets are up in the main hall. You should definitely run for something. Admissions directors really look at your accomplishments sophomore year. I'm running for class secretary. I wanted to run for treasurer but LG Wong already signed up and everyone knows she's a math freak—I heard she dreams in numbers. Is that possible? Anyway, I really need to win. So this year it's secretary. Next year I'll run for treasurer."

"Well, I'd been thinking about maybe running for class vice president. Does that sound insane?" I hoped not. It was a building block for my seven-point plan.

"Not at all. I'll be your campaign manager if you want."

"But won't you be kinda busy running for secretary?"

"Yeah, but it'll look good on my college apps."

So before class, I walked over to the sign-up sheet. I wasn't signing up yet or anything. I just wanted to check out my competition. Charlie had signed up for secretary, and LG Wong was the only name under treasurer. There was also only one person signed up for sophomore class president—but you'll never guess who.

Peter Hutchison!

I wanted to scream. So I did—fortunately, at the exact same moment that the warning bell rang for homeroom. So no one was tempted to call 911.

Maybe I should run for class president instead of vice president . . . Hmm . . . It seemed like the perfect way to kick Hutch's butt. *And* it would look good on my college applications. I could beat Hutch, couldn't I?

Couldn't I?

chapter twenty-eight

Drama that day was intense—for a few reasons. First, when I walked into class, Cate Maduro practically ran over to me.

"Smile, Paisley! Say Brie cheese!" She snapped my picture, even though I was looking like a total goober trying to figure out why she would want a picture of me. "I'm adopting you for the Adopt-a-Pop program."

What?!

"No!" yelled Bean, stepping in front of Cate. "She's *my* Adopt-a-Pop. I knew her first. Paisley, look at me. Okay, now look really sad." Bean took my picture too. This was weirdly amazing.

"What are you guys doing?"

"We're reaching out to help a less-fortunate popular student," said Cate.

"And sharing our mental wealth," Bean added, trying not to laugh.

I could tell they were joking. At least I *thought* they were joking.

"Don't be afraid. We just want to help you," said Cate really sweetly.

"I'm *not* one of those popular people!" I snapped, playing

my part. Although I kind of was, but, honestly, I didn't think I needed anyone's help.

"Maybe we can share her," Cate said to Bean, looking hopeful.

"Yes, let's share her." Bean smiled, throwing her arm around Cate's shoulder. "Two unpopular brains are definitely better than one."

"You guys! I am not some freaky rah-rah! Really!"

Cate and Bean looked at each other, shaking their heads.

"Paisley, it's okay." Cate touched me gently on the arm.

"Acceptance is the key to inner peace," Bean said, smiling kindly.

"I'd better not see any of those pictures online—or anywhere else, especially on YouTube." I was kind of pissed, but I was also secretly flattered. I couldn't believe that anyone would actually take Miss UnPleasant's homework assignment seriously. How cool was that?

Teddy Baedeker was finally back in school, looking basically the same. I debated whether or not to say anything to him about last Friday night. I kind of wanted to, but then it might really embarrass him if he knew that I saw him in his underwear, crying. Besides, my apology to Mandy Mindel hadn't gone very well. Teddy seemed okay, so I sent him a brain-wave apology and hoped he would get it.

"Okay, people!" Mr. E. announced. "Let's pull our chairs into a circle—wait, where have I heard that before?" he asked, all dramatic with a British accent.

My butt clenched. Uh-oh.

"I'm hearing a lot about this 'How to Be UnPopular' column," Mr. E. said, holding up a copy of *The Fly*. "Let's talk about it."

What? We all looked around at each other, but nobody said a word. Mandy was looking at the floor. Teddy chewed nervously on his lower lip.

"Okay, so is Miss UnPleasant serious or kidding or maybe both?"

A Library Girl raised her hand.

"Louise?"

"I think she's serious and I think she's . . . mean."

Mean?! A rolling wave of snickers and laughs.

"Mean?!" Cate asked, all perturbed. "Everything she wrote was dead on."

"Yes!" yelled Bean and a few of the AV Guys. A few others mumbled agreement.

"It's divisive," said Charlie Dodd. "It calls attention to the problem but it also contributes to the problem."

"How so?" asked Mr. E.

"Well, making it unequivocally clear that there are two groups at this school—the Pops and the UnPops."

"Yeah dude, because there are," said Clint, shaking his head.

Mandy Mindel raised her hand uncertainly.

Mr. E. pointed at her. "Mandy?"

"I like her. I . . . I like the way she uses irony to make a point." Mandy talked at the floor with her hands folded neatly in her lap. "There's a huge divide between the popular students at this school and everyone else," she said, glancing up for a second and catching my eye. "And some of them are vicious. They treat us . . . They act like we're only here for their amusement." She mushed her nose around with the back of her index finger.

"What I can't figure out," Cate said, "is who *thinks* like an UnPop but *acts* like a Pop."

I gulped, glancing around the circle, waiting to see who would speak next.

"Paisley, what do you think?" asked Mr. E.

Oh crap. "Well . . . I'm pretty sure I know the real identity of Miss UnPleasant." I had my serious face on, waiting until everyone in the room was looking at me. "It's Mr. Canfield."

Everyone burst into hysterics, even Mr. E.

"All right. That's enough for now," Mr. E. said. "But this is interesting stuff, and worth thinking about. Personally, I hope we'll see more from Miss UnPleasant."

OMG. Mr. Eggertson was a fan!

The rest of class, we were working with our scene partners shooting lines. So I got to sit facing Clint Bedard, which wasn't such a bad way to spend time. But it was a little hard to concentrate—Clint was wearing some girl's lip gloss again.

SIDEBAR

Shooting lines is not as violent as it sounds. It's basically just you and your scene partner saying your lines back and forth quickly without trying to do any acting. It really helps you memorize your lines and get a sense of the flow of the scene before you start thinking about blocking.

BTW—*blocking* is what you call figuring out where you move and what you do in a scene. It's sort of like choreography for actors. None of the movement in a scene happens by accident—at least it's not supposed to. (More on that later!)

"So, I'm handsome and dashing and delightful, and you are . . . kind of a total b—"

"Babe?" I cocked my head, smiling.

Clint laughed. "Yeah, that too." He leaned in. Our knees almost touched. "Otherwise I wouldn't put up with that nasty-ass sharp tongue of yours."

"A sharp tongue comes from a sharp mind." I smiled smugly.

"Excellent. You're already in character. I guess I'll start then."

Clint slowly read from his script. It sounded like he was reading a foreign language.

> CLINT AS PETRUCHIO:
>
> Good Morrow, Kate—for that's your name, I hear.
>
> ME AS KATHERINE:
>
> Well have you heard, but something hard of hearing.
>
> They call me Katherine that do talk of me.
>
> CLINT AS PETRUCHIO:
>
> You lie, in faith, for you are called plain Kate,
>
> And bonny Kate, and sometime Kate the curst . . .

"No way I can memorize this." Clint slapped his script on his knee. "I don't even know what I'm saying."

"Just try. We'll figure it out."

He shook his head but kept reading.

> And bonny Kate, and sometimes Kate the curst,
>
> But Kate, the prettiest Kate in Christendom,
>
> Kate of Kate Hall, my super-dainty Kate—

"Great. At least I know what super means. Who knew *super* was such a Shakespearean classic?"

"Keep going," I said. "You're doing great." Clint sighed. I was feeling a little frustrated too—I just wanted to run my hands through that hair. Oh, maybe I'd get to do that in our scene! That could count as blocking, right?

> For dainties are all Kates—and therefore, Kate,
>
> Take this of me, Kate of my consolation:

I watched him read, wondering what his bedroom looked like. I hoped we could rehearse at his house sometime—not in his bedroom, of course. I just wanted to see where he lived and see his stuff and what he had on his walls . . .

> Hearing thy mildness praised in every town,
>
> Thy virtues spoke of, and thy beauty sounded—

"I have *no* idea what I just said." He shook his head.

Frankly, neither did I, but I folded my arms and stared at him until he continued.

> Yet not so deeply as to thee belongs—
>
> Myself am moved to woo thee for my wife.

"What?! No way I'm marrying *you*. You're a total . . . *shrew!*"

"Well, yeah, that's kinda the point. Have you even read this scene yet? You have to win me over. You have to *persuade* me to like you."

He sighed.

"You know, if you're not even gonna try, then forget it."

"Wow. You really *are* in character. How could I not want to win you over?" he said, batting his eyelashes.

I sighed and looked away. Bean and Cate were working on a scene from *The Odd Couple*. Clint was hot, but suddenly it seemed like a lot more fun to be working with a girlfriend on a comedy. Why did we get stuck with Shakespeare?

The bell rang and everyone scrambled for their stuff.

I was headed out the door when Clint started walking with me and threw his arm around my shoulders.

"Hey Red, wanna do something next Saturday night?"

Whoa. I stopped. "What?" *What?!* "Um, you mean like a date?"

He pulled me along and we kept walking up the main hall together, his arm still around me. "Yeah, but kinda homework too. Don't you think our scene will be a lot better if we actually get to *know* each other?" He gave me that smirky flirty grin.

"I guess." OMG. Clint Bedard just asked me out—on a date! I was giddy and giggling on the inside but extremely cool on the outside. Then suddenly, I started to sweat. Could I handle being alone with Clint Bedard? My head might explode—or worse. "Um . . . Hey, the Walnut Festival carnival thing is happening that weekend . . . "

"Well, yeah. We could stop by," he said, smiling.

I was excited but completely unprepared. Never—even in my dreamiest, most delusional flash fantasies—had this crossed my mind. Suddenly this romantic soundtrack soared through my brain-speakers. This feeling melted from my brain—down, down, down.

And then Jen, Candy Esposito, and Bodie stepped into the main hall from the quad, just as we were walking by.

I remember it as this beautiful slow-motion moment. Jen did

a full-on double take, her mouth fell open, and a wad of pink gum flew out. Candy froze, looking sick like she had accidentally taken a huge gulp of Coke instead of Diet Coke. Bodie just stared at me looking totally confused—or was it amused? Whatever.

Clint and I passed by them without breaking our stride. And it felt . . . *good.*

"So, what do you say?" Clint asked.

"Yeah. Okay, sure," I said with a big grin.

"Cool. I'll pick you up on my bike around seven thirty. You're not afraid of motorcycles, are you?"

"Course not." I shrugged. That might have been a lie. "This is me." I peeled off to the right toward my locker and waved like a dorkasaurus. He winked at me and kept walking.

Holy shiitake mushrooms! I had never been on a motorcycle before. But more to the point—I had never been on a real date before. You know, where the guy actually comes to your house and picks you up?

Wait. Wait! WAIT!!!

Didn't I kind of sort of tell Eric Sobel that I would meet *him* at the Nut Festival?

Oh crap.

SIDEBRA

Guys who wink fall into two categories.
1) The skanky, trying-too-hard category, when . . .
- they don't have a clue what to do next after they say something stupid.
- they actually think a wink will persuade you to do something you don't want to do.
2) The effortlessly cool category, when . . .
- they know exactly what they're doing and how charming they really are.
- they don't care about trying to persuade you because they love the thrill of the flirt—which makes them, of course, totally irresistible.

chapter twenty-nine

YOU'RE SO CUTE WHEN YOU'RE MAD

Ugh! I slammed my locker shut. Normally, I would be happy to get a locker stalker note. But not today. For starters, no one wants to be told they're cute when they're mad. Really. What an insult. And secondly, *everyone* has seen me mad lately—Jen, Bodie, Eric, Hutch, Mr. Canfield, Cate, Bean. So it could be *anyone* writing these notes—except for Canfield. I hoped. Ew.

I slipped the locker stalker note into my notebook and slammed it shut.

Jen was back to serving me up a double ice-berger with cheese, which was fine. I didn't have anything to say to her anyway. Amy and Carreyn were terminally inconsistent, one day choosing sides, the next, trying to build a bridge of peace by running messages back and forth between us.

"No! Tell her again I don't have her green sweater at my house." I was seriously annoyed. "I've looked. I never even borrowed it!"

"Okay, okay." Amy backed up. "Jeez, don't shoot spit on the messenger."

"Sorry." I wiped my mouth with my sleeve.

"Why are you wearing that old ratty shirt?" Carreyn asked me.

I was wearing the cowgirl-cool shirt that Bean had given me. "It's not ratty, it's vintage—and it's *paisley*." I spastic jazzed her. "Get it?"

"Um, not really. It looks like it smells."

I decided right then to go with Bean the next time she invited me thrifting.

Amy flipped open a copy of *The Fly*. "Any new ideas on who wrote this 'How to Be UnPopular' thing? I'm searching for clues."

"Oh my gag, I read it again last night in the tub before I loofahed," Carreyn answered. "It's sooo sad. Whoever this Miss UnPleasant is, she's obviously filled with self-hatred because she's not popular."

My mouth fell open. But I quickly covered with a very convincing yawn.

"I don't know," said Amy, looking back at *The Fly*. "She makes some pretty good points."

"I'm so sure. Like what?" Carreyn snapped.

"Like how all the Pops walk alike, talk alike, and dress alike. Like how the UnPops have more freedom . . . to be weird or unweird or whatever."

"Well, I don't want to be weird," said Carreyn, so missing the point.

"I do." They both looked at me. "I *do*! Don't you?" I asked Amy.

"I *am* weird. You have no idea how exhausting it is to appear this normal all the time."

I laughed. "This is you trying to be normal?" I made the uh-oh face and we all fell off the bench giggling.

Bean and Cate were weaving their way through the crowd in sophomore hall, taping flyers to the wall and handing them out. Oh man, did they stand out. Bean was wearing her vintage power polka-dot suit with white, shiny, wet-look go-go boots. Cate was in her usual retro drag. I think it was more forties that day, a pencil skirt and tight little shawl-collar blouse on top with these open-toe platform sling-backs.

"Hey, Drama Mamas!" I called.

Carreyn wrinkled her nose, giving them the up-down.

"Hey Paisley." Bean handed me a flyer. "Join the revolution!"

"Doubt you know her," Cate said, looking from me to Amy to Carreyn. "But if you do, *please* beg her to write again."

MISS UNPLEASANT—WRITE ON!

We desperately need your insightful,
snarky commentary.
If you want it, you've got an ongoing column on
UnPop Culture at Pleasant Hill High.
Contact me, please!

Miriam Goldfarb, editor
The Fly

OMG. Was this for real?!

"You have *got* to be kidding." Carreyn was reading over my shoulder. "Miss UnPleasant is a crazy you-know-what."

"You say crazy you-know-what." Bean did this hip-hop girl, finger-wagging head wave, pointing right at Carreyn. "I say crazy what-you-know."

Everyone laughed, except for Carreyn, who didn't know what to do. She just gave Bean the stink-eye.

"So, girls." Cate fingered her tight pearl choker and looked from Amy to Carreyn. "Has anyone adopted you yet for the Adopt-a-Pop program?"

Amy and Carreyn shook their heads. I think they were a little afraid of her.

"Oh, I'm sorry. That's too bad." Cate tried to look sorry for them. "We'll put the word out to all our unpopular friends."

"We've adopted Paisley," said Bean, hanging her arm over Cate's shoulder. They both smiled at me like goobery proud parents. "With the proper mentoring, we believe there's hope for her." I smiled back like any hopeful UnPop protégée would.

"Hey!" Bean yelled suddenly, pointing down the hall. "Peter! What are you doing?!" Hutch was ripping down all the flyers that Bean and Cate had just taped up. What a brainless buttcap!

"Just cleaning up some trash in the halls," he answered innocently, walking over to us.

Carreyn laughed like that was the funniest thing she'd ever heard.

Cate leveled her eyes at Hutch and draped her hands on her hips. "Miss UnPleasant is not trash, Peter. She's a valuable hidden resource at this school. We've got to find her."

"Her BS is boring. I don't want to read any more of that

crap in *The Fly.*" Hutch tossed a big wad of crumpled flyers at a garbage can like he was shooting a free throw. It hit the back rim and bounced over onto the ground.

"More arc," said Amy.

Hutch just laughed. "Hey girls, I'm running for class president. Will you vote for me?"

What nerve! And he didn't even pick up his trash.

Bean cocked her hip out and put her hand to her mouth, pretending to contemplate his question. "Hm . . . Nope. Definitely not." She smiled.

"I will," Carreyn chirped. "Absolutely!"

"I'd rather go on a roller-skating date with the entire JV football team," said Cate matter-of-factly.

Amy gave her a funny look.

"Oooh, that sounds hot. Need a chaperone?" Hutch chuckled like the creep he knew he was.

Carreyn giggled. The rest of us did not.

Cate smiled warmly. "Gosh Peter, that was so thoughtful and clever. Maybe I *will* vote for you. Oh wait. You're a misogynistic philistine. Never mind."

"Yeah, I'm sure it's mutual." Hutch turned to Amy and me. "What about you guys? Gonna vote for me?"

"Maybe," answered Amy.

"I'm not sure yet. Who's running against you?"

"No one. Guess they're all afraid of me." He shrugged and walked off down the hall.

Bean stared after him. "Someone better run against that

cretin." She turned back to me and did the prom queen wave. Elbow, wrist. Elbow, wrist. "See you later, Pais."

"Cute shirt, Paisley." Cate winked at me as she turned to go.

"Oh my gag. Did you see that?" Carreyn whispered. "That lesbianic chick winked at you."

"She's just trying to freak you out."

"It's working," Amy and Carreyn said at the exact same time.

"You guys!"

"Excuse me, but why were they even talking to us?" Carreyn asked. "I do *not* want to be seen with girls like that."

"Like what?"

"You know. Like weird and loserish and . . . gangly."

"Carreyn, you're such a snob."

"Thank you."

I let that one go. I had bigger things to think about—like my new campaign for sophomore class president.

That's right.

Game on!

chapter thirty

I couldn't wait to start brainstorming my campaign strategy, but first, this flyer. An ongoing column on UnPop Culture?! I read and reread the flyer as I walked to the library. Wow. Maybe this could replace Yearbook and be the new seventh point on my seven-point plan? *This is Paisley Hanover, UnPop Culture columnist, reporting live from the gym.* Oh wait. It's by Miss UnPleasant. Not me. And did I even know anything *about* UnPop Culture?

Bean ran up next to me, still clutching her stack of flyers, and fell into step. "Really. Come on. Who do you think it is?"

"Really? I think Miss UnPleasant sounds a lot like Cate Maduro," I said.

Bean's eyes got all big. "I *know*. I thought that too. But don't tell her I said that. Gotta go," she said, waving her flyers and hurrying off in the other direction.

And if I *did* write more Miss UnPleasant columns, how would I keep people from finding out it was me—and then *hating* me? If tracking an IP address is as easy as Eric Sobel made it sound, then I couldn't send anything from my laptop. If people found out, I'd have to change schools or . . .

I had a traumatic flash fantasy of being chased down the hall by an angry, screaming mob of Pops lead by Candy Esposito, Bodie, and Jen. They cornered me in the quad near the base of the bronze hornet, shouting ugly accusations as they pelted me with chicken nuggets. Carreyn was especially vicious. She dipped her nuggets in honey barbecue sauce and *then* fired them at me.

Oh God, if people found out, I was going straight to Pleasant Hell.

I looked up just then and saw Eric Sobel walking out of the library. Perfect! I had an idea.

"Hey, Eric," I said, running to catch up. "Have you seen this?" I waved the Miss UnPleasant flyer in his direction.

"Hey." He grabbed the flyer and read it. "Wow."

"Yeah, wow. How's your plan to expose her coming along?"

"Um . . . slowly." He sighed. "*The Fly*'s weblog is password protected. I'm still working on it. Know any good hackers?"

I laughed. "Nope. Sorry." Like I would say anything if I did. I shrugged and waved. "But I'll keep thinking."

I went into the library and casually leaned against the windowsill, keeping an eye on my locker. At the same time, I scribbled in my notebook, making a list of pros and cons for doing the ongoing column.

Charlie Dodd was speed-typing at one of the library computers nearby. Come to think of it, Charlie was kind of a computer brainiac. I'd have to keep that to myself. I looked around. These computers were a good twenty-five feet from the magazine lounge. Two of the five computers were basically concealed behind the end of a reference shelf. Hmm. I could hide in plain sight. If I typed my columns at home and transferred them to a jump drive, then I could quickly submit them to *The Fly* website from one of the library computers. I checked around for security cameras . . .

No! This was crazy. It would be too much work on top of homework and soccer and Drama and running for class office. But it sure would be fun to keep empowering the UnPops and see what Miss UnPleasant could inspire them to do next week. Hmm . . .

"Hey, Paisley," said Charlie, waving the "Miss UnPleasant—Write On!" flyer. "Have you seen this?" He shook his head. "Gold. Pure college-admissions gold."

"What do you mean?"

"Shhhhh! Library voices, please," said Ms. Whitaker softly, waving at us. I waved back.

"Are you kidding?" asked Charlie, trying to whisper. "I'd kill to be Miss UnPleasant. To have a platform to write satirical social commentary about high school while you're *in* high school—and do it anonymously? Gold. I've been trying to write a 'How to Be UnPopular' column. It sucks. I thought maybe I could ghost it for her, but her voice is snarky, and snark is not my forte. Whoever she is, if she accepts this offer, I bet she can write her own ticket to any college in the country."

"You think?"

"With the grades and the test scores? Definitely. Assuming

that she lives through it and doesn't get stripped and duct-taped to the bronze hornet by a mob of angry Pops."

"Yeah . . . " I nodded slowly, picturing that exciting possibility.

"Have you signed up for vice president yet? Three people are already on the list."

"Actually, I've decided to run for president instead."

"Really?" He sounded shocked. "You really think you can beat Hutch?"

"Yes, I do—and I look forward to it." I left Charlie sitting there speechless, looking quite envious of my newfound confidence.

When I got down to the main hall, I scoped out the sign-up sheets. Good thing I changed my mind. Now there were *four* people signed up to run for vice president of the sophomore class. And it was only the second day of sign-ups. LG Wong was still the only name under treasurer. Some C-list girl had signed up under Charlie for secretary. I scanned over to the list for president—and stopped dead.

There was a new name on the sign-up list for sophomore class officers.

OMG.

Miss UnPleasant was running for president.

chapter thirty-one

It took all my self-control not to mention anything to Cate and Bean when I went thrifting with them that weekend. It was just too surreal to think about me running against . . . well, my pen name.

Cate and Bean were calling this our first Adopt-a-Pop field trip and I played along mainly because I needed to find something to wear for my *Taming of the Shrew* scene. And Bean said she wanted to take me to her favorite second-hand clothing store. So we hopped a bus and entertained ourselves playing the "where are they going?" game. Every time a new passenger got on the bus, we made up stories about them. It basically went like this.

A young man wearing a baggy suit got on carrying a small bouquet of flowers.

"He's going to visit his girlfriend in the hospital," Bean whispered. "Her appendix almost ruptured, but she's gonna be fine. And then in three weeks, he's gonna dump her."

Cate leaned in toward us. "He's going to the cemetery to put flowers on his father's grave." Her eyes got all big. "He goes every Saturday afternoon and he always wears his father's suit—

because he murdered him and has to pretend to be grieving to keep the cops off his trail."

"You guys are dark," I said. "I hope he's just going to Nordstrom to buy a suit that fits."

Finally we got off the bus and started walking through this semi-sketchy neighborhood. We passed an old bowling alley that was boarded up and a self-storage place where a few people with shopping carts were organizing their stuff.

"So, how's it going with Clint Bedard?" Cate said his name like it was a dirty word—the good kind of dirty.

"Fine." I tried not to blush, but I couldn't help it.

"Pais, what?" asked Bean, smiling. "Come on, dish."

For some reason I felt safe talking to them. "It's kinda crazy," I said, laughing, a little embarrassed. "Promise you won't say anything to anyone?" I pressed the crosswalk button.

"Promise!"

"I have a major below-the-belt crush on him. I can barely concentrate when we're practicing our blocking and he's whipping me around in his arms." I sighed, blowing out a mouthful of air. "I don't get it."

We ran across the street.

"What's not to get?" Cate asked. "He's sexy."

I nodded. "He's definitely different from other guys at our school, you know?"

"That's because he's confident," said Bean. "And he doesn't care what anybody thinks. And he's tall."

I nodded. "But it's more than confident. It's like he's . . ." I struggled to find the right word. "It's like he's *manfident*. He just *knows* what to do with a girl."

"Ooooh," said Cate provocatively. She and I laughed. Bean just looked at me.

"But Clint and I don't have anything in common, other than our scene."

"Are you sure?" Bean asked coldly. Cate raised an eyebrow.

"Are you saying I'm manfident?" I smacked Bean on the arm. "Thanks!"

"I'm not saying anything." Bean shrugged.

"*I'm* saying you should spend some time with him and *find* something in common." Cate winked.

"There it is!" Bean shouted. "The Second Coming thrift store. Prepare for miracles, girls!"

Cate and I followed Bean inside. It was kind of dark and smelled like my Grambo's glove drawer.

Cate immediately took charge. "Okay, so I'm seeing you in something long, of course, maybe with an empire waist, with either poofy sleeves or sexy little straps."

"Or something with a tight little lace-up bodice," Bean suggested.

"Sexy? I can't be sexy."

"Everyone can be sexy. It's all up here." Cate tapped the side of her head. "Okay, fan out and start flipping hangers."

We found six long dresses that might work, but one didn't pass the stink test. Then we holed up in a dressing room. Cate sorted the possibilities while I got undressed.

"You guys, I signed up to run for class president." I looked at Cate and then Bean. "What do you think?"

"Yes!" Bean cheered. "You've got to beat that pompous sexist buttcap."

"That's so weird!" Cate practically jumped. "Yesterday at lunch, I signed up Miss UnPleasant for class president!"

"That was you?"

Cate nodded, raising an eyebrow.

"Isn't that the best idea?" Bean asked. "Miss UnPleasant infiltrates the establishment and brings it down!" Bean and Cate burst into hysterics.

"I'll be managing her write-in campaign for class president." Cate added.

I stepped into the first dress, feeling a little freaked. Did they know? Were they making fun of me? Was this a trap? Wait, how *could* they know? "Genius." I nodded. "Pure genius. Of course, she doesn't stand a chance against *me*." I smiled, but I meant it. Miss UnPleasant wasn't real. No one would actually vote for her. "Hey, can you zip this?"

Bean zipped up the back of a purple velvety dress. I looked at my reflection in the full-length mirror and cringed. "It's huge. I look like Barney."

Bean unzipped it, nodding, and handed me the next dress.

"Canfield immediately crossed Miss UnPleasant's name off the list. But I'll just sign her up again and again and again."

This was fascinating. I mean, why would anyone want to act

like Miss UnPleasant really existed? "Why? Just to bug Canfield?" I asked.

Bean giggled. "Cate's in love."

"It's true. Miss UnP is a goddess. I worship her."

OMG! Miss UnPleasant has a better social life than I do! "Cate, what if she's butt-ugly?"

"It doesn't matter," Cate mooned. "I love her for her mind, her wit, her deep social insights."

I burst out laughing. This whole thing was just too bizarre. "You are way weirder than I thought!"

"Love is the flower you've got to let grow," Cate responded wistfully.

"That's beautiful." I rolled my eyes. "I never realized you were such a romantic. So, you think I should run?"

"You should definitely run," Bean urged. "It'll be fun to run against you. And Peter Hutchison is scum of the universe. Miss UnP will kick his butt! Or, you know, you will." She smiled.

Cate stood in front of me, lacing up the black bodice part of the next dress. "Take a big breath and exhale." She pulled really hard on it and tied it in a bow.

"I can't breathe," I gasped, taking a quick breath. Stitches popped. Oops. "Well I hate to burst your bubble, girls, but *Miss UnP* can't run for class president. She isn't real."

Cate cocked her head and looked me in the eye. "She may not be real to you. But she's very real to me."

"Me too." Bean studied the dress I was wearing. "That's the one!" she squealed. "Turn around. I love it! Don't even try the others."

"What do you think, Cate?"

She nodded slowly. "Elizabethan hottie. Clint's gonna like you in this."

I looked in the mirror. Bean was slouched against the wall behind me while Cate tried to hold my hair up. That bodice was holding most things in and pushing a couple of things out, making it appear like I actually had some shape. Wow. I didn't look like me at all. I hardly recognized myself.

On the walk back to the bus stop, I casually mentioned that Clint Bedard had asked me to go to out with him next Saturday night.

Bean stopped suddenly. "Like . . . like on a date?"

"Yeah, kinda. But also like homework for our scene. I think we're going to the Walnut Festival."

"Clint is going to the *Walnut Festival?*" Cate asked, grinning.

Bean shushed her. "What did you say to him?"

"I said yes."

"Oh my God!" Bean walked around in a circle, huffing.

"What?" I asked. "You said he was hot."

"He is, and *tall!* It's one thing to be crushing on him from a distance, and another to start dating him!" She glared at me and marched off down the sidewalk.

I turned to Cate. "What? I don't get it."

Cate and I stopped, watching Bean stalk off to the bus stop at the end of the block. Cate turned to me and sighed. "If girls like you start dating guys like Clint Bedard, then who will girls like us have to date?"

What? I blinked a few times trying to do the math in my head, but I was totally confused. "Wait, I thought you liked *girls?*" I asked.

"That's not the point!" She shook her head, then looked me hard in the eyes. "Why do you care anyway?"

"Because we're friends."

"Since when? Seventh grade? Or last week?"

I looked at her, trying to understand what she was saying. And then it hit me. Oh my God. She was hurt—of course, she'd never admit it. Did I ice her out after seventh-grade Spanish? Did I ice her out just like Jen was icing me out? God, what a buttcap. "Cate, I'm sorry. I—I just hope we're friends now—friends enough that we can be honest."

She looked away, slowly shaking her head. "You want me to be honest? Okay. Guys don't like me. I don't know why. Whatever." She shrugged. "So this one girl kissed me, and it was pretty damn fun, and then I told everyone I was a lesbian—basically to freak out my parents. But they were *soo* accepting, *soo* supportive, *soo* there for me." She threw up her hands. "And I was *soo* annoyed. You have no idea." She sighed. "I don't know what I am. I guess . . . I guess I'm still undecided."

For the first time since seventh-grade Spanish, I felt like the real Cate Maduro was actually talking to me. I gave her a big hug.

She looked at me kind of awkwardly. "Thanks. FYI, I'm pretty sure Bean has a major below-the-belt crush on Clint Bedard too."

I looked at her to see if she was kidding. She wasn't. "Oh no. I had no idea. I thought . . . I just—"

"There's the bus. Come on!" Cate pulled me up the sidewalk and we ran a half block to the bus stop.

The three of us climbed on the bus and worked our way to the back row.

"Bean, hey, I didn't know you were into Clint, like for real. I wouldn't have—"

"Whatever." She rolled her eyes at me. "Girls like you never know."

Girls like me? God, who does she think I am? I looked at Cate hoping that she would say something to back me up. But she looked away and then pulled out her phone and started reading her text messages.

The three of us rode back on the bus in silence. I stared out the window replaying over and over what Cate had said. *If girls like you start dating guys like Clint Bedard, then who will girls like us have to date?* Sure, there were never enough popular guys to go around, I knew that. But it never occurred to me that there weren't enough *unpopular* guys to go around either, or that there was some sort of unspoken boundary. If I went on a date with Clint, would I be just another piggy insensitive Pop? *Am* I even popular anymore? Do I want to be? I couldn't figure out anything or anyone anymore, especially myself.

chapter thirty-two

I pushed all of that out of my mind. I had work to
do. Because that night, I decided to take my first stab at answer-
ing Miriam Goldfarb's rally cry. Better me than Charlie Dodd, I
figured—though I *did* admire his crafty thinking.

I sat in bed with Dyson on my lap and brainstormed into
my notebook. I wanted to write something even better than
before—something that made people really think. But it wasn't
coming together. At all. I just wasn't sure what I was trying to
say. I put on my Dumbe Blonde T-shirt for inspiration. I didn't
have the guts to wear it to school yet. But I always had the best
bizarro dreams when I wore it as a sleep shirt.

What *is* UnPop Culture anyway? I guess I knew, but I
didn't *really* know. And so far, I'd scratched out everything I'd
written. It all sounded stupid or forced or whatever. So I got
out of bed and I went online to Wikipedia, typed in "Pop
Culture," and read the definition. Basically, it means everything that's popular right now. So that would make UnPop
Culture everything that *wasn't* popular right now? Oh, crap.

I started a new text file and typed, "Miss UnPleasant's Ongoing Column," except that I'm not the best typist and so I

actually typed, "Miss UnPleasant's Ungoing Column." I was about to fix it, but then I stopped. Wait a second. Maybe UnPop Culture isn't just about *being* unpopular or *feeling* unpopular . . . Maybe it's about being *un*-everything—unpredictable, unapologetic, unperfect, unappreciated, undiscovered, undecided.

A flood of excitement rushed through me. OMG—that's it!

I started speed-typing. Miss UnPleasant's second column— "Un Is More Fun!"—practically flew out of me. I submitted it to *The Fly*'s website and was in bed by midnight.

I was lying there, petting Dyson, listening to his power-purr and trying to fall asleep. But I couldn't shake this thing about Bean. I buried my nose in Dyson's black fur. I loved the way he smelled, sweet and dusty.

So Bean was crushing on Clint. How much did that suck? I mean, no—not that she was crushing on him, but that I felt like I had to *do* something about it now. Because Bean was, like, my friend. Oh, that was weird. Three weeks ago, just the idea of being friends with Bean—the idea of Bean *wanting* to be friends with *me*—would have been totally crazy. And now the crazy thing was that it wasn't crazy at all.

I didn't blame her for being surprised and mad. There aren't a lot of hot desirable UnPop guys—especially guys as tall as her. And she couldn't exactly go out with some rah-rah guy or some jock. She'd lose all credibility.

But truthfully? It kind of bugged me that she was crushing on Clint. There, I said it. I'm an awful person. Still, I had to call it off. I *had* to. Even if I did have a major below-the-belt crush and desperately wanted to know him better. I would do something nice for my friend. Besides, lots of guys are taller than I am. And there was Eric Sobel, who was more and more a real person and not just a lickable torso in one of my flash fantasies. And hey, there was always my locker stalker, right?

I started to drift off. And then I remembered what Cate had said as we were walking to the bus stop. Did guys really not like her? She was so pretty and confident and clever. Or was that just her way of explaining things to me—and maybe explaining things to herself?

chapter thirty-three

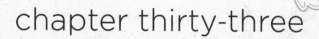

Charlie Dodd was my official campaign manager,
but Amy and Carreyn were helping out too. I guess Carreyn had
decided that I wasn't so bad after all, or more likely, that helping
me run for president might somehow help her. So on Sunday,
they all came over to my house to brainstorm. The night before,
Carreyn had dyed her hair red in a show of solidarity with me. I
screamed when I opened the front door.

"Okay, for starters, we need posters, locker stuffers, and a really
memorable slogan," I said, sitting down at the kitchen table.

"I have a few ideas." Charlie pulled out a yellow legal pad and
showed us his list. Charlie's great, but his slogans were not.

Paisley for President!

Pais for Pres!

Hand the reins to Hanover!

Good Ideas—Great Leadership!

"Leadership, scholarship . . . " He tapped his pen on his
yellow legal pad.

"Chip and Dip?" I laughed. Charlie snorted and Amy nearly
spit up her Diet Coke. Carreyn glanced at Charlie and giggled.

"I was thinking of something a little more offbeat. Maybe a play on words?" I pulled my notebook out of my bag and flipped to the last scribbled pages and read from a list of possible slogans.

Building Sophomore Bridges

Connect the Dorks

Redhead & Shoulders Above the Rest!

Go Red to Get Ahead!

Paisley Hanover—Not Just Tho—

I stopped. I was suddenly having a painful flashback of my Yearbook headline disaster.

"A Pattern of Success!" my mom yelled from the other room.

I groaned as loudly as possible. "How about 'Cool, Calm, and Connected'?" I tossed out.

"That's pretty good," said Amy. Carreyn nodded in agreement.

"I know!" Charlie blurted. "'*Fun* of a Kind Girl!'" They all fell out of their chairs at that one.

I rolled my eyes. Hilarious.

"Or maybe I should go with 'Spastic Jazz Hands Working for You!'" I spastic jazzed them.

Charlie pulled back and tilted his head like a dog trying to understand. "I kinda like that."

"It was a joke."

"Wait, what's this?" Amy grabbed my notebook.

Oh God, please don't let it be another doodle of Eric Sobel kicking a heart-shaped soccer ball.

"'Spastic Jazzed for the Job!'" she read from my list. "It's perfect!" She set my notebook on the table and drew an arrow and smiley face pointing right at "Spastic Jazzed."

"I like that one too," Charlie said, sounding surprised. "Yeah, I think that works! It shows that you can laugh at yourself. Plus, it's memorable and it's *ownable*. Hutch can't use a tagline like that. And no one's gonna confuse that slogan with Hutch's slogan, you know?"

"What's his slogan anyway? Do we know?" I asked.

"Yeah." Charlie flipped through his yellow legal pad. "Go with a Proven Winner. Go with Hutch—I'm Open!"

I read it a couple of times. My shoulders fell. "Damn. That's good."

"Yeah." He nodded. "It's pretty perfect for a star wide receiver running for president." I nodded. He was right.

We were all silent for a second.

"Paisley—Power to the People!" Mom shouted again.

"Thanks, Mom!" I crossed my eyes and everyone laughed.

"I think that's sweet." Carreyn shrugged.

"No."

"Speaking of sweet. Did you guys see the necklace that Bodie gave Jen?" Amy asked.

"And when exactly would I have seen that?" I asked sarcastically.

"Oh, right." Amy shrugged. "Sorry."

"It looks *really* spendy." Carreyn nodded with obvious envy.

"Guys like Bodie shouldn't get to have money too," said Charlie. "It's just not fair to the rest of us."

"Jen's *so* lucky." Carreyn sighed.

"Whatever." I flipped the pages of my notebook, looking for other slogan ideas.

"Hey, how's your website coming?" Charlie asked me. "Mine's in beta, we're going live on Monday."

"My website? What website?"

"Paisley, come on. You've gotta have a website these days. Voters expect it. And college admissions officers love it. Total competitive advantage." Amy and Carreyn were looking at Charlie like he was an alien life form. "A personal website is like a college app on steroids. You gotta do it."

I nodded, trying to process what he was saying without laughing. Was he serious? Did I really need my own website? Was PaisleyHanover.com even available? With my luck, some web geek in Scotland had already bought the domain name. "Okay, good suggestion. I'm on it as soon as we nail my fabulous, memorable slogan." I so didn't have time to worry about it right now.

Amy jumped out of her seat. "Spastic Jazzed for the Job! Spastic Jazzed for the Job!"

"Spastic Jazzed for the Job," I repeated. "Paisley Hanover— Spastic Jazzed for the Job! What do you guys think?"

"Let's do it," said Charlie. Carryen nodded.

"Yay!" Amy ran a victory lap around the table, giving me a low five as she rounded my side. I tried to imagine that my official campaign slogan was "Spastic Jazzed for the Job!!!"

Oh man. It was crazy enough that it might work. Or maybe I was just crazy.

Un IS MORE FUN!

Okay, people—let's all move our brains into a circle for a lively class discussion! Today's topic:

What is UnPop Culture?

Who wants to share first?

Me! Me! Me!

Yes. That's correct. UnPop Culture is all about *you*!

It's about listening to the *Un*Usual all-in-your-head voice and grooving to the *Un*Predictable tunes of your own personal soundtrack. It's about throwing a big bash every day for what makes you *Un*Normal and letting your freak flag fly! It's the art of being *Un*Popular, *Un*Perfect, *Un*Forgettable, *Un*Decided, *Un*Sane, *Un*Cool, *Un*Discovered, *Un*Apologetic.

Sound familiar? That's right. It's UnEquivocally YOU.

Aren't you sick of scrambling up the Pleasant Hill Higherarchy? I know I am. Come on, people! Let's quit this Brat Race, because I've got the inside dish—there *is* no finish line!

Come on, people!

Just say "No!" to that popularity poison pill.

Just say "Whoa!" to that too-cruel-for-school brattitude.

Just say "I don't think so" to those perfectly plasticky popular clones and hunky homogenerous varsity jerks.

SIDEBRA

*Un*Pleasant Questions to Ponder for Future Class Discussions:

1. Ever wonder why the Pretty-in-Pop girls act like we're just extras in their *fabulous* lives?
2. Ever wonder why some Pop bullies are too cruel for school, as if we're just here for their vicious amusement?
3. Ever wonder how some Pop varsity jerks get away with murder, and never even mess up their hair?

I have. It's called *Preferential Treatment* by the oh-so-Pleasant Hill administration. Yep. Hate to pee in your bubble bath, kiddos, but our star athletes get all the perks, and they make this a Pleasant Hell for the rest of us.

Take a hall pass on the in crowd and join the *Un* crowd instead. Everyone's welcome and everyone's got the power—it's called UNdividuality. What a concept.

Okay, people, listen up! Your homework assignment this week is multiple-choice:

1. Tap into your UnPop Power—wear your *Un*-side out.
2. Be yourself—Be Un of a Kind and be proud!
3. Take back the quad—it's not just for Pops!
4. Take back Pleasant Hill—it's your school too.

Big kiss, class dismissed!

Miss UnPleasant

LETTERS TO THE EDITOR

Dear Flies,

Miss UnPleasant needs to get on meds and get a life. What a miserable beyatch. And if she really feels so strongly, than [sic] why is she hiding behind some stupid fake name?

Keep up the bad work, Flies—

A Varsity Hornette, Junior

Dear Editor:

I was extremely disappointed to read the column by Miss UnPleasant in the last edition of *The Fly*. Do we really need this kind of negativity in our school newspaper? I don't think so. I consider myself popular and all of my friends are popular too, and we are NOT trapped. The next time that you are tempted to run a piece like this, you should remember that popularity is <u>earned</u> by people who have style and confidence and social skills and athletic ability. Too bad the bitter, untalented, unpopular students at this school don't get this.

Signed,

Anonymouse [sic]

PS: Popular students have feelings too.

Dear Madame Editor,

When I read "How to Be UnPopular" by Miss UnPleasant, I laughed out loud. Finally someone is calling these snotty bullies and brats on their entitled behavior. I hope she will write another column, because this school needs to hear from someone who has the guts to point out what makes Pleasant Hill feel like Pleasant Hell.

Sincerely,

Cate Maduro, Sophomore

Dear Fly Paper Editor:

"How to Be UnPopular"—what a provocative op-ed piece! When I consider the true identity of its author, Miss UnPleasant, I am reminded of the Jackson 5 hit "One Bad Apple."

After my first reading of "How to Be UnPopular," I was quite certain that this anonymous author was a disgruntled, unpopular loner, the type of person who lurks in the shadows of PH and does nothing more than take up space on our crowded bleachers. Upon further readings and reflection, however, I now suspect that the real Miss UnPleasant is actually a disgruntled, *popular* loner. While that may sound like an absurd oxymoron, I assure you that it is not. In fact, I myself am a popular loner.

Having said that, I too prefer to remain anonymous.

The primary support for my thesis is reflected in Miss UnPleasant's keen knowledge of certain events, events that only an in-the-know Pop could possibly be aware of and, therefore, reference.

I would caution Miss UnP not to dismiss the merits of all popular students simply because of the unsavory and selfish behavior of a few, which I admit can be quite odious. In conclusion, let me refer your readers, including Miss UnP, to an excerpt from the deliciously addictive chorus of "One Bad Apple":

One bad apple don't spoil the whole bunch, girl.
Ooh. I don't care what they say.
I don't care what you heard now.
Ooooooh! Ooooooh!

Yours truly,

Sir Pleasantly Laughs-a-Lot

chapter thirty-four

After the second Miss UnPleasant column ran in *The Fly*, things got crazy. That day at lunch, I was in the main hall hanging one of my campaign posters when I noticed Candy Esposito and a bunch of other Pops marching into Canfield's office, looking outraged. I don't know what they said, but I'm pretty sure they weren't nominating Miss UnPleasant for homecoming queen.

When they all marched out, I overheard Hutch asking Bodie, "And what the hell does she mean by *homogenerous?*"

"Dude, what do you think?"

They were heading toward me, so I quickly turned to face the wall, adding another piece of tape to my poster.

"I'm gonna crush her!" Hutch sounded really mad. "I'm gonna out her and I'm gonna bring her down."

Yikes.

Homogenerous? I pulled my copy of *The Fly* out of my bag and skimmed my Miss UnPleasant column. Whoops. Typo! I'd been going for homogeneous. Different thing *entirely.*

The next morning at carpool, some dweeby freshman climbed

into the minivan wearing what looked like his dad's undershirt over his clothes—except it had "<u>UN</u>DISCOVERED" written across the back with black electrical tape.

In Drama, three Library Girls showed up wearing matching cute baby-doll tees, "<u>UN</u>IMPRESSED" written across the front in black felt pen. Cate Maduro swished her hips around, pointing out the slab of duct tape stuck to her butt. "<u>UN</u>DE-CIDED" it said. Bean Merrill was wearing a cowgirl-cool belt with a big "UN" buckle made of aluminum foil.

And at morning break, I kept passing people in the halls—kids I didn't know and, frankly, had never even noticed before—with "Un" signs safety-pinned to their backpacks.

UnNormal

UnDetected

UnApologetic

UnSane

It was everywhere. It was endemic. It was historic. It was *unbelievable*.

It had to be a really, really long flash fantasy.

But no. LG Wong had brought a bunch of stick-on name tags and was handing them out to people. Throughout the day, I kept seeing *Hello, my name is . . .*

UnPerfect

UnEven

UnAppreciated

UnForgettable

I didn't know what to think, and I sure wasn't going to say anything. I just watched in amazement. And then I remembered—that day at the first *Fly* meeting? Ms. Whit was so totally right. Writing is *power*.

The next day was even better. Because the next day was Backlash Day. A bunch of Pops showed up at school sporting signs and name tags and T-shirts that said things like:

UnTouchable

UnDisturbed

UnDaunted

UnTarded

UnFazed

UnAffected

UnShakable

The fact that even the Pops couldn't ignore it? That they had to get in on it in order to defend themselves against it? It was like a small, seriously viral miracle.

And then came the day when the Uns took back the quad.

I was sitting in the main hall at lunch, trying to get caught up on my American History homework, when there was this crazy roar. I stood up and looked out over the quad. The Pops were swatting and screaming like they were being attacked by a swarm of bees. A corner of the quad—the sunny corner, the corner nearest to senior hall—was totally and completely overrun by a flash mob of colorful, weird Uns in all shapes and sizes, laughing and talking. Hey, there was Mime Guy juggling with Teddy Baedeker! Someone must have sent out a text message that spread like bad news and got the UnPops to the quad en masse the second the lunch bell rang. In a few minutes they'd all be lining up for the conga.

Yep, the conga. See, all week, Cate and Bean had been rolling out Miss UnPleasant's write-in campaign for sophomore class president. Canfield kept crossing Miss UnPleasant off the sign-up list, but that didn't slow down Cate and Bean—they signed her up fourteen different times. And every day at lunch, there was a Miss UnPleasant conga line. They marched and danced from one end of sophomore hall to the other and back again, waving signs, cheering, and chanting that day's UnSlogan. And every day, the parade got bigger and bigger and bigger. Even Uns from other grades joined in.

If I had spent all summer coming up with a master plan to promote UnPop Culture and the whole Un thing, I doubt I could have come up with something that would have worked nearly this well.

But I was starting to worry that maybe it was working *too* well. With a growing following of Library Girls, Mathletes, AV Guys, and weird-ass freakazoids, Miss UnPleasant's message was attracting

SIDEBRA

UnSlogans!
Monday: "Vote for Miss UnP to Support Diversity!"
Tuesday: "Join the Un Crowd!"
Wednesday: "UnNormal and Proud!"
Thursday: "The Power of Un Is Way More Fun!" *

* On Thursday, the Miss UnPleasant parade/conga line danced all the way down to the main quad and halfway through it before the Pops attacked them with water balloons and everyone screamed and scattered, laughing all the way back to sophomore hall. Which only proved their point—the power of Un *is* way more fun.

a lot of people no candidate had even noticed before, much less tried to reach.

I did my best to act really annoyed by the whole thing. I mean, I kind of had to or I'd blow my cover. But secretly, I was all butterflies and rainbows inside. I was even a little jealous—Cate and Bean and the whole Miss UnPleasant crew were having so much fun! A lot more fun than us boring candidates, all taking ourselves so seriously. As I passed out my paisley-patterned playing cards stamped with "Paisley 4 Pres!" that my mom had found online, I had to wonder if my pen name was jeopardizing my own candidacy. But no one would really vote for her, would they?

Then Cate and Bean started a membership drive. If you signed up to join the UnCrowd, this *un*official club they were starting, you got to choose three Un stickers that they'd had printed up. By Wednesday, people had started wearing them on T-shirts and slapping them on binders and lockers just because they were funny, even if they had no intention of voting for Miss UnPleasant—even if they weren't in our class.

Hutch was pissed. But his dad is in like marketing or promotions or something, so he had a few hundred little yellow plastic footballs printed with HUTCH FOR PRESIDENT. When Hutch passed them out at lunch one day, it was like the most brilliant idea. I was totally annoyed. But then Hutch's little balls turned into a big, chaotic game of Tweak the Freak, and one of the Trost twins got smashed in the head and needed stitches.

Canfield confiscated all of the footballs and threw them away in two giant trash cans. Oh, poor Hutch. Guess he'll just have to go buy more balls.

On Thursday, we heard about the campus-wide assembly to discuss the whole Miss UnPleasant thing. Apparently the principal had received a number of complaints from outraged Pop parents and students who were demanding that Miss UnPleasant be silenced and whoever was responsible be punished. They were even calling for the resignation of the *The Fly's* editor and faculty advisor.

The forum would take place in the quad during third and fourth periods on Friday—which meant no Drama. Secretly, I was relieved. Over the last week, every day in Drama with Clint had been excruciating. Our big *Acting Out* performance was coming up on Monday night, and our scene together was getting better. At least now we both sounded vaguely Shakespeare-ish, even if Clint still didn't seem to know what he was saying half the time. But even with our amateurish fumbling, there was something . . . *yikes* about the whole thing. Every time Clint grabbed me and pulled me up against his chest and whispered, "Nay hear you, Kate: in sooth you scape not so," I totally dissolved. Which, of course, made it hard to be like, "Um, yeah, so the Walnut Festival on Saturday? Sorry. Can't make it after all. Bean loves you."

Off topic, off topic. So anyway, the forum. It was going to take place in the quad on Friday before lunch, and there would be equal time for people speaking for and against Miss UnPleasant. Whoever wanted time at the mic just had to sign up in advance either Pro Miss UnPleasant or Anti Miss UnPleasant.

And then I had this brilliant idea.

The best way to hide from any suspecting minds was in plain sight, right?

So I signed up to speak.

chapter thirty-five

Friday morning, things were insane. Almost all of the PH student body had squished into the quad, probably for the first time ever. Most people were just milling around waiting to watch the action. But some people were holding signs. "Miss UnPleasant for President!" "Shun the Uns!" From where I stood up near the podium with all the other speakers, I could see that there was even a local news team doing a live report from our parking lot.

Ms. Whit was in a very animated discussion with a few of the faculty members. Canfield was standing with his arms crossed, talking to our principal. They both looked stressed and annoyed, like they'd much rather be off at McDonald's chowing down on Egg McMuffins.

The Dumbe Blondes had taken over the circle around the base of the big bronze hornet. The bongo guy was drumming and they were all softly singing, "Kumbaya, Miss UnP, kumbaya. Kumbaya, Miss UnP, kumbaya."

Ms. Whit stepped up to the podium and quieted everyone down. The Dumbe Blondes would not be silenced, but they did bring their Kumbaya down to a haunting whisper. Then Ms.

Whit thanked everyone for attending and introduced Miriam Goldfarb, editor extraordinaire of *The Fly*.

"Hello, peoples!" Miriam announced in her nasally voice. "Is this great or what?! When was the last time anyone got pissed enough to gather in the quad and duke it out? Right on, peoples!"

Peoples from both camps cheered because, hey, she was right.

"I am here speaking today because I am the"—pause—"editor of *The Fly* and thus, the decider. Yes, I approved Miss UnPleasant's columns."

A wave of boos and cheers filled the quad.

"Okay, all right, pipe down, peoples. Obviously, you don't *all* agree with Miss UnPleasant's point of view. And that's cool. She doesn't"—pause—"agree with all of you either. But can't we agree today that anyone should have the right to express his or her views—as long as they are nonviolent? I mean, hey, this is a democracy! This is the United Screwed-Up States of America, and every voice counts! I say give Miss UnPleasant's piece a chance! Thank you."

Miriam bowed a few times and then stepped to the side. In the meantime, a yelling war had broken out between the Pops, who were booing, and the UnPops, who were screaming and cheering. It was hilarious, and incredible. I couldn't believe I had started this. I couldn't believe we were all here because of something I had *written*.

The first to speak out against Miss UnPleasant was the tag

team of BS1 and BS2, wearing their cheerleading uniforms. Of course.

"Hello, fellow Hornets," said BS1.

A lot of people clapped and yelled "Hello!" back.

"Thank you for your support. We are here to say that we have been deeply wounded by Miss UnPleasant's hurtful words. As you know, we are Varsity Hornettes, so we know what it's really like to be popular. And I just have to say that we are not trapped, we are not bullies, we are not brats. We are happy, nice people—and we *do* have power at this school. We have power because we have *earned* it!"

The Pops cheered and whistled.

"Obviously," BS1 continued, "this Miss UnPleasant person is clueless. We don't think that someone who has no idea what they're talking about—and obviously *no* school spirit—should be allowed to write mean lies, and hurt so many good, beautiful people. Thank you."

The Pop crowd cheered like maniacs.

When they finally quieted down, BS2 leaned into the mic. "Ditto," she said with a smirk, igniting another insane explosion of cheering and stomping.

Then Cate Maduro stepped up. She was wearing a T-shirt that said "UnEven and Proud."

"I don't agree," she said, leveling her gaze at the crowd. "Yes, I realize it's *shocking* that someone like me doesn't agree with two *Hor*-nettes. I think Miss UnPleasant has a ton of school spirit— but she's disappointed and she's pissed off! She cares enough to write that Pleasant Hill *does* feel like Pleasant Hell. And for those of you wondering, no, I didn't write those columns—but I sure wish I had. Miss UnPleasant has shined her high beams on the bad behavior of the Pops at this school and the bad-ass behavior of the UnPops. She has empowered the UnPops by encouraging them to let their freak flags fly. I say, Miss UnPleasant's got the power!" Cate raised her hand in a fist and saluted the crowd. "Power to the UnPops! Power to the UnPops! Power to the UnPops!"

The UnPops went crazy, picking up the chant and screaming and stomping and waving signs, holding their clenched fists high in a show of UnPop solidarity.

Cate had a huge smile on her face as she passed the mic to Bentley Jones.

"Good morning! I'm Bentley Jones. Sophomore. I'm here to show my support for Miss UnPleasant."

"Boo!" someone shouted.

"This debate is not about whether or not you agree with Miss UnPleasant's opinions. I certainly don't agree with everything she's written. This is about freedom of speech, which is one of our inalienable rights as freshmen, as sophomores, as juniors, as seniors, as people of this world. Without freedom of speech, we cannot have an open dialogue. And an open dialogue is vital for a healthy society."

The Dumbe Blondes cheered and raised their signs high.

"PH may be a small society, but it *is* a society nonetheless. It's important for us to hear diverse voices that raise our awareness of social issues and raise our consciousness. I applaud Miss UnPleasant. Yes, she has criticized us, but I ask you, if we can't handle criticism from an *insider*, then how can we possibly handle criticism when we're out in the real world?"

A bunch of people cheered at that. Not the Pops, though.

"Let us look at her criticism as an opportunity to improve ourselves. I ask you to focus not on where Miss UnPleasant is wrong, but rather on where she is right. Thank you for being here and for having a voice in freedom."

I really liked that Bentley Jones. I realized I had to spend more time with her, even if she *was* the next generation of Yearbook Royalty.

Then suddenly it was my turn to speak. OMG. I'd gotten so caught up in everyone else's speeches that for a second a blanked on whose side I was on. Cate nudged me toward the podium. I pulled myself together and stepped up.

"Hi, I'm Paisley Hanover," I said, smiling out at the crowd. "I'm speaking today because I think Miss UnPleasant is a *coward!*"

The Pops cheered.

"And I'm not just saying that because I *am* a Pop. Or at least, I'm close to being one," I said, catching Candy Esposito's eye and winking.

"Sure, Miss UnPleasant raises some good points about our school, but I think the way she's doing it is pathetic. She's hiding behind the safety of anonymity. She's hiding behind this bogus Miss UnPleasant name! If she has something to say to us, then I invite her to step forward—right here, right now—and identify herself. I'll be happy to give up my time and pass her the mic." I squinted at the crowd. People started looking around suspiciously.

Ooh, this was fun. Then I had an even better idea. "Given her obviously twisted brain and tweaked sense of humor," I said, "she's probably even one of the speakers today. She's probably standing up here right now." I cocked an eyebrow and turned to Miriam and Bentley and Cate and Ms. Whit, who were all looking nervously at each other.

"Come on, Miss UnPleasant! Come clean! Who are you?"

I waited. I was really into it.

"Take responsibility for your words!"

A few voices from the crowd joined in.

"Yeah!"

"Right on!"

"Step up, coward!"

A few more clumps of people cheered and yelled.

I waited a little longer, feeling giddy with podium power. And then I kind of went off the deep end.

"That's what I thought. Miss UnPleasant, you're a gutless, two-faced coward! Whoever you are, don't mess with Pleasant Hill's best!" I paused for dramatic effect, slowly raising *two* clenched fists. "*More* power to the Pops! *More* power to the Pops! *More* power to the Pops!"

I smiled in triumph as the crowd went crazy, cheering and clapping and whistling. It was like a wall of sound being pushed on top of me. I looked out and saw Bean and Charlie, and over there, Amy. And suddenly my smile felt stamped on my face. They all looked just . . . stunned. My eyes swept over the quad. I caught sight of Jen and Bodie, laughing and clapping, and Hutch whooping. My stomach swished dangerously. Uh-oh. I hadn't thought this through very well. I took a step back from the podium—I spotted Eric Sobel taking pictures. Then he lowered his camera, and my eyes locked with his. But I couldn't read his expression. What *was* that? I took another step back and bumped into someone. I turned to apologize, and there was Cate, glaring at me.

When I first came up with this idea, I thought I was pretty darn clever. And that line about Miss UnP being one of the speakers? Genius, right? No one in a million years would think she was me. But now this gross feeling was creeping up my arms and legs and making my scalp prickle. My stomach twisted as I realized, finally.

That look on Eric's face? It was disappointment.

He may not have known that I was Miss UnPleasant. But I knew.

I was the gutless, two-faced coward.

chapter thirty-six

I couldn't face anyone at lunch. I mean, really. What had I been thinking? So instead I started walking down to the deserted end of sophomore hall where I almost never go—and nearly tripped over Clint Bedard. He was stretched out on the grass reading.

He covered his eyes from the sun and squinted up at me, smiling. "Hey, Red."

How could it be that I'd literally trip over the first and last person I wanted to see right now? That warm feeling was spreading again somewhere below my belt and—God, who was controlling the heat settings in my body? I just stood there for a second, trying to figure out what to do. I knew what I *had* to do. Finally, I dropped down onto the grass next to him.

He kept squinting at me. "What's up?"

"You weren't at the assembly?" I asked, pulling out a blade of grass.

He flashed me that what-do-you-think? look. But all he said was, "I've been reading."

Well, that was a relief at least. He hadn't seen me cluelessly toss aside my morals—and my friendships. "Is it good?" I asked, gesturing at the book.

"It's okay," he said, flipping it over and resting it on his chest. "What's up?" he asked again.

Well, no time like the present, I guess. I took a deep breath. "Um, I know I said yes last week, but . . . but I don't think I can . . . go out with you."

"What?" He laughed, and then looked over at me a little confused. "Wait, this weekend or ever?" he asked, sitting up.

Oh, this sucked. I didn't want to lie to him, but I couldn't really explain the real reason. And the truth was, I *did* want to go out with him. I *so* wanted to go out with him. If only he *knew* how much I wanted to go out with him. But at the same time, it kind of scared me. I mean he kind of scared me. Well, not him really, it was more me around him that scared me.

"This weekend . . . " I said, trailing off. Coward.

"Really?" he asked. He could tell I was totally hedging. He scratched his beautiful thick head of hair. "Why not?"

Oh man. I should have planned this better. "Well, I just . . . I don't know. I just don't think it would be a good idea."

"What, did you run it by your popular posse, and they didn't sign your permission slip?"

"No! No, it's not like that at all. It's just that . . ." I scrambled for something to say.

"Yeah, okay." He shook his head. "I know how it works." He snapped his book shut and stood up. I looked down at the grass, waiting for an onslaught of angry words. But they didn't come. When I looked up again, Clint was already halfway across the lawn, headed for the lockers.

I'd done this thing for my friend, right? I'd done this for Bean. I should feel good about it, right? So why did I feel so much worse?

chapter thirty-seven

I just sat there, out in the boonies of sophomore hall, slumped over with my chin in my hands. No matter what I said, it always seemed like the wrong thing. The wind was starting to kick up now, blowing the grass around me in twisting waves. I looked up just as the sun disappeared behind a big dark cloud. Then it started to sprinkle. Perfect.

I leaned back and closed my eyes. The light rain felt cool on my face, and I didn't care if I got a little wet. I *wanted* to get wet. I wanted to wash this feeling away, this feeling of dumbness and dread. I felt like I had really blown something that could have been—I don't know. Like different and real and special.

I thought about my Drama scene with Clint. Could I fix this? Probably not. Clint and I were supposed to perform on Monday night. Ugh! Now with him feeling completely disgusted with me, thinking I'm some ridiculous rah-rah clone who can't think for herself . . . Who would want to woo that?

It started raining harder, so I got up and ran for the covered hallway. It was bad enough to *feel* like a rat. I didn't want to *look* like a wet rat too.

I wandered down the hall toward the crowded section and my locker, so in a depressed daze that I almost bumped right into Jen.

"Pais, hi." She touched my arm. "God, I've been looking all over for you." Jen was trying to smile, but I could tell she was upset. "Your speech was really great. You put the screws to that Miss UnPleasant. You're so right. She is a gutless coward."

I tried to smile back. I knew she was trying to be nice, but her compliment just made me feel worse. Was that even possible? Yes.

And then I noticed her necklace. It was a small but chunky silver *j*—with a sapphire or something as the dot—hanging from a short silver chain. Wow. Bodie's got money *and* style.

It was almost the end of lunch, and the halls were getting really crowded because of the rain. I watched Jen's face brighten.

"Hey, Hutch," she said all perky. Ugh. I didn't turn around.

Jen grabbed my arm and led me away from the crowd back toward the sophomore boonies. When we were a safe distance away, she burst into tears.

"What?" I stopped. "What is it?"

She shook her head, trying to cover her face with one hand, pulling me along past the few loners and dweebs and outsiders who stared at us as we walked by. When we got to the end of the hall where it was deserted, she rounded the corner and collapsed against the wall, sobbing.

"Jen, what happened?"

She shook her head. "It's bad, Pais, really bad."

I tried to imagine what could be so bad. Not so bad that she would cry but that she would come to me after everything that had happened. And to tell you the truth, I wasn't completely sure I trusted her. Was this just another setup?

"Why are you telling me?" I asked.

"You're the only one I trust. You're the only person I *can* talk to."

I eyed her. That was a switch.

"I did something . . ." She let out this big sigh. "I did something really . . ."

I waited for her to finish, but she started crying again, so I put my hand on her shoulder. I didn't know what to say. I still wanted to be mad at her, but Jen hardly ever lets her guard down. I was starting to worry. "You did something . . . bad?" I asked, trying to get her talking again.

"No!" She wiped her nose. "I mean, yeah, I did something stupid, but that's not the bad part."

The rain was coming down hard by then, hitting the roof like dancing pebbles. "What's the bad part?"

She gritted her teeth and sort of growled. These weren't sad tears. She was crying because she was angry, frustrated.

"Jen, what? What? Tell me."

"Oh, that stupid, stupid party. I hate those people! If only I hadn't gone. I so wish I had never gone."

"What party? Hutch's party?"

She nodded, dropping her head into one hand.

Okay, wait. That really confused me. I thought she *loved* those people. I thought that party was where she bonded with her new best girls and hooked up with Bodie.

"God, I'm such an idiot, I'm such a fool." She wiped under her eyes, careful not to smear her mascara. "There was this bathroom in the pool house." She shook her head. "Before the party, some sick creep—"

The warning bell for sixth period rang. Crap!

She wiped the tears from her face and tried to sniffle herself together. "Damn! I've got a test in sixth. I have to go."

We ran back toward our lockers, weaving our way through the crowded hallway.

"Want to talk tonight?" I asked, spinning the combination lock on my locker.

"Yeah. Can I come over?"

"Sure." She hadn't come over since before Labor Day weekend. I gave her a big hug. "Yeah, that'd be great." I wondered for the thousandth time what happened at that party. Whatever it was, it couldn't have been good.

I opened my locker—and another folded note fell out. I looked at it there on the ground. Jen looked at it too. Then she looked at me, puzzled.

Finally, I picked it up.

RIGHT ON, BABY.
MORE POWER TO THE POPS!

"I have a secret admirer." I shrugged, feeling more embarrassed than proud. "I've been getting anonymous notes in my locker since the first day of school."

"You're kidding." She tilted her head, thinking. "That's weird. I've been getting anonymous notes in my locker too."

"You have?" Damn. Suddenly I didn't feel so special.

"Yeah. But they're definitely *not* from a secret admirer."

chapter thirty-eight

I slammed my locker closed and took off for Biology. On the way, I passed a scraggly group of UnPops. OMG! They flipped me off! Whoa. And then all of them flashed the UnPop Power fist. I almost ran right into a pole.

I ran all the way to class and dropped into my seat, panting, just as the final bell rang. I was so distracted by what Jen had told me that I forgot to turn off my phone. About ten minutes into sixth period, it buzzed in my pocket.

I discreetly slipped it out and flipped it open. It was a text. From Charlie Dodd? That was weird.

Hutch bought his speech online!

No way! Was that true? I texted back under my desk.

Hw do u kno?

He told me.

Disgusting. What a lazy, pathetic cheater. I had to think about this. No way was I letting him get away with that on top of everything else. But what could I do? It's not like I could just run through the halls screaming, "Hutch bought his speech online!" Like anyone would even care. No. I had to be able to prove it.

I stared at the whiteboard, not thinking at all about how cells multiply.

And then it hit me. Maybe I *wouldn't* have to prove it. Maybe all I had to do was get people wondering . . .

Suddenly, I knew what to do. And I knew I had to write it that day if it was going to make it into the next edition of *The Fly*, which would be coming out right before the election.

And honestly, I was so charged up I couldn't wait. Besides, my weekend nights were becoming weirdly UnSocial with all the time I'd been spending writing "How to Be UnPopular" columns. So in Biology, I got to work. I pretended to be attentive, taking detailed class notes, but really I was scribbling a bunch of UnPleasant ideas in my notebook. By the end of class, I knew I had a killer secret weapon.

I waited until the end of the day. Then about halfway through final period, I stuffed my notebook into the back of my jeans and pulled my top over it. I asked to use the hall pass to go to the bathroom. But this was no bathroom break.

I speed-walked down the hall and ducked into the library. It was pretty dead in there. But I couldn't risk Ms. Whit seeing me. I quickly ducked behind the magazine rack and hauled booty for the reference shelves. Then I opened my notebook.

When the coast was clear, I crept out from behind a bookshelf. I checked over one shoulder and then the other. Then I slid into the chair in front of the computer closest to the book shelves—the one with the most protective cover. I knew I had to move fast. I went to *The Fly* website, clicked on SUBMISSIONS, and started speed-typing right into the submissions window. I finished in less than two minutes, and leaned back to double-check my bad typing. I made a few corrections and hit the SUBMIT button.

I stood up, feeling pretty darn pleased. Maybe everything would work out okay after all. I turned to leave, but then stopped. I had this weird feeling. I looked around and didn't see anyone. I turned the other way—and there was Ms. Whit, staring at me from across the room with her arms folded over her chest. I'd already used my Get Out of Jail Free card on the first day of school. What could I do? I smiled, shrugged, and bolted.

As I rounded the corner into the hall, I ran smack into Charlie Dodd.

He seemed surprised for a second, or maybe just preoccupied. But he wouldn't look me in the eye. Then he shook his head. "Nice one, Paisley."

I didn't know if he was talking about my disastrous speech at assembly this morning or me running into him just now. "Uh, sorry," I said lamely. "Hey, thanks for the tip about Hutch."

"Yeah, no worries." He looked at his feet, tugging nervously on the bottom of his black XXL polo shirt like he was trying to decide what to say. And for Charlie, that was bizarre. When he finally looked at me, he had this weird expression on his face. But all he said was, "Good to know the real you, Paisley." Then he turned and walked into the library.

Talk about mixed signals. What was up with Charlie Dodd?

And then I had this horrible sinking feeling. I remembered Charlie's stunned expression at the assembly . . . and I groaned. Oh no. Thanks to my brilliant More-Power-to-the-Pops speech, had I just lost my campaign manager too? Or was it more than that?

chapter thirty-nine

It poured rain all weekend—there were flood warnings and everything. I sat on the couch eating like a whole bag of Pirate's Booty, watching bad reality TV, while I worked on my campaign speech for president.

I felt totally crappy.

I'd managed to alienate practically all of my friends and romantic possibilities in a single day. Was that like some kind of world record?

And Jen never showed up Friday night. She ignored my texts and my calls. God, I was such a sucker. And by Saturday afternoon, it was clear the Walnut Festival wasn't happening. The TV news said it was being postponed till next Saturday.

It's not like I was going anyway. Who would I go with? Not Cate, not Bean, not Carreyn, not Amy, not Jen, not even Charlie Dodd. Eric thought I was a shallow idiot after hearing my totally UnInspired anti–Miss UnPleasant speech. God, the look on his face when he lowered his camera . . . I'd never forget it.

And what *about* Eric? I still liked him. Was that so bad? Was it bad to like two guys at once? It's not like I could just switch my feelings on and off like a floor lamp. And Clint—Clint thought

I was a total Pop snob. Ugh, I couldn't even begin to imagine what our *Acting Out* performance would be like on Monday. Total disaster.

I must have fallen asleep on the couch. I don't know. I just remember being startled when my dad came bounding down the stairs in his running gear, including his dorky neon yellow vest over a rain jacket. I sat up, my heart pounding.

"Hey Pais, come on! Let's go for a run."

"Dad," I grumbled. "It's *pouring* out there."

"I know! It's gonna be great!" He started doing his quad stretches. "Nothing better than a run in the rain to clear your head. It's a meditative outdoor shower. It's an endorphin-powered brain rinse. Come on!"

I just looked at him. "No thanks." I sighed. I was so inside my own head space that if I cleared it, I wasn't sure I'd even exist anymore.

"We could talk while we run?" he suggested.

"Yeah, but I really have to work on my speech," I said. "Thanks anyway." I waved and fell back onto the couch, closing my eyes.

"Can't wait to hear it!" He ran out the back door and into the pouring rain.

By Saturday night, I was stuffing handfuls of Pirate's Booty into my mouth. Just stuffing and stuffing, I was so mad. I couldn't believe the mess I'd gotten myself into. I really wished that Mom wasn't off at a Yogilates retreat. I actually *wanted* to talk to her for a change.

Then I stopped. I was having this horrible, dawning realization as I listened to the rain coming down.

OMG, I didn't even *have* to cancel with Clint. I didn't even *have* to make it into this whole big thing. The rain would have taken care of it for me. Oh God, this was the worst. I wish I hadn't even thought of it. I dug back into the bag of Pirate's Booty.

Wait.

No.

Of *course* I had to say something to him on Friday. I mean, I wasn't just calling off our date. I was calling off *Clint*. And I was doing it for Bean. It wouldn't have been fair otherwise . . . I mean, that's why I'd done it, right? For Bean? Or was I just telling myself that? I mean, I knew I was sort of afraid, you know, of the way Clint made me *feel*. But if I was going to be totally straight with myself, I guess I was also sort of afraid of . . . of what some people might think.

Suddenly my bones felt like lead. Oh God, I really was the worst of the gutless cowards. What was I going to do?

chapter forty

On Monday morning, I was still feeling so crappy that I didn't even want to go to school. It was only *Acting Out* and my curiosity about Miss UnPleasant's latest column that got me out of bed.

Carpool was painful. No one would sit next to me. Two Library Girls scowled at me over their shoulders, whispering back and forth. Sleeping-braces-kid flashed the UnPop Power fist with a nasty grin, then closed his eyes and went back to sleep. The dweeby UnDiscovered freshman turned to me. "*More* power?" He shook his head sadly. "Really? I thought you were one of the *nice* ones."

Ouch. That one really hurt.

Charlie Dodd wasn't in carpool. Charlie Dodd was *always* in carpool. I guess he didn't want to get stuck ignoring obnoxious, podium-power me all the way to school. I couldn't really blame him.

I stared out the window, trying to focus on my day. *The Fly* probably wouldn't be out until just before lunch, so I should spend all morning campaigning wherever I could—especially in the outer limits of sophomore hall. The election was only a day away, and I had a lot of damage-control to do. I really needed to score big with the fringe factor if I was going to crush Hutch. And after my crazy speech in the quad . . . Oh God. Would we find out the fate of Miss UnPleasant today, I wondered, or would the administration wait to read her next snarky column and then decide? I shook my head. Ugh, I didn't want to think about it.

Fortunately my shipment of PAISLEY POWER temporary tattoos had arrived on Saturday along with my bags of customized pink and green M&M'S. Half of them said *Paisley 4 Pres!* The other half said *Spastic Jazzed!*

Yes, it's true. Hutch had inspired me—I refused to let him be the only one with shameless self-promotional treats and toys.

Before homeroom, I set out for the far end of sophomore hall. As I was handing stuff out, I got some major UnPop brattitude from a bunch of girls. They actually flung my M&M'S back at me. Then a few AV Guys flashed the UnPop Power fist—one of them even turned his clenched fist around like he was threatening to hit me. OMG. Creepy. But most people were like, "Thanks, cool, whatever," just happy to be getting candy for free.

Not LG Wong. She was standing with a clump of dog-eared Library Girls. She took one look at the temporary tattoo I gave her and laughed in my face. "*Paisley Power?* How perfect," she said all snarky. "*More* power to you, Paisley."

The Library Girls all snickered.

I got out of there fast—and ran into Bean and Cate near the far end of the hall. The air between my teeth hissed as I sucked in a breath. Uh-oh. This might hurt.

They were rehearsing their scene. I watched them for a few seconds until Cate noticed me and stopped. I stood there awkwardly. She put her hand on her hip and raised her chin. "Miss UnPleasant is *not* a coward," she said, zapping me with her crazy laser-beam blue eyes.

I glanced at Bean and then back at Cate. Then I heaved this huge, heavy sigh. "I know. I know," I finally said. "I got a little carried away up there. I'm really sorry. Believe me."

"Why did you even say that?" Bean asked, looking at me in total disbelief.

I couldn't tell them the truth. I so wanted to, I realized. But I couldn't. So I stood there, not knowing what to say. They looked at me. I looked at them. And then I just blurted, "It was for my campaign. You know, for visibility. I—I didn't mean all that stuff. I just wanted to . . . to stand out and be . . . um, controversial."

Cate gave me this long yeah-right look.

"Hey, here's a peace offering." I handed each of them a few temporary tattoos and a bag of Spastic Jazzed M&M'S. "Don't hate me, okay?" I asked, looking from one of them to the other.

"Don't worry," said Cate. "I don't care enough about you to hate you."

Um, did that mean she was still mad at me?

"Yum, chocolate! Thanks, Pais." Bean ripped open her bag of candy and dumped half of it into her mouth. "I don't agree with *all* your campaign tactics," she said around a mouthful of

M&M'S, "but I do agree with some. You need any help passing stuff out?"

"Actually, yeah. That'd be great," I said, thinking of the UnPops who'd flung my M&M'S back at me. "Thanks. Come by my locker at lunch, okay? See you guys in Drama." I waved, heading back down the hall toward Popularity Place.

Lunch. OMG. I'd almost forgotten. *The Fly* would be out. I was dying to read my little UnPop Quiz and see how people reacted—nothing like juicy gossip to get tongues wagging. By the end of lunch, practically everyone in our class would know that Hutch didn't write his own campaign speech. What a skeezy creep cheater. And who would vote for him then?

chapter forty-one

Clint wasn't at school. Or maybe he just cut Drama because he was too disgusted to look at me. I wondered if he was even going to show up for *Acting Out* that night.

I sat on a windowsill doodling in my notebook, watching the others rehearse their scenes for the last time. Charlie Dodd and Teddy Baedeker were still using their scripts a little. Bean and Cate were having a hard time rehearsing because they kept cracking each other up. Svend, the cool foreign exchange student, was rehearsing with Mandy Mindel. She actually looked like she was having fun for a change. I smiled.

Mandy saw me and gave me a shy smile. I waved back, surprised. I was even more surprised when they got to the end of their scene and she walked over to me. "Hi," she said, twisting her hands in front of her. "Um . . . did Miss UnPleasant ever . . . ever um, say anything to you?" she asked, looking up at me for a second. "I mean, after the assembly?"

"Nope. Not yet," I said, shaking my head. "I was kinda harsh, though. I'm not sure she'd *want* to talk to me." I laughed like, *Oh, silly me and my crazy podium-power.*

"Well, if you um, if you figure out who it is, will you . . . will you tell me?" she asked. "I really want to talk to her."

I nodded, wondering what Mandy wanted to say to Miss UnPleasant.

"Okay, um, thanks." She gave me this little wave down by her hip, and then walked back to Svend.

At the end of class, I found Bean and Cate. "Hey, you guys feeling ready for tonight?"

"Yeah, ready to burst into hysterics!" Bean said giddily. "What about you?"

"I don't know. I don't know where Clint is. I hope he shows tonight."

"I'll call him," said Cate. "He'll show." She looked at me but didn't smile.

Was she still mad? I couldn't tell. Then I remembered something, and my heart started beating fast.

"Oh, hey Bean," I said, feeling awkward all of a sudden. "Um, Clint and I decided to bag our date on Saturday. It seemed kind of stupid. I mean, other than *Taming of the Shrew*, we don't really have much in common. And after tonight, you know, that'll be over, so . . ."

"Really?" She looked super happy. "It seemed stupid?"

The damage was already done with Clint, I'd decided. I might as well share the good part and make Bean happy. "Well, I mean, we're so . . . different. What would we even talk about?" I said. "Just thought you'd want to know."

Cate shot me a knowing glance and then smiled. "Maybe there's still hope for you."

I smiled back.

At lunch, I made a beeline for *The Fly* stack in the main hall, trying not to walk too fast.

When I saw the headline, I caught my breath. "Miss UnPleasant Writes On!" Yes! I didn't bother reading the article and skipped straight to my column.

MISS UnPLEASANT'S UnPOP QUIZ

Okay, people. Heads up—pencils down! It's time for your first UnPop Quiz.

1. Which incredibly popular hottie has a secret crush on sweet, adorable me?
2. Which candidate for sophomore class president bought his speech online?
3. Which BP flirts shamelessly with one hot guy just to make another—the one she *really* likes—jealous?
4. Which Varsity Pom stole her mom's credit card to get a nose job?
5. Which sophomore rah-rah is getting love notes in her locker?
6. Which brainy babe ignored an invite to speak at the assembly because she has way more power if she stays UnNonymous?

Pop goes the weasel!

Big kiss, class dismissed!
Miss UnPleasant

After about five minutes, it was clear that my Miss UnPleasant plan had worked—only, maybe a little *too* well. I ran back to my locker to meet Bean and pass out more Paisley promo paraphernalia. But all during lunch, I couldn't help listening in on people's conversations everywhere we went.

"Number three," said Carreyn, sitting with Amy on our bench reading *The Fly*. "'Which BP flirts shamelessly with one hot guy just to make another—the one she *really* likes—jealous?'"

"That would be *all* of them," said Amy matter-of-factly.

I saw Charlie run up to Hutch at his locker and show him *The Fly*. Hutch said an unpleasant expletive very loudly and slammed his locker. I suppressed an evil chuckle.

Then Eric walked up to Hutch and Charlie. I couldn't hear them, but it looked like they were talking about something serious. Eric turned and stared at me. He looked, I don't know, worried or something. He didn't smile or wave. Then he looked back to Hutch. Weird.

But I didn't think much of it. I was too distracted. The UnPop Quiz had caused this delicious cacophony of speculation and accusations. It started slowly, like popcorn popping, and then got faster and louder and crazier. I couldn't help but smile.

"How could any popular hottie have a crush on *her*?"

"Hutch."

"Of course it's Hutch. He's the only guy running for president."

"Are you getting love letters in your locker?"

"No. Are you?"

"Hey, I'm not a rah-rah!"

When Bean and I turned the corner, BS2 and BS1 were heading toward us on their way back to junior hall. And they were really going at it.

"I didn't tell *anyone* you stole her card. Not a single person!" cried BS2.

"You liar!" BS1 snarled. "You're the only one who knew!"

OMG. That one I just made up!

"It's true! She *does* have more power if she stays anonymous."

"A lot more power."

"Yeah, but if anyone finds out who she is, she's totally dead."

And my smile totally faded.

chapter forty-two

Acting Out started at 7:00. It was 6:50, and there was still no sign of Clint.

I peeked out through the side of the curtain. The audience was really filling up. People were chattering away. Logan Adler and a bunch of Dumbe Blondes had gathered in the back, holding up signs in a silent protest. "THE ARTS ROOL!" "DRAMA QUEENS GIVE ME THE CLAP!" "I SUPPORT PERFORMANCE ANGZIETY!" "HOMERUN!"

Grambo and my parents were in the third row, sitting next to Mr. and Mrs. Merrill, studying the program, probably reading my mini bio over and over. OMG! A few rows back on the other side, I spotted Jen and Amy and Carreyn—and *Eric Sobel!* What was he doing here?! Oh right, probably just taking photos for Yearbook.

Even so, I got a jolt of chills and pulled back from the curtain. Now I was sort of relieved that Clint hadn't shown up. I wasn't sure I wanted Eric to see me wrestling around in Clint Bedard's arms. I wasn't sure *I* wanted to be wrestling around in Clint Bedard's arms. Okay, who was I kidding? I wanted to. I so wanted to. But it totally freaked me out at the same time.

I wouldn't have to worry about it if Clint didn't show up, though.

I found Cate and Bean backstage doing relaxation exercises in front of the girls' dressing area. I almost squealed, they looked so great. They were both dressed like old men with funny hats and neckties and plaid pants. They were even wearing men's dress shoes! I love those guys.

"Break a leg!" I said to them.

"You too," said Bean.

Cate shook out her arms. "I am so damn nervous!"

"Don't worry. Your scene is hilarious. Everyone's gonna love it."

"Have you seen Clint yet?" Bean asked.

"Nope." I sighed. "I'm pretty sure he's not coming."

"No, I mean, he's here. He's right behind you."

Was she kidding?

I turned around. Clint was standing right there, holding a garment bag over one shoulder.

"Hey!" I broke out into a huge goobery grin, but I couldn't help it. I was so happy to see him. "You're here?!"

"Yeah, I'm here. You think I'd blow this off just 'cause you blew me off?"

Cate and Bean looked at each other, then at me. "Clint, I'm sorry I—"

"Save it. Whatever." He walked away to the guys' dressing area and went inside.

Cate and Bean looked at each other again.

"Holy molé," said Cate. "You blew him off? I thought you said you both decided it was stupid to go out."

"Well . . ."

"Pais, he likes you," Bean whispered, sounding like she had just solved a big mystery.

"No, he doesn't. Not anymore, if he ever did. Trust me."

"No, I think he does." Cate nodded. "I've never seen him like that. Oh, I can't wait to watch you two go at it in your scene!"

Bean didn't seem all that disappointed, actually. I guess maybe it had never occurred to her that guys like Clint Bedard could ever like girls like me. Frankly, it had never occurred to me before either.

"Well, I guess I should come clean," Bean said, blushing. "I feel kinda bad now, after what you did, Pais . . . But you know Svend, the exchange student? He just asked me out today at lunch. Can you believe it? Apparently tall gangly blondes remind him of home. And Svend told me he's *very* homesick."

What?! OMG. Well, that explained it. I couldn't believe that I'd killed my date with Clint! *Aaaaaaah!* I could have screamed. Instead, I gave her a big hug.

Mr. Eggertson gathered us all together and delivered a quick pep talk. Then he went onstage to introduce *Acting Out*. And then the curtain went up.

Charlie Dodd and Teddy Baedeker opened the show with their "Who's On First?" scene. Teddy was playing this dopey ding-a-ling who couldn't get anything straight, and Charlie was playing this over-thinking, frustrated control freak. And I have to say they were both *really* good. Even though they screwed up some lines, they really got the crowd laughing.

Then a few other groups did their scenes—some were pretty good and a few were pretty awful. Then Cate and Bean did their *Odd Couple* scene. I watched from the wings, so I couldn't see the audience but I could sure hear them, and they were laughing like crazy. I could hear my mom, and I just knew she and Mrs. Merrill were crying with laughter.

I looked across the stage. Clint was standing in the wings in the shadows on the far side. A huge tidal wave of nervousness smacked into me. We were next! *Aaaaaaah!*

Cate and Bean's scene ended, and the audience went nuts, clapping and cheering. I was so nervous. I already had swamp pits. Cate and Bean took a quick bow. Then the lights went down. As Bean moved offstage and I moved on to my position, Bean whispered, "Go Pais!"

I took my place, waiting for the lights to come up. And when they did . . . OMG! Holy molé was right! I blinked a few times. The audience hooted and whistled. Clint was standing across from me looking like some sexy, bad-ass swashbuckler. He was wearing these tight black pants tucked into knee-high black boots. And his off-white shirt was loose and billowy and—I swear to God—open practically to his belly button. Talk about an Elizabethan hottie! I started to pant with fear. At least I think it was fear.

"Good morrow, Kate," said Clint in his stage voice. "For that's your name, I hear."

"Well have you heard, but something hard of hearing." I walked around him in a half circle, and then cocked my head, full of attitude. "They call me Katherine that do talk of me."

He laughed in his mocking yet flirtatious way. "You lie, in faith, for you are called plain Kate, and bonny Kate and . . . "

Thank God, the minute I started speaking my lines, my fear transformed into energy. I was totally in it. And Clint was right there with me. He became Petruchio like I had never seen in our rehearsals. He was dashing, charming, flirtatious, confident, and really Shakespeare-ish.

We didn't just deliver our lines. We moved around the stage like we were sparring and dancing and flirting all at the same time. It was intense. I couldn't tell if I was just one hundred percent in character or if he was really making me *feel*. And then we got to the really, really intense part of the scene.

Of course, we were speaking Shakespeare. But Clint was basically saying, "I really dig you. You're hot, and I want to marry you." And I was all, "No way! You're not good enough for me—even though I'm way hot for you. But I'd never admit it in a million years." And it was full of all this sexual innuendo and plays on words like tail and stinger and tongue. Oh boy, that William Shakespeare!

Then Clint grabbed me and pulled me up against his chest and whispered in my ear, "Nay hear you, Kate: in sooth you 'scape not so." He had tiny beads of sweat on his forehead. I wanted to reach up and wipe them off, but I had to stay in character.

"I chafe you, if I tarry," I replied, struggling a little to get away—but not too hard since, let's face it, both Katherine and I kind of melted whenever he whispered in our ear.

Clint spun me around and held me in his arms while I struggled to break free. His chest felt warm against my back, and I could feel him breathing hard. I kept struggling to get out of his grip. And then? I heard my dress rip.

Uh-oh.

I looked down as the front of my dress pulled away from the poofy shoulder part. Good thing I was wearing a really cute bra! A few people in the audience laughed. I heard a camera speed-clicking. But I didn't break. I just clutched the front of my dress, holding it up, and looked at Clint like I was furious.

"No, not a whit," he said. "I find you passing gentle." I struggled again and spun around, but he grabbed both of my wrists and stared into my eyes, holding me close. "'Twas told me you were rough and coy and sullen, and now I find report a very liar. For thou are pleasant, gamesome, passing courteous, but slow in speech, yet sweet as springtime flowers . . ."

I was so caught up in the words, and the emotion *behind* the words, that I began to lean toward him. God, I wanted to kiss him. And I almost did. But then at the last possible second I remembered that we were up onstage in front of my parents, my grandmother, and about a hundred other people, including Eric Sobel. I suddenly pulled back, turning my head to the side. Wow. That was close.

It went along like that for a few more steamy minutes. I struggled—holding my dress together—pretending not to like him, trying to push him away, while Clint tried to wear me down with his honesty and his charm and his open shirt. And boy, was it working. Whoops! Did I say Clint? I meant Petruchio.

And then before I knew it, our scene came to an end. Clint held me in his arms, leaning over me like he was about to kiss me. My head was dropped back, but still our mouths were just a few inches apart. He was panting. I was panting. I looked into his eyes and they were hungry. And for a second I thought he really was going to kiss me. And honestly? I hoped he would. I really didn't care who was watching anymore.

But then the audience began to clap and scream and cheer. Someone whistled like a teenaged boy. I'm pretty sure it was my Grambo, because she does that kind of thing. Then Clint drew me up so I was standing, and he let me go. I almost fell over. I was so . . . so . . . I don't know what. But then he grabbed my hand and pulled me back next to him, and we did our little bow. When we straightened up, he turned and hugged me, lifting me up so that my toes came just off the floor.

I could barely breathe. I was having a major below-the-belt meltdown.

Then the lights went down. And I'm sure this time—his lips brushed my cheek.

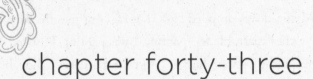

chapter forty-three

Backstage, Clint and I didn't talk. I hung out with the girls and he went over to the guys. I had a lot to think about, and maybe he did too. I don't know.

After the show, Amy came up to me and gave me this big hug. "Pais, that was amazing! You're a really good weird-ass drama freakazoid!"

"Thanks," I said, laughing. Maybe I was.

Carreyn came over and gave me a quick hug. "Wow. That was *hot!* I've got to read more Shakespeare. Okay, well, any Shakespeare." She laughed.

My parents and Grambo came up and did the whole proud parent and grandparent thing. It was a little embarrassing, especially when Grambo high-fived me. But fortunately Bean's and Cate's and everyone else's parents were doing the same proud parent thing. I looked over at Clint, but I didn't see anyone who looked like his family. And then, thank God, the parents retreated to a safe distance where they could swap embarrassing parenting stories or whatever it is they do.

I was sort of hoping that Eric and Jen would come over and

say something to me, but they didn't. I watched them walk out the door toward the parking lot. Oh well.

Then Clint grabbed me from behind. I could smell it was him. Mmmm. I closed my eyes and melted back into his arms. "That was fun," he said, lifting me up and spinning me around. "Maybe even more fun than a regular date."

I didn't say anything for a second. I just inhaled and smiled like a goober and nodded. I was a little afraid of what might come out of my mouth. But at the same time, I was like really feeling the emotion behind the words. And you know what? That was it. I decided I was going to say it. So what if I sounded like an idiot? At least I'd sound like a fearless idiot.

I turned to face Clint. "Hey, um . . . I know I called off our date. You know, the date that the rain probably would have called off anyway and I, um . . . I'd kinda like to propose a rain date. You know, I mean . . . if you're up for it."

I looked at him hopefully, waiting for some response. But he just stared at me, eyes squinted.

And then he finally said, "Red, you are *trouble*." He picked me up and swung me around again. We both laughed. I felt like I was going to melt and slip right through his arms.

I had a hard time sleeping that night. I lay in bed with Dyson, mainlining my customized "Paisley 4 Pres!" M&M'S while so many thoughts and questions swirled through my head. Mostly I was wondering why Jen had reached out to me like that, then never showed up at my house and now wasn't talking to me again.

I traced a pink M&M in my notebook and then wrote "Why" in it. And what happened in that bathroom at that stupid party? I was almost tempted just to ask Hutch. He must know *something*. It happened at his house.

I traced another one and wrote "What happened?" and chased it with an arrow, then scribbled "Flush Hutch!"

And then I kept rehearsing my speech in my head, especially the big audience laughs. I knew it was going to be a tight race and I didn't want to be insanely nervous. Hutch probably never got nervous. At least he never seemed nervous. Ugh. I hated Hutch.

And what about Eric? Eric. Eric. Eric. I so blew it with him when I made that drunk-with-podium-power anti–Miss UnPleasant speech. God, what could he think of me after that steamy scene with Clint? If he even thinks of me at all.

But what was really keeping me awake was Clint. I couldn't stop playing the mental movie of our scene over and over and over again trying to relive the experience—and I mean the *whole* experience.

I'm pretty sure when I *did* fall asleep, it was with a smile on my face.

chapter forty-four

Something felt weird the day of the speeches. For starters, Hutch was being really nice to me. At morning break he came up to our bench, acting all friendly.

"Hey, Team Paisley!" he said, interrupting my speech—I'd been practicing all morning. "Brought you guys a good-luck sticky bun." Carreyn's eyes lit up, but Amy and I were instantly suspicious.

"Is it poisoned?" Amy asked, poking it with her finger.

"Are you hoping I'll choke on it and not be able to give my speech?"

"Choke? No way. The speeches are gonna be fun today. I know yours is gonna be crazy good."

"Thanks," I said uncertainly. "You too."

I saw Eric Sobel in the hall at lunch while I was passing out our *I'd Vote for Paisley* buttons.

"Hey," I mouthed to him across the crowded hallway.

He didn't say anything. He just stared at me, like maybe he recognized me but wasn't quite sure. I guess he was still annoyed at me for bashing his imaginary girlfriend Miss UnPleasant at the assembly last week. Either that or . . . or he felt weird about me after watching my steaming hot scene with Clint. Ergh.

After lunch, everyone in our class started gathering outside the gym for the speeches assembly sixth period. It was a warm sunny day, so everyone waited until the last minute to go inside. Carreyn and Amy were both doing their best to pump me up.

"You're gonna do great!" Amy cheered. "Just be the Fun of a Kind Girl we all know you are!"

I laughed nervously. "I'll try," I said.

Carreyn nodded and gave me a little pat on the back. "Don't get all freaky nervo. Your speech is awesome. Really. I know because I've heard it like ten times. High five!"

As we goofily high-fived, I caught sight of Hutch and Charlie Dodd talking. "Since when did those two become friends?" I asked.

Amy and Carreyn turned to look. "That's beaucoup bizarro," said Carreyn. "I thought Hutch hated Charlie."

"And in reverse," added Amy.

"Yeah," I agreed, watching Hutch and Charlie get into it. "Weird."

"Hey, Pais, good luck!" Bean chirped as she and Cate walked by on their way into the gym. "I'll be vibing you positive energy." She wiggled her fingers at me.

I just laughed. What a goof.

Cate stopped and gave me a quick hug. "You know I love Miss UnPleasant, but I still like you as a friend. Kick Hutch's butt for us, okay?"

"Looking forward to it," I said, smiling.

Mr. Eggertson and a few other teachers were trying to herd all of us into the gym. He smiled at me and tapped his chest three times. That was Drama class code for "feel the emotion behind the words."

I tapped three times back.

I kind of hoped I'd see Jen walking in, but it didn't happen.

"Come on people, take your seats," Mr. Canfield barked into the microphone. "We've got a lot of speeches to get through."

All of the candidates running for sophomore class office were seated in a row of chairs in front of the bleachers. I was between LG Wong and Hutch. Ugh. The gym was buzzing. It was so noisy, I couldn't think—which was probably a good thing because thinking made me more nervous, and more nervous made me have to pee.

I turned around and waved at Amy and Carreyn sitting in the front row of the bleachers, then scanned the crowd for Jen. I finally spotted her a few rows up, but she was all caught up in a conversation with Eric Sobel. Fortunately, Bean was sending me more positive vibes with her wiggling fingers.

Clint Bedard was practically the last person into the gym. He probably got busted trying to skip the assembly. I watched him climb up the side of the bleachers and squeeze in next to Cate. He caught my eye and gave me a clipped military salute. Whoa. Certain parts of my body did the wave. God, how does he do that to me?

I had practiced my speech so many times that I basically had it memorized, but I still wanted to be able to look at it just in case I had a total brain freeze. Even though I felt solid about my message and my jokes, I still had butterflies in my butt. And my sweaty palms kept rolling my speech up into a little paper baton.

I leaned down the row of jumpy, twitching candidates and mouthed "Good luck!" to Charlie Dodd. He looked particularly uncomfortable and winced more than nodded in my direction. Why did he have a laptop on his knees? Oh, I hoped he wasn't going to do some obnoxious flow-chart presentation with his speech.

I snuck a peek at LG Wong's notes on her lap. They looked like some math equation. She probably *does* dream in numbers. Then she turned to me. "Don't you just love the democratic process? I think I'm gonna puke."

"Me too," I said with a nervous giggle. That was funny. Was LG Wong funny? I couldn't figure out why *she* was nervous about her speech. No one was even running against her. She could stand up there and do an interpretive dance of the Pythagorean Theorem and win.

Just then, Mr. Canfield stepped back up to the podium and explained how it all would work. The candidates for secretary would go first, then the treasurers, then the VPs, and then the presidents. Great. I had plenty of time to make myself queasy.

Kirby Scarborough went first. I really tried to listen, but she lost me when she started connecting her childhood butterfly collection to her being a social butterfly now, and somehow that made her the most qualified to be secretary.

Charlie went next, but he left the laptop on his chair. Was he going to be the AV guy for Hutch's speech? That was weird. Why would he do that?

But Charlie was great. His entire speech, he acted like he was running for secretary of state instead of secretary of the sophomore class. He talked about his plan to negotiate a peace alliance between the sophomore and junior classes and his desire to spend as much time in face-to-face talks with Poms and BPs as possible because popularity was definitely a foreign policy to him. And his big idea was to impose economic sanctions on the freshmen by forcing them to pay a toll every time they walked through sophomore hall. It was good. Everyone laughed. I was definitely voting for him.

Keep it funny. Keep it funny. Keep it funny. I exhaled deep breaths, trying to pay attention to the other candidates' speeches. But I couldn't stop rehearsing mine over and over. I was stuck in my head—and there was no indie-groovy soundtrack playing this time. It was more like fingernails on a chalkboard.

Finally—thank God—it was time for the presidential candidates. I snapped to and sat up straight in my chair.

"The first of our two candidates for sophomore class president hardly needs an introduction." Mr. Canfield chuckled, smacking his fish lips together. "I'm sure you all know Peter Hutchison! Come on up, Hutch!"

The audience clapped and whistled and cheered. Canfield clapped like a total suck-up.

Hutch bounded up the stairs, pretending to trip at the top step, which got everyone laughing. Crap. Physical comedy. Everyone loves physical comedy. He stepped behind the podium and launched into his speech, raising both arms.

"Friends, Hornets, countrymen, lend me your ears!" He looked down at his notes. "Whoa! Wrong speech. I bought that one online last week but it seemed a little too old-school."

People laughed. Not me.

"Seriously, I'm running for president for three simple reasons—all things I truly believe in and genuinely value. Leadership, scholarship, and chip and dip!"

More laughing.

Hey! I shot Charlie an evil look. That was *my* line! He didn't look at me. What was going on?

"Okay, I guess that's four reasons, but you get the idea." Hutch chuckled.

"I'm a leader on and off the field, I'm a serious student—even though I don't always act like it outside of class, *and* I throw killer parties!" People laughed again. "So if I am elected class president, each and every one of you will be invited to my next party!"

Everyone went nuts at that one, whistling and whooping. Except for me.

"Because bringing people together is one of my favorite extracurricular activities. Know what I'm saying?" He nodded with sort of a creepy grin.

More laughing and whistling.

"Okay, okay, but I'm not up here because of me—I'm up here because of *you*. I want to work for you! I love this school and I want to make this class the best sophomore class in history! And I can do it. I'm a guy with connections and I can get things done. Trust me with the awesome responsibility of being your class president, and I promise you, I will not drop the ball." He laughed at his own bad joke. "I'll totally be open to your ideas, your suggestions, and your propositions—especially if you're a really hot babe."

Laughs, then a few of boos, and then more freakin' laughs!

"Go with a proven winner, go with Hutch—I'm open!" He faked catching a football and doing a touchdown spike on the stage. "Thank you! Thank you!"

The audience clapped and cheered.

What an idiot. What a cocky jerk. I had this thing in the bag.

Hutch was beaming as he hopped down the steps. He gave a few people in the front row of the bleachers knuckle knocks and then strutted back over to his seat and plopped down next to me, flashing a big ol' winner's smile. Then he laughed, like he was in on some private joke.

"And now our second and final candidate for sophomore class president, Paisley Hanover!" Mr. Canfield clapped politely.

I confidently climbed the steps to the stage while the audience clapped and cheered. Of course, my friends were hooting and whistling and screaming like rowdy lunatics. I had a hard time un-smiling as I flattened out my speech on the podium.

I was just about to begin when Hutch hopped back up onstage and grabbed the mic off the stand in front of me. "Before you get started, Paisley, a few of us varsity jerks have a special treat for you."

He turned to the audience. "I think you're all *really* gonna like this."

chapter forty-five

The audience was suddenly going nuts. People were talking, then booing at Hutch and yelling.

"Sit down!"

"You had your turn!"

"Come on, man! Give her the mic!"

What was going *on?* I turned to Canfield and spread my hands, like *do something!* He stood up but looked as surprised as I was.

"Hutch, sit down!" Canfield yelled over the crowd. "You gave your speech! We're on a schedule here. This is Paisley's time."

I tried to grab the mic back, but Hutch held it up over his head. So then I tried to be cool, acting like maybe I had a clue what was going on.

The audience started stomping and chanting. *"Paisley! Paisley! Paisley!"* The gym filled with this deafening, chaotic roar. It was pretty cool, but I was so pissed at Hutch, it was hard to enjoy the moment.

Hutch seemed to be pleading his case to Canfield, but I couldn't hear a thing he was saying. Canfield just kept shaking his head.

Then Hutch turned away from Canfield. "Charlie, roll video!" he yelled into the mic, pointing at Charlie Dodd. "Roll it! Now!" Charlie looked completely terrified.

The audience was still chanting and stomping. *"Paisley! Paisley! Paisley!"*

And then everyone went totally silent. Hutch and Canfield turned to look up at the screen behind me.

Okay, seriously. What. Was. Going. On?!! I traced the cord from the projector to . . . Charlie Dodd's laptop?!

No. No. This couldn't be happening. Charlie Dodd?!! What—? Unless . . . Were they showing that stupid Spastic Jazz Hands video on YouTube? Oh, please. That was so old. Get over it, people. I looked at Eric Sobel, frowning. He saw me and quickly looked away.

I refused to turn around. It was so stupid. I couldn't believe that Hutch could get away with this, or that Charlie was in on it. Fine. I'd just stand there until it was over and then calmly start my fabulous speech.

I watched the audience. Everyone was looking at the screen behind me. It was actually kind of cool. In their faces, I saw confusion, fascination, boredom, curiosity. Some people were shaking their heads.

Wait. Why wasn't I hearing the humiliating, ridiculous rap that went with the video?

This tangy, sour, metallic taste started bubbling up from my stomach. But the voice in my head kept me focused. *I will not turn around, I will not turn around, I will not turn around—*

I couldn't help turning just a little, just enough to see Hutch looking up at the screen. He was sporting a big ol' smile.

I will not turn around, I will not turn around, I will not let Hutch screw with my confidence! I turned back to face the audience.

Cate and Bean and Clint were all staring up at the screen with confused, curious expressions. Amy and Carreyn were leaning forward, their mouths hanging open. Jen held her hand up to her mouth, watching in total fascination. Eric Sobel looked like he was in physical pain.

Don't look. Don't turn around. Just keep breathing. Just keep breathing. Don't look. Don't turn around. Just keep breathing. Just keep breathing. Whatever it is, it'll all be over soon.

Suddenly, the audience erupted. "No way!" someone shouted. People were gasping and pointing at the screen, yells, boos, hisses, laughter. "Oh my *God!*" Carreyn screamed. Everyone in the gym, even the teachers watching from the side, started talking all at once.

"What?!"

"No!"

"Oooooh!"

"Rewind!"

I couldn't stand it anymore. I turned and faced the screen.

It was . . . It was hard to be sure what it was at first. It looked like the back of my head and part of one shoulder. And there was a little red flashing graphics arrow, pointing at a few barely legible words on the computer monitor in front of me.

I tilted my head to read them.

Big kiss, class dismissed!

Miss UnPleasant

Oh, God. No.

The audience was going crazy, hissing and booing and screaming.

I watched the image of myself peek over one shoulder, looking utterly guilty, and type a little more. Then I stood up from the computer, looking quite pleased with myself, and stuffed my notebook into the back of my jeans. I turned to leave. But then I tensed—you could see me do it. I looked around furtively, like a criminal. And I froze. You could see my eyes looking off beyond the camera. My face slowly got really huge as the camera zoomed in, giving everyone a nice view up one nostril. It stayed like that for a second before suddenly pulling back to show me all bug-eyed. Then I smiled this weird smile, shrugged once, and ran off. The screen went dark.

There was some laughter, some shouts, more chatter, more confusion.

"Fellow classmates!" Hutch boomed into the mic. "I give you . . . Miss *UnPleasant!*" He gestured grandly toward me, then slipped the mic back on the stand. He clapped, nodding at me with a huge crap-eating grin on his face, and hopped off the stage.

My heart pounded and my ears got all hot. I felt my nose break out in a cold sweat. And I swear, it felt like my stomach had shot out my butt. The audience kept blasting me with a strange mix of nasty sounds—mostly boos and angry hoots and heckles, some stomping and laughter and yelling, and a few lonely cheers and claps. It even smelled really nasty. Maybe it was just my BO, but the whole place suddenly reeked of teen revenge.

Mr. Canfield glared at me. I think his head was actually vibrating.

Everyone was talking and shouting and making these weird, angry faces. My ears rang. I breathed fast and hard. And even though everyone seemed to be saying something, the only words I could hear crashing around the gym were:

"Paisley Hanover! Miss UnPleasant?"

"Paisley Hanover? Miss UnPleasant?!"

"Paisley Hanover! Miss UnPleasant!!!"

It was like being trapped in the spin cycle of some nightmarish washing machine. I wanted to run off the stage and out the door and never come back *ever*. But I couldn't move. I started feeling dizzy. Soon I was praying that I'd just pass out or die. Then this would end and I could be carried off to the nurse's office on a stretcher.

Mr. Canfield had stepped up to the microphone. He was trying to quiet everyone down. "People, that's enough! That's enough! Okay, okay, okay! Let's give Paisley a chance to speak." The room got quiet. The only sound left in the whole gym was this gigantic, excruciating silence.

Canfield turned to me. "Paisley? Do you have something you'd like to say to us?"

Um. I stood there blinking at the audience. My head

really hurt. Then I finally realized that the only way to end my pain was to start my speech. So I gripped both sides of the podium and looked back out at the crowd, searching for a friendly face. Some were mocking me, but most looked like they couldn't wait to kill me with their bare hands. The look on Jen's face actually made me want to kill *myself* with my bare hands.

But then I saw Bean beaming at me with a big, proud, goobery grin. And I remembered the advice my dad had given me at the breakfast table: "Even if you make a mistake or forget to say something, no one will notice but you—so just keep on going with a smile on your face."

So I smiled. But my mouth was so dry that my upper lip stuck to my front teeth. I casually tried to un-stick my lip while smoothing my speech out on the podium.

"Hi," I squeaked into the microphone. Whoa. I cleared my throat. "Hi! I'm Paisley Hanover and I'm running for class president."

Silence.

"Good thing I have a big mouth, because I have some really big ideas for you."

More silence.

"Doesn't a hula hoop–athon fund raiser for homecoming sound like fun?"

Nothing.

"Or how about a sophomore hall clean-up-party-slash-scavenger-hunt?"

Silence.

Oh crap.

"I'll bet you're gonna love this idea"—I really tried to sell it—"Smoothie Tuesdays!"

A few snickers followed by another long silence.

Help. Help! HELP! I'm dying up here.

I looked down at my speech, trying to flatten the curled edges, and skipped ahead to the next paragraph. "Have you ever wondered if your biggest embarrassment could turn into your biggest break? I sure have." I jumped out from behind the podium and spastic jazzed the crowd.

The audience groaned and hissed.

OMG. OMG. OMG. OMG! I'm screwed. I'm so totally screwed.

Some guy yelled, "You got a new biggest embarrassment, Hanover!"

Sure, *everyone* laughed at that. Ha ha ha.

I looked down at my typed speech. "Um . . . Have you ever felt frustrated because you couldn't find Pirate's Booty or . . . or other tasty snacks in the . . . "

I took a deep breath and crumpled my speech into a tight sweaty wad. For a while, I just stood there, feeling everyone's eyes on me. Waiting. Waiting. And then . . .

And then I kind of lost it.

"Surprise!" I spastic jazzed the crowd. "Yep. Yep." I nodded, taking it all in. "I am Miss UnPleasant."

A few people whistled and yelled not-so-nice things.

"Yes, me. I am scary, bad-ass Miss UnPleasant . . . *Boo!*" I shouted. "Big kiss! Class dismissed!"

I started to giggle. All of a sudden, this felt like the most hilarious, absurd moment of my life.

"I didn't plan this. I mean, who could plan this? No one!" I grabbed the mic off the stand and walked around the stage like Oprah, only I was giggling way more. I jumped out at the audience again. "*Boo!*" Then I went into absolute hysterics, laughing so hard I could barely get the words out. "No one could. No one would! I was just . . . crazy one night. *Crazy pissed off!*" I let my smile fade. "It just happened . . . one Friday night . . . It happened by accident." I stared out at the crowd. A lot of people were looking really sorry for me. But I didn't care.

I realized then that I was holding a microphone, on a stage in front of almost four hundred students—and I could say *anything*.

"Okay, people—listen up!" I snapped my fingers. "Let's all move our brains into a circle!" I walked to the front of the stage. "Have you ever seen something go down at this school, something *really* ugly, and you wanted to do something to stop it, but you didn't? And you know you only wimped out because you didn't want to be the quote-unquote *uncool one* or break some unspoken social rule?"

Nobody said a word. I sat down on the front edge of the stage and looked right at Hutch. He didn't flinch.

"I have," I said. "And I felt like total crap. And I . . . I just couldn't shake it. I was pissed! So I started typing. And I typed and typed and typed all night. I know, I know, you're thinking, big deal, Paisley, so you're bitter and you couldn't sleep. You should've taken an Ambien or one of your mom's Valium, but don't trash our beloved school!" I thought about it for a few seconds. "Yeah, I dunno. I was surprised too. But I didn't want to sleep—I wanted to *wake up!*

"Because what is up with all these *stupid* rules?! I am *so* sick of them! I am *so* sick of who's in and who's out, who it's okay to talk to and what it's okay to wear, who you can date and who you can't date, who gets to sit where at lunch and what classes make you cool and what classes make you a geek or a freak or a loser." I took a breath. "God, aren't *any* of you sick of this crap too?"

Some scattered claps and cheers.

"Who even makes these rules up anyway—and why do we *all* follow them?"

More solitary claps and cheers from various pockets of the crowd. Oh, thank God—Eric Sobel was clapping. Amy and Bean both screamed, "Yeah!" And LG Wong let rip a series of loud whistles. I liked that girl more and more.

I looked down at my hands while the smattering of clapping faded. Wow. I've got to stop biting my cuticles.

"So, why am up here?" I stared at the row of candidates sitting in the front, each looking at me completely baffled and/or disturbed. Even Hutch. "Oh, right. Yeah. Would I make a good class president? I dunno. I really don't." I shrugged. "All I know is that I care about this school and I think about this stuff. And I think about everyone, really—not just the popular people, or the unpopular people."

If this had been my Academy Awards acceptance speech, the music would have started right about now. But it wasn't, and it didn't. So I stood up and kept talking.

"Popular. What does that even mean? All I know is that I don't want it. I don't *want* to be more popular. I just want to be more *me*. I'm a *closet weirdo!*" I shouted.

A lot of people laughed.

"Sure, I can pass for normal, but why should I want to? Why should I *have* to? What is normal, anyway?" I looked out at the crowd. "Does anybody out there hear what I'm saying? Is *anyone* getting this?"

A small burst of hoots and applause.

"I don't just want to go to school every day. I want to go to my *life*. And if that makes me *unnn* . . . cool or *unnn* . . . popular, well then, good! Because some days I feel really *unnn* . . . everything. I mean, I can't be the only one, can I?" I scanned the entire audience. Uh-oh. Maybe I can be. I hadn't thought of that.

"Come on, people! I've *seen* you over the last couple weeks! I *know*. If you've ever felt a little *un*normal or *un*sane or *un*discovered or *un*cool, *un*perfect, *un*apologetic, *un*decided, *un*fashionable, *un*forgettable, *un*predictable, *un*usual, *un*whatever, then maybe you can relate to why I wrote that stuff! Maybe you can even relate to *me*. Un *is* way more fun!"

The gym was totally silent again.

Crap. I seemed to be going backward.

I stood there in the middle of the stage and looked down at my feet. Oh well. I tried. I should just end it. "Okay, well, that's all I have to say." I started to put the mic back into the slot on the stand, when I realized something and grabbed it back. "But whether I'm Miss UnPleasant or Paisley Hanover, I'd vote for Paisley. And I hope you will too."

The crowd started to grumble and rumble and gurgle and churn. A few people started clapping. A few more started standing up. Then Bean and Clint and Amy and a bunch of Library Girls and AV Guys started yelling, "*Paisley! Paisley! Paisley!*" And— OMG, I couldn't believe this! More and more people stood up, and then this whole chunk of the audience was clapping and cheering, and chanting. I couldn't even understand what they were saying at first. Then it came clear, and I smiled the hugest, most goobery smile I've ever smiled in my life.

"*Un! Un! Un! Un! Un! Un! Un!*"

Even some of the teachers joined in. What *was* this? Like some crazy teen movie?! I just stood there looking out at the crowd, completely amazed.

Before I could think what to do next, Canfield grabbed the microphone from me and said something about how everyone should be sure to vote tomorrow and get hustling to seventh period so classes could start on time. And then the assembly was over.

I went straight for Charlie Dodd. He looked like he was going to crap in his pants.

"Et tu, Charlé?" I asked coldly. He tried to laugh, but he

couldn't even convince himself it was funny. "You suck." I turned and walked back to my chair to get my stuff.

A lot of people came rushing up to me, mostly people I had never really talked to before. And they said all these things to me all at once. But the one comment I'll never forget was Mandy Mindel saying "Thank you." That's all she said, then ducked out of the crowd and out the door.

Bean gave me a great big hunched-over hug. "I knew you were a closet weirdo! I knew that's why I liked you!" she squealed. "I'm a closet weirdo too!"

"No. You're just a weirdo!" And we both laughed.

Amy stood a few feet away, watching some Uns swarm around me. When things calmed down, she finally came over. "I can't believe it was you all along. It seems so obvious now. Who else could have known all those things?"

I didn't know what to say to her.

"I'm really mad at you," she said.

"Sorry."

"No, I'm mad because you never *talked* to me about this stuff before! I can totally relate."

"You can?"

"You have no idea. And you're a hella good liar. That's kinda scary, actually."

But a lot of people kept their distance. Carreyn and Jen stood back with their arms crossed, watching Amy and me, and obviously dishing. Eric Sobel was getting into it with Hutch, who looked like he was trying to explain himself. And Cate hadn't moved from her spot on the bleachers. She was the only person still sitting there. Clint was long gone. I waved to her. But she didn't wave back. She just stared at me, upset or mad or disappointed. I couldn't tell.

I walked over to Eric and Hutch. "Hey Eric, what did you think?" I asked, buzzing with adrenaline.

Eric turned from me to Hutch and back to me. He seemed embarrassed. "Not really sure what I think yet . . . But the speech was pretty cool. Nice save."

"Thanks." I slid my gaze over to Hutch. "Thanks again for the sticky bun, Hutch," I gushed. "It was *crazy* good just like you said." I smiled and turned to go. "And great speech!" I called over my shoulder.

I was headed for the gym doors—and that's when Canfield tapped me on the shoulder.

"Meet me in my office, Paisley. Now."

chapter forty-six

On the way to Canfield's office, people were looking at me really weird. Some kids smiled and stared, like we were in on some geeky secret. A few flashed me the UnPop Power fists with big grins. But others acted like I'd just turned them in for cheating on their American Lit test. It was a rush having this UNderground connection with so many people I really didn't know. But I also felt exposed. Okay, totally naked—like not-even-wearing-a-tuba naked.

When I got to Canfield's office, he was talking on the phone. He waved me in, so I sat down in the low, wobbly Fink Fast chair and waited for my butt to start sweating, wondering what brilliant clichés were going to come out of his fish lips this time. Finally he hung up.

He looked at me, shaking his head. "That was quite a show, Paisley."

I smiled. Was he serious?

"Very *un*pleasant to watch."

Duh. Of course not.

"I called you in here to let you know we'll be reprinting the ballot for sophomore class elections—and your name won't be on it."

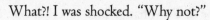

What?! I was shocked. "Why not?"

"Frankly, you amaze me. How anyone could write such ugly, mean-spirited words about our exemplary school and student body and then expect to represent this school and its students is beyond me." He was cold. "You have really disappointed me, Paisley. And you've disrespected this school and your classmates. I'm sorry. But you are clearly *not* leadership material. I'm terminating your candidacy as of right now."

My mouth fell open. "You can't do that! I have all the signatures required to run." I felt my nose break into a sweat.

"Oh yes, I can. The administration has the right to deny any student running for class office at Pleasant Hill High. Check the school bylaws."

"But I *am* leadership material! Didn't the audience at speeches prove that? I mean, don't you think it takes a real leader to challenge things, and . . . and inspire people, and point out what's wrong with something and try to make it right?"

He gave me his big fish-lipped smile. "I didn't read a lot of hope in your Miss UnPleasant negative propaganda."

I wasn't exactly sure what propaganda meant, but I sure wasn't going to let him know. I'd look it up later. "It's not propaganda. I think it's called satire, Mr. Canfield. You know, using irony and sarcasm to make a point?"

"You can call it whatever you want, but you're off the ballot. And another thing." He pointed at me, hairy nostrils flaring. "You won't be writing anything ever again by Miss UnPleasant. Got it?" He waved me out of his office. "Ba-bye."

I stormed down the hall. What a pig. Just because he couldn't stand being criticized, he was going to shut *me* down? I didn't think so. Check the school bylaws? Yeah, I thought I would.

I marched straight to the library and up to the front desk.

"Ms. Whit, can you help me find a copy of the Pleasant Hill High bylaws? I need to see them right now." I pounded on the countertop. My heart was thumping hard and fast in my chest, and I could feel the sweat on my nose cooling in the air-conditioned library air.

"Paisley, what's wrong. Are you okay?" Ms. Whit asked, looking alarmed.

"No! I'm not okay! Mr. Canfield just told me I that can't run for class president because I'm not leadership material! He's reprinting the ballot—and my name won't be on it!"

"All right, all right, calm down."

"And that means Hutch will automatically win even though he's a bully and a liar and a cheat! Is that what Canfield considers leadership material?" I was nearly panting, I was so mad.

"Paisley," Ms. Whit whispered. "Library voice please. Let's go into my office."

She closed her door. "Why would Mr. Canfield not let you run for class office?"

"Because I'm Miss UnPleasant."

"What?" She suddenly looked very excited. "*You* are Miss UnPleasant?"

I nodded.

She covered her mouth, then laughed, and I mean laughed hard. "Right on, sister! You're a little radical trapped in the body of a popular girl. Cool. Good for you for stirring the pot. Good for you for making people think."

"Really? Thanks. I guess. People are really pissed, though. Not just Canfield." Then I told her everything Canfield had said to me.

Ms. Whit stood up. "Wait right here."

I had never thought of myself as a radical before. But Miss UnPleasant is definitely a radical, and she came out of my brain, right? So part of me must be a radical. Why are there so many parts of me? It's so confusing. There's the popular me, the unpopular me, the rah-rah, the closet weirdo, the radical, the girl who just wants to be liked, the girl who likes Clint, the girl who likes Eric. Who was the real me anyway?

Ms. Whit came back in carrying a thick binder and started flipping through it. "Okay, here it is. Class elections."

I sat up eagerly watching her read. She shook her head slowly. "Hmm. He's right. Damn! Oops." She looked up at me. "Sorry. The bylaws state that the administration has the right to terminate the candidacy of any student deemed to be an inappropriate student leader. Inappropriate is defined as unlawful, negligent, below a C minus average, or inclined to influence other students in a negative manner."

Ergh! I clenched my fists super tight. I was so angry, and— and I hated that Canfield was doing this to me! I hated feeling helpless. Then I burst into tears—not because I was sad but because I was furious, and indignant, and, well, PMS-ing a little. It's true.

"I'm so sorry, Paisley."

"It's not fair! I've worked hard for this and now . . . " I blubbered a little more. "I can't believe Hutch is going to win all because of Miss UnPleasant! He's such a jerk. He's the whole reason I wrote the column in the first place. And talk about unbelievable? Miss UnPleasant has a thriving write-in campaign for president— which is completely ridiculous! And now *I* can't even run!"

Ms. Whit looked up from the binder, like she had just thought of something really interesting. She quickly scanned the bylaws again. "That's it!"

"What's it?" I whined.

She jumped up out of her chair. "Paisley, you have to launch your own write-in campaign. The bylaws don't say a word about write-in candidates and who may or may not be eligible."

"Really?" I blew my nose. "Really?!" I started to feel a lot better. "But the election's tomorrow!"

"You'd better get going. You've got a lot to do!"

"Yeah, I do!" I was feeling pumped up again.

Ms. Whit left me in her office so I could pull myself together and formulate a plan. What was I going to do? And who could I get to help me? And more importantly, would anyone even vote for me now that they knew the real me?

I texted my mom. I had to get out of there and away from school, fast.

NQA shtl pls!

She called me right back. Mom's not the best texter.

"Horrible," I said into the phone. "Yes, please! Right now. I'll be by the vending machines. Thanks, Mom."

I ran to my locker to grab my stuff. It was almost the end of seventh period, and I really didn't want to be caught in the halls when the bell rang. I opened my locker, grabbed my bag, and shoved in a few books—not that I'd have any time for home-work tonight. And that's when I saw it.

Another locker stalker note.

I looked around, really fast, checking both ways down the hall. Then I opened it quickly.

I'D VOTE 4 ANYONE BUT YOU.
YOU'RE UNDERLIEVABLE.

chapter forty-seven

What?! OMG. My locker stalker had turned on me! And he was obviously a sophomore. *And* he must have just stuffed this in here!

I looked into all the classroom windows across the lawn to see if anyone was spying on me, but I didn't see anything suspicious. The bell was going to ring any minute. So I just stuffed the note in my pocket, slammed my locker shut, and took off jogging down the hall with my bag bouncing awkwardly against my hip.

On my way down the main hall to the vending machines, you'll never guess who I ran into coming out of Canfield's office.

Peter Hutchison.

He had this big dumb-ass grin on his face. Canfield must have just told him that my name was not going to be on the ballot.

"Hey Paisley, I heard you're history."

I stopped. "Oh yeah? I'm a lot of things, Hutch—but I am *not* history."

"Come on, Pais, don't be mad. Look, I'm . . . I'm sorry. Really. I didn't know *this* would happen. Come on, peace!" He threw open his arms, like he wanted to hug me. "Share the sugar."

I snorted out my mouth like a horse. "What?! Yeah right. Like that's ever gonna happen."

"Don't be mad. Come on. Don't be mad 'cause I'm gonna win. I can't help it, dude. It's genetic."

I just laughed at him. He was such a clueless social loser that I almost felt sorry for him. But no. I was too pissed. "*Dude, I'm not mad—I'm motivated. So watch out.*"

I left him standing there trying to figure out what I meant.

I guess he couldn't think of anything smart to say because he yelled after me, "Are you just PMS-ing again?"

I sat on a wall at the front of the school waiting for my mom, scribbling in my notebook.

> I am *not history.*
> I am *not* history!
> I am NOT history!
> I am *not a loser.*
> I am *not giving up.*
> I am *not going away.*

And I felt really good, like superhero good, so I kept scribbling in this frustrated manic rant that Miss UnPleasant would have been proud to call her own.

I am not who I was last year.

I am not who I was last <u>week</u>.

I am not a rah-rah.

I am not my reputation.

I am not who the vice principal thinks I am.

I am not perfect.

I am not <u>trying</u> to be perfect.

I am not afraid to say no.

I am <u>not</u> just PMS-ing.

I am not kidding.

I am not falling for that.

I am me! (If only I knew who that really was!)

On the way home, I started telling Mom about my disastrous speech and everything else that had happened, but I didn't get very far. Mom totally freaked.

"*You're* Miss UnPleasant? No." She practically stopped the car. "No!"

I nodded at her, like *Yes I am! I just said so!*

"*You* wrote those biting, sarcastic, popularity-bashing columns?"

"Mo-om, whatever, yeah! I just said that!"

"Paisley Hanover." She sounded seriously stern, like I was in big trouble. But then she started to giggle and she kept giggling like she was about to lose it. "This is going to be a little embarrassing for me."

"Embarrassing for *you*? Mom, this isn't about *you*! And by the way, I'm proud I wrote those columns. Miss UnPleasant is way cooler than I'll ever be."

"Oh honey, no! I'm proud you wrote them too. Really, I'm impressed—surprised, but impressed. It's just that . . ." She started to laugh again. "It's just that I've said some rather pointed things to a few parents about Miss UnPleasant and her obviously rotten parents."

"What?! You've been talking about her? I mean me?" I started laughing a little too. It all seemed so surreal. "Saying like what?"

"Like . . ." She turned to me, making one of her funny whoops-I-really-blew-it faces. "I said she's clearly an intelligent but extremely angry girl who needs therapy immediately."

My mouth dropped open. "Mo-om! That's so harsh."

"I didn't know it was *you*." She shrugged. She looked at me all sweet and loving. "Honey, *do* you need therapy? If you do, it's perfectly okay. You know how I feel about therapy. It's always better to ask for help than to suffer in sil—"

"Mo-om, no!" I rolled my eyes. But then I thought about it for a second and got very serious. "Well, after today, maybe I do need therapy—I need *speech* therapy!"

We both howled at that stinker. Mom loves bad puns almost as much as I do.

"What did your friends think when they found out?"

"Well . . . I don't know really. Bean thought it was cool, and

Amy, but everyone else . . . not so cool. No one wants to talk to me. I guess I'm officially unpopular with almost all my friends."

"Oh honey, I'm sorry. But you can't always be who your friends want you to be." She squeezed my leg.

We drove on in silence for a while and I thought about what Mom had just said. It finally hit me. As much as I wanted everyone to like me, I realized that everyone wasn't going to like the *real* me. I loved my friends and I needed my friends, but I was never going to be just who they wanted me to be. And that was okay. I mean, no one was who they seemed to be on the surface. Nobody was the person they wore to school every day.

I looked down at my notebook in my lap and put a big bold X through the E. That was the moment my notebook became my *not book*. Totally *not* what it seemed—just like me.

I opened it to the page of my "I am not" rants, adding:

I am *not just who my* friends want me to be.

"So, Mom? Did you ever think you'd have an unpopular little radical trapped in the body of a popular girl?"

She laughed. I love it when I can make Mom laugh.

"Actually, yes, even if you do scare some people. But Pais, look on the bright side. You know what? Our gossip street-value just went way, way up. We are gossip rich!" she screamed, honking the horn like we had just won the lottery. I slid down in my seat, trying to hide. My mom can be so over-the-top weird sometimes.

When we got home, I went straight to up my room, closed the door, and turned on some music. Part of me wanted to curl up with Dyson and listen to music till I fell asleep. It had been an off-the-chart, Stressy-Bessy day. I was fried, but I knew I needed a plan. I needed a strategy. I needed to make a lot of noise in a short period of time and I had no idea how. So I sat down at my computer and started typing ideas, anything that came to mind.

But suddenly, it's like my phone wouldn't stop buzzing.

Amy texted.

Whr ru?

I didn't reply.

Eric texted.

Listnin spt 6:30? Nd 2 tlk

I didn't reply—but I wanted to.

Jen texted.

Cnt bleev u did dis 2 me! hu RU Nyway?

Wow. I thought I was dreaming when I got that one. And no, I didn't reply. It made me feel so sad. I was starting to wonder if Jen and I would ever be real friends again. But I couldn't think about it right now.

I started typing a bunch of ideas:

Locker stuffers telling people to write me in.

New signs?

Name tag stickers?

Something to make a lot of noise?

I dug through the drawers of my desk and night table, looking for anything that might help. Safety pins, binder clips, paper clips, nail polish, a mini harmonica. What could I use to reach four hundred people that I already had at my disposal? I found a plastic whistle. That could help. No. I grabbed the wad of sticky notes. These could work.

I knew I definitely needed a good locker stuffer. So I started thinking. What do I say? What do I say?! WHAT DO I SAY?! Just keep it simple, just keep it clear, and don't sound like a bitter loser. I started typing.

VOTE PAISLEY HANOVER!

I'm off the ballot but I'm not out of the race—
I'm still spastic jazzed for the job!

Please WRITE IN Paisley Hanover
for sophomore class president.

I hit SAVE and transferred the file to my jump drive.

Dyson had hopped up onto my lap, and I was curling my fingers under his neck, getting his power-purr going. And then I felt his name tag. I pulled it up and looked at it. Hmm . . . I could make a bunch of these tonight at Pet Stuff.

Then I speed-texted a message:
Realy nd yr hlp W campain!
Sofmr hall @ 9:00 2nite. Pls?
I sent it to Bean, Cate, Amy, Carreyn, Eric, and Clint. It

would be interesting to see who, if anyone, showed up. Really interesting.

Mom and Dad were way into the idea of my write-in campaign.

"Glen Canfield is a boob." Dad looked up from the mail he was opening. "He always has been. I know, I went to high school with him."

"Glen? Gross." It creeped me out to think that Mr. Canfield was a real person with a first name.

I explained my plan to them and asked if they would drive me around, then over to school to stuff lockers. Dad couldn't wait. He changed his clothes and came downstairs wearing jeans and a black turtleneck. He pulled a black knit cap down really low and slipped on sunglasses.

"Dad, what are you doing?"

"I'm driving the getaway car, right?"

"You are so embarrassing. I'm driving with Mom."

"Oh no, no. I'm staying home. Someone has to be here when you call from the police station."

"Come on, Viv. We're not doing anything illegal, just making a little adventure out of it."

She shook her head. "No thanks. You kids have fun!"

Dad drove me to Kinkos and I had them print out five hundred flyers on bright pink paper. Then we drove straight to Pet Stuff, where I made twelve round, pink dog tags. The machine engraved this in each tag:

I'D VOTE
FOR
PAISLEY

Wow. They looked pretty cool. These were for my core supporters—whoever agreed to pass out flyers at school tomorrow. But first, we had to get through tonight.

chapter forty-eight

When Dad and I got to school, it was quiet and dark. We parked at the far edge of the parking lot, then made our way up to sophomore hall. Amy and Bean and Eric were already there, standing in the shadows talking. I could have screamed, I was so happy to see them.

"Hey you guys!" I gave each of them a hug. "Thanks for showing up!" OMG! Did I just hug Eric Sobel?! I did!

My dad whispered, "Shhhhhhh. This is a commando mission." My dad could be such a goober.

I gathered everyone into a little pod. "I need your help," I whispered. "I've been canned. Canfield took my name off the ballot for class president because of Miss UnPleasant."

"No way!" said Amy and Bean.

"Way." I handed each of them a stack of pink flyers, and they started reading. "I have a ton of these. So we need to get a flyer into every sophomore locker."

"Cool." Eric nodded.

Amy joined in, "Write on, Miss UnPaisley!"

Bean gave me another hug. "Yes! Power to the UnPops! We're bringing Peter Hutchison down!"

But just as we were about to spread out and start stuffing lockers, there was this loud noise. It came screaming up the hall. So much for our commando mission.

Clint Bedard on his motorcycle. He screeched to a stop. We all stood there a little shocked as he got off his bike and pulled off his helmet.

"Hey, sorry I'm late." He smiled at me, then noticed Eric Sobel. He ran one hand through his hair, looking a little perturbed.

I was speechless to see him there at all.

Fortunately, Dad jumped in. "No problem. We're glad you made it." He patted Clint on the back. What? No! "Right on! Power to the UnPops," Dad cheered the group. OMG. I couldn't wait until I got my license.

Clint read the flyer, digging it. "I love an anti-authority chick. Yeah. Let's make this happen."

Eric Sobel gave Clint a cold, scrutinizing stare, like he was eyeing his competition. But he didn't say a word.

We spread out, going up and down sophomore hall, stuffing every locker with my pink flyers. Little conversations kept suddenly igniting and ending.

"Can I talk to you?" Eric asked me after a little while. "Look. Sorry about the video. Sorry about what happened at the assembly."

"You were involved in that?"

"I was before I knew it was you. And then when I found out, I was a little freaked. But the whole thing snowballed out of control. I didn't want it to go down like that, really. But Hutch is a stubborn bastard. So, you know, I just wanted to say sorry."

Wow. "Thanks." I'd have to process all this later. There was way too much to do right now. But I smiled at Eric Sobel like a total goober.

Amy came up to me. "Oh my God," she whispered. "Jen's mortified and beyond mad. She said you really embarrassed her and trashed her in front of all her Pop friends. I don't agree, but she thinks you wrote those columns just to hurt her."

"That's ridiculous!"

"I know. But everything that happens to anyone these days is all about Jen. Don't tell her I said that, okay?"

"Don't worry. We never even talk anymore." I couldn't see Amy's eyes. It was too dark. But I was pretty sure she understood why.

I walked over to the box of flyers, shaking my head. It sounded like Jen was lost in space. Or more like lost in her own head space.

Bean reached in for another bunch of flyers. "Hey Bean, have you talked to Cate?" I asked, using my library voice. "Is she mad? She looked mad after my speech."

"Well, not mad really, I don't think." Bean twirled a piece of hair over and around her index finger. "It seems more complicated than that. You should talk to her about it. I know she wants to talk to you. I just think she's still trying to figure it all out for herself."

We went back to stuffing lockers. Every time I stuffed a flyer into a locker, I thought about my locker stalker. I guess he didn't like the Miss UnPleasant side of me. That had to mean he was a Pop. Hmm . . .

When we were finally finished, Dad took us all to Millie's for a late-night breakfast. He was even cool enough to sit at the counter and pretend not to know us. Thank God.

We were all sitting in one of those big round booths, scribbling "WRITE IN PAISLEY" on bright-colored sticky notes as quickly as possible. Then I talked strategy while everyone chowed down.

"Okay, tomorrow morning, I need boots on the ground early, passing out more flyers, slapping sticky notes on lockers and poles, making noise, making sure everyone knows to write me in, and showing support." I reached into my Pet Stuff bag. "I got these for you guys." I passed out the pink dog tags. "Chokers for the girls and, I don't know, belt loop thingies for the guys?"

"Yay! I love jewelry," Bean squealed.

"Dog tags? Nice." Amy nodded. "Very Un . . . Expected."

"No way," Clint said adamantly, putting up his hands. "I'm not wearing this on my belt loop." Then he flashed that smile. "I'm wearing mine as a choker too. Chokers are sexy." He raised his eyebrows seductively.

We all laughed, except for Eric, who was staring at Clint. "Oh yeah? Dude, you think you're so bad-ass. Well, I'm wearing mine as an *earring*." He held it up to one ear, smiling like a goof, the same goof I had seen doing that crazy dance on the soccer field.

Everyone screamed at that one. I laughed so hard I thought I was going to pee. But then I reminded myself that I was sitting at a table with Eric Sobel *and* Clint Bedard—plus Amy, an old friend, and Bean, a new friend. Wow. I watched them all talking and laughing and eating while I was secretly having a warm and fuzzy, people-are-beautiful moment.

So much had already happened this year. I looked at Clint and then Eric, then back to Clint, realizing that a whole lot more was *still* going to happen this year—I just didn't know what. But I did know that whatever happened with the election tomorrow, I *was* living the best year of my life.

chapter forty-nine

The day of the elections was a crazy Hornets' nest of activity. Posters were up on every wall in all the halls, and everyone—especially me!—was excited, buzzing around and passing out buttons and flyers and stickers.

The ballots wouldn't officially open until the beginning of lunch. But that didn't stop us all from campaigning like overcaffeinated overachievers. Amy and Bean were great, shamelessly getting the word out about my new write-in status. Eric and Clint were much more on the down low, but still slapping sticky notes on people, working opposite ends of our class's social food chain.

I guess Eric chickened out on his earring idea, which was kind of a relief. I didn't want him to feel too weird supporting me. I just appreciated his help. I mean, he could have just hung with Hutch like all of the other Pops in our class.

But Clint was wearing his pink choker with pride. And he was right—he did look sexy.

Hutch and a bunch of his varsity jerk and Pop buddies had taken over the lawn in sophomore hall, tossing around a new load of soft and squishy, hospital-safe mini yellow footballs, all printed with "Vote Hutch—I'm open!" Jen and Carreyn were helping to pass them out and—oh my gag!—wearing tight little baby-doll T-shirts that said "I'm a Hutch's Honey" across the front. That explains why Carreyn didn't show up last night—not that I really expected her to. By the looks of it, she was probably in the bathroom all night anyway—poor Carreyn was sporting tragic Easter-egg pink hair. I guess her home-salon effort to remove her red-hair-show-of-solidarity hadn't quite worked out.

And wow. I didn't know why Jen was so mad at me for trashing her reputation. She seemed to be doing a pretty good job of trashing it herself.

Amy walked up to them and casually patted Jen on the back. OMG. She put a WRITE IN PAISLEY sticky note on her back! I love Amy.

Charlie Dodd ran up and down our hall, frantically passing out pens that said *Vote Charlie Dood for secretary!* Bean showed me hers. Perfect. That one was going to stick. He tried to hand me a pen. I ignored him.

The voting stations for all four classes had been set up in the quad, each at a table in a different corner. It was pretty much the only day of the year when it was safe for any student at our school to cross into to the sacred ground of the quad.

At morning break, I ran straight out there to check out the action. The bronze hornet was covered in signs for various candidates from all classes. It was a tradition. But still, the pink paper plate that I had tied around the hornet's neck like a choker definitely stood out. "I'D VOTE FOR PAISLEY!"

Yes! Even the Pleasant Hill Hornet was behind me.

I ran back up to sophomore hall. We were already out of flyers and sticky notes, but I still wanted to be there, urging people to write me in. I spotted Amy sitting on the grass sharing a sticky bun with Bean and Clint. Aw, that's so cute.

I was going over to join them, but then I saw Cate and a bunch of Uns marching down the hall in a sloppy but enthusiastic clump, blowing on party noisemakers and chanting "Join the Un Party!" "A vote for *Un* is a vote for Fun!" "Write-on, Miss UnP! Write-in Miss UnP!"

Oh man, this had to stop. I raced over to Cate, waved her down, and pulled her out onto the edge of the lawn where we wouldn't get bonked by a yellow football.

"Cate, come on, why are you *still* doing this? I really appreciated it before, when it was all just a joke but now—"

"It's never been just a joke," she snapped. The Un Party moved on without her, chanting and weaving down the hall.

"But now you're just hurting my chances of beating Hutch. Come on—*no one's* actually gonna vote for Miss UnPleasant!"

She looked me in the eye. "I'm not doing this for you, Paisley. I'm doing this for me."

"What do you mean?"

She squinted and frowned and finally shrugged. "I don't know what I mean."

There was so much chaos going on around us, it actually

seemed like the perfect place to be having a personal conversation. "Cate, Miss UnPleasant isn't real. *I'm* real."

She blinked her eyes a few times and looked away. Oh no. Oh God. I hoped she wasn't going to cry. "Yeah but who *are* you? I'm still trying to figure that out."

"Well, that makes two of us." I kinda half laughed. "But don't be mad at me, please. Help me out here."

"I'm not mad at you, I'm just . . . I'm just . . . " She looked away, then finally turned to me. "I'm just kinda heartbroken, I guess." She wiped underneath each eye and exhaled hard, trying to pull it together. "That freaked me out yesterday."

I was surprised. "Why? I thought you'd like me *more*."

"I do." She tucked a piece of dark hair behind her ear, looking really sad. "But I sort of had this fantasy that Miss UnPleasant was a lot like me, and that we'd become best friends, and that I wouldn't feel so lonely in this Pleasant Hell." She wiped her nose and looked away. "And that maybe, maybe she even liked girls." Oh wow. I hadn't thought of that. Cate twirled her party noisemaker around in her hand, then pretended to smoke it like a cigarette. "But now . . . I don't know. That fantasy is over, up in smoke," she said, fake exhaling.

I felt like I had somehow let her down. "Sorry if I disappointed you."

She shook her head. "That's okay. It's not your fault. It's me. I get disappointed all the time."

I gave her a hug. "Me too." Over her shoulder, I could see Jen acting like a brainless bimbo. "Cate, I need your help. I really don't want to lose this election. Is there any way you could get the Uns to endorse me and start chanting about writing in *my* name for president? Otherwise, Hutch is gonna win this and then we'll both be disappointed."

Cate looked a little better. Then she laughed. "Okay, but only if you give me one of those foxy pink chokers."

"Deal!"

At the beginning of lunch, Team Paisley sprinted down to the quad and staked out a choice yelling spot right next to the sophomore voting station. We stood on the bench, chanting, "Write in Pais-ley! Write in Pais-ley! Write in Pais-ley!"

Our group got bigger and louder and way more diverse as Miss UnPleasant's supporters gradually joined in. I was smiling and waving to Hutch, who had gathered with his Pop posse near the hornet. They were all staring at us like we were freaks, especially Jen and pink-haired Carreyn. Poor Carreyn.

As Hutch walked up to the voting station, he scratched his eyebrow, giving us the finger. What a classy guy, what an exemplary leader.

Our chant got even louder. *"Write in Pais-ley! Write in Pais-ley! Write in Pais-ley!"* He swirled his finger in circles a few inches from his ear, and mouthed "Crazy!" I just laughed, watching him grab a ballot from the stack and lean over to vote.

He looked up suddenly with this crap-eating grin on his face. "Hey Paisley, have you seen the ballot yet?" He waved it at me. No, actually, I hadn't. So I snatched it out of his hand.

I gasped—yes, I really gasped. Holy shiitake mushrooms! Oh

crap. Oh no! Canfield was more of a pig than I ever imagined. He was a rabid revengeful fetal pig! Amy and Bean and Cate were all trying to read over my shoulder. Eric and Clint grabbed their own copies of the ballot.

I felt the bottom fall out of my world and sank down onto the bench. Under *Class President*, there was a box to vote for Peter Hutchison. Under that it read: *Any write-in votes for Paisley Hanover will not be counted and will automatically disqualify your entire ballot. None of your votes will count.*

Everyone slowly stopped chanting my name, trying figure out what was going on.

The Pops all started chattering and laughing. Yup, Jen and Carreyn were front and center. Jen was all leaning into Bodie in the submissive-needy-girlfriend pose.

Hutch stood there laughing at me.

Some girl yelled, "Hutch, you suck!" OMG. It was Mandy Mindel.

"This is no election," Bean said to him. "It's *Preferential Treatment* by Pleasant Hill." She bounced her hand under her blond hair with this dopey vacant smile.

"Whatever, Beano."

Clint stepped into Hutch's face. "Dude, be a man. I'm pretty sure this isn't how a democracy works."

"Oh, thanks for the tip, dude."

"You play filthy dirty, you scum sucker," Cate said coldly.

Hutch didn't say anything. He just tried to laugh it off.

Then Eric stepped up and calmly asked, "Hutch, do you

really want to win like this? I mean, seriously, I've always thought of you as a winner. This isn't how a winner plays the game."

Yells of support popped around the crowd that had gathered.

Hutch looked a little confused, like he was actually thinking about what Eric had said. "Yeah, dude. This blows. I want to win, but not like this."

I wanted to pound on him so bad, and I would have if he hadn't weighed like twice as much as me. "Oh really? Then why'd you set me up like that at the speeches?"

"I thought it'd be funny! That's all. And yeah, I was sick of all your Miss UnPleasant crap."

"You know what? That's really hilarious. Miss UnPleasant never would've existed if it hadn't been for you and your shidiot behavior."

He looked at me puzzled.

"What you did to Mandy and Teddy that night after the game."

Hutch's face showed a flash of recognition, then he looked away, scratching the side of his nose with his knuckle. The crowd around us was silent, waiting for him to say something. But I knew he wouldn't.

"Hutch, why don't you do the *right* thing for a change?" I called.

He turned and stared at me like he was thinking hard, trying to figure out what to do. And then I realized something. Hutch had no idea what was the right thing to do—and he probably never did. For a second I almost felt sorry for him. Almost.

"So . . . um. Well, what do you want me to do?" he said, suddenly frustrated. "I can't change the ballot!" Hutch looked at all of us and then at his Pop buddies, who had gathered around.

"I have an idea," said Eric. "You write in Paisley Hanover. And you get everyone else to do it too." A bunch of us cheered at that. OMG! He's gorgelicious *and* a genius! "We'll force the administration to do the election over again."

He looked at Eric and sighed. "Dude, I *don't* want to win like this. I don't." He turned back to me. "So if I do that, what do I get from you, Paisley?" he asked in his trying-to-be seductive, creepy way.

"Nothing," I snapped.

Bean and Cate clapped politely. Then Amy joined in.

"Dude, listen. This way, you get the chance to, like, win for real," said Eric.

Hutch shook his head. "Crap." He leaned over and started writing on his ballot. Then he held it up and showed his vote to everyone, starting with the Pops. "Everyone write in Paisley Hanover!" he yelled. "We're throwing the election!"

A wave of reactions followed—from angry shouts of "Dude, no!" to cheers of support for Hutch from our side.

Eric smiled at me. And yes, I was smiling at him too.

Hutch slowly turned around until I could see his ballot.

I craned my neck. I squinted.

Under Class President, Hutch had written

PAISLEY HANOVER

What? WHAT?! I could feel my eyes bulging.

He dropped his ballot into the box and walked off.

No! NO!! *Aaaaaaaah!* The soundtrack to the shower scene from *Psycho* blared from my brain-speakers in these sharp pulsing shrieks. No. No! NO! I felt this creeped-out icky feeling, thinking of all the times Hutch had teased me or grabbed me and tried to hug me. Gross! Yuck. Hutch was my locker stalker? Hutch?! No. I wanted to puke in a purse! No!!!!!!!!

I stumbled away from the bench, grabbing my head. I felt completely disoriented. Clint caught me as I was about to tumble to the ground. Then Clint and Amy and Bean and Cate were talking to me in slow-mo-underwater-speak that made no sense. What? What were they trying to say? I didn't even care. I just wanted to get out of there. I took a few steps back from the group and then I ran from the quad as fast as I could.

chapter fifty

Eric eventually found me at the listening spot, stretched out on the grass with my ear to the ground.

"Hey," he said. "You okay?"

I opened my eyes. He was panting like he'd just finished a run. I closed my eyes again. "I dunno."

I had been lying there for a good half hour or so, trying my best to have an out-of-body experience.

Eric stretched out on the grass next to me. Neither of us said anything for a long time. I liked that about him. We both just lay there looking up at the clouds. The warning bell rang for sixth period, but I didn't budge and he didn't either. And then the starting bell for sixth rang.

I closed my eyes again. But I kept seeing Hutch's all-caps handwriting. Uck! So I opened them again.

Why do I always want to know everything and have everything all figured out? Lying there, I realized that sometimes it's much better not to know.

I didn't care about the election anymore. I didn't care if I won or lost or got any votes at all. I didn't want to be like Charlie "Dood," so obsessed with planning my future that I couldn't enjoy what was happening right now. A lot of great things were happening *right now* and I hadn't planned any of them!

Eric pointed up at the clouds. "Dumb varsity jock chasing a cool indie chick."

I laughed.

"UnSane redhead chasing her tail. Two o'clock."

We both laughed.

"It was pretty crazy in the quad after you left."

I didn't want to think about it anymore.

"Jen voted for you."

I looked at him. "You're kidding."

"She showed me her ballot before she stuffed it in the box."

Wow. That was a shocker. Maybe she did still like me a little—or maybe she just wrote in my name because Hutch did and she was a "Hutch's Honey." I'd never know. All I knew was that if we somehow got to be friends again, it would never be the same as it had been before school started. But I guess that was okay. Neither were we.

"Hey." Eric rolled over on his stomach. "Wanna go to the dance Friday after the game?"

OMG. Was he serious? I turned to look at him. He seemed serious. But he did have that crush on his idea of cool, edgy Miss UnPleasant. "Are you asking me or asking Miss UnPleasant?"

He smiled. "I'm asking you."

I smiled too. But on the inside, I felt like a screaming, windblown, frizzy nerve. I'd been riding this crazy emotional roller coaster for so long without a safety bar, holding on for dear life. I turned to him. "Don't be too nice to me, okay? I might burst into tears."

Eric didn't say anything. Finally, he reached over and grabbed my hand and just held it. "That'd be okay," he said at the clouds.

Wow. This guy could melt my heart. I remembered the first time I really liked him, when I saw him almost cry after getting the MVP award at the soccer championships. For a change, I didn't want to melt into the earth and hide from embarrassment. I kind of wanted to melt into him. OMG. Did I just say that?! Yes! I totally did!

You're probably wondering if this was all just another flash fantasy—I know I was for a second. But it wasn't. It was real. I was going out on a date with Eric Sobel on Friday night. And I was spastic jazzed for it! And then I suddenly remembered something else. I had a Nut Festival rain date with Clint Bedard on *Saturday* night!

I had a date with my above-the-belt crush *and* my below-the-belt crush all in the same weekend? OMG! How was I going to manage that?

In the movie version of my life, this is where the camera pulls up and away to a high crane shot (or a helicopter shot, pending budget) and the soundtrack swells, but it's not just in my head for a change—it's in digital surround-sound. And you can see two small people lying in the middle of a big green soccer field smiling and holding hands.

And then my voice-over would say something smart and kind of deep like, *Have you ever had the feeling that you were destined for greatness? And that the whole reason you're even on the planet is to do something unique and totally amazing? Not that you would ever admit that to anybody. Whoops!*

The UnEnd

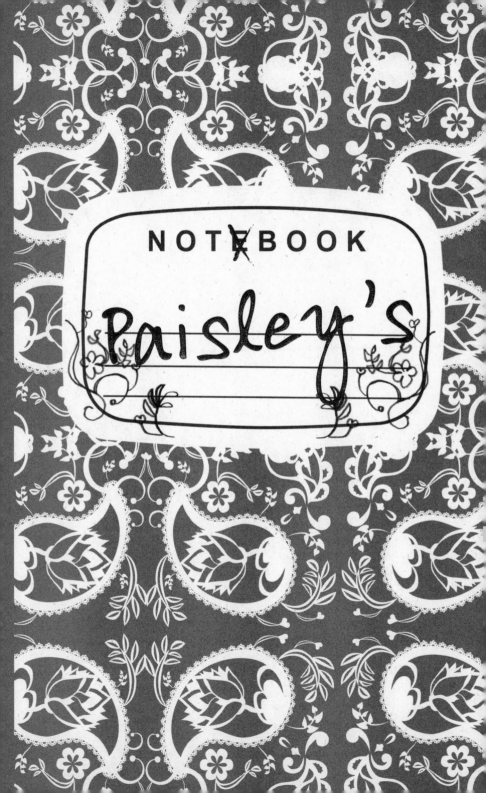

NO PEEKING!!!!

Paisley Hanover—
Something clever
Something clever
Something <u>cleverer</u>
Anything!
Welcome to Never Clever Land
Clever is Crazy Being Polite
Paisley Hanover—Crazy in Polite Ways
Ugh.
Brainy Babe
Quirky Turkey
Strange but True
Hope on a Rope
Dork on a Fork
Fun for All, All for Fun!
A Punny, Funny Friend
Funny Weird
Funny Ha Ha
Funny Weird <u>and</u> Funny Ha Ha
More Laughs than a . . .
More Fun than a Barrel of
Sophomores
Sophomore of the Good Stuff
Sophomore of a Good Thing
Paisley—Not Just Those
   Sperm-Shaped Thingies
Focused on Fun
Focused, Fun, Fabulous!
Little Miss Funshine
Freckles and Funshine
Freckles are Fun
One of a Kind
Fun of a Kind
Fun of a Kind Girl
Fun for Your Life

Tickled Think
The Sizzle <u>and</u> the Steak
Functional <u>and</u> Fashionable
Smart, Stylish, and . . .
   totally stupid!
Shigoogley!
<u>What?</u>
Irony. Irony. Try irony.
Paisley Hanover—
   I Should Have Overslept!
That's good. That's kind of funny.
No, not so funny.
Paisley Hanover—Write On!
Will Write for Clothes
I'm Dying Here!
Not as Popular as Candy
Will Write for Candy
I'd Vote for Candy

??? !!! ...
⁉

Sidebra

When I bought this at the beginning of school, it was a totally normal notebook. Now it's my <u>NOT</u>book and totally un-normal like me. But I won't tell you why. You'll have to read it to figure that out. I <u>will</u> tell you it's kind of my journal, my sketchbook, and my scrapbook all in one doodle-icious mess. It's filled with secrets, notes, confessions, daydreams, and a lot of things I probably never should have said. Basically, it's a peephole into my life and my slightly tortured brain. I'll bet you can relate.

Write on,

Paisley Hanover

REASONS MY LIFE IS OVER TODAY:

• Made a TOTAL fool of myself trying to get into Yearbook class.

• Got stuck in Drama with the socially disabled and hair-impaired! *(my so-called best friend!)*

• Jen basically dumped me.

Why? WHY?! What did I do?

(((The CRAZY·OMETER)))

TODAY I FEEL . . .

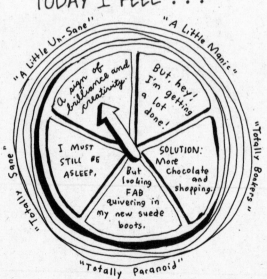

I AM NOT A RAH-RAH. I AM NOT MY GPA. I AM NOT SURE.

THINGS I WISH I'D SAID:

"Hey, no worries.
I'll just take Drama."

THINGS I WISH I'D NEVER SAID:

"Paisley Hanover—FUN of a kind girl!"
(Punctuated by me doing spastic jazz hands.)

Don't ask.

I AM NOT JUST PMS-ING. I AM NOT MY REPUTATION.

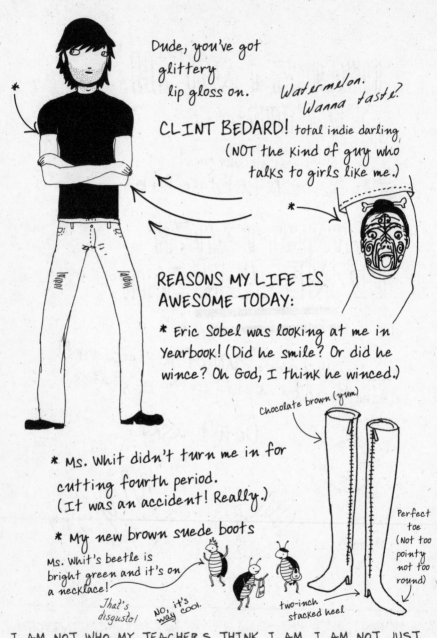

Secret crushes:
ERIC SOBEL

Not-so-secret crushes:
ERIC SOBEL

He never speaks!

He can't help it. He's SHY.

Like THAT's ever going to happen, Pais!

Eric Sobel! SO pop, sweet, adorable, shy, sexy. (NOT the kind of guy who talks to girls like me—for so many different reasons.)

WEIRD PLAY
(My vocab prep for SATs)

WEIRD OF THE DAY:

in·sa·tia·ble [in-sey-shuh-buhl]
 -adjective
not satiable; incapable of being satisfied or appeased:
She has an insatiable hunger for ~~sticky buns, gossip,~~ shoes.

SOMEBODY'S GIRLFRIEND. I AM NOT JUST SOMEBODY'S EX.

PEOPLE WHO SECRETLY WANT TO **<u>KISS</u>**/KILL ME:

Eric Sobel?

Clint Bedard?

My new secret admirer?
(Affectionately known as my <u>locker stalker</u>)

PEOPLE WHO SECRETLY WANT TO KISS/**<u>KILL</u>** ME:

Ms. Madrigal!

Candy Esposito!

Whoever pinched my butt during the so-called TRUST exercise in Drama.

BM?

CB?

CM?

I AM NOT MY HAIR. (THANK GOD!!!) I AM NOT A WIMP. I AM NOT A

POP QUIZ!

1) Who's been getting notes in her locker from a secret admirer?

2) Who thinks she's going to become "mucho popularo" by trying out for cheerleading?

3) Who did fifteen perfect pull-ups with his shirt off while I watched his gorgeous shrink-wrapped torso and totally forgot to breathe?

FRECKLES ARE SEXY

Who wrote that?!
(Must figure out who makes E's like backwards 3's!)

PICKLES ARE SEXY

That's disgusto

Answers: 1) Me! 2) Jen (My soon-to-be-ex best friend!) 3) Eric Sobel (Yum!)

LOSER. I AM NOT GOING TO BE QUIET. I AM NOT GOING TO HIDE.

UNPOP QUIZ!

1) Who basically asked me to kiss him on the first day of Drama?

2) Who got dropped on her butt by a bunch of geeks, losers, and Library Girls? _Bummer_ OUCH!
        Sorry Pais!

3) Who said, "I don't hate you, Paisley, you're just _so_ Pleasant Hill?"

NOTE INTERCEPTED IN CLASS

Found this under my chair in Drama. Real subtle.

PH is not only so PH, she can't even act. How did this no-talent rah-rah get into our class?

I heard she got bounced from Yearbook because she dances like a total freak.

What? That makes NO sense.

Answers: 1) Clint Bedard (He's like some delinquent.) 2) Me! 3) Cate Maduro (Duh. Obviously she hates me. See above. But why?)

The bottle-rocket bomber? No way!

I AM NOT WHAT ANYONE SAYS ABOUT ME BEHIND MY BACK.

THIS FLYER CHANGED MY LIFE.
(It's a long story.)

Hey,
I thought **I** changed your
life! It was
my idea to go the Fly
meeting.
-Bean

THE FLY IS OPEN!
for business this year

Despite senseless draconian budget cuts,
The Fly is still in business.
Come to a lunch meeting to learn how you
can join our new all-volunteer staff
and discover the many joys of journalism—
long hours, no pay, great parties.
We need writers, editors, field reporters, columnists,
photographers & coffee sherpas.
No experience or scruples required.

"Zipper or button?"
Thanks, Charlie! Duh.

Come on, *peoples*, step up!

WHERE: Room 107
WHEN: Friday @ noon

You can KILL the budget
but you CAN'T silence the pen...
or the computer...
or the website...or whatever.

Or the kumbaya singers.

OR the bongo players!

I AM NOT PERFECT. I AM NOT <u>TRYING</u> TO BE PERFECT.

AM I CRAZY??

or did Cindy Kutcher get a boob job
over the summer?

Gotta get the scoop.

They were a b-day present from her parents!

Disgusto!!

WAYS MY MOM IS
CRAZY:

Fake tap-dances when she's happy
or nervous.*

Always tries to hug and kiss me.

Obsessed with Yogilates.
(What is that anyway?!)

*OMG. Maybe that's where spastic jazz
hands came from! It's GENETIC!

I AM NOT GOING AWAY. I AM NOT WHAT SOME GUY WANTS ME TO

RUMORS I
HEARD/ IGNORED/ STARTED:

Ms. Whitaker, our new librarian,
is a radical socialist. (Heard it.)

Not true. She's actually
a radical socialite.

Foxy Señor Abbott is married to
a Bolivian heiress. (Started it.)

I got kicked out of Yearbook class because I
dance like a freak. What?! (Tried to ignore it.)

*Well Pais,
you kind of do!*

INCREDIBLY BORING
Personal **REFLECTIONS:**

I KNOW SOMETHING HAPPENED TO JEN AT HATCH'S
POOL PARTY. BUT WHAT I DON'T KNOW IS WHY SHE HASN'T
TOLD ME ABOUT IT. SHE NEED TO TELL ME EVERYTHING.

BE (OR DO). I AM NOT WHAT SOME GIRL WANTS ME TO BE (OR DO).

IDEAS FOR HOW TO BE
MORE POPULAR?

Get super cute
new boyfriend (jock? BP?).

Buy more clothes.

Bigger boobs? ← *Like THAT's ever going to happen!!* *If it does, call me! -Clint*

Happened! Total humiliation. → Get on YouTube.

Start catchphrase or trend. *Me too!! ox Cate*

Start a club.

Lose 10 pounds. *Brilliant idea... Popular but DEAD!*

Lose 100 pounds.

Be mean to everyone below me
on the social food chain. —

candy

Candy Esposito
So pop.
So perfect.
SO ruining my life!

I AM NOT WHO I WAS LAST YEAR. I AM NOT WHO I WAS LAST WEEK.

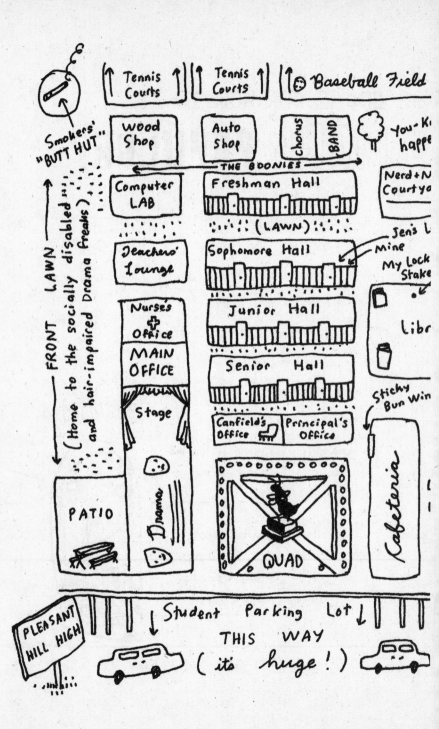

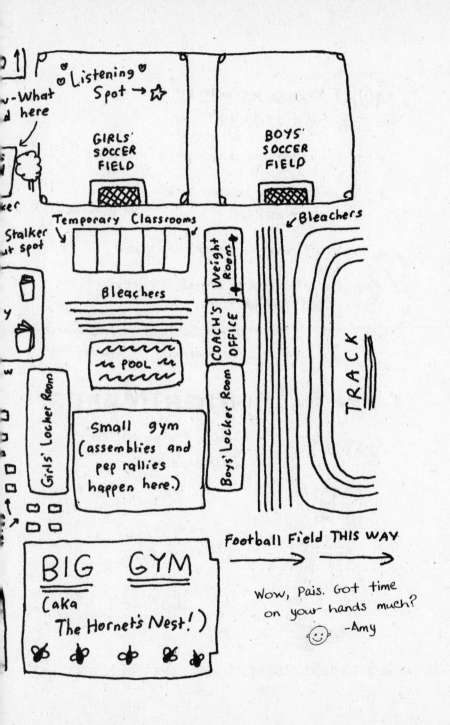

(MORE) Reasons my life is over today:

* My life is one big crazy anxiety dream!

* I'm already way behind on my PSAT vocabulary words.

  Look up repugnant.

* Jen isn't playing soccer this year!!

  So tragic! She's one of our best forwards!

* Made a total fool of myself in front of Eric Sobel! AGAIN!

  Silent library scream Aaaaaaaaaaah!

  Already told you. Offensive. Repulsive. Disgusting. Duh!
  —Charlie

Crazy Reality NIGHTMARES:

Jen is trying out for cheerleading!

Oh my Gag!

I know. Is she Pleasant Hill high?

You guys!!! We're all going to be mucho popularo!

I AM NOT SCARED. (OKAY, I AM SOMETIMES, BUT NOT

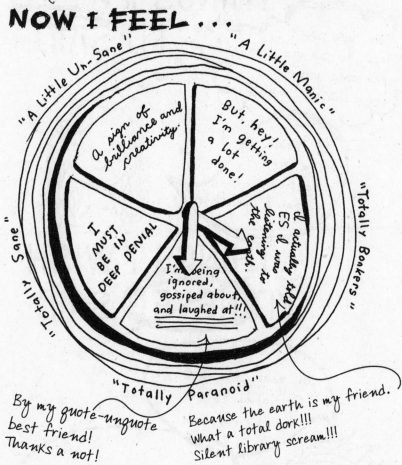

(((The CRAZY-OMETER)))
NOW I FEEL...

"A Little Un-Sane"

"A Little Manic"

A sign of brilliance and creativity.

But, hey! I'm getting a lot done!

"Totally Bonkers"

I actually told ES I was listening to the earth.

I MUST BE IN DEEP DENIAL

I'm being ignored, gossiped about, and laughed at!!!

"Totally Sane"

"Totally Paranoid"

By my quote-unquote best friend! Thanks a not!

Because the earth is my friend. What a total dork!!! Silent library scream!!!

OMG. You didn't really?

I did. ☹

THAT SCARED.) I AM NOT APOLOGIZING FOR WHAT I WANT.

REASONS MY LIFE IS ~~AWFUL~~ TODAY:

* **DWIGHT CASHEL'S BLOG**

* **CATE MADURO.** What a PSYCHO!
What did I ever do to her?

* **SPASTIC JAZZ HANDS** is the new
"hiya" wave at my school. Seriously.

Think about it.
Tu hablas denial?

NOT exactly the trend
I wanted to start.

Just wait, Pais.
It gets WORSE.

I AM NOT A GOSSIP. (WELL AT LEAST I TRY.) I AM NOT A WALLFLOWER.

some sort of clerical error, Ms. Madrigal announced. to me.
Highly suspicious, I thought immediately. But no one else
seemed the least bit suspicious. Were I a betting man,
which I am not, I would wager that Ms. Madrigal, our
beloved yet masochistic yearbook advisor, had planned
the whole thing—the mix-up and the headline slam-off. I
suspect that after a long, hot summer, she had developed
quite a hunger for student suffering, craving the acrid
smell of our mental anguish much like a vampire craves
pulsing, warm blood and will do anything to get it. (Please
note: my brother was in Yearbook for three years. I've
heard all about Ms. Madrigal's devious ways.)

OMG! That never even occurred to me.

Despite my suspicions, I thoroughly enjoyed watching
that spunky Paisley Hanover sweating it out, pitted
against the lovely, gifted, caramel-coated Candy Esposito.
(Who says that God doesn't give with both hands?) The
headline slam was quite a revelation as fine sport and
entertainment. (I am going to suggest that we do it as an
icebreaker at the next Scrabble party.) It was reminiscent
of the gladiators of ancient Rome. Only these gladiators
were thrown to the literary lions armed with no weapons
save their wit—and they were super cute.

SPUNKY?! What an insult!

What a total dork!

I love Scrabble. Who wrote that?

they?

After a three-minute brainstorming period, during which
poor Paisley looked like a frightened, disoriented beagle
caught in the headlights of an 18-wheeler, and Candy
looked...well, you all know how Candy looks, Paisley
bravely went first. Her headline, Fun of a Kind Girl, wasn't
bad. But she had some sort of spasm or petit mal seizure
as she announced her headline to the class and kept
flapping her hands around uncontrollably. It was weird.
Of course, Candy won the last spot in Yearbook with her
outstanding headline, "Sweet, Nutty, Mouth-Watering
Candy." I voted for her. Twice.

BEAGLE?!!! Okay, okay, I'll take spunky.

Uptight & annoying—yes! Squeaky clean...not so much!

THINGS I WISH I'D SAID:

"Teddy! Howdy partner!" ✓

✓ "Gosh, thanks, Cate.
You're just ... so <u>Unpleasant</u>."

THINGS I WISH I'D NEVER SAID:

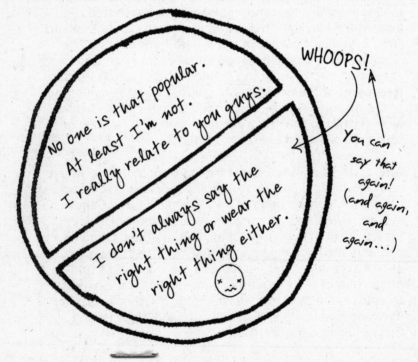

No one is that popular.
At least I'm not.
I really relate to you guys.

WHOOPS!

You can say that again! (and again, and again...)

I don't always say the right thing or wear the right thing either.

I AM NOT WHO MY PARENTS WANT ME TO BE SO THEY CAN BRAG TO

KILLER QUOTES FROM THE GEEK CHORUS:

(Bean Merrill, Charlie Dodd, Cate Maduro, LG Wong (and her LG posse))

"So, Paisley, what's it like being one of the chosen people at PH?" —LG Wong

"Leave her alone." —Bean

"Does it hurt your head being so popular? Does the pressure just make you want to kill yourself?" —Cate

"She's not that popular." —Charlie

And I thought the POPS were the only McNasties at my school.

Tu hablas denial?

Who keeps writing this?!!

ALL THEIR FRIENDS. I'M NOT EATING THAT! I AM NOT KIDDING.

PEOPLE WHO SECRETLY WANT TO
(KISS)/KILL ME:

NOBODY

PEOPLE WHO SECRETLY WANT TO
KISS/(KILL) ME:

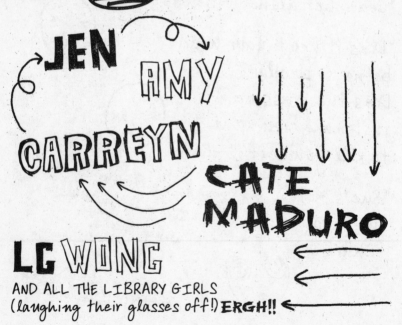

JEN
AMY
CARREYN
CATE
MADURO
LG WONG
AND ALL THE LIBRARY GIRLS
(laughing their glasses off!) ERGH!!

I AM NOT WHAT I WEAR. I AM NOT A TEASE. I AM NOT DESPERATE.

PLEASANT HILL HIGH'S
THE FLY

HORNETS STING COUGARS

Wow. This looks just like The Fly! You're good, Pais.

I'm going to Princeton. Don't burst my bubble!

Freshman Charlie Dodd marches to his own beat at the car wash fundraiser for new band uniforms

PLEASANT HILL PROFILE:

What a PERV!

Football Coach Dave Cave builds summer personal training business and muscles for moms at Bigwood Athletic Club.

I think he's kinda foxy.

Sophomore standout Bodie Jones catches air before dunking the ball at the buzzer for the varsity victory over Cougars hoopster rivals.

CAN'T WE ALL JUST NOT GET ALONG? By Miriam Goldfarb pg 10-11

oh my gag!

NOTES FROM THE FLY LUNCH MEETING:

1. The Fly is no longer an accredited class. It's a <u>club</u>! — Pun intended!

2. The Fly has sick parties.

3. Miriam Goldfarb is a weirdo. (But a cool, independent weirdo. Hmmm...)

4. OMG! The budget for Drama was almost cut too?!

Thank God that didn't happen!

I know!

Look up jingle-ism
Whoops. I meant jingoism! noun

It's kind of like fanatical (football) patriotism. (I looked it up) ox Bean

♡ They're a couple! ♡ ♡

How do you know?

Read his blog. It's hilarious!

Black and yellow just like our school colors! Very clever.

DUMBE BLONDE

but I just laughed at her, staring her down through her thick eyeball-distorting glasses. And then she said in her adorable, nasal voice, "Logan, you imbecile, you need three (pause) credible sources, and (longer pause) Wikipedia is not one of them." We debated that point for a good hour while we made punctuation mosaics out of macaroni. That night, I lay in my narrow, swayback upper bunk tossing and turning and tossing and turning but I couldn't get her adorably nasal voice out of my head. And suddenly, I knew it was looooove. That was a fact. But there was no fact-checker on the planet who could prove it.

Aw!

FYI: You don't need blond hair to be a Dumbe Blonde. You just have to be an authority-questioning, arts-loving activist.

PS FYI: Dumbe is misspelled on purpose. You know, it's like satire?

I don't get it.

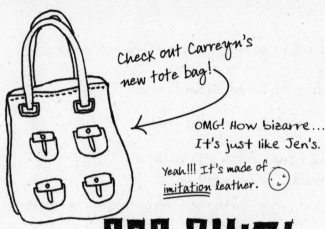

Check out Carreyn's new tote bag!

OMG! How bizarre... It's just like Jen's.

Yeah!!! It's made of <u>imitation</u> leather.

POP QUIZ!

1) Who's turning into a freaky-meanie cheerleading zombie?

2) Who's turning into the freaky-meanie cheerleading zombie's clone?

3) Which popular sophomore found another note from her locker stalker?

HOT 4 YOU!

It's Teddy Baedeker!

That's disgusto!

Who? Who?! WHO?!

~~ES? CB? EM? CB?~~

Must set up a stakeout and spy on my locker

Answers: 1) Jen (duh!) 2) Carreyn (Double duh!) 3) Me! (Yay! Someone really likes me!)

I AM NOT AFRAID TO TRY. I AM NOT AFRAID TO FAIL.

UNPOP QUIZ!

1) Who's jealous of Clint Bedard?

2) Who can juggle like a total pro?

3) Who thinks that Paisley Hanover is
   A-list popular? (Hilarious!)

Answers: 1) Charlie Dodd (But he totally denies it.) 2) Teddy Roedeker
(Wonder what other things about him would surprise me?) 3) Le Wong

Oh gosh, maybe I _am_ A-list popular!
Wow! Wouldn't that be super-duper?
Let me think...Hmmm...I have lots
of really cute clothes, a really big
mouth, and super small boobs,
and...Oh, never mind.
Definitely _not_ A-list popular!

PAISLEY'S PERSONAL POP QUIZ:
(I told you you'd be tested later.)

I am named after...

a) my grandmother who loves to sew ← Sew what?!
b) those sperm-shaped thingies
c) my older brother, Gingham ← Ew. Gross!
d) Paisley, Scotland

He's very comfortable →
with himself, but kind
of plain and often
"checked-out"! (Ha ha!)

Great city, but
named after those
sperm-shaped thingies!

REASONS MY LIFE IS AWESOME TODAY:

NONE. ZERO. ZIP.

THINGS I WISH I'D SAID:

(Still too stunned and sad to think of anything smart... or clever... or funny...)

I kind of want to puke, but every time I try, I keep seeing my own reflection!

THINGS I WISH I'D NEVER SAID:

Let's have a powwow pig-out party.

Static clingy.

I'm not sure I really trust Bodie. I know he's supposed to be a great guy and all. But what if he's just using Jen?

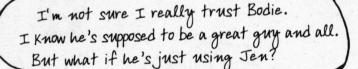

I AM NOT MY BAD HAIRCUT. I AM NOT MY BAD HAIR DAY. I AM

(((The CRAZY-OMETER)))

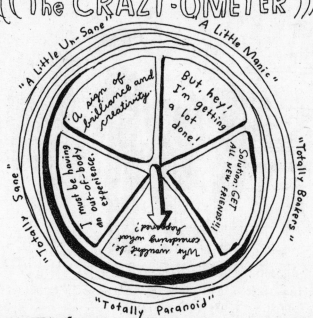

"A Little Un-Sane" "A Little Manic"

"Totally Sane"

"Totally Bonkers"

A sign of brilliance and creativity.

But, hey! I'm getting a lot done!

I must be having an out-of-body an experience.

Solution: GET ALL NEW FRIENDS!!!

Why wouldn't he considering what happened!

"Totally Paranoid"

POWERFUL PERSONAL DISCOVERIES:

Never leave the house without...
shoes and a cell phone!

No one is always who they seem to be!!!

OUCH!

NOT MY AVATAR. (BUMMER! SHE'S SUPER HOT AND SUPER BAD!)

CRAZY ANXIETY DREAM:

Crying... Crying... Crying... Crying

←Puddles of Tears

My quote-unquote friends will cry oceans of tears at my funeral, then fall into deep depressions and go on to live very long, unfulfilling, loveless lives because they can never escape the memory of how unbelievably nasty they were to me.

And it was all PREMEDITATED!

Am I CRAZY?

Or was Cate Maduro actually nice to me? I think she's kind of cool.

→ Uh, yeah! What did you think?

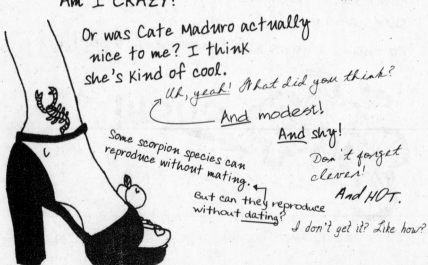

__And modest!

__And shy!

Some scorpion species can reproduce without mating.

Don't forget clever!

But can they reproduce without dating?

And HOT.

I don't get it? Like how?

COOL (ANCIENT) MOVIES TO RENT:

Heathers

Say Anything

The Breakfast Club

Dazed and Confused

Ferris Bueller's Day Off

Fame

Dirty Dancing

10 Things I Hate About You

(OMG! It's based on <u>Taming of the Shrew</u>.)

UNPOP QUIZ!

Who doesn't?!

Um, like Jen, Carreyn, BS1, BS2, Bodie, Hutch, Candy Esposito...

1) Who thinks that popularity is poison?

2) Who has the best goody-goody schoolgirl act of anyone?

3) Who performs road-kill surgery like a cool, calm pro?

My sweet, snuggly, crazy Kitty Dyson. (Yes, he was named after that vacuum cleaner. I know, I know. It's a long story...)

ACTUALLY, NO. <u>This</u> is how I feel. Yikes! Crap.

OMG
OMG
OMG
OMG

PUKE in a purse!!!

Dyson sent my angry vent letter!

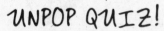
Answers: 1) Cate Maduro 2) LG Wong (Wonder what she's really like outside of school?) 3) Cate Maduro

REASONS MY LIFE IS OVER TODAY:

→ old
* My friends aren't talking to me!

There. I added "old." — What am I? Your sidekick?!

My OLD friends aren't talking to me.

REASONS MY LIFE IS AWESOME TODAY:

OLD
* My friends aren't talking to me!

* Bean! (She gave me this cowgirl cool vintage paisley shirt. How sweet!)

Thanks Bean. I love it! You're a great sidekick.

* Drama class! (CB said the love word to me, and I said it back!

OMG! No way!

WAY! But it was only during a concentration exercise in Drama.

THINGS I WISH I'D SAID:

How come your cat never e-mails me? (Amy!)

Bye-bye, Cate. Everyone's favorite no-talent rah-rah just kicked your booty!

POWERFUL PERSONAL DISCOVERIES:

I am a drama queen **ROCK STAR!**

* Eric Sobel is so vicious.
No, he's beyond vicious—he's EVIL!

(Nerds in love)

SECRET CRUSHES: ♡ ♡

Teddy Baedeker on Mandy Mindel (?)

OMG NIks! Love them.
They're cuter
than Muppets.

Oh my gag! Disgusto.

Excuse me, but nerds
need love too.

I AM NOT HOW MY BUTT LOOKS IN THESE JEANS. I AM NOT GOING THERE.

PEOPLE WHO SECRETLY WANT TO ⟨KISS⟩/KILL ME:

CLINT BEDARD?

→ (Is that even possible?)

Don't take this the wrong way but...NO.

Thanks a not!

I so hope you're kidding.
He's disgusto.

MY LOCKER STALKER?

↖ Your what?!

PEOPLE WHO SECRETLY WANT TO KISS/⟨KILL⟩ ME:

JEN

↕

Duh!

Um, Pais. I don't think it's a secret.

CATE MADURO

Carreyn

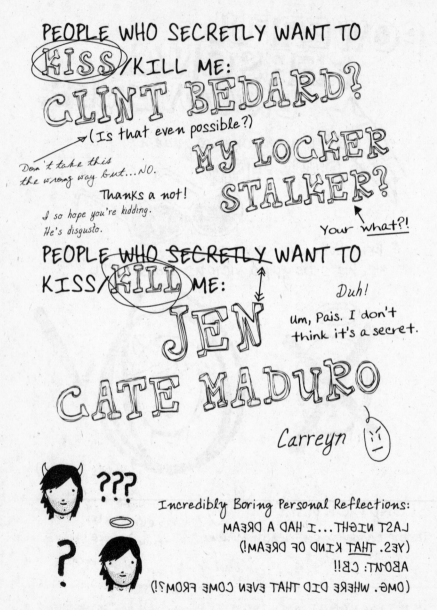

???

?

Incredibly Boring Personal Reflections:
LAST NIGHT...I HAD A DREAM
(YES. THAT KIND OF DREAM!)
ABOUT: CB!!
(OMG. WHERE DID THAT EVEN COME FROM?!)

I AM NOT CRYING. I AM NOT TOO SENSITIVE. I AM NOT

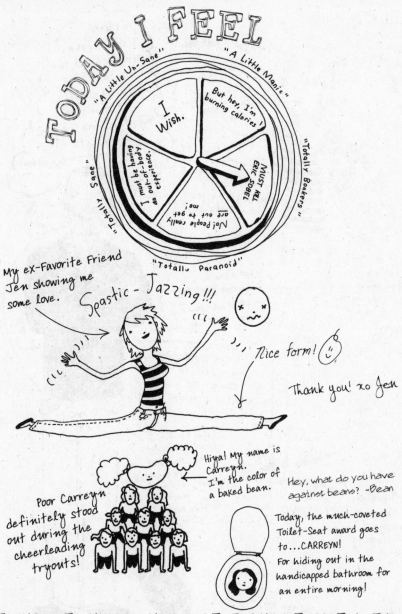

TALKING TO YOU OR YOUR CAT. I AM NOT JUST A TYPO.

ZZZZZZZZZZZZZZLLLL ZZ CRAZY ANXIETY ZZZZ DREAMS: ZZZ ZZ ZZZZZZZZZ

Sorry, Pais.
That wasn't
a dream.

Okay, so I'm standing up in front of the class doing
this totally embarrassing spastic jazz hands dance
and singing this utterly humiliating beat-box-like rap
song that makes me sound like a total idiot and I'm in
a video on YouTube!!! Aaaaaaaaaaaaaaah!

Rock on, Red!
And that editing
was mad. ◁——Don't you mean bad?

No, little dude,
it was mad.

CRAZY REALITIES:

I swear to God, Jen totally lost it
and ACTUALLY said this to me.

"Just get away from me, Paisley! Go <u>away!</u>
You're always telling me how I'm doing it wrong.
You're always trying to make me feel like crap!
I'm sick of it! I'm sick of you!"

What is up with her? Whatever. I am SO over her.

I really like your friends.   Me too!

I AM NOT MY YEARBOOK PHOTO. I AM NOT BETTER THAN

AM I CRAZY

Or did the Hornettes steal my spastic jazz move for their cheerleading routine?!

You are crazy AND the Hornettes stole your spastic jazz move for their cheerleading routine.

Hey, I thought you weren't talking to me?!

I'm not. I'm writing.

RUMORS I HEARD/IGNORED/STARTED:

- I'm secretly dating the bottle-rocket bomber. Me! Paisley Hanover!! (HEARD IT.)
- Cate Maduro goes to a therapist to be deprogrammed after every pep rally. (STARTED IT.)
- Candy Esposito is way into Eric Sobel. (IGNORED IT.)

Who even cares?!

ANYONE ELSE. I AM NOT WORSE THAN ANYONE ELSE.

POP QUIZ!

1) Who claimed she wanted "qual time" with me but really just wanted backup? Ergh!!

2) Who was hanging all over ES all night?

3) Who scored the game-winning field goal and uses words like "homage"?

Answers: 1) Jen (I'm never falling for that one again!)
2) Candy Esposito (Duh! Hate her! She gets everything I want! Whoops.
Did I just write that? I did.) 3) Eric Sobel

WEIRD OF THE DAY:

hom·age [hom-ij or om-ij] -noun

A tribute or formal public acknowldgment of reverence or respect:
His totally humiliating video paid homage to her totally humiliating moment in Yearbook.

Not homage like the ho'nettes. It's a soft "h" or silent "h," like ohmage. Like OMG.

Wait a minute. Reverence? Respect? Was he kidding?

Like OMG! When did YOU turn into such a total nerdathon?

INCREDIBLY BORING PERSONAL REFLECTIONS:

ERGH! I SO CAN'T FIGURE OUT ERIC SOBEL. I DON'T WANT TO LIKE HIM—BUT I DO. BUT SO DOES EVERY OTHER GIRL AT THIS SCHOOL. AND I SO HATE BEING ONE OF THE CROWD. HATE IT! I AM NOT GOING TO LIKE HIM. IT'S DONE. IT'S DECIDED. BUT WAIT, WHAT IF HE LIKES ME? NO, THAT'S TOTALLY RIDICULOUS. BUT...WHAT IF HE DOES?

I AM NOT ON A BUDGET. (WHOOPS. NEVER MIND.) I AM NOT

UnPOP QUIZ!

1) Who held up hilarious misspelled signs
   at the football game?

2) Who will burn to a crisp in the popular wing of
   hell with all the other cute, well-dressed wimps
   for what she didn't do after the football game?

3) Who danced in the parking lot like
   goofy crazed teenagers?

Answers: 1) The Dumbe Blondes (Love those guys!) 2) Me
(Hate myself! And Hutchi!!) 3) Clint Bedard and Cate Maduro
(I so wish I had been with them Friday night.)

FAKING IT. I AM NOT SIGNED UP FOR THIS CLASS. (NOT AGAIN!)

I CAN'T SLEEP!

(WHY? I'M SOOOOOOOOOOOOOO TIRED.)

Why? Why? Why? Why? Why? Why? **WHY?** Why did that happen? Why didn't anyone do anything? Why didn't <u>I</u> do anything? I'm such a wimp-out loser. What am I afraid of? What are we <u>**ALL**</u> so afraid of? The popular people? The <u>**MORE**</u> popular people? That's insane!!! That's sad. They're sad. I'm sad.

<u>Sad</u> + Mad = **BAD**

Varsity Jocks. Varsity jokes. **VARSITY JERKS!**

Boozers vs. Losers

Uncool but Uncruel

If you write it enough times, it doesn't look like the same word or even mean anything!

Popular. Popular. Popular! Popular?

Gotta be popular! More. More! **MORE!**

Poor. Bore. **SNORE**. Got to be more Popular.

Why does **EVERYONE** try so hard to POPULAR?

POOPULAR is more like it.

I AM NOT UNPOPULAR. I AM NOT POPULAR. I AM NOT

Popular = mean, cruel, cloney, phony

FUN Popular = different,
cool, weird,

unweird

Do I even WANT to be popular?

Does anyone really?

WHY? WHY? WHY?!

Why try so hard to be popular
when I can be...

UNPOPULAR

Hmmmmmm...

PLAYING THAT GAME. I AM NOT ASLEEP. I AM NOT A SHEEP.

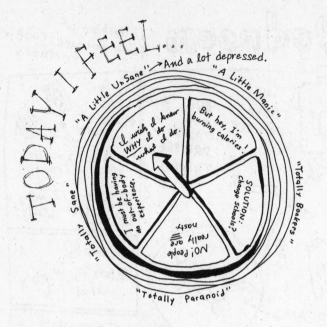

TODAY I FEEL...

"A Little UnSane" → And a lot depressed.
"A Little Manic"
"Totally Sane"
"Totally Bonkers"
"Totally Paranoid"

I wish I knew WHY I do what I do.
But hey, I'm burning calories!
SOLUTION: change schools?
No! people really are nasty.
I must be having an out-of-body an experience.

REASONS TO HATE MYSELF / MY LIFE / MY SCHOOL TODAY:

* That look on Mandy Mindel's face when I apologized.
* The fact that Teddy Baedeker didn't even come to school.
* The way I feel right now.

I AM NOT THE STUFF IN MY PURSE. I AM NOT PUKE IN A PURSE.

REASONS TO LOVE MYSELF / MY LIFE / MY SCHOOL TODAY:

Don't forget STICKY BUNS!

* At least I apologized. Well, I tried.
* Drama! & Mr. E. & William Shakespeare & Clint Bedard! OMG!!! You are so friggin' lucky!
* Thank you, Candy Esposito, for getting the last spot in Yearbook!

I hate you! (In that I-love-you-and-wanna-be-you kind of way!) ox Bean

Wait. I thought you hated her?

Does anyone really need a reason to love? -Cate

She's such a weird you know what?!

You say weird you-know-what, I say weird what-you-know! (Picture my finger wagging in your face, girlie.)

Smart punster troublemakers!

SUSPENSION IS FOR BRIDGES.

Write on!

I AM NOT A FAD. I AM NOT A PHASE. I AM NOT A MISTAKE.

Dear Mom and Dad,
Today I learned a lot at school...
1) Eric Sobel is possibly more of
   a creep than I ever imagined.
   Unbelievable!

2) Mr. Canfield (our lame, ridiculous
   vice principal) has this self-contained
   torture chamber in his office.
   I call it the Fink Fast chair.
   (Get it?)

That's pretty funny, Red.
I always just called
that chair "friend."

Seat covered in sticky, non-breathable
vinyl to make your butt sweat.
(It's probably a fire hazard!)

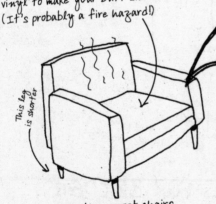

This leg is shorter

Oh the stories I
could tell...
I should write
a memoir!

One back leg is a
little shorter
to keep you—the
presumed-guilty—
off balance.

Lower than most chairs
to keep you feeling small!

And now I call
the Fink Fast chair
"friend" too.

3) I think I missed my calling as a bad kid.
   I'm a <u>really</u> good liar!

AM I CRAZY

OR

IS ES REALLY THE GOOD GUY HERE?

CRAZY REALITIES:

⌐Oh here it is. I found it!

• Jen has totally lost it. <u>School spirit</u>?! She's confusing school spirit with the truth. Is she Pleasant Hill <u>high</u>?

• Canfield didn't believe me—even when I finally told the TRUTH. That's no surprise. He's Pleasant Hill low!

• Canfield is as desperate to be liked by the Pops as everyone else!

I AM NOT DOING <u>THAT</u>. I AM NOT JUST WHO MY FRIENDS WANT ME TO BE.

POWERFUL PERSONAL DISCOVERIES:

* If you lie once, it's really hard to get someone to believe you next time.

THINGS I WISH I'D SAID:

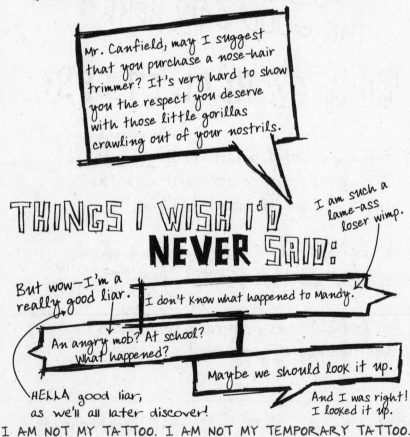

Mr. Canfield, may I suggest that you purchase a nose-hair trimmer? It's very hard to show you the respect you deserve with those little gorillas crawling out of your nostrils.

THINGS I WISH I'D NEVER SAID:

I am such a lame-ass loser wimp.

But wow—I'm a really good liar.

I don't know what happened to Mandy.

An angry mob? At school? What happened?

Maybe we should look it up.

HEllA good liar, as we'll all later discover!

And I was right! I looked it up.

I AM NOT MY TATTOO. I AM NOT MY TEMPORARY TATTOO.

WEIRD OF THE DAY:

ma·lign [muh-lahyn] -verb
to speak evil, harmful untruths
about someone; slander, defame:
There are many people in line to malign
PETER HUTCHISON.

I thought it was <u>untruths</u>?

Oh right. Whoops!

There is no one in line to
malign Bentley Jones.

She's awesome.

*Awesome?
She's <u>PERFECT</u>.*

*Charlie!
I know you wrote
that! ⟶ I know. I hate her.*

PEOPLE WHO SECRETLY
WANT TO KISS/~~KILL~~ ME:

HUTCH

I AM NOT THE SONGS ON MY IPOD. I AM NOT A CLONE.

PEOPLE I SECRETLY WANT TO KISS/~~KILL~~:

HUTCH
JEN
BODIE
MR. CANFIELD
ALL THE POPS

PEOPLE I SECRETLY WANT TO KISS/~~KILL~~:

→ MISS UNPLEASANT
ALL THE UNPOPS
MY CAT DYSON

Me too!
Me three!
She's baaad.

You are so weird!

What?! He's really handsome.

Disgusto!

What the hell is a SIDEBRA?

Sidebra?

HOW TO BE UnPOPULAR

Okay, people—listen up! Let's all move our chairs into a circle. Welcome to the first day of UnPop Culture, Pleasant Hill High's sick new social studies class. Please note: This class will be graded on a slippery slope, zit-free freaks talk alike, walk alike, dress alike, think alike— oh wait, you're not allowed to think when you're popular. Silly me.

Tragically, the Pops don't get to explore the free world ~~~~~~ fun fringe benefits

Okay, people! Here's your homework assignment:

If you're one of the fortunate UnPops at Pleasant Hill High, please reach out to one of the needy students and adopt a Pop. Be sure to keep a picture of your adopted Pop in your locker or on your phone to remind you of their pathetic rah-rah daily existence. By

People actually did this!!

sharing your mental wealth with a Pop, someone less fortunate than you will have at least three well-balanced thoughts a day. Hooray! *Wow! That Miss UnPleasant sure is clever!*

And maybe, if we're lucky, one day Pleasant Hill won't feel like Pleasant Hell.

Big kiss, class dismissed!
Miss UnPleasant

These must be the ideas that pop into your head at 4:00 AM.

I AM NOT MY PHONE. I AM NOT GOING TO DIE WITHOUT MY PHONE.

I'M SO CONFUSED...

That Miss UnPleasant is such a cool bad-ass—or some geeky guy in the computer lab!

SECRET CRUSHES:

Eric Sobel on Miss UnPleasant

OMG! Candy Esposito still has it for Bodie! (I wonder if Jen Knows?)

She does.
DON'T bring it up.
She's feeling insecure enough already.
Seriously.
   —Amy

*Amy on Dyson

Me on ES (It's back!)

(Could ES be my LS?)

*P.S: It's no crush.
   It's true love.

I AM NOT A BENCHWARMER. I AM NOT ABOUT TO GIVE UP.

WEIRD OF THE DAY:

neo·pop·u·lar [pop-yuh-ler] -adjective
new and different type of popular characterized
by individuality rather than commonality:
If everyone in school would just be themselves,
then we'd all feel neopopular.

Just made that one up in carpool!
But I kind of think it works.

It definitely works.

Ditto

Double ditto

Paisley, you're sooo deep.

Double ditto!

Can I use that on my
college apps? -Charlie

OMG! People are really doing
Miss UnPleasant's homework
assignment! **ADOPT-A-POP**

Cate and Bean
adopted me!

PEOPLE THINK MISS UNPLEASANT IS... SERIOUS

MEAN 😝

DEAD-ON

DIVISIVE ← 🙁 Hmmm...

A POP WHO THINKS

LIKE AN UNPOP 🙂

OMG. He's wearing
some girl's
lip gloss again!

What can I say?
Chicks dig me.

POWERFUL PERSONAL DISCOVERIES:

I **LOVE** Shakespeare,
especially when I'm staring at C13.

See?

SILENT LIBRARY SCREAM!!!!!!
How did he get my notebook?!

I AM NOT PROCRASTINATING. (WELL, MAYBE JUST A LITTLE.)

INCREDIBLY BORING PERSONAL REFLECTIONS:

OMG! OMG! OMG! OMG! OMG! OMG! OMG! OMG! CLINT BEDARD ASKED ME (ME!) ON A DATE! MY HEAD IS ABOUT TO EXPLODE. OF COURSE I SAID YES.

Red, relax. It's just homework for our scene.

EXTREMELY <u>NOT</u> SILENT LIBRARY SCREAM!!!!!

I let him borrow the mirror in my compact. Sorry. —Cate

MUST BE MORE CAREFUL

MUST BE MORE CAREFUL WHERE I LEAVE THIS NOTEBOOK!

Yep. I found another one.

YOU'RE SO CUTE WHEN YOU'RE MAD.

I HATE MY LOCKER STALKER. HE'S GETTING OBNOXIOUS.

Bean handed me one of these today. I couldn't believe it! They were everywhere...

MISS UNPLEASANT— WRITE ON!

We desperately need your insightful, snarky commentary.
If you want it, you've got an ongoing column on UnPop Culture at Pleasant Hill High.
Contact me, please!

Miriam Goldfarb, editor
The Fly

PROS
COULD REPLACE YEARBOOK
ON MY SEVEN-POINT PLAN
TO EMPOWER AND
INSPIRE THE UNPOPS
MAKE CHARLIE DODD
INSANELY JEALOUS

CONS
A LOT OF WORK
DO I KNOW ANYTHING ABOUT UNPOP CULTURE?
DEATH BY CHICKEN NUGGETS IF FOUND OUT

I just might love Miriam Goldfarb. **HOW COOL IS SHE?**

Hutch **HATES** Miss UnPleasant.

Makes me **LOVE** her even MORE!

Hutch is running for class president?!

Makes me **HATE** him even **MORE** . . .

and inspires me to... puke in a purse? ☺

Cate called Hutch a misogynistic philistine.

Makes me **LOVE** her even more! But wait. What is a

misogynistic philistine? Gotta look that up.

AND MOTIVATES ME! I'M RUNNING FOR PRESIDENT TOO!

Basically, it's a woman-
hating idiot. – Cate
PS: Love you too!

RUMORS I HEARD/ IGNORED/ STARTED:

* Miss UnPleasant is full of BS. (Heard it.)
* Miss UnPleasant is really Cate Maduro (Started it.)
* Miss UnPleasant will be pelted to death by an angry, screaming mob of Pops hurling chicken nuggets and then go straight to Pleasant Hell. (Started it in my own head and then tried to ignore it but couldn't.)

OMG! You'll never guess
who's running for sophomore
class president:
Peter Hutchison
Me
And...Miss UnPleasant!!!
Hilarious.

OMG. Cate
signed her up!

She couldn't help it.
She's in love.

It's true. She's a goddess.

I AM NOT <u>SO</u> BACK-IN-THE-DAY. I AM NOT MY FRENCH HORN.

WEIRD OF THE DAY:

man·fi·dent [man-fi-duhnt] -adjective
Bold, sexy, and self-confident, especially
when it comes to knowing how to treat a woman:

He whipped me around in his arms like a manfident
rogue until I felt weak in the knees and
delicately collapsed against his chest that
rose and fell with his every hot breath.

Sigh...I better sit down. Oh wait.
I am sitting down. -Bean

Hmm...Let me think. Do I want to look like
an Elizabethan hottie onstage with CB or
do I want to look like Barney?

Purple and velvety
and HORRIBLE.

Elizabethan hottie dress.
(Even I looked
almost sexy in it.)

I AM NOT DISGUSTO. I AM NOT JEALOUS. I AM NOT THE ENEMY.

THINGS I **WISH** I'D SAID:

Hey Cate, wanna eat lunch with me?
(Like three years ago in seventh grade!)

THINGS I WISH I'D **NEVER** SAID:

Hey you guys,
guess who asked me out?
Clint!

Dear Mom and Dad, **NOT**
Today I learned a ~~lot~~ at school...

1) Cate is actually <u>undecided</u>.

2) Bean has a major below-the-belt crush
on CB too.

3) "If girls like you (me) start dating guys
like Clint Bedard, then who will girls like
us (Cate and Bean) have to date?"

Why would anyone want to date
guys like Clint Bedard?

Wow. Never thought about it
that way before.

Because he's HOT!   Me neither!

Like a pile of steaming dog crap.

Girls, please—there's enough of me
to go around.

OMG! I hate him!
What a snoop.

I AM NOT YOUR COMPETITION. I AM NOT GROUNDED! (PLEASE?).

~~Different by design~~

~~Break out of the mold. Break your own mold.~~

~~Break out and break free!~~ ← ———— Brilliant! Sounds like an ad for zit medicine.

~~Color outside the lines. Live outside the box.~~

~~Don't repeat...~~ something. ~~Don't compete...~~ something again.

~~Don't be a sheep. Don't be asleep.~~ Don't...ERGH!

Okay. Think like a Dumbe Blonde.   That's kind of funny.
How to be...   No, not so funny.

What am I trying to say?????

~~Be YOU-nique!~~   www.PaisleyHanover.com
                     ?????

~~Dare to be different. Dare to scare. Dare to shave your hair.~~ Oh crap.

UnPop Culture??????? What is that anyway?

IT'S OFFICIAL!

I AM RUNNING FOR CLASS PRESIDENT!

I need a GREAT slogan. And locker stuffers and
posters and...and I don't have much time!

Building Sophomore Bridges

Connecting the Dots

Connect the Dorks

Head and shoulders above Hutch

Redhead & Shoulders Above the Rest!   Don't you need at
                                       least a little cLASS
Go Red to Get Ahead!   for that job?
                                       (Arg! Argh)
Paisley Hanover—Not Just Those sperm-shaped thingies!

Spastic ~~Jazz Hands Working~~ For You!

(Spastic Jazzed for the Job!) ← ☺   carreyn's hair
                                     is SO moody!
Spastic Jazzed to crush Hutch!

OMG! Carreyn dyed her hair RED!   Carreyn Hates Me Hair   Carreyn Likes Me again Hair

                                                            No it's NO!!

Uɴ IS MORE FUN!

Take a hall pass on the in crowd and join the *Un* crowd instead. Everyone's welcome and everyone's got the power—it's called UNdividuality. What a concept.

Okay, people, listen up! Your homework assignment this week is multiple-choice:

1. Tap into your UnPop Power—wear your *Un*-side out. ← *They actually did this!*
2. Be yourself—Be Un of a Kind and be proud!
3. Take back the quad—it's not just for Pops! *AND this!*
4. Take back Pleasant Hill—it's your school too.

LETTERS TO THE EDITOR

and we are NOT trapped. The next time that you are tempted to run a piece like this, you should remember that popularity is <u>earned</u> by people who have style and confidence and social skills and athletic ability. Too bad the bitter, untalented, un-popular students at this school don't get this.

Good thing they have social skills!

Signed,
Anonymouse [sic]

Hi! I'm Mickey Mouse's invisible shy cousin!

bullies and brats on their en-titled behavior. I hope she will write another column, because this school needs to hear from someone who has the guts to point out what makes Pleasant Hill feel like Pleasant Hell.

Sincerely,
Cate Maduro, Sophomore

Love her!

One bad apple don't spoil the whole bunch, girl.
Ooh. I don't care what they say.
I don't care what you heard now.
Oooooooh! Oooooooh!
Yours truly,
Sir Pleasantly Laughs-a-Lot

Love HIM! (Whoever he is...)

OMG! OMG! OMG! OMG!
THINGS ARE CRAZY! MISS MNP HAS STARTED AN UNOFFICIAL REVOLUTION! UNS ARE EVERYWHERE! (WAIT. IS THIS JUST A REALLY LONG FLASH FANTASY?) NO ONE SUSPECTS IT'S ME! AT LEAST I DON'T THINK.

Life is happening SO fast,

I barely have time to write anything!

Backlash day was amazing!

UnTouchable

UnDisturbed

UnDaunted

UnTarded

UnPhased

UnAffected

UnShakable ← Yeah, right!

HELLO my name is **UNFORGETTABLE**

MISS UNPLEASANT'S CAMPAIGN IS A LOT MORE FUN THAN MINE.

UNSLOGANS!

Monday: "Vote for Miss UnP to Support Diversity!"

Tuesday: "Join the Un Crowd!"

Wednesday: "UnNormal and Proud!"

Thursday: "The Power of Un is Way More Fun!"

HELLO my name is UnPerfect

HELLO my name is UnEven

HELLO my name is UnAppreciated

I just signed up to speak out against Miss UnPleasant at the school forum. (Am I a genius or what?!)

I'd say you're an OR WHAT!

Um.... Yeah! What's up with you?!

Most definitely. Actually, calling you an OR WHAT is very kind.

I AM NOT EASY. I AM NOT EASILY DEFINED. I AM NOT MY SHOE SIZE.

PEOPLE I WANT TO KILL:
BS1 & BS2
JEN & BODIE
HUTCH
MYSELF! (What was I thinking?!!)

PEOPLE I WANT TO KISS:
MIRIAM GOLDFARB
BENTLEY JONES (Love her!)
THE DUMBE BLONDES, ESPECIALLY BONGO GUY
CATE MADURO

AM I CRAZY...
Or did Jen just say that I'm the only one she
can trust and really talk to?
I must be crazy.

NICE NECKLACE! ⟶

What in the hell happened at that party?!
I'm going to explode if I don't figure it out!!!!!!!!

I AM NOT MY SHOES. (BTW, MY SHOES ARE SUPER CUTE!)

YES, I GOT ANOTHER ONE...

RIGHT ON, BABY.
MORE POWER TO THE POPS!

Now I know my LS has to be a Pop—or maybe just a moron. Probably both.

But the really weird thing? Jen's been getting notes in her locker too. ???

But NOT from an admirer. Hmmm...

I'm sitting in biology trying to pay attention. **SNORE!** A text from CD? That's kind of weird. (He better not be my locker stalker!)

OMG! Hutch is such a skeazer, lame-ass, slime-bag, scum-of-the-universe CHEATER! I am not just going to sit here and take this.

I HATE HUTCH!!!!

Guest columnist?

How to be UnEthical   How to be UnFair

How to be UnBelievably Lazy

by Peter Hutchison

MISS UNPLEASANT'S CRYSTAL BALL?
MISS UNPLEASANT'S VOODOO DOLL?
MISS UNPLEASANT'S UNPOP QUIZ?

I AM NOT MY FAT POCKETS. I AM NOT WHAT I ATE TODAY.

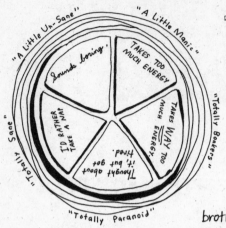

TODAY I FEEL...
TOO DEPRESSED TO FEEL ANYTHING.

It's raining. I have NO friends, at least no friends that I like or like me. I have NO boyfriend. I have NO dates. My mother doesn't love me anymore—she only loves Yogilates. My brother never returns my calls. My dad just went running in the pouring rain. I'm depressed. Totally depressed. I should be working on my speech but I can't concentrate—and I can't stop stuffing my face with Pirate's Booty! If I eat any more I will turn into one big giant Pirate's Booty. What is that anyway? "Pirate's Booty." A pirate's butt? I don't know—but it doesn't sound pretty. If I ever have any good ideas for my speech, they'll go right here:

I AM NOT THE POSITION I PLAY. I AM NOT KEEPING SCORE.

I WONDER IF

Miss UnPleasant will get the boot
or get to write again?
Ooh, wondering that really made me tired. I
have to put my head down. The mail just arrived.
Should I get up?
No. It'll take too much energy.

The doorbell just rang.

OH CRAP...

OMG! Guess what just arrived?! My shipment
of temporary tattoos and Paisley for Pres,
Spastic Jazzed M&M's. Yes. Chocolate! Wahooo!!!

My shameless self-promotion.

How cool is that?
Thanks for the inspiration, Hutch! ⟶

Carpool was painful this morning.
But not half as painful as
being pelted by M&M's.
Those Library Girls have
surprisingly strong
arms. Must be from
lugging all those
books around.

OUCH!

OUCH!

OUCH!

I AM NOT MY BAD MOOD. I AM NOT WEARING THAT.

THINGS I WISH I'D NEVER SAID:

More power to the Pops! More power to the Pops!

I don't think I can go out with you.

Podium power is a gateway drug!

MISS UnPLEASANT'S UNPOP QUIZ

Okay, people. Heads up—pencils down! It's time for your first UnPop Quiz.

1. Which incredibly popular hottie has a secret crush on sweet, adorable me?
2. Which candidate for sophomore class president bought his speech online?
3. Which BP flirts shamelessly with one hot guy just to make another—the one she *really* likes—jealous?
4. Which Varsity Pom stole her mom's credit card to get a nose job?
5. Which sophomore rah-rah is getting love notes in her locker?
6. Which brainy babe ignored an invite to speak at the assembly because she has way more power if she stays UnNonymous?

Pop goes the weasel!

Big kiss, class dismissed!
Miss UnPleasant

IT WORKED! (ALMOST TOO WELL.) EVERYONE WAS GOSSIPING LIKE CRAZY!

Clint's not in Drama. Everyone's rehearsing but me.

This is what I would look like in my Taming of the Shrew Elizabethan hottie dress if I get to wear it onstage which I probably won't because I'm an idiot and insulted my scene partner, and now he's not talking to me or even coming to Drama class and he probably won't show up tonight for Acting Out!

He showed up. Oh my God...

Oh my God is right!

He more than showed up! He showed his whole chest! *Girls, girls, girls, get a grip!*

WHY?

WHAT HAPPENED?

Will I ever find out what happened at that stupid party?! It's killing me!!! (And maybe killing my friendship with Jen.)

→ FLUSH HUTCH! ←

It's speeches day. I have butterflies in my butt. Something feels weird...

OMG OMG OMG OMG OMG OMG
OMG OMG OMG OMG OMG OMG
OMG OMG OMG OMG OMG OMG
OMG OMG OMG OMG OMG OMG
OMG OMG OMG OMG OMG OMG
OMG OMG OMG OMG OMG OMG
OMG OMG OMG OMG OMG OMG
OMG OMG OMG OMG OMG OMG

I'D VOTE 4 ANYONE BUT YOU. YOU'RE UNBELIEVABLE.

Everyone hates me!
Even my locker stalker has turned on me.
!!!!!
Is that "OH MY GOD" or "OH MY GAG"?

I am not history.
I am <u>not</u> history!
I am NOT history!
I am not a loser.
I am not giving up.
I am not going away.
I am not who I was last year.
I am not who I was last <u>week</u>. Good. Who were you last
I am not a rah-rah. week anyway?
I am not my reputation.
I am not who the vice principal   Excuse me!
   thinks I am.   What's wrong with that?
I am not perfect.
  I am not <u>trying</u> to be perfect. Thank God.
I am not afraid to say no.   That would be boring!
I am <u>not</u> just PMS-ing.
I am not kidding.
I am not falling for that. Are you sure?
I am me!
(If only I knew who that really was?!)
  I am not just who my friends want me to be.
    But are you falling for him?

They're
pink.

I'D VOTE
FOR
PAISLEY

For my core supporters.
Love those guys! ♡

(You never know ♡ ♡
   who's really there for you
   until you need them!)

FOXY!

I love jewelry!

I AM NOT MY MOST EMBARRASSING MOMENT. I AM NOT

GUESS WHAT?
I <u>AM</u> LIVING THE
BEST YEAR OF MY LIFE.

Every year is the best year
of your life! ox Bean

You're so deep. I know.

The day of class elections
WAS **INSANE**!

And that was before
I found out about ...

POOR CARREYN. ANOTHER
HOME DYE-JOB DISASTER.

No, not Carreyn's pink hair

Something much MUCH

WORSE!

Puke.

OMG
HOLY SHIITAKE
MUSHROOMS!

THAT'S DEFINITELY "OH MY GAG!"

MY MOTHER'S DO-OVER. I AM NOT A DISAPPOINTMENT.

I AM NOT ALONE. I AM NOT HISTORY. I AM <u>NOT</u> <u>FINISHED</u>.

Big thanks to many—the legendary, loving, and lovable Charlotte Sheedy; her ace assistants, Meredith Kaffel and Hilary Costa; my trusted and beloved readers: Angela Drury, Wendy Merrill, Sasha Cagen, Julie Mason, and Lisa Webster; my inside high-school spy Michael McAlister; my unofficial but not unappreciated editor Andy Garrison; my friends and family who propped me up and/or ignored my absence while writing this book; the incredibly enthusiastic, talented, and patient team at Dial Books (AKA Team Paisley): Lauri Hornik, Regina Castillo, Lily Malcom, and design-goddess Jasmin Rubero; and the amazing illustrator Alli Arnold who created the visuals for Paisley's world.

Special thanks to everyone who has ever lived through high school, especially the Pops and UnPops who lived through it with me. You are all an inspiration!

My biggest thanks goes to my editor Jessica Garrison, who transformed my dirt clod into a sparkling gem. Without her vision, tenacity, support, smarts, to-do lists, friendship, and undying positive energy, Paisley Hanover would not exist. Thank God we found each other! OMG. Did I just say that? I totally did.